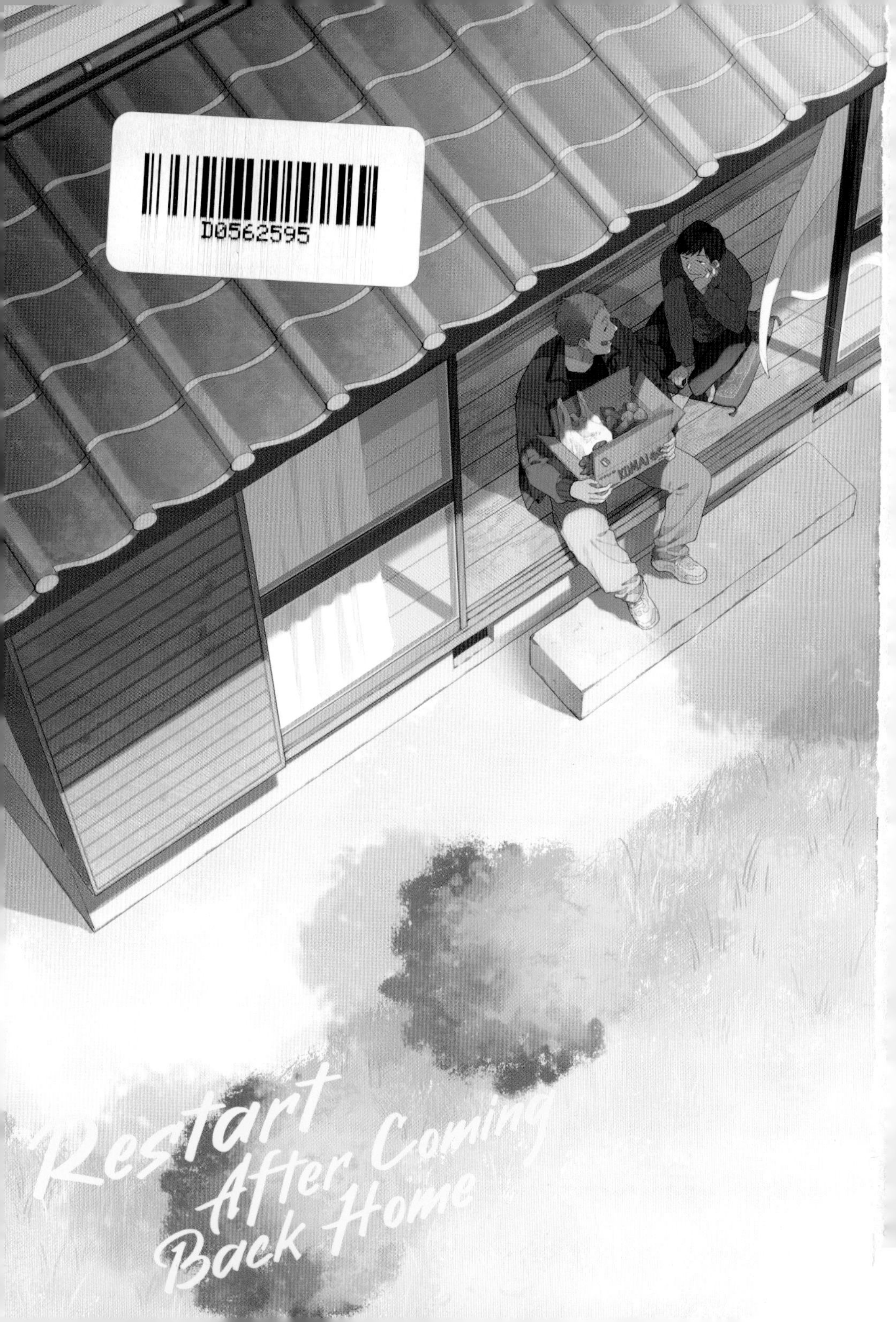
Restart After Coming Back Home

CONTENTS

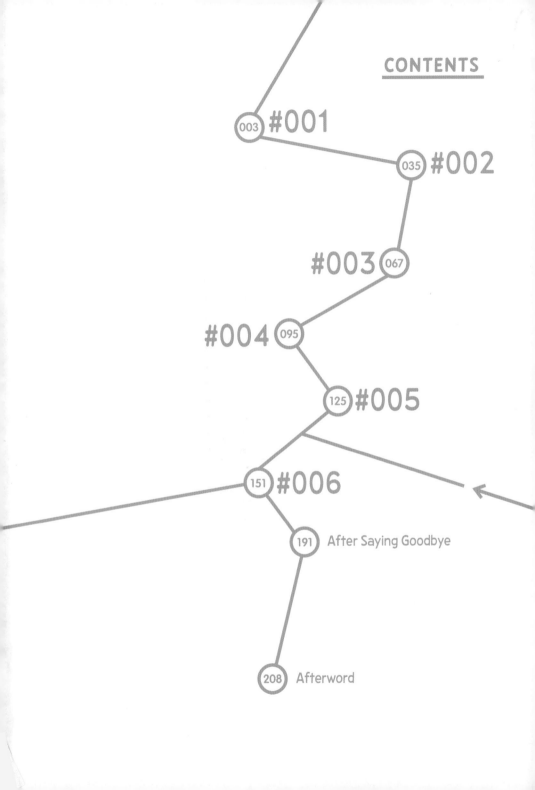

#001

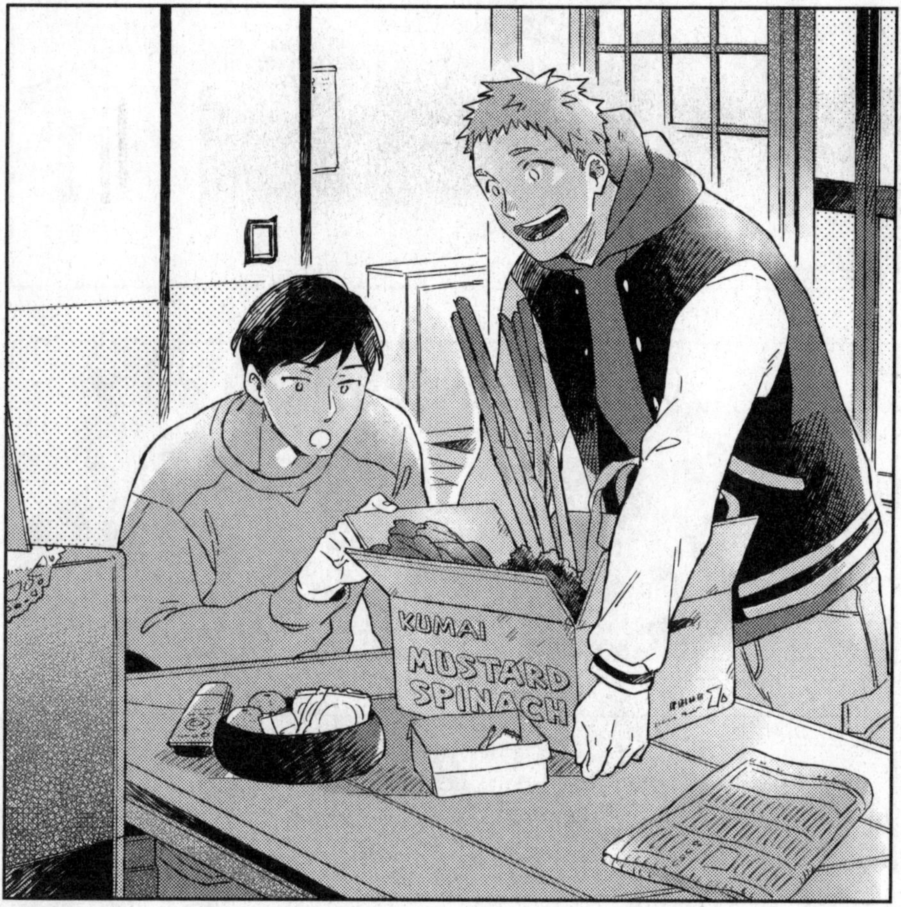
KUMAI
MUSTARD
SPINACH

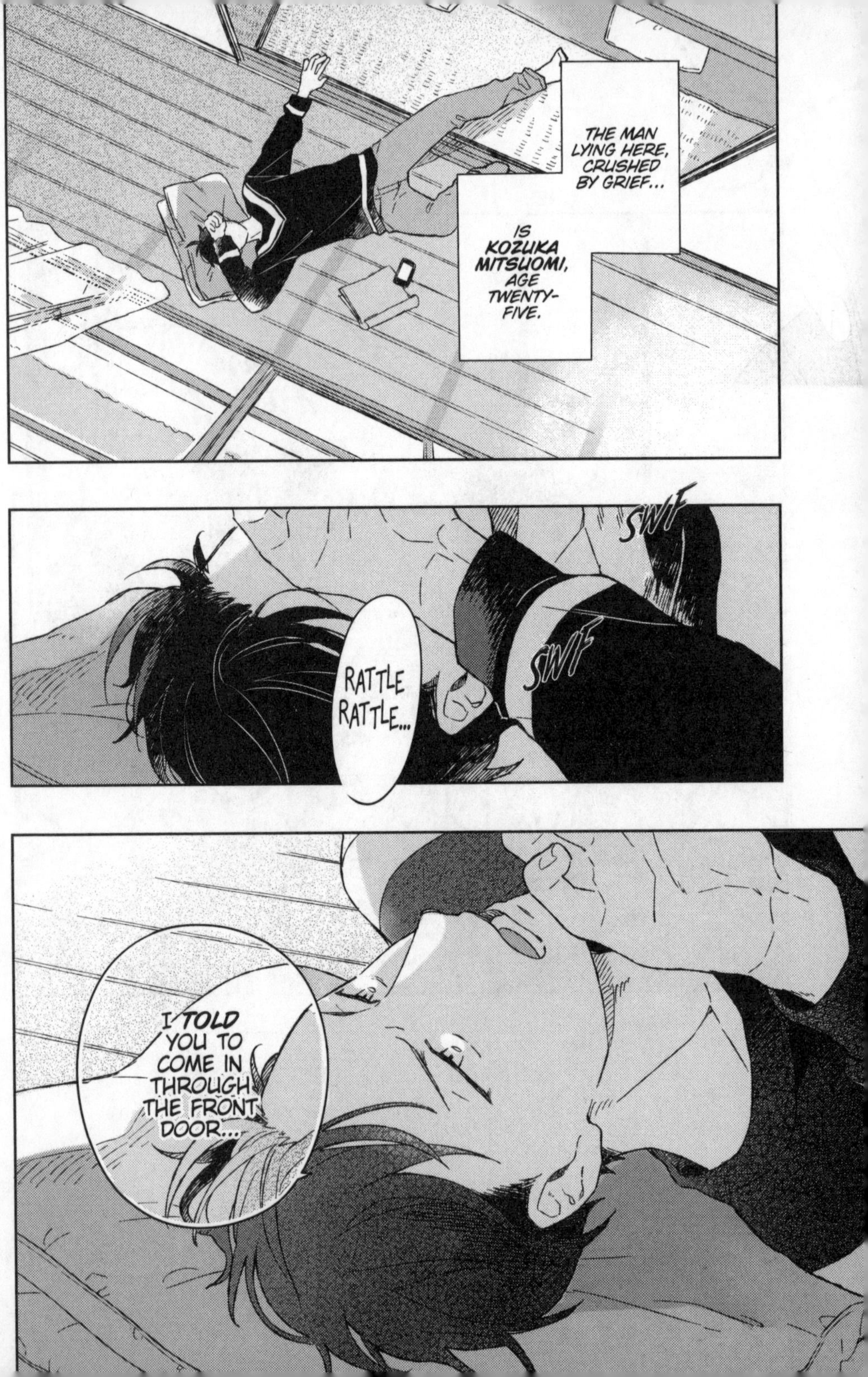
THE MAN LYING HERE, CRUSHED BY GRIEF...
IS KOZUKA MITSUOMI, AGE TWENTY-FIVE.
SWIF
SWIF
RATTLE RATTLE...
I *TOLD* YOU TO COME IN THROUGH THE FRONT DOOR...

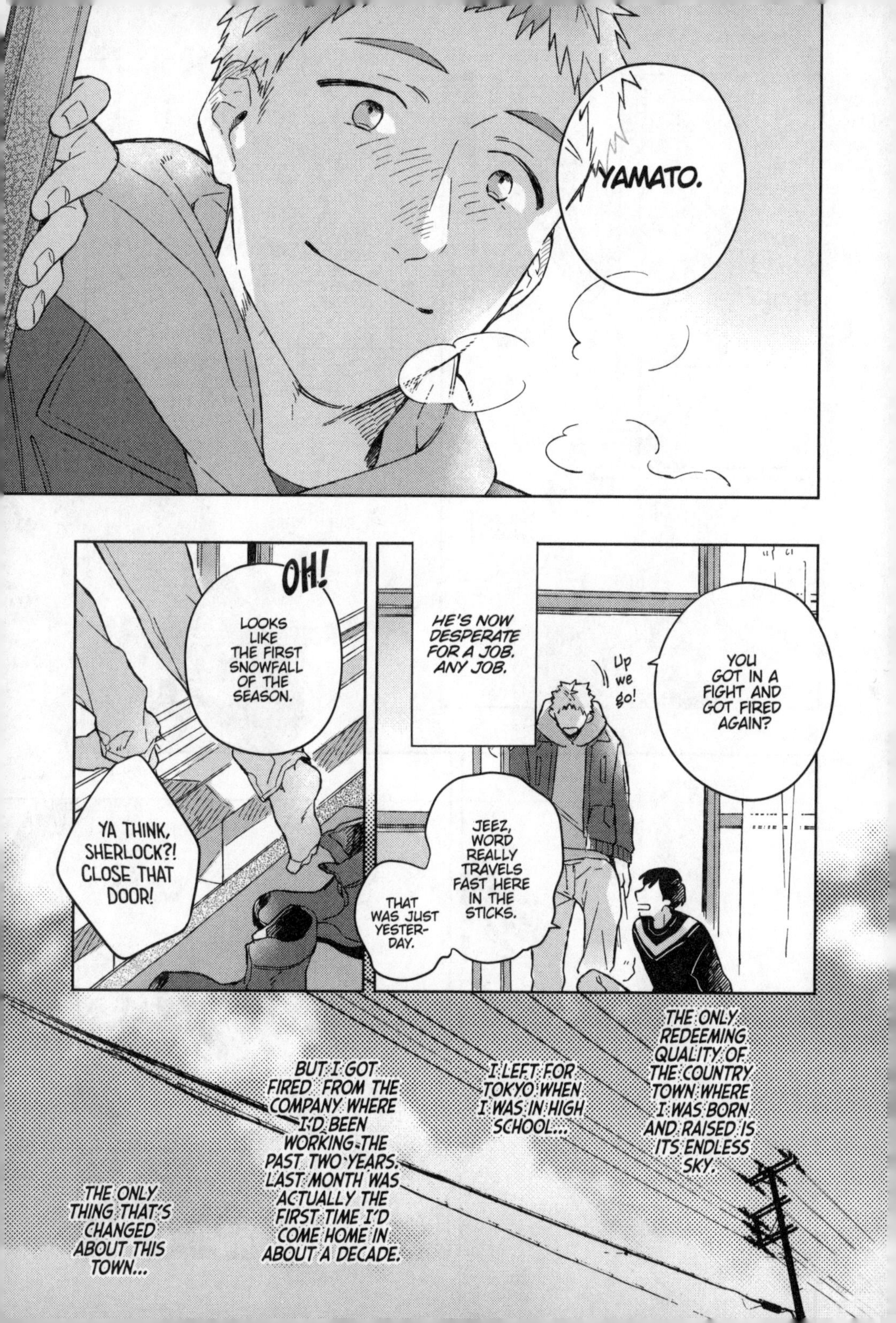
YAMATO.
YOU GOT IN A FIGHT AND GOT FIRED AGAIN?
Up we go!
HE'S NOW DESPERATE FOR A JOB. ANY JOB.
JEEZ, WORD REALLY TRAVELS FAST HERE IN THE STICKS.
THAT WAS JUST YESTER-DAY.
OH!
LOOKS LIKE THE FIRST SNOWFALL OF THE SEASON.
YA THINK, SHERLOCK?! CLOSE THAT DOOR!
THE ONLY REDEEMING QUALITY OF THE COUNTRY TOWN WHERE I WAS BORN AND RAISED IS ITS ENDLESS SKY.
I LEFT FOR TOKYO WHEN I WAS IN HIGH SCHOOL...
BUT I GOT FIRED FROM THE COMPANY WHERE I'D BEEN WORKING THE PAST TWO YEARS. LAST MONTH WAS ACTUALLY THE FIRST TIME I'D COME HOME IN ABOUT A DECADE.
THE ONLY THING THAT'S CHANGED ABOUT THIS TOWN...

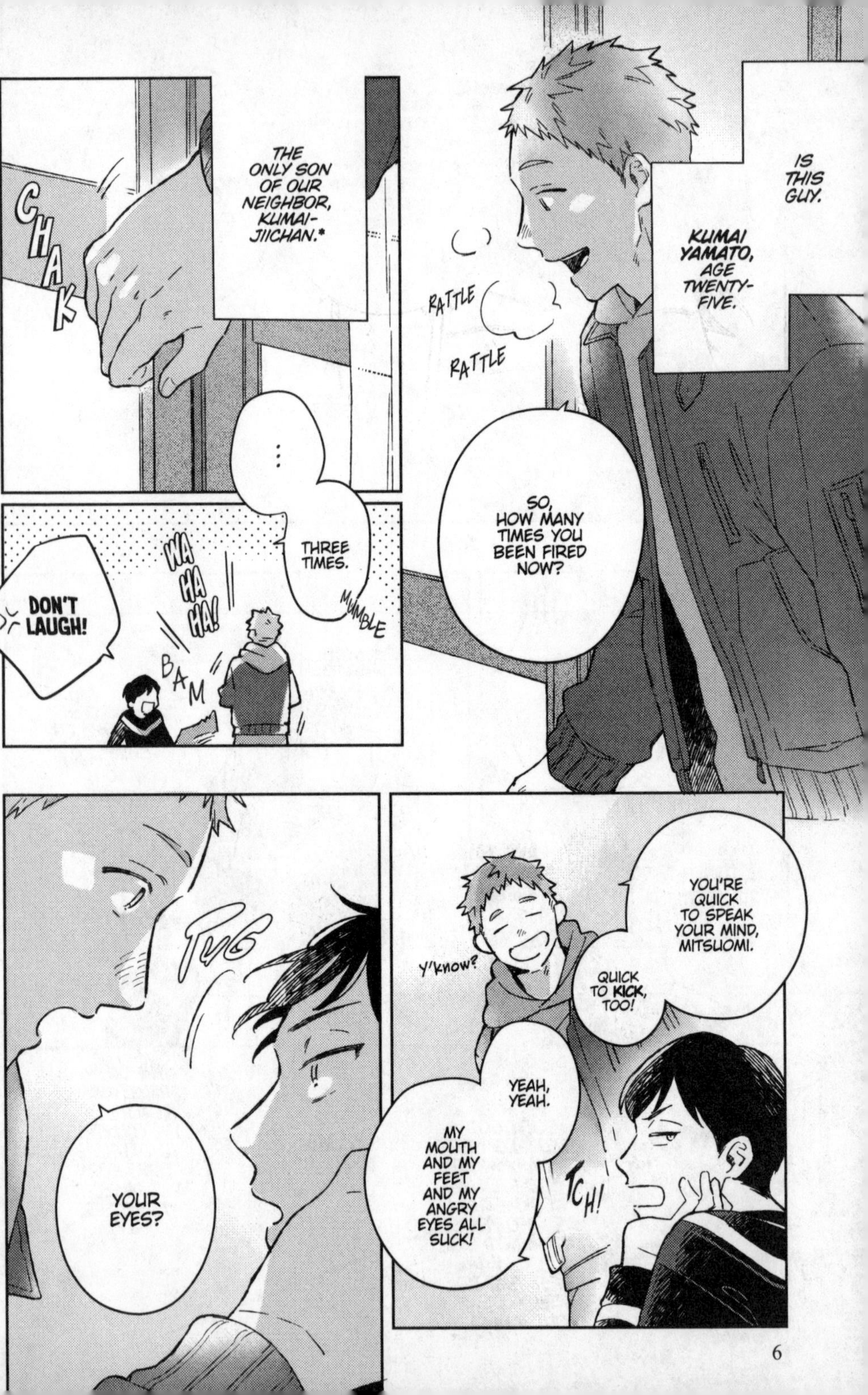
CHAK
THE ONLY SON OF OUR NEIGHBOR, KUMAI-JIICHAN.*
IS THIS GUY.
KUMAI YAMATO, AGE TWENTY-FIVE.
RATTLE
RATTLE
SO, HOW MANY TIMES YOU BEEN FIRED NOW?
...
THREE TIMES.
MUMBLE
WA HA HA!
BAM
DON'T LAUGH!
YOU'RE QUICK TO SPEAK YOUR MIND, MITSUOMI.
Y'KNOW?
QUICK TO KICK, TOO!
YEAH, YEAH.
MY MOUTH AND MY FEET AND MY ANGRY EYES ALL SUCK!
TCH!
TUG
YOUR EYES?

* Jiichan is an affectionate term meaning "grandpa" or an elderly man.

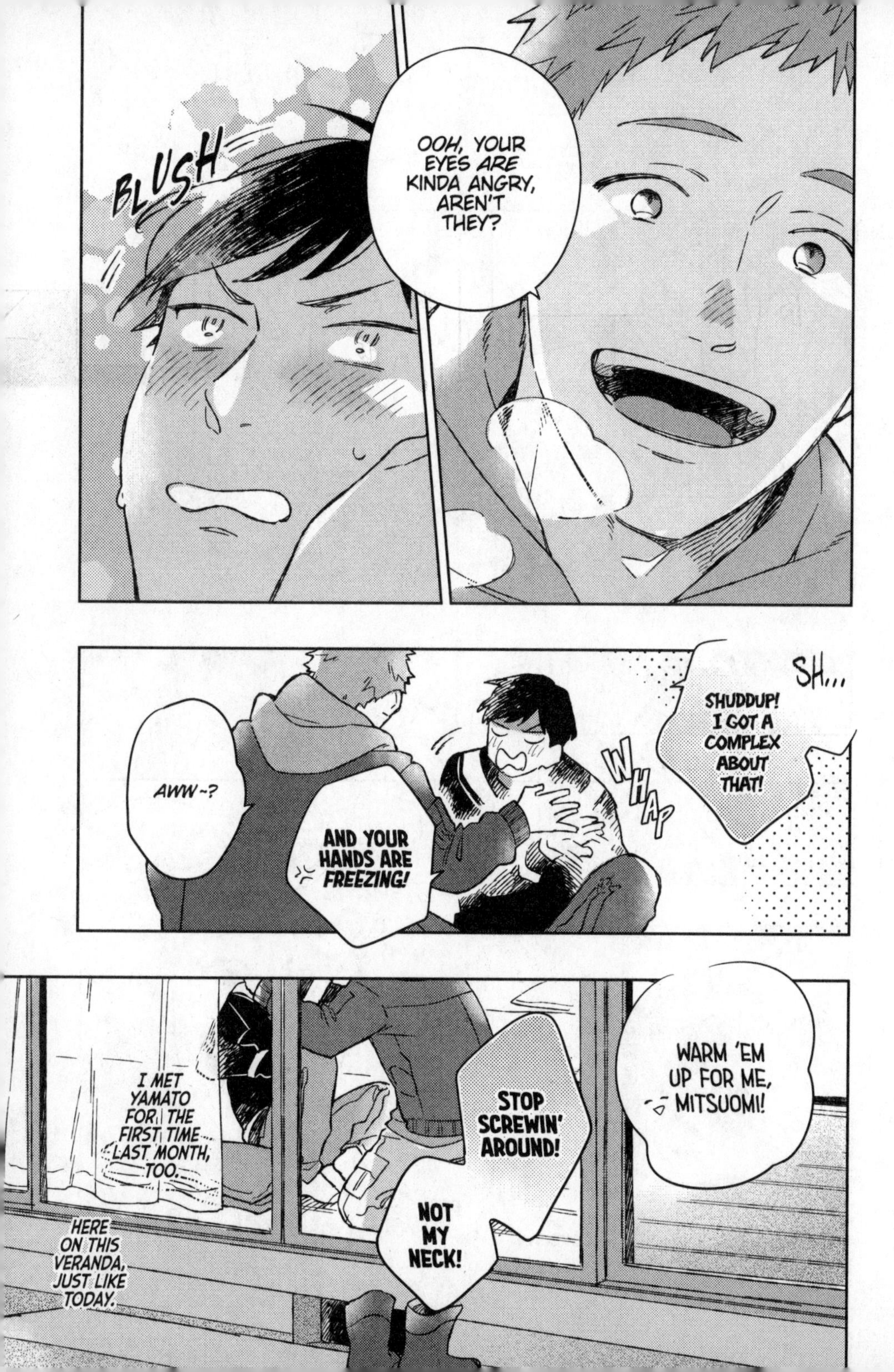
OOH, YOUR EYES ARE KINDA ANGRY, AREN'T THEY?
BLUSH
SH...
SHUDDUP! I GOT A COMPLEX ABOUT THAT!
WHAP
AWW~?
AND YOUR HANDS ARE FREEZING!
WARM 'EM UP FOR ME, MITSUOMI!
STOP SCREWIN' AROUND!
NOT MY NECK!
I MET YAMATO FOR THE FIRST TIME LAST MONTH, TOO.
HERE ON THIS VERANDA, JUST LIKE TODAY.

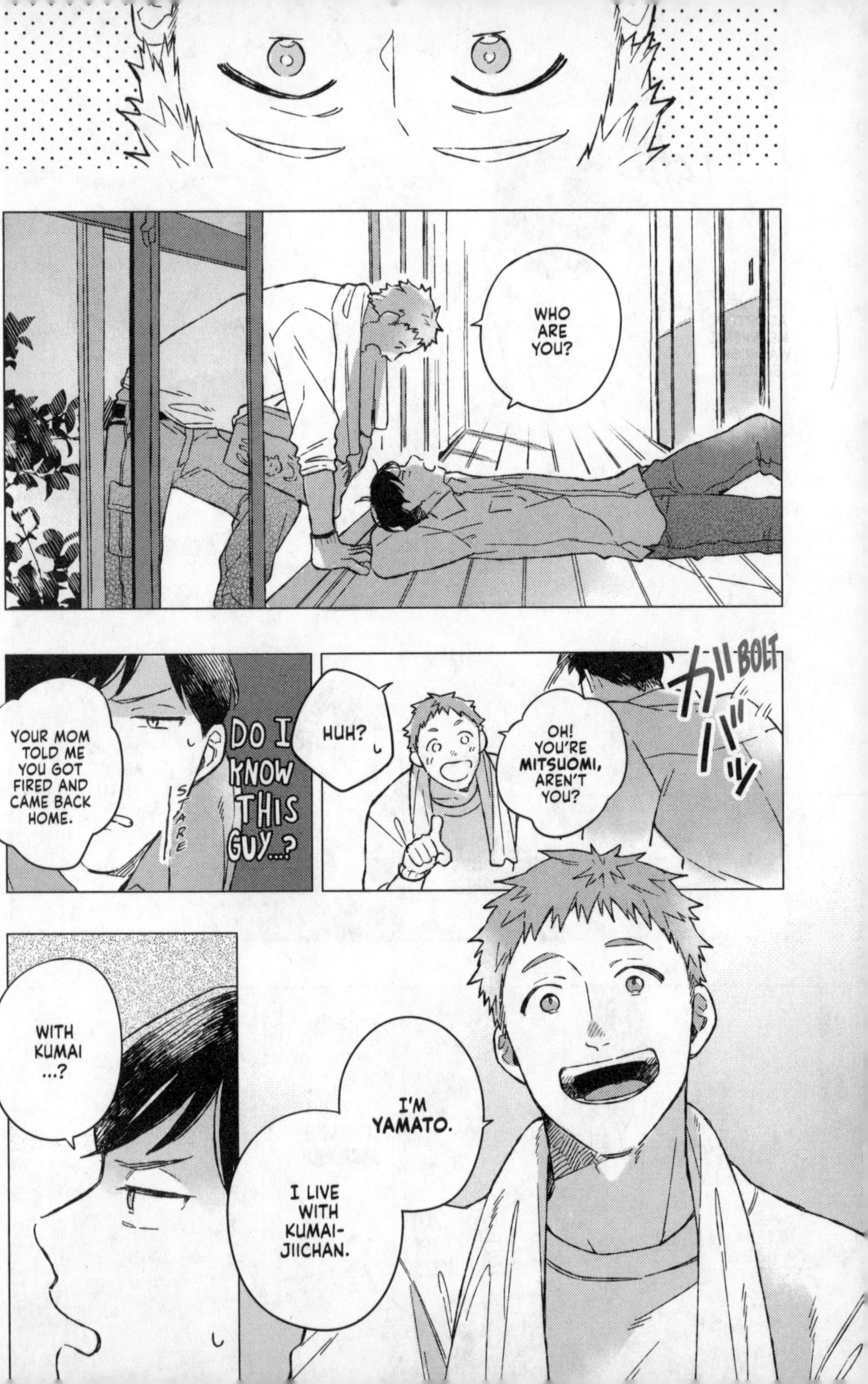
WHO ARE YOU?
BOLT
OH! YOU'RE MITSUOMI, AREN'T YOU?
HUH?
DO I KNOW THIS GUY...?
STARE
YOUR MOM TOLD ME YOU GOT FIRED AND CAME BACK HOME.
I'M YAMATO.
I LIVE WITH KUMAI-JIICHAN.
WITH KUMAI ...?

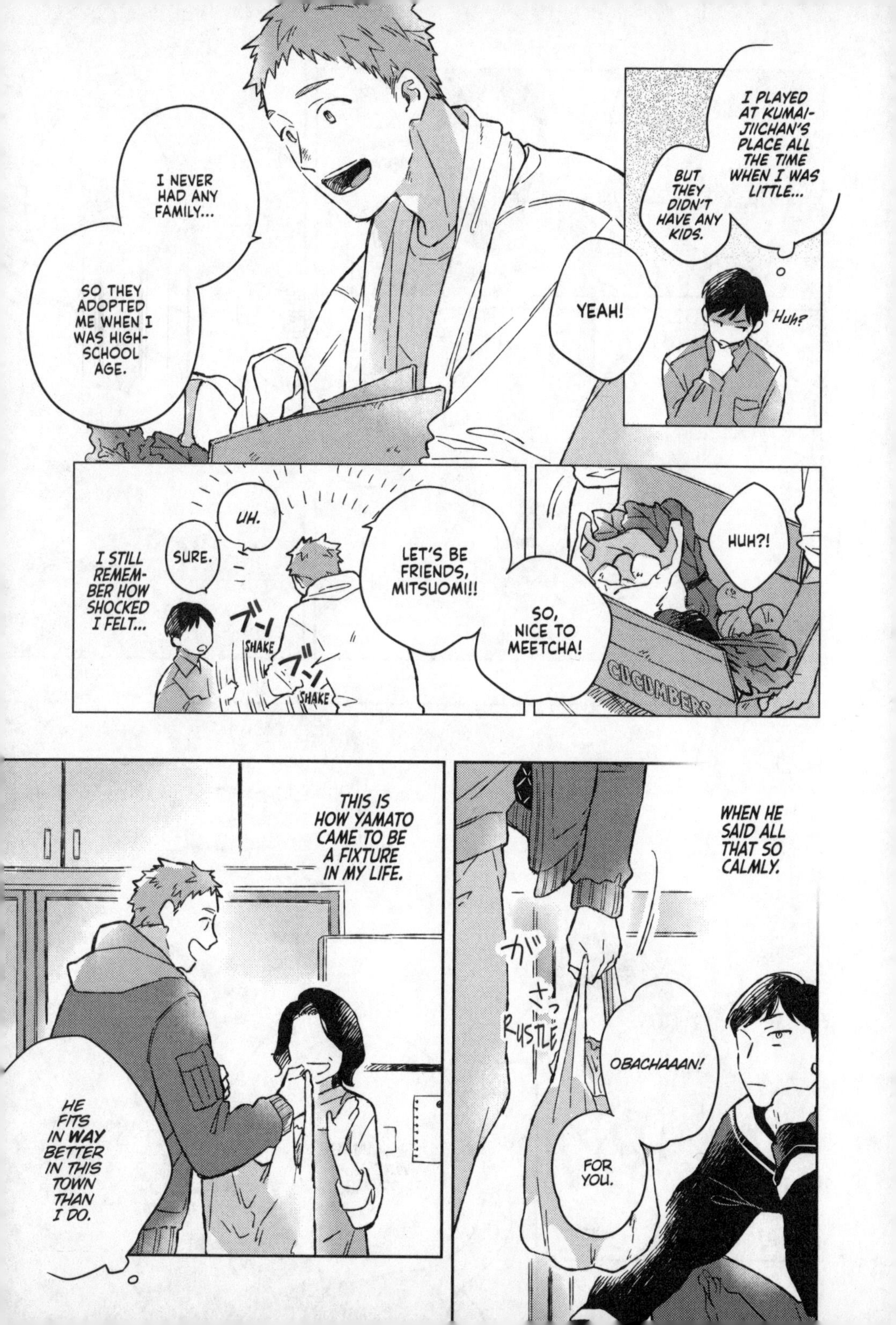
I PLAYED AT KUMAI-JIICHAN'S PLACE ALL THE TIME WHEN I WAS LITTLE...
BUT THEY DIDN'T HAVE ANY KIDS.
Huh?
YEAH!
I NEVER HAD ANY FAMILY...
SO THEY ADOPTED ME WHEN I WAS HIGH-SCHOOL AGE.
HUH?!
SO, NICE TO MEETCHA!
CUCUMBERS
LET'S BE FRIENDS, MITSUOMI!!
UH.
SURE.
ブン SHAKE
ブン SHAKE
I STILL REMEMBER HOW SHOCKED I FELT...
WHEN HE SAID ALL THAT SO CALMLY.
OBACHAAAN!
FOR YOU.
ガさっ RUSTLE
THIS IS HOW YAMATO CAME TO BE A FIXTURE IN MY LIFE.
HE FITS IN WAY BETTER IN THIS TOWN THAN I DO.

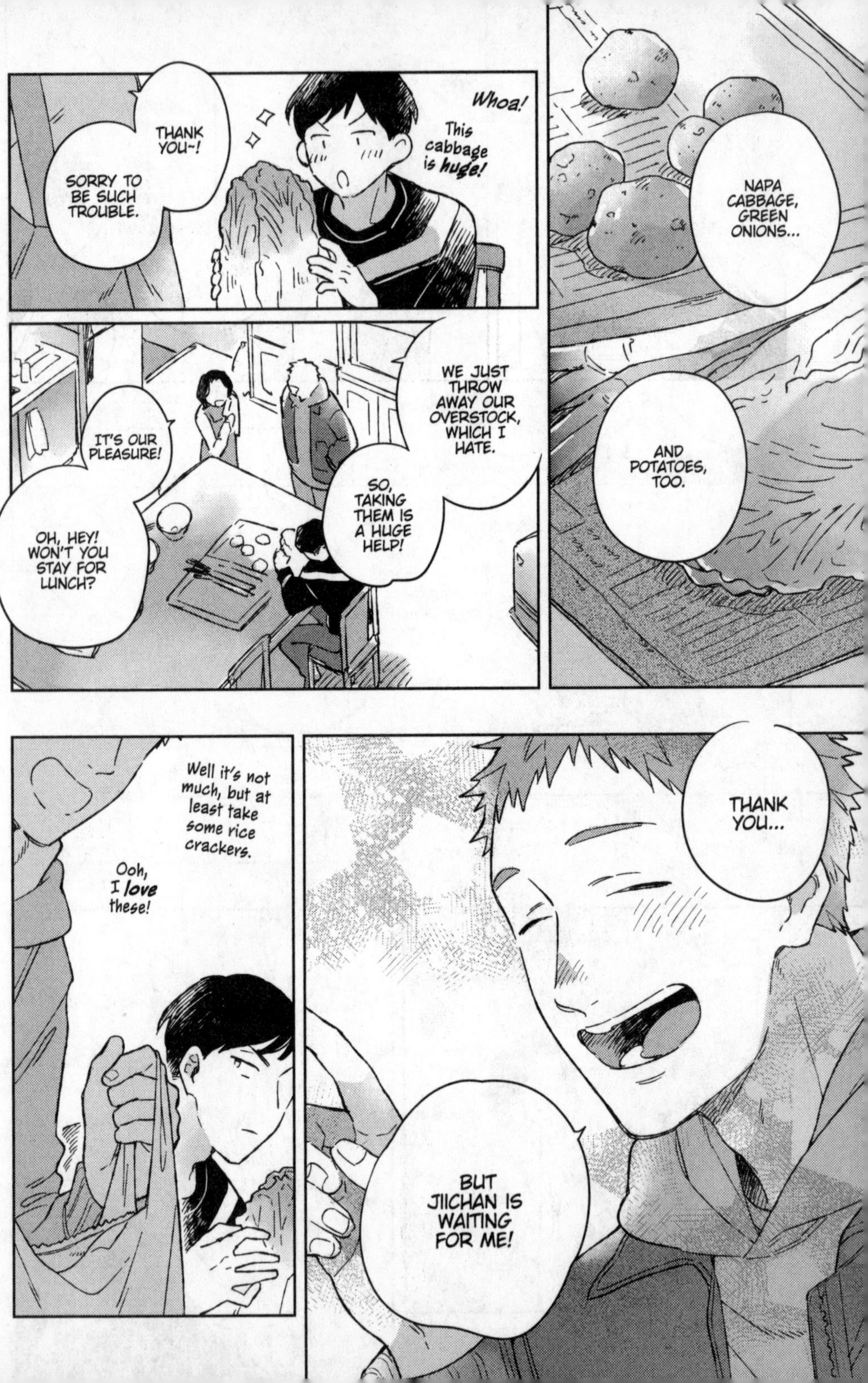
NAPA CABBAGE, GREEN ONIONS...
AND POTATOES, TOO.
Whoa! This cabbage is huge!
THANK YOU~!
SORRY TO BE SUCH TROUBLE.
WE JUST THROW AWAY OUR OVERSTOCK, WHICH I HATE.
SO, TAKING THEM IS A HUGE HELP!
IT'S OUR PLEASURE!
OH, HEY! WON'T YOU STAY FOR LUNCH?
THANK YOU...
BUT JIICHAN IS WAITING FOR ME!
Well it's not much, but at least take some rice crackers.
Ooh, I love these!

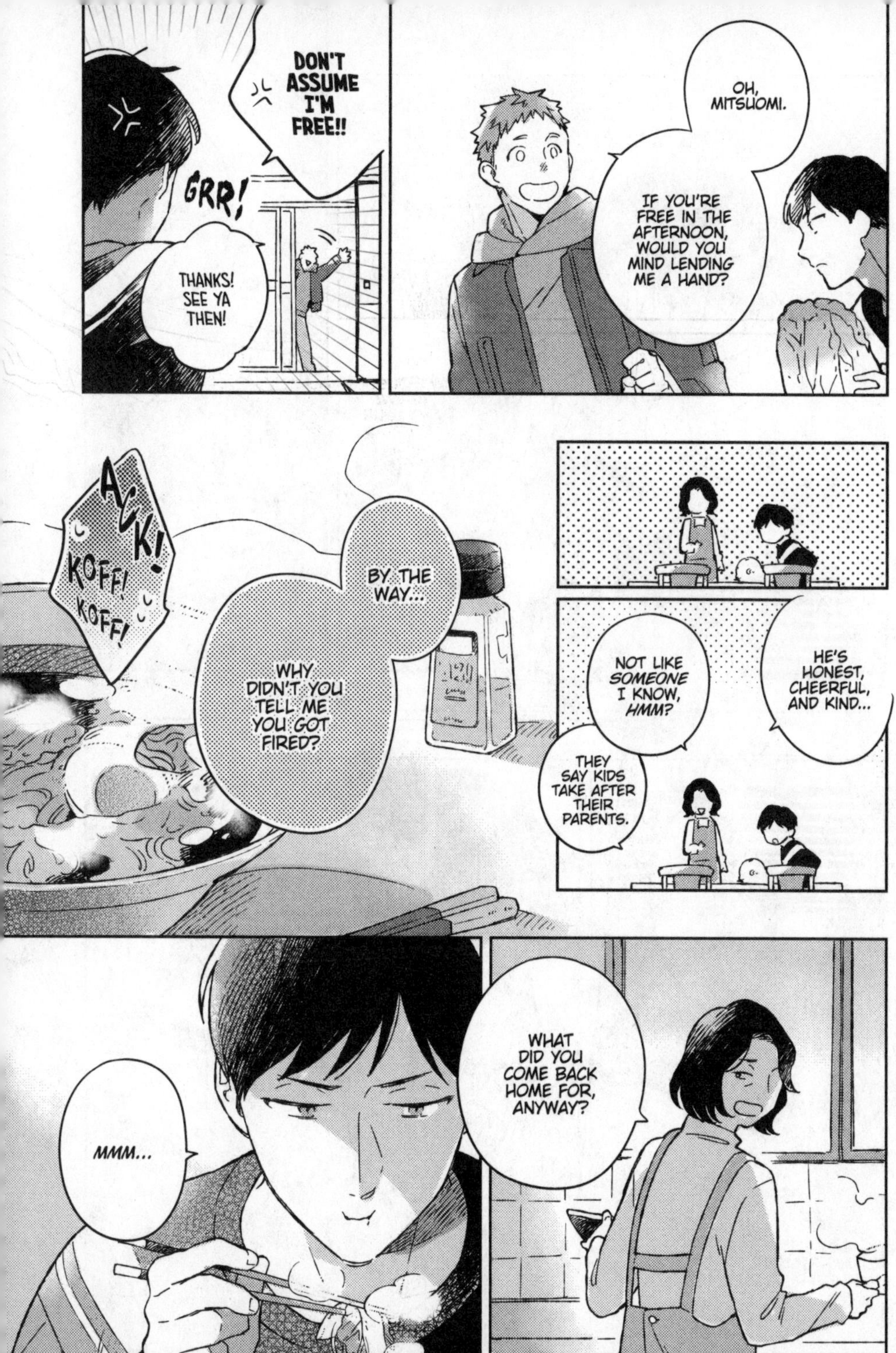
OH, MITSUOMI.
IF YOU'RE FREE IN THE AFTERNOON, WOULD YOU MIND LENDING ME A HAND?
DON'T ASSUME I'M FREE!!
GRR!
THANKS! SEE YA THEN!
HE'S HONEST, CHEERFUL, AND KIND...
NOT LIKE *SOMEONE* I KNOW, *HMM*?
THEY SAY KIDS TAKE AFTER THEIR PARENTS.
BY THE WAY...
WHY DIDN'T YOU TELL ME YOU GOT FIRED?
ACK!
KOFF! KOFF!
WHAT DID YOU COME BACK HOME FOR, ANYWAY?
MMM...

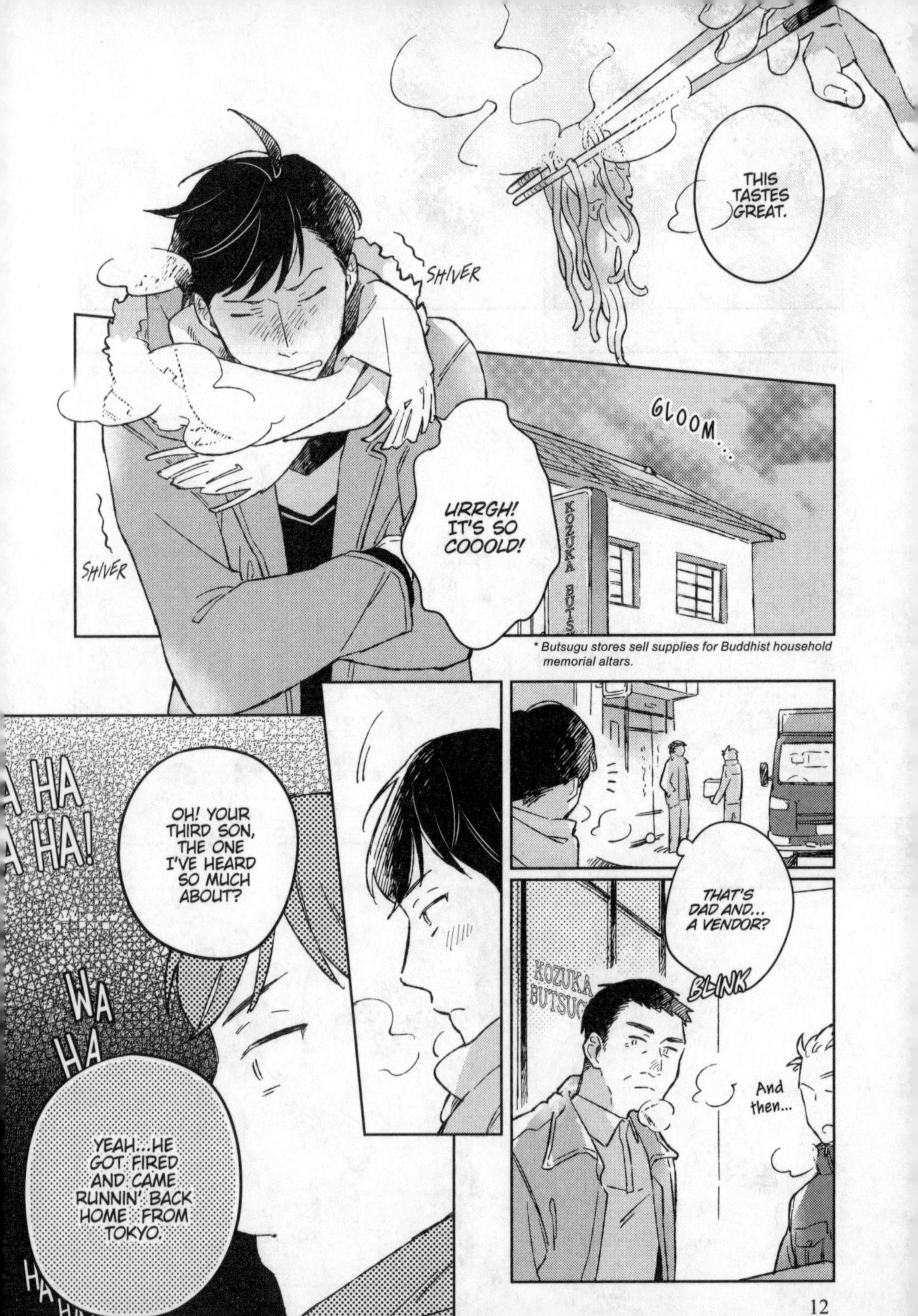
THIS TASTES GREAT.
SHIVER
GLOOM...
URRGH! IT'S SO COOOLD!
SHIVER
KOZUKA
THAT'S DAD AND... A VENDOR?
BLINK
KOZUKA
And then...
A HA HA HA HA!
OH! YOUR THIRD SON, THE ONE I'VE HEARD SO MUCH ABOUT?
WA HA HA
YEAH...HE GOT FIRED AND CAME RUNNIN' BACK HOME FROM TOKYO.
HA HA!

* Butsugu stores sell supplies for Buddhist household memorial altars.

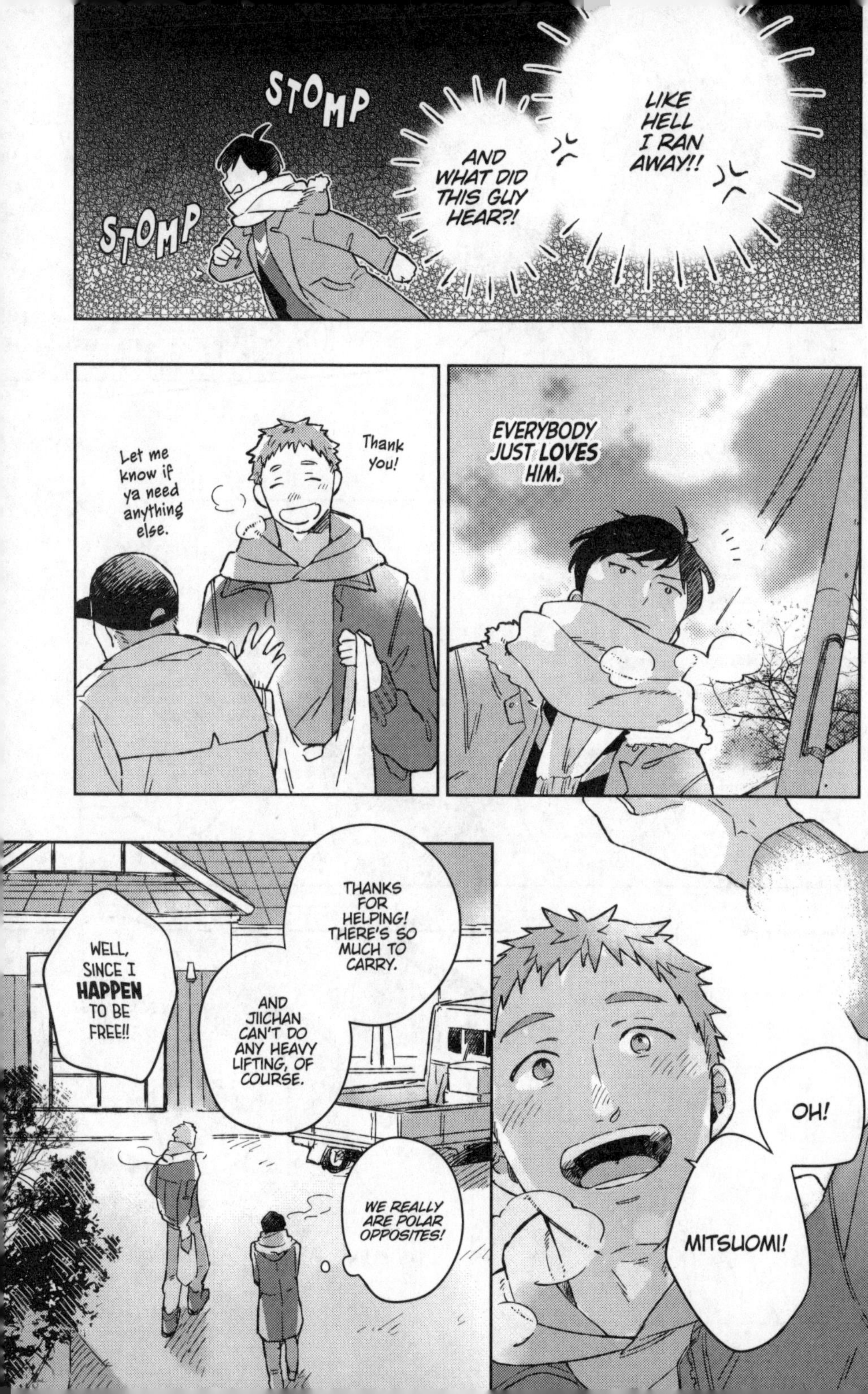
LIKE HELL I RAN AWAY!!
AND WHAT DID THIS GUY HEAR?!
STOMP
STOMP
EVERYBODY JUST LOVES HIM.
Thank you!
Let me know if ya need anything else.
OH!
MITSUOMI!
THANKS FOR HELPING! THERE'S SO MUCH TO CARRY.
AND JIICHAN CAN'T DO ANY HEAVY LIFTING, OF COURSE.
WELL, SINCE I HAPPEN TO BE FREE!!
WE REALLY ARE POLAR OPPOSITES!

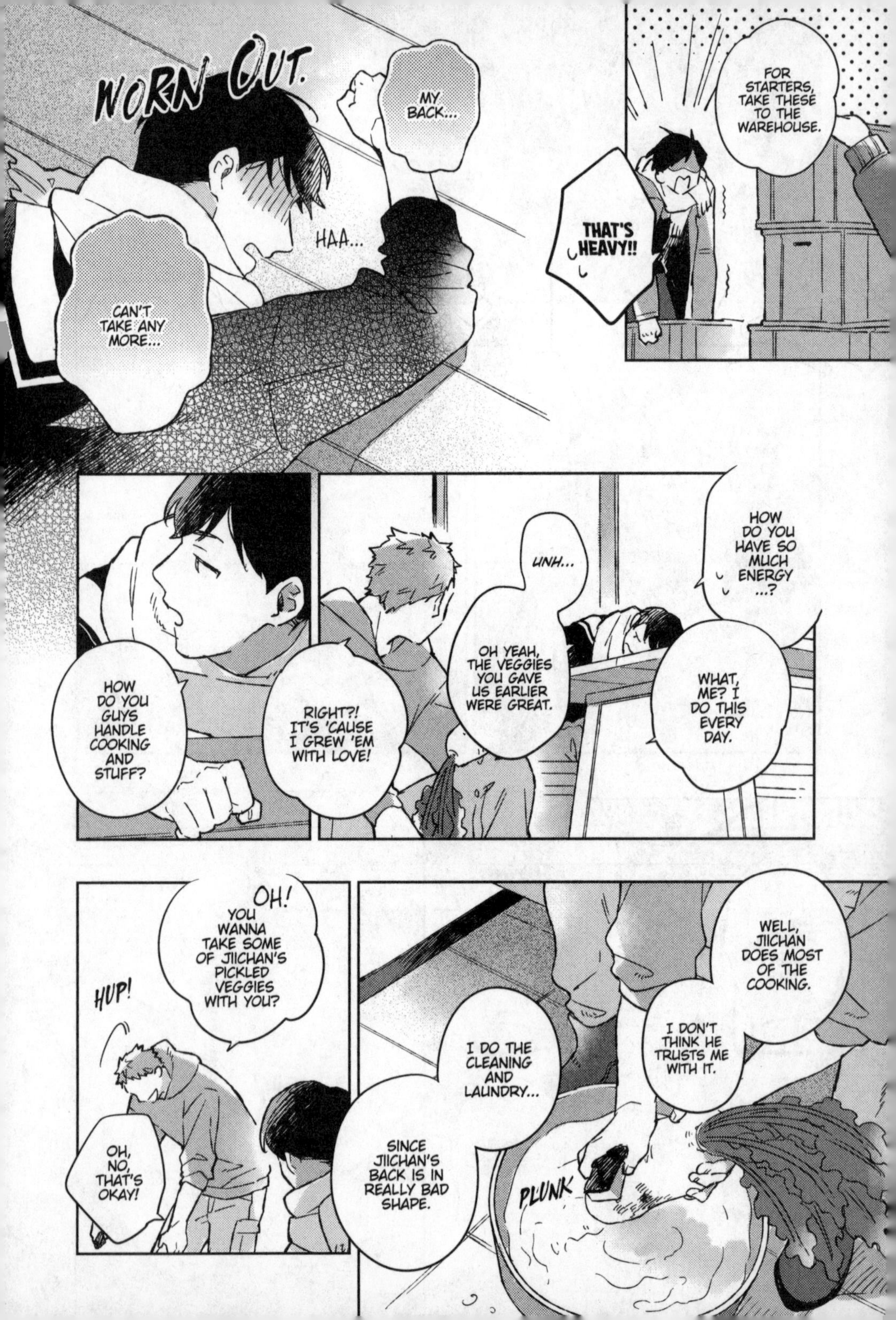
FOR STARTERS, TAKE THESE TO THE WAREHOUSE.
THAT'S HEAVY!!
WORN OUT.
MY BACK...
HAA...
CAN'T TAKE ANY MORE...
HOW DO YOU HAVE SO MUCH ENERGY ...?
UNH...
WHAT, ME? I DO THIS EVERY DAY.
OH YEAH, THE VEGGIES YOU GAVE US EARLIER WERE GREAT.
RIGHT?! IT'S 'CAUSE I GREW 'EM WITH LOVE!
HOW DO YOU GUYS HANDLE COOKING AND STUFF?
WELL, JIICHAN DOES MOST OF THE COOKING.
I DON'T THINK HE TRUSTS ME WITH IT.
I DO THE CLEANING AND LAUNDRY...
SINCE JIICHAN'S BACK IS IN REALLY BAD SHAPE.
PLUNK
OH! YOU WANNA TAKE SOME OF JIICHAN'S PICKLED VEGGIES WITH YOU?
HUP!
OH, NO, THAT'S OKAY!

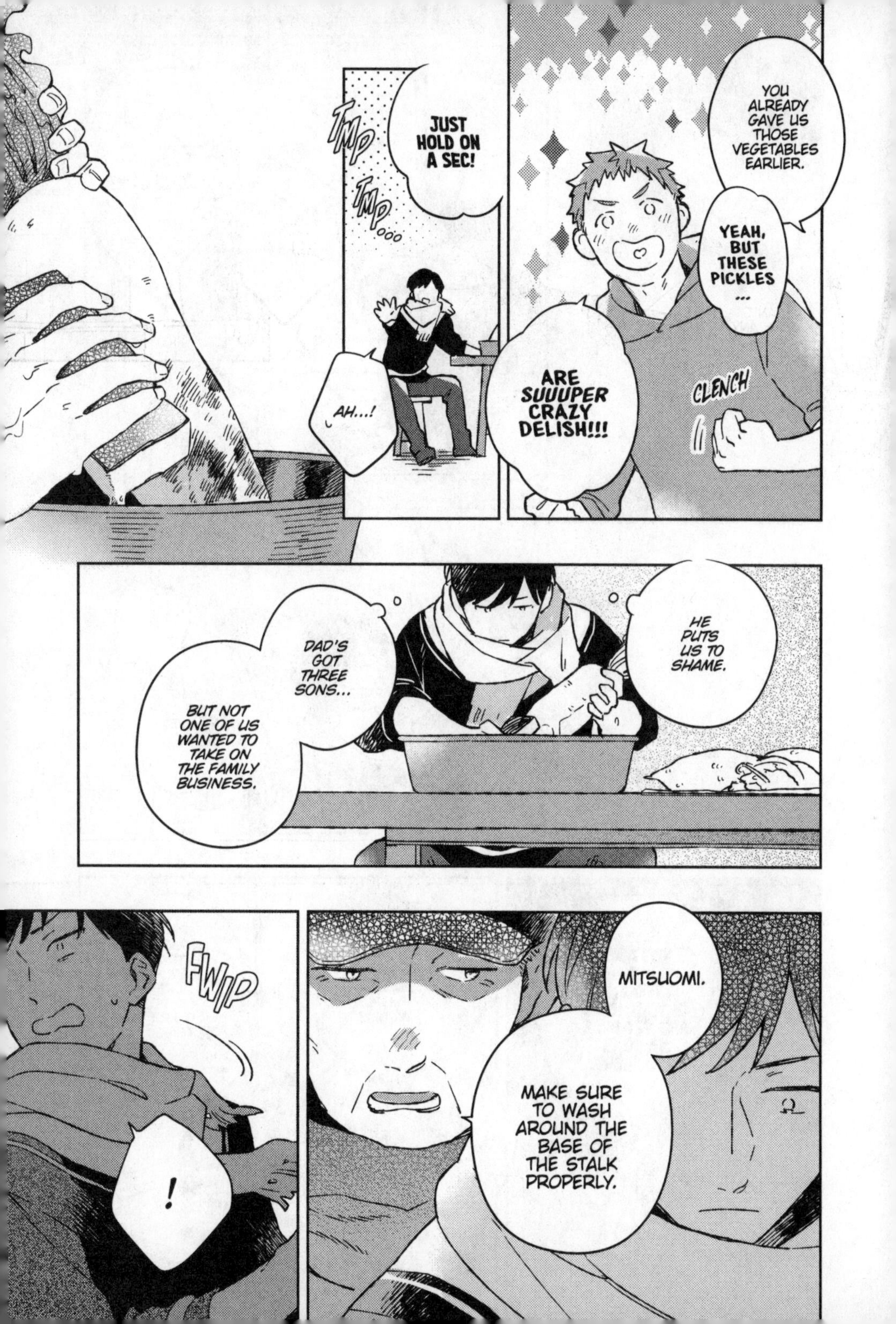
YOU ALREADY GAVE US THOSE VEGETABLES EARLIER.
YEAH, BUT THESE PICKLES ...
CLENCH
ARE SUUUPER CRAZY DELISH!!!
JUST HOLD ON A SEC!
TMP
TMP...
AH...!
HE PUTS US TO SHAME.
DAD'S GOT THREE SONS...
BUT NOT ONE OF US WANTED TO TAKE ON THE FAMILY BUSINESS.
MITSUOMI.
MAKE SURE TO WASH AROUND THE BASE OF THE STALK PROPERLY.
FWIP
!

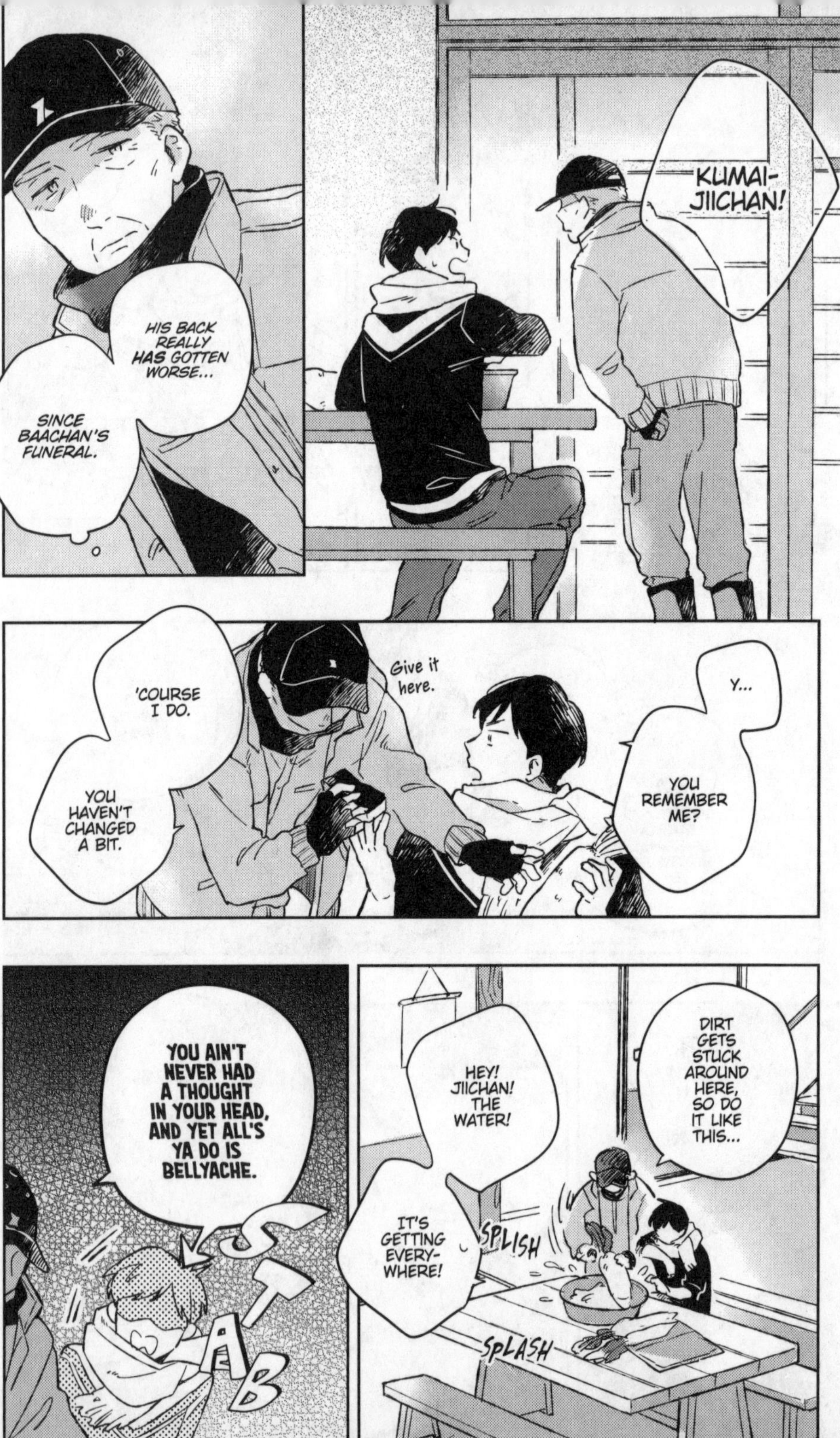
KUMAI-JIICHAN!
HIS BACK REALLY HAS GOTTEN WORSE...
SINCE BAACHAN'S FUNERAL.
Y...
YOU REMEMBER ME?
Give it here.
'COURSE I DO.
YOU HAVEN'T CHANGED A BIT.
DIRT GETS STUCK AROUND HERE, SO DO IT LIKE THIS...
HEY! JIICHAN! THE WATER!
SPLISH
IT'S GETTING EVERY-WHERE!
SPLASH
YOU AIN'T NEVER HAD A THOUGHT IN YOUR HEAD, AND YET ALL'S YA DO IS BELLYACHE.
STAB

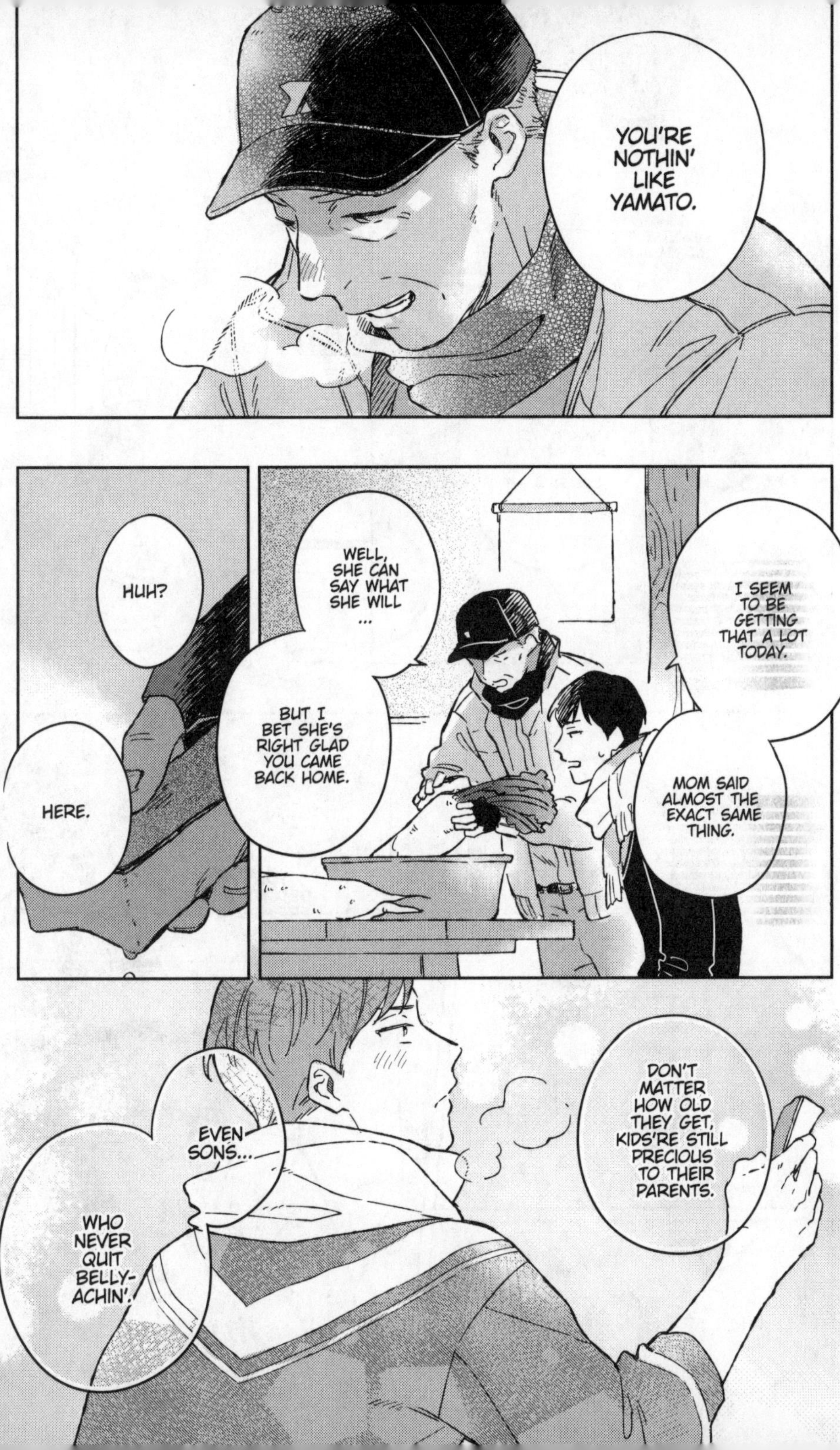

YOU'RE NOTHIN' LIKE YAMATO.
I SEEM TO BE GETTING THAT A LOT TODAY.
MOM SAID ALMOST THE EXACT SAME THING.
WELL, SHE CAN SAY WHAT SHE WILL ...
BUT I BET SHE'S RIGHT GLAD YOU CAME BACK HOME.
HUH?
HERE.
DON'T MATTER HOW OLD THEY GET, KIDS'RE STILL PRECIOUS TO THEIR PARENTS.
EVEN SONS...
WHO NEVER QUIT BELLY-ACHIN'.

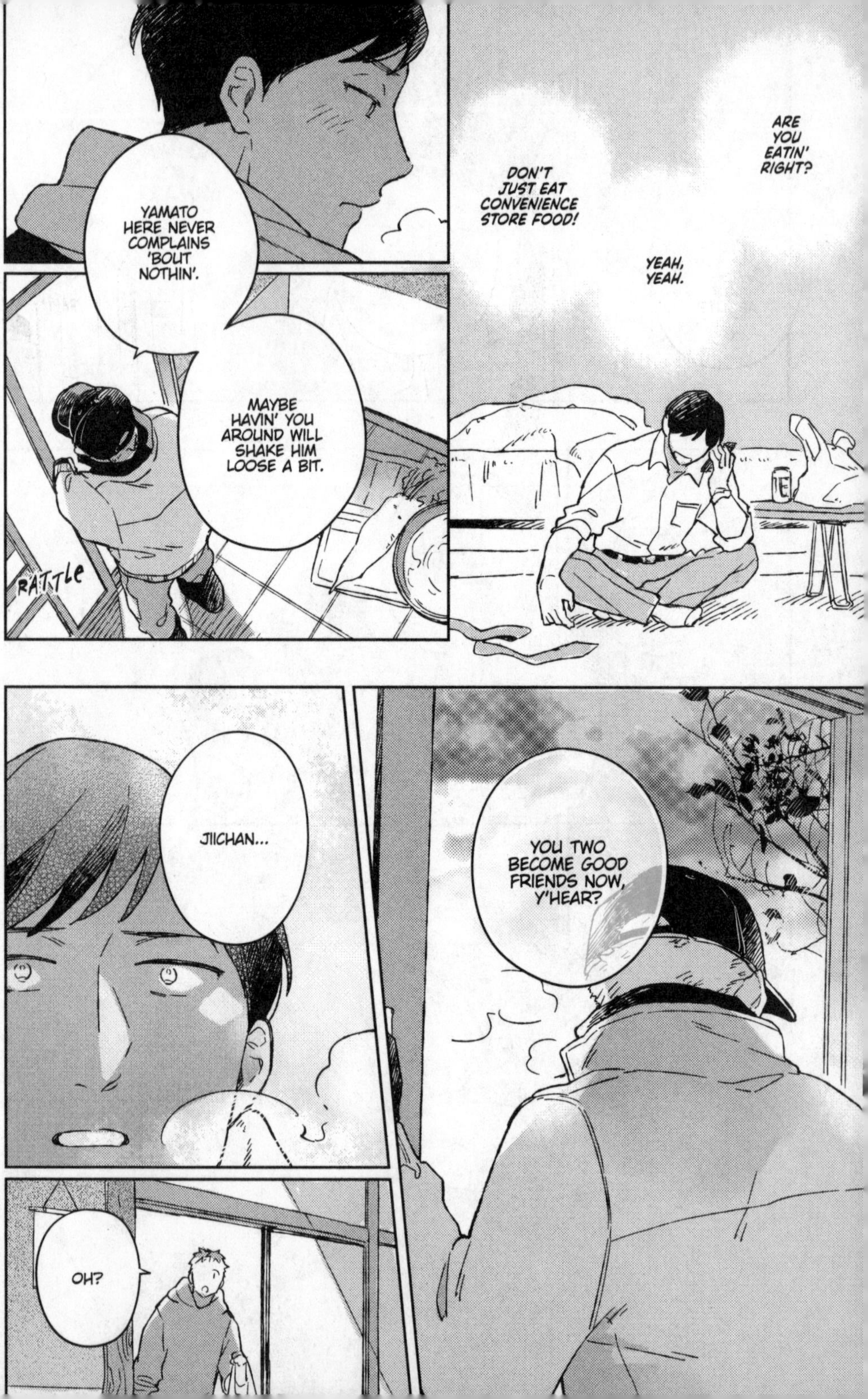
ARE YOU EATIN' RIGHT?
DON'T JUST EAT CONVENIENCE STORE FOOD!
YEAH, YEAH.
YAMATO HERE NEVER COMPLAINS 'BOUT NOTHIN'.
MAYBE HAVIN' YOU AROUND WILL SHAKE HIM LOOSE A BIT.
RATTLE
YOU TWO BECOME GOOD FRIENDS NOW, Y'HEAR?
JIICHAN...
OH?

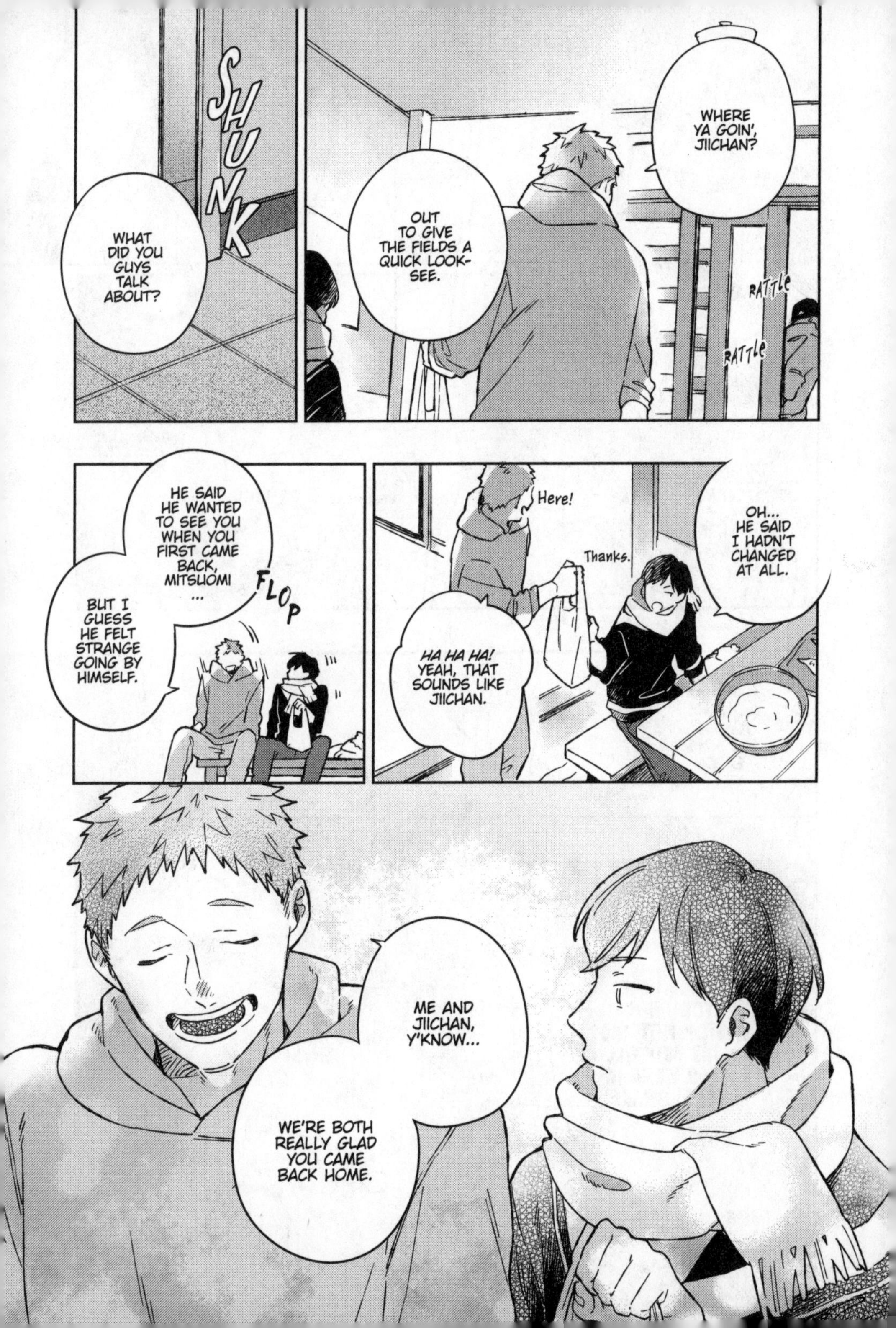
WHERE YA GOIN', JIICHAN?
OUT TO GIVE THE FIELDS A QUICK LOOK-SEE.
RATTLE
RATTLE
SHUNK
WHAT DID YOU GUYS TALK ABOUT?
OH... HE SAID I HADN'T CHANGED AT ALL.
Here!
Thanks.
HA HA HA! YEAH, THAT SOUNDS LIKE JIICHAN.
HE SAID HE WANTED TO SEE YOU WHEN YOU FIRST CAME BACK, MITSUOMI...
BUT I GUESS HE FELT STRANGE GOING BY HIMSELF.
FLOP
ME AND JIICHAN, Y'KNOW...
WE'RE BOTH REALLY GLAD YOU CAME BACK HOME.

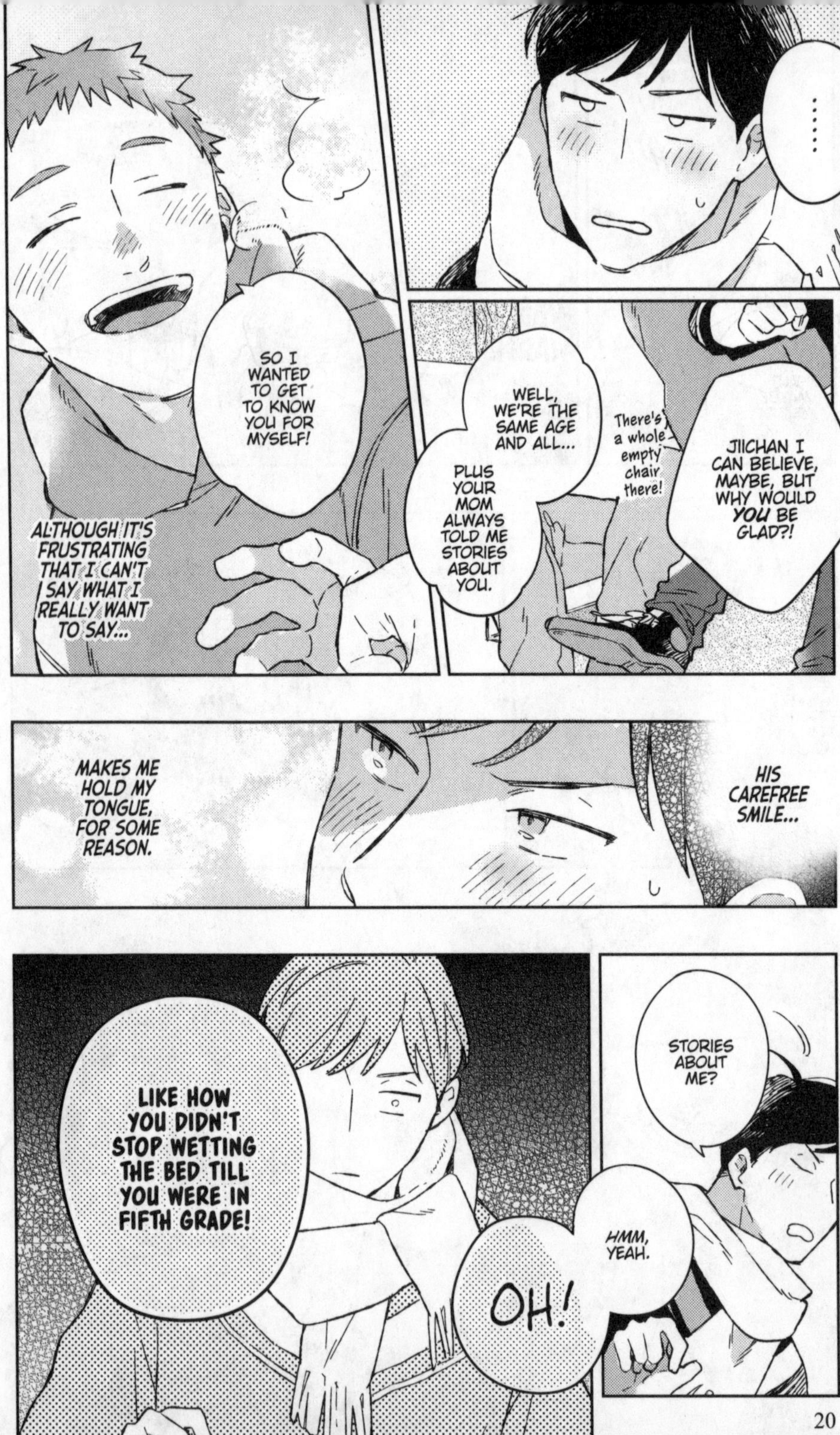
......
JIICHAN I CAN BELIEVE, MAYBE, BUT WHY WOULD *YOU* BE GLAD?!
There's a whole empty chair there!
WELL, WE'RE THE SAME AGE AND ALL...
PLUS YOUR MOM ALWAYS TOLD ME STORIES ABOUT YOU.
SO I WANTED TO GET TO KNOW YOU FOR MYSELF!
ALTHOUGH IT'S FRUSTRATING THAT I CAN'T SAY WHAT I REALLY WANT TO SAY...
HIS CAREFREE SMILE...
MAKES ME HOLD MY TONGUE, FOR SOME REASON.
STORIES ABOUT ME?
HMM, YEAH.
OH!
LIKE HOW YOU DIDN'T STOP WETTING THE BED TILL YOU WERE IN FIFTH GRADE!

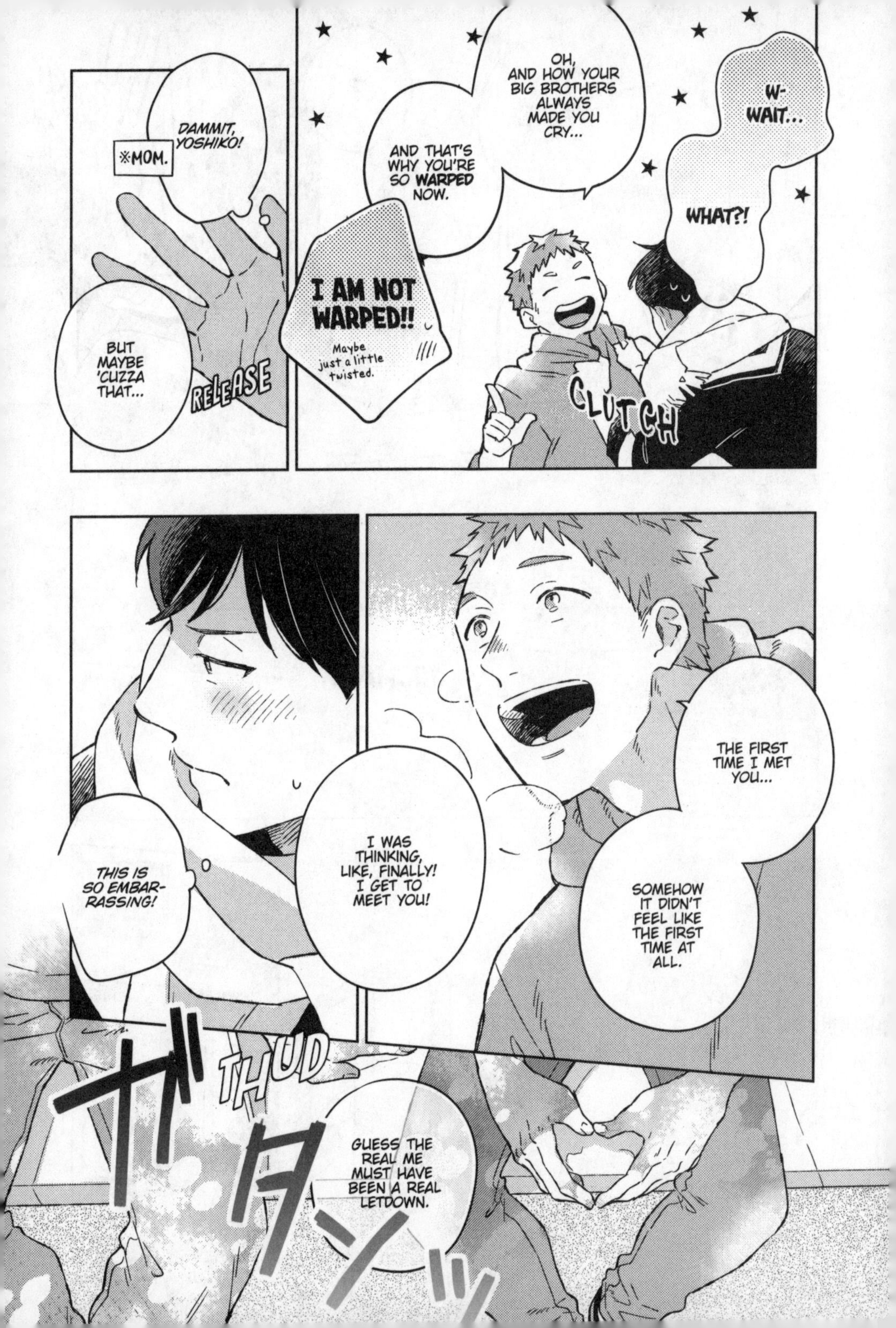
W- WAIT...
WHAT?!
OH, AND HOW YOUR BIG BROTHERS ALWAYS MADE YOU CRY...
AND THAT'S WHY YOU'RE SO WARPED NOW.
I AM NOT WARPED!!
Maybe just a little twisted.
CLUTCH
DAMMIT, YOSHIKO!
※MOM.
RELEASE
BUT MAYBE 'CUZZA THAT...
THE FIRST TIME I MET YOU...
SOMEHOW IT DIDN'T FEEL LIKE THE FIRST TIME AT ALL.
I WAS THINKING, LIKE, FINALLY! I GET TO MEET YOU!
THIS IS SO EMBAR-RASSING!
THUD
GUESS THE REAL ME MUST HAVE BEEN A REAL LETDOWN.

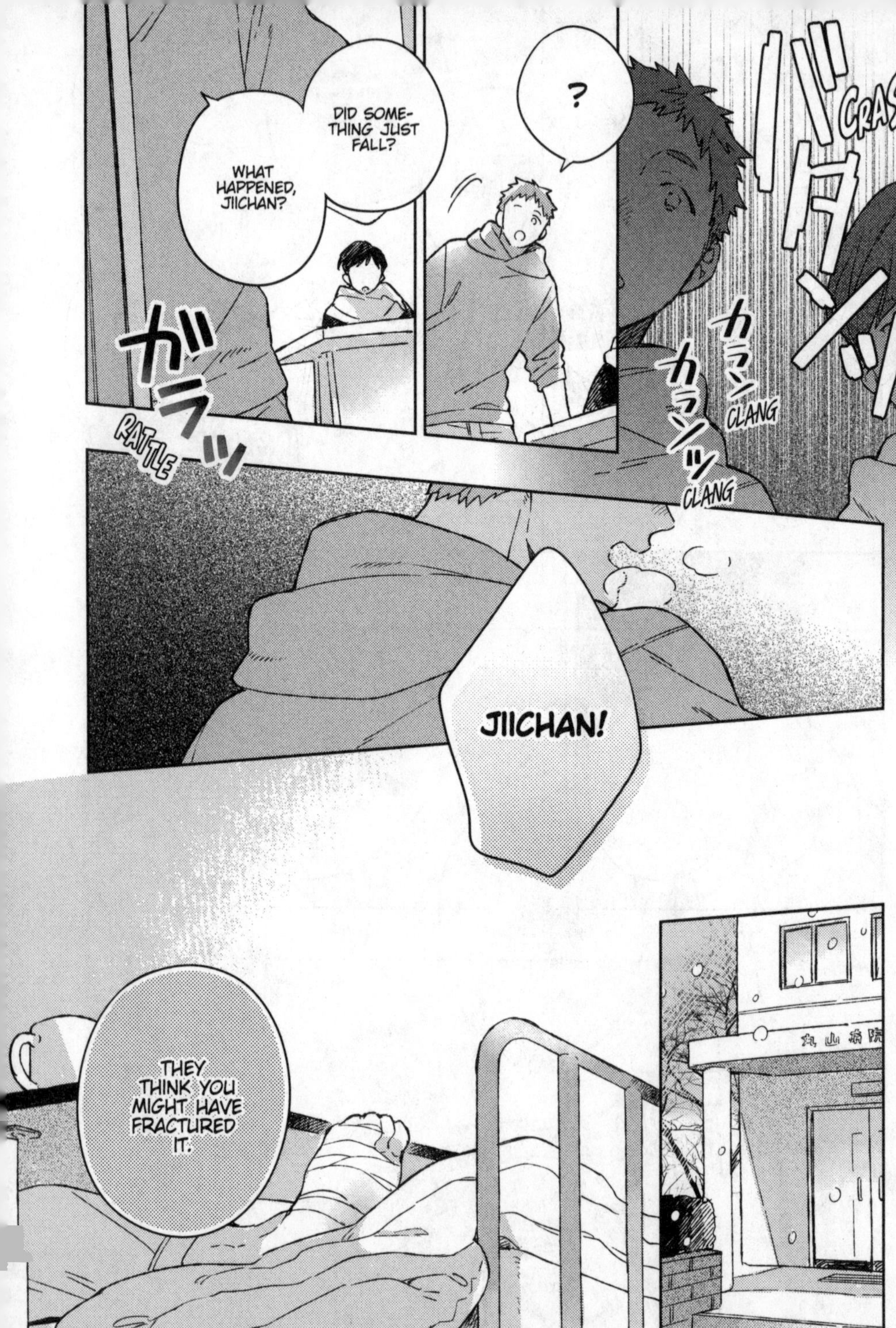
バダンッ
CRASH
カランカランッ
CLANG
CLANG
?
DID SOME-THING JUST FALL?
WHAT HAPPENED, JIICHAN?
ガラッ
RATTLE
JIICHAN!
丸山病院
THEY THINK YOU MIGHT HAVE FRACTURED IT.
Sign: Maruyama Hospital

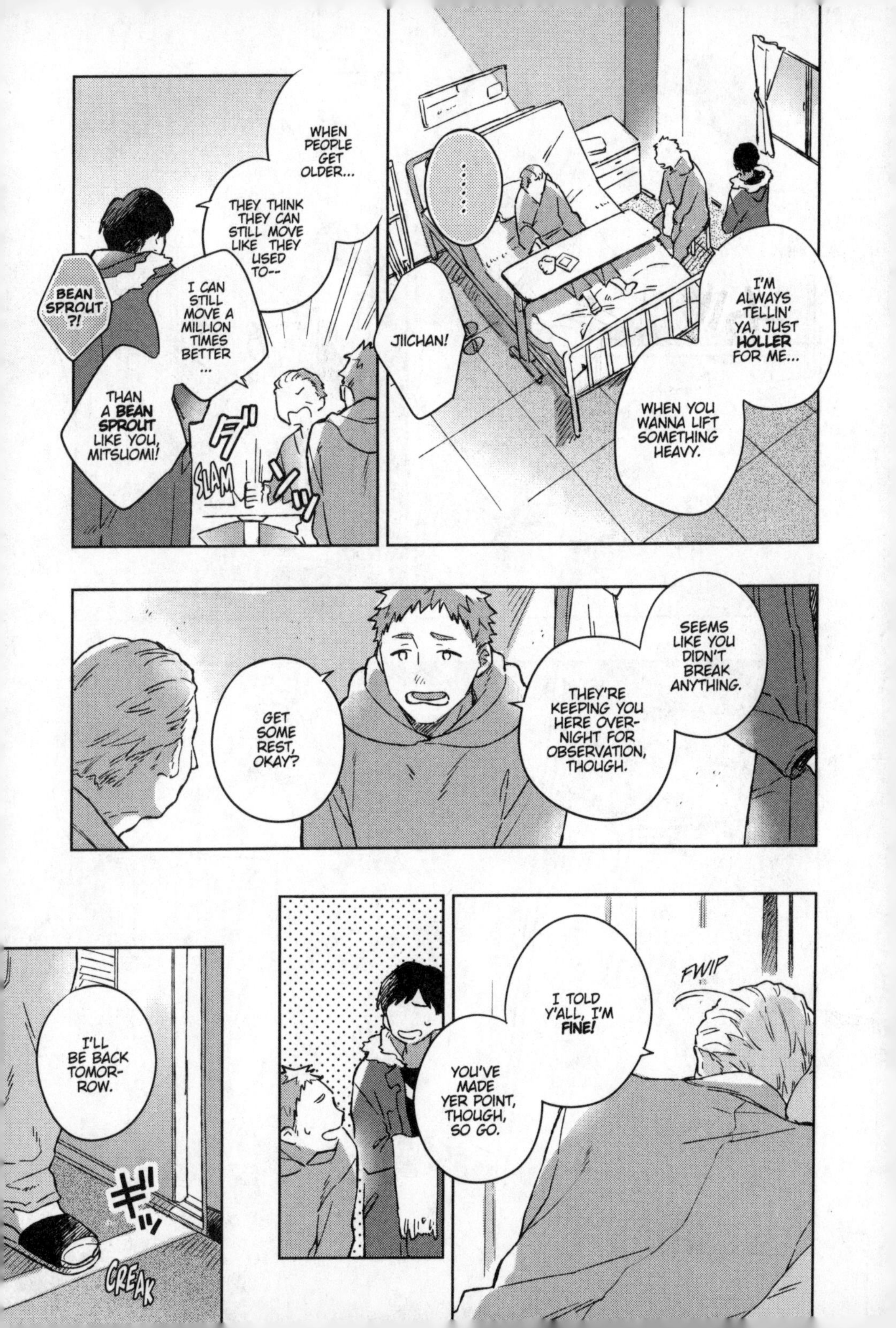
......
I'M ALWAYS TELLIN' YA, JUST **HOLLER** FOR ME...
WHEN YOU WANNA LIFT SOMETHING HEAVY.
JIICHAN!
WHEN PEOPLE GET OLDER...
THEY THINK THEY CAN STILL MOVE LIKE THEY USED TO--
I CAN STILL MOVE A MILLION TIMES BETTER...
THAN A **BEAN SPROUT** LIKE YOU, MITSUOMI!
SLAM
BEAN SPROUT?!
SEEMS LIKE YOU DIDN'T BREAK ANYTHING.
THEY'RE KEEPING YOU HERE OVER-NIGHT FOR OBSERVATION, THOUGH.
GET SOME REST, OKAY?
FWIP
I TOLD Y'ALL, I'M **FINE!**
YOU'VE MADE YER POINT, THOUGH, SO GO.
I'LL BE BACK TOMOR-ROW.
CREAK

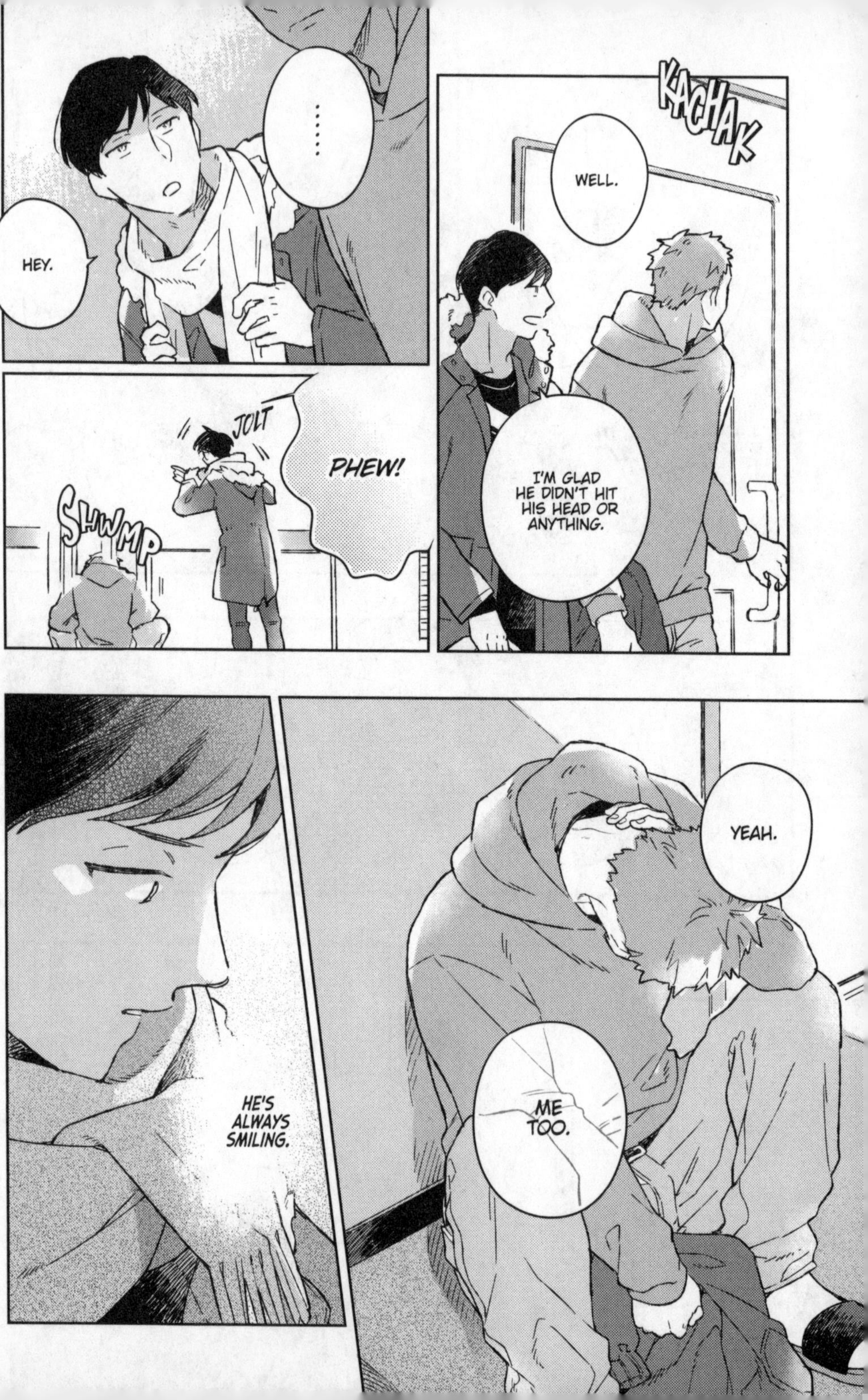
KACHAK
WELL.
I'M GLAD HE DIDN'T HIT HIS HEAD OR ANYTHING.
......
HEY.
JOLT
SHWMP
PHEW!
YEAH.
ME TOO.
HE'S ALWAYS SMILING.

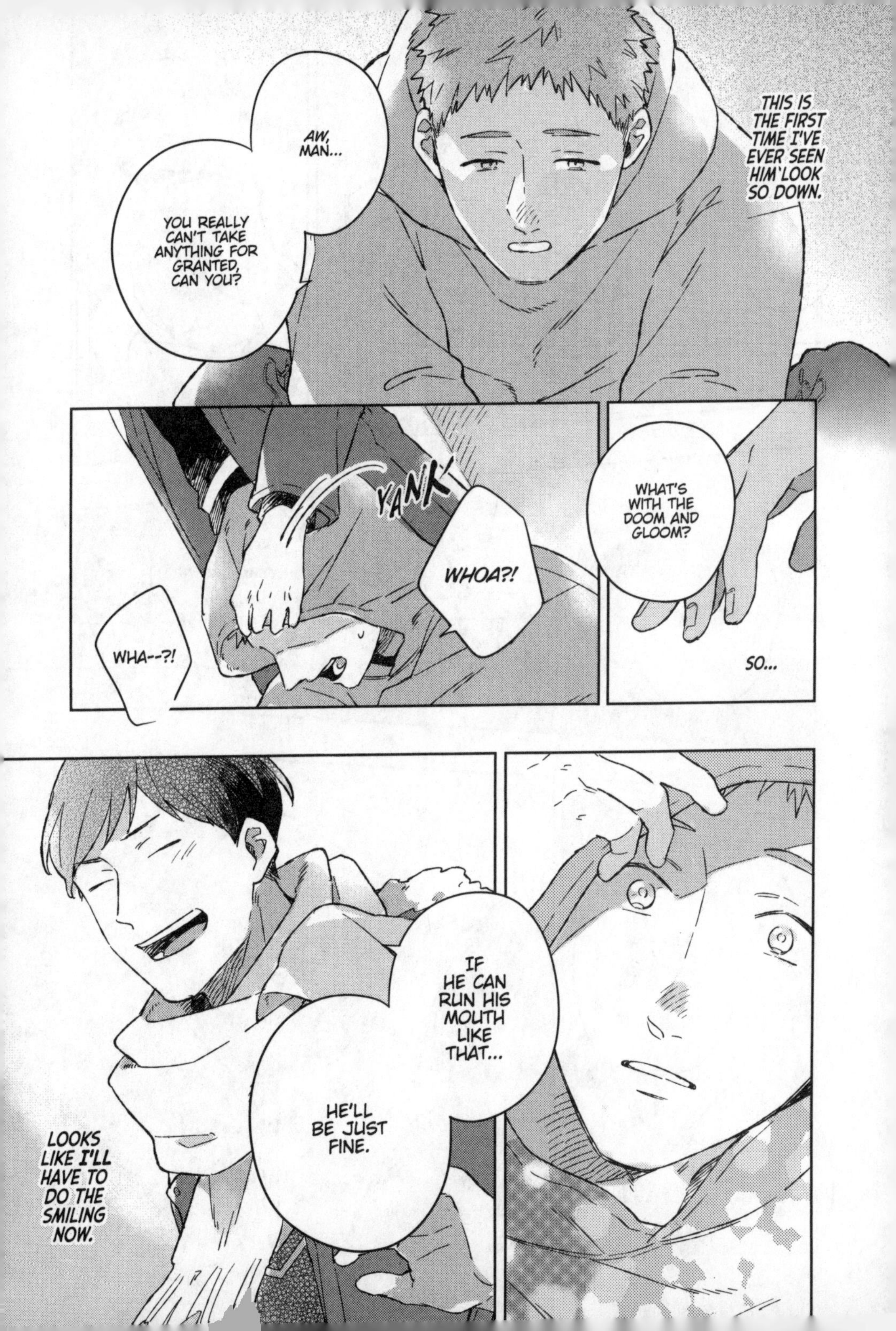
THIS IS THE FIRST TIME I'VE EVER SEEN HIM LOOK SO DOWN.
AW, MAN...
YOU REALLY CAN'T TAKE ANYTHING FOR GRANTED, CAN YOU?
WHAT'S WITH THE DOOM AND GLOOM?
SO...
YANK
WHOA?!
WHA--?!
IF HE CAN RUN HIS MOUTH LIKE THAT...
HE'LL BE JUST FINE.
LOOKS LIKE I'LL HAVE TO DO THE SMILING NOW.

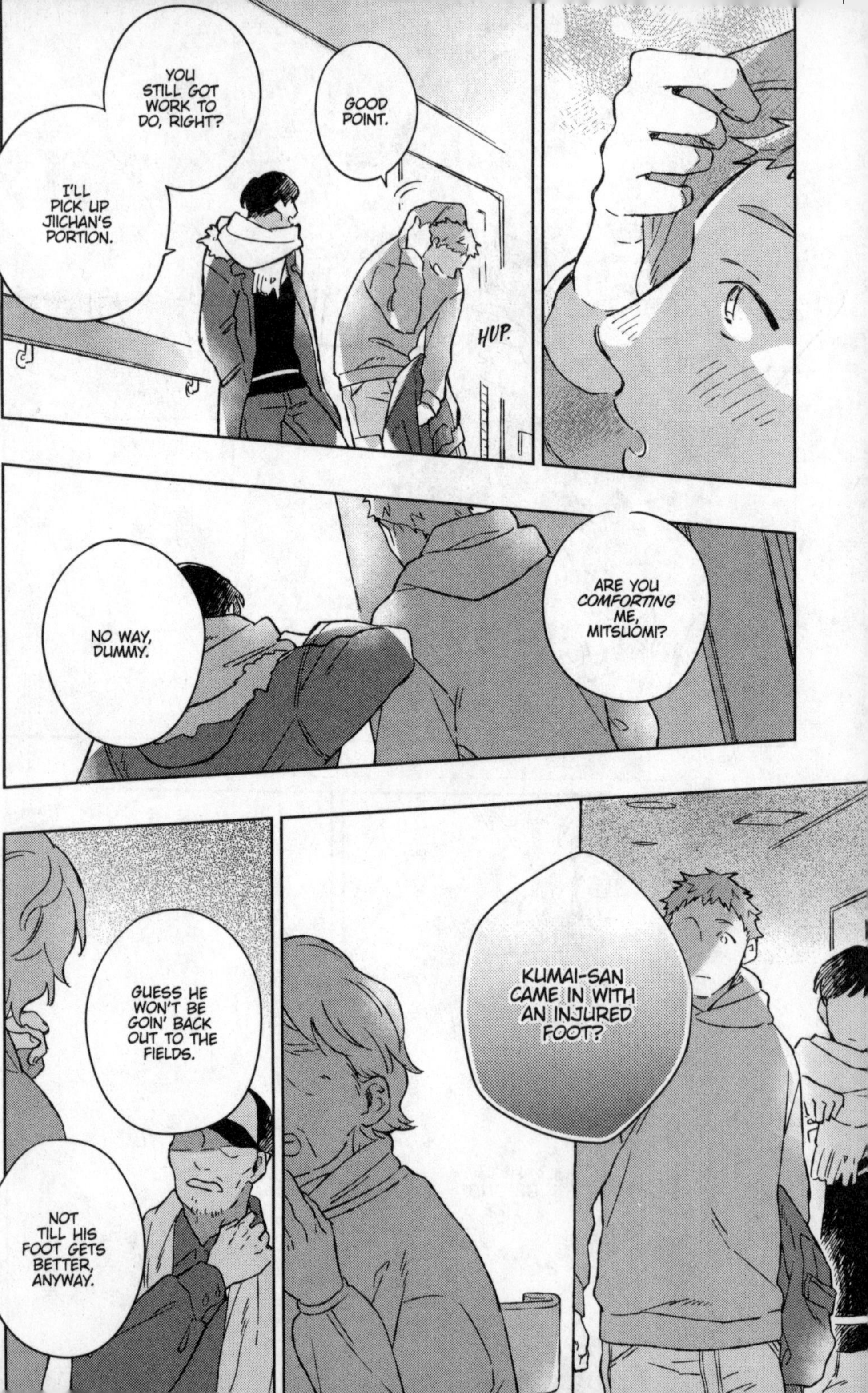
GOOD POINT.
YOU STILL GOT WORK TO DO, RIGHT?
I'LL PICK UP JIICHAN'S PORTION.
HUP.
ARE YOU COMFORTING ME, MITSUOMI?
NO WAY, DUMMY.
KUMAI-SAN CAME IN WITH AN INJURED FOOT?
GUESS HE WON'T BE GOIN' BACK OUT TO THE FIELDS.
NOT TILL HIS FOOT GETS BETTER, ANYWAY.

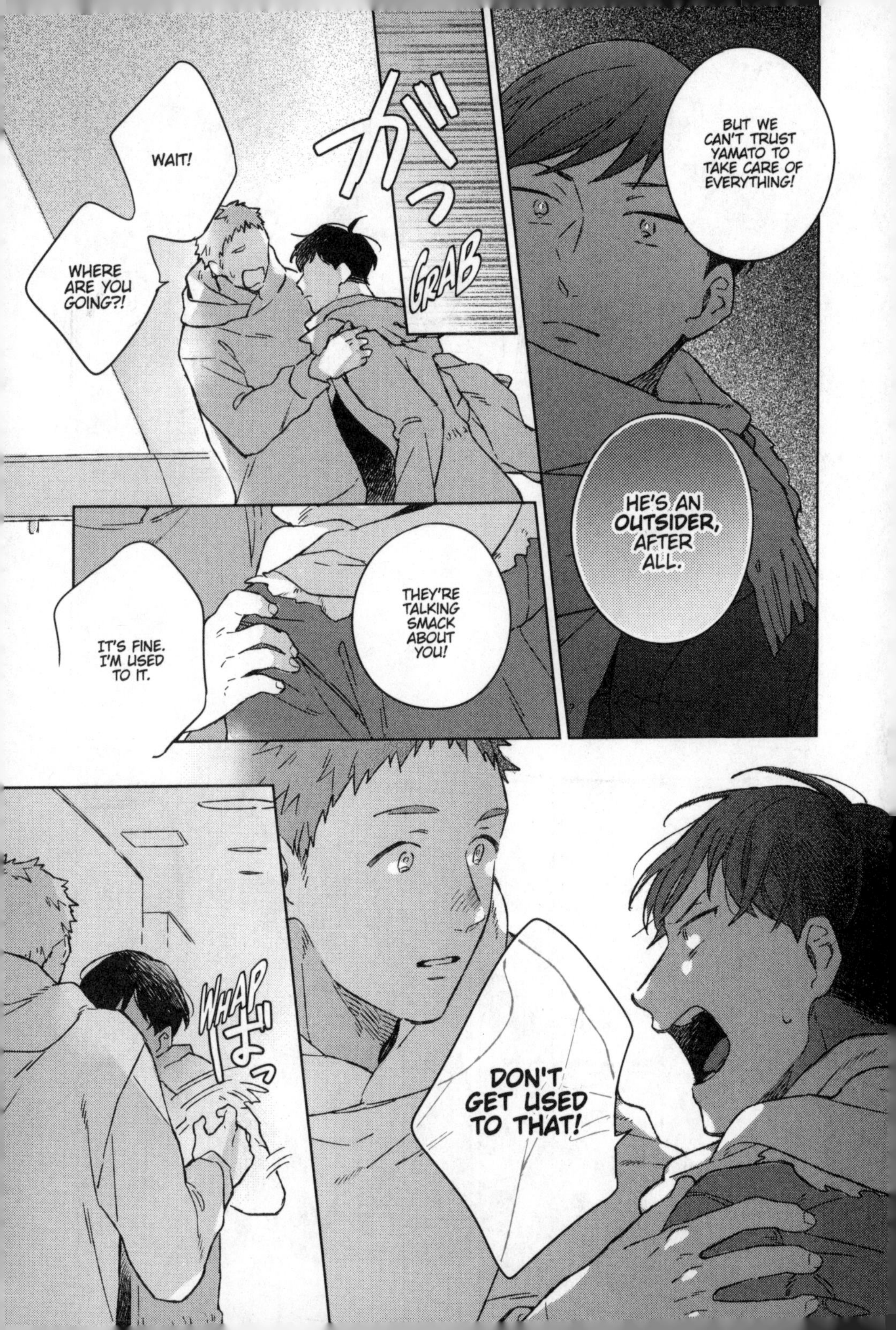
BUT WE CAN'T TRUST YAMATO TO TAKE CARE OF EVERYTHING!
HE'S AN OUTSIDER, AFTER ALL.
がっ
GRAB
WAIT!
WHERE ARE YOU GOING?!
THEY'RE TALKING SMACK ABOUT YOU!
IT'S FINE. I'M USED TO IT.
DON'T GET USED TO THAT!
WHAP
ぱっ

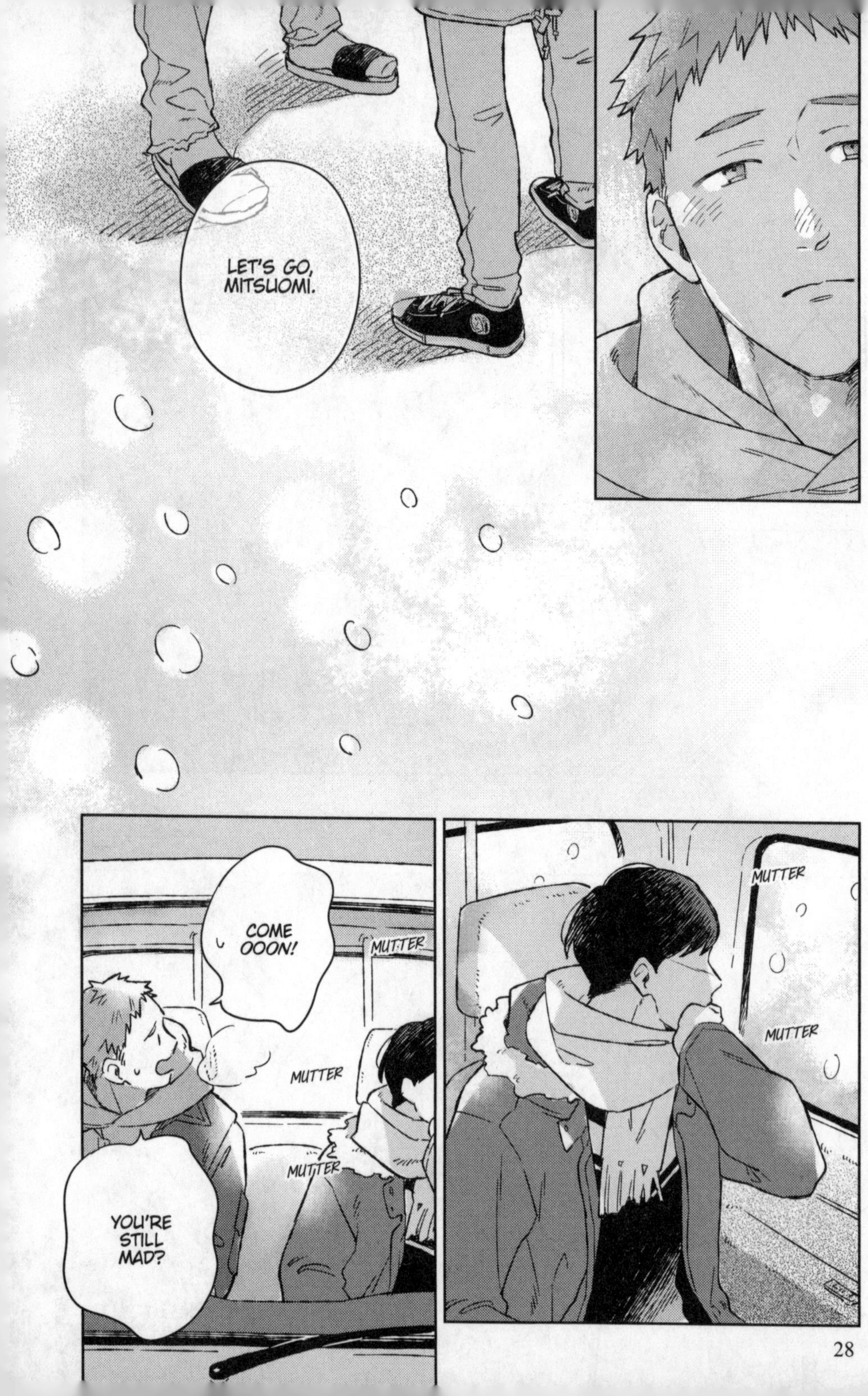
LET'S GO, MITSUOMI.
MUTTER
MUTTER
COME OOON!
MUTTER
MUTTER
MUTTER
YOU'RE STILL MAD?

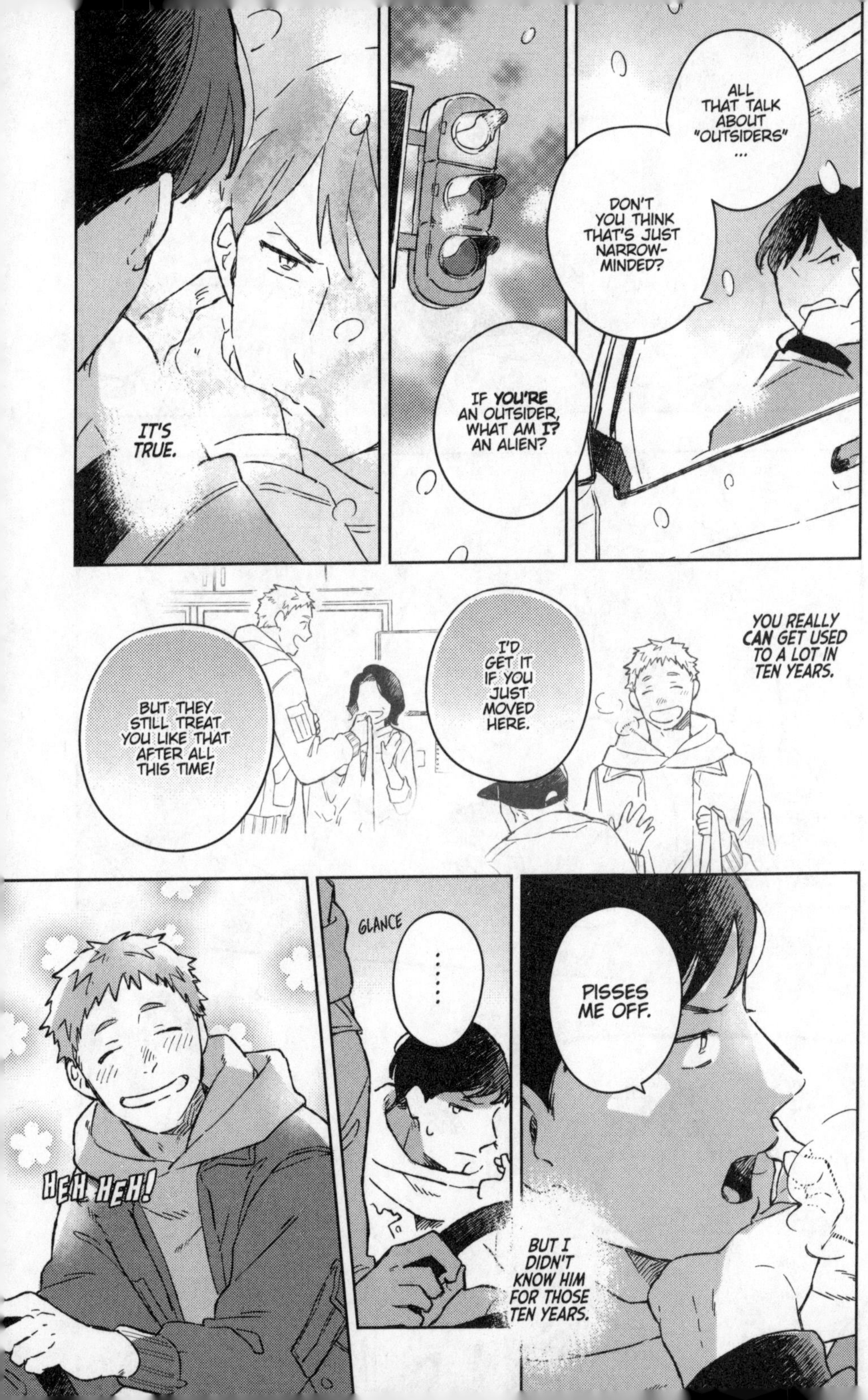
ALL THAT TALK ABOUT "OUTSIDERS" ...
DON'T YOU THINK THAT'S JUST NARROW-MINDED?
IF YOU'RE AN OUTSIDER, WHAT AM I? AN ALIEN?
IT'S TRUE.
YOU REALLY CAN GET USED TO A LOT IN TEN YEARS.
I'D GET IT IF YOU JUST MOVED HERE.
BUT THEY STILL TREAT YOU LIKE THAT AFTER ALL THIS TIME!
PISSES ME OFF.
BUT I DIDN'T KNOW HIM FOR THOSE TEN YEARS.
GLANCE
......
HEH HEH!

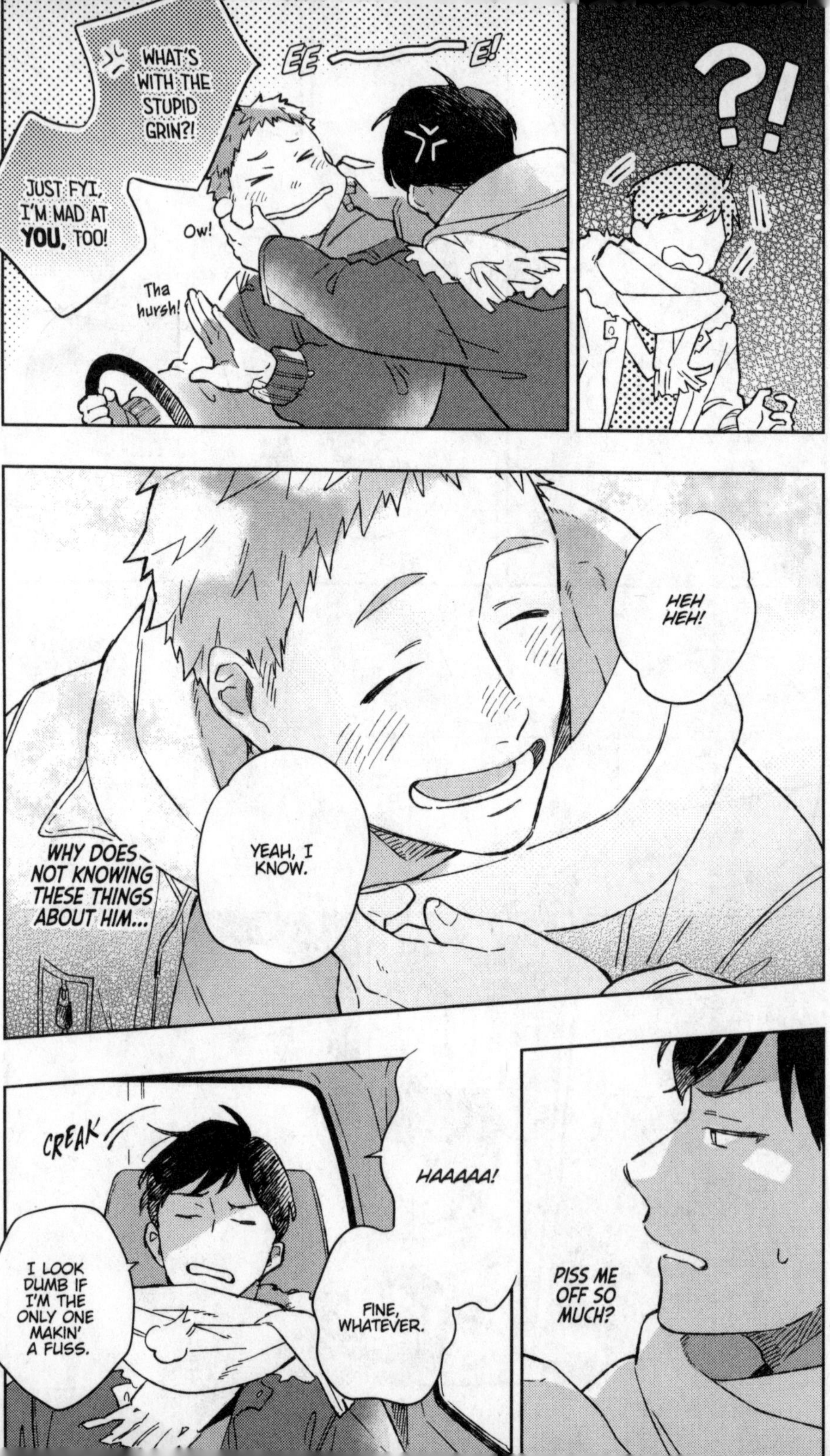
?!
EE——E!
WHAT'S WITH THE STUPID GRIN?!
JUST FYI, I'M MAD AT **YOU,** TOO!
Ow!
Tha hursh!
HEH HEH!
YEAH, I KNOW.
WHY DOES NOT KNOWING THESE THINGS ABOUT HIM...
PISS ME OFF SO MUCH?
HAAAAA!
FINE, WHATEVER.
CREAK
I LOOK DUMB IF I'M THE ONLY ONE MAKIN' A FUSS.

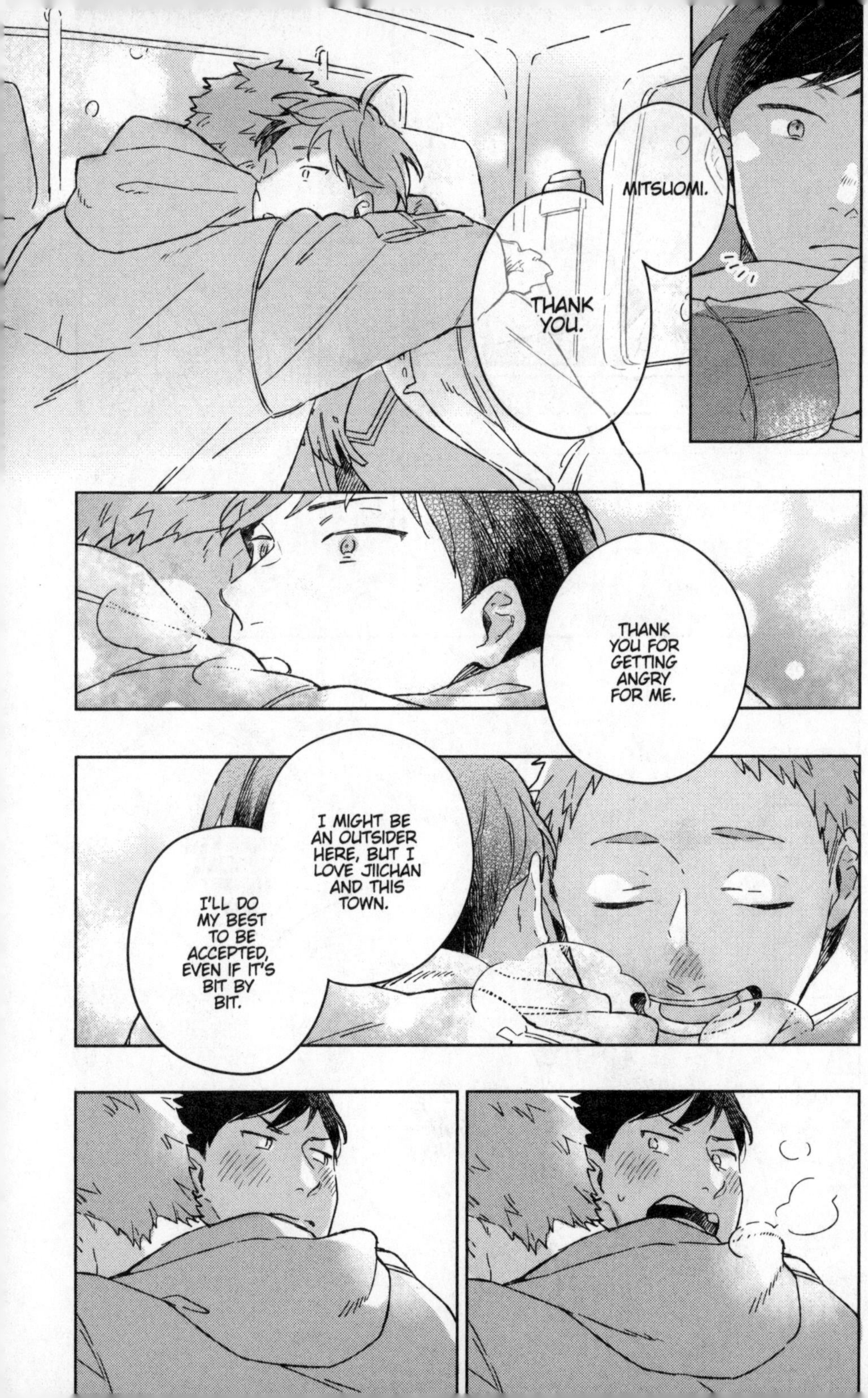
MITSUOMI.
THANK YOU.
THANK YOU FOR GETTING ANGRY FOR ME.
I MIGHT BE AN OUTSIDER HERE, BUT I LOVE JIICHAN AND THIS TOWN.
I'LL DO MY BEST TO BE ACCEPTED, EVEN IF IT'S BIT BY BIT.

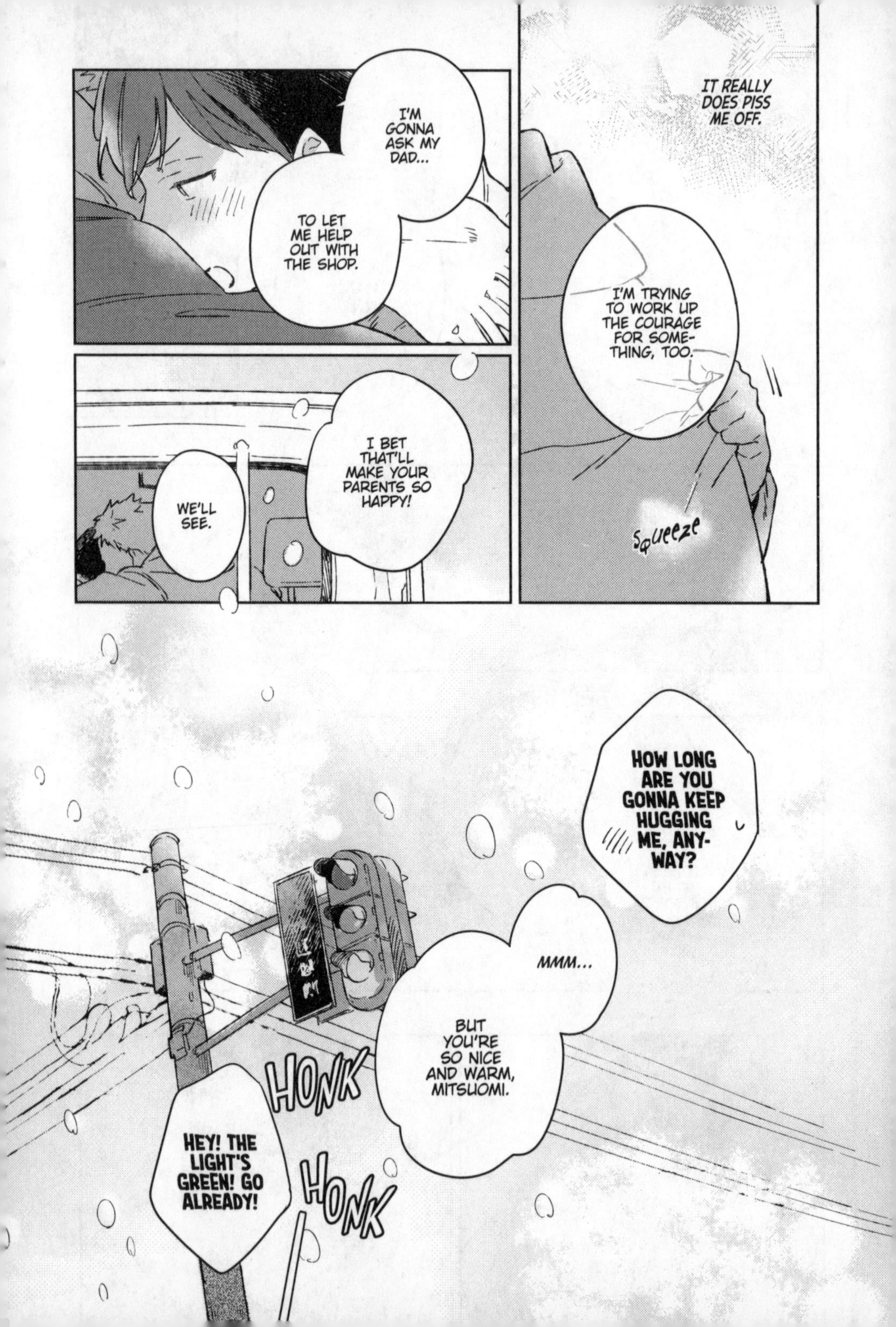
IT REALLY DOES PISS ME OFF.
I'M TRYING TO WORK UP THE COURAGE FOR SOMETHING, TOO.
squeeze
I'M GONNA ASK MY DAD...
TO LET ME HELP OUT WITH THE SHOP.
I BET THAT'LL MAKE YOUR PARENTS SO HAPPY!
WE'LL SEE.
HOW LONG ARE YOU GONNA KEEP HUGGING ME, ANYWAY?
MMM...
BUT YOU'RE SO NICE AND WARM, MITSUOMI.
HONK
HEY! THE LIGHT'S GREEN! GO ALREADY!
HONK

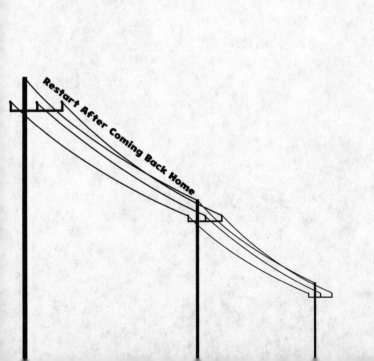

Restart After Coming Back Home

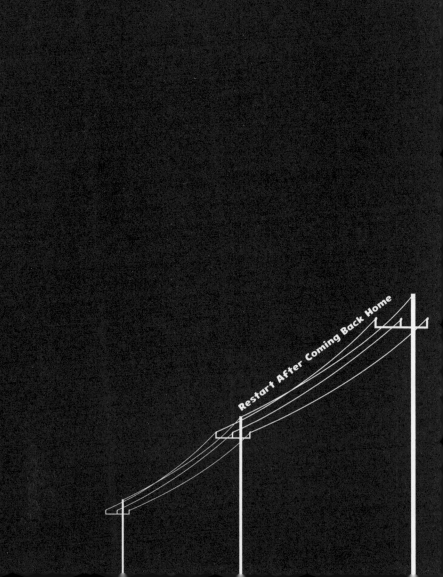

Restart After Coming Back Home

#002

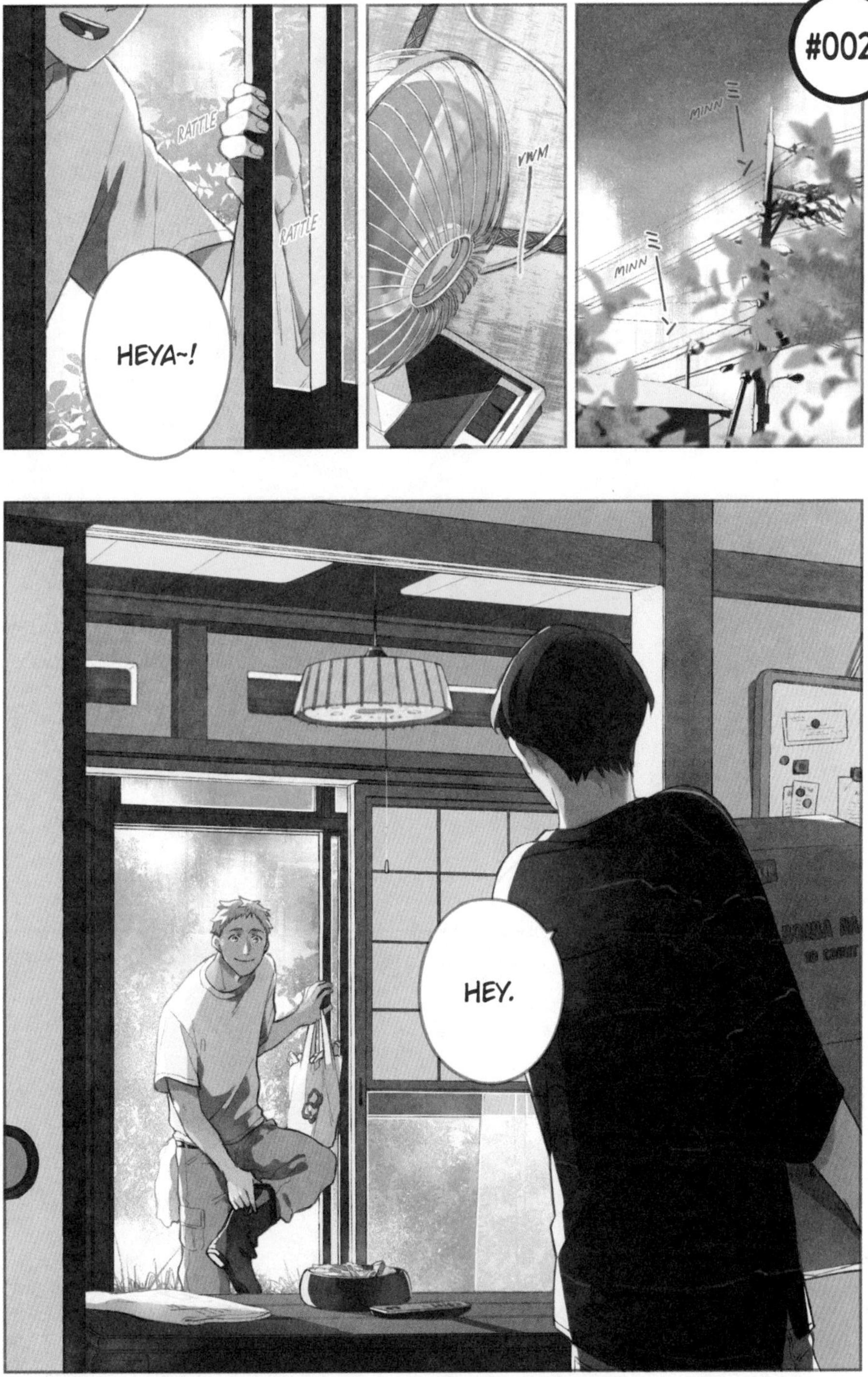
MINN
MINN
VWM
RATTLE
RATTLE
HEYA~!
HEY.

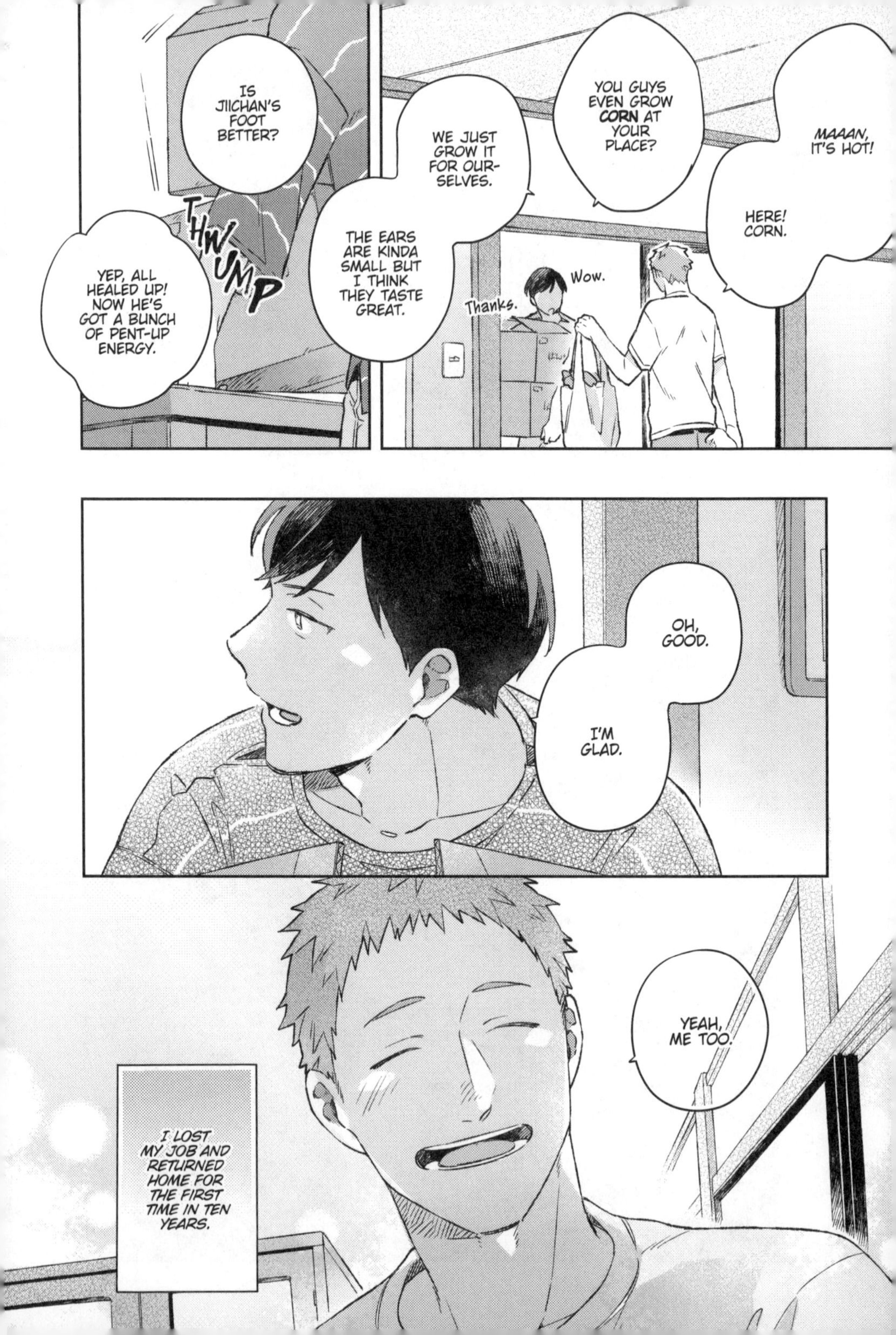
MAAAN, IT'S HOT!
HERE! CORN.
YOU GUYS EVEN GROW CORN AT YOUR PLACE?
Wow.
WE JUST GROW IT FOR OUR-SELVES.
THE EARS ARE KINDA SMALL BUT I THINK THEY TASTE GREAT.
Thanks.
IS JIICHAN'S FOOT BETTER?
THWUMP
YEP, ALL HEALED UP! NOW HE'S GOT A BUNCH OF PENT-UP ENERGY.
OH, GOOD.
I'M GLAD.
YEAH, ME TOO.
I LOST MY JOB AND RETURNED HOME FOR THE FIRST TIME IN TEN YEARS.

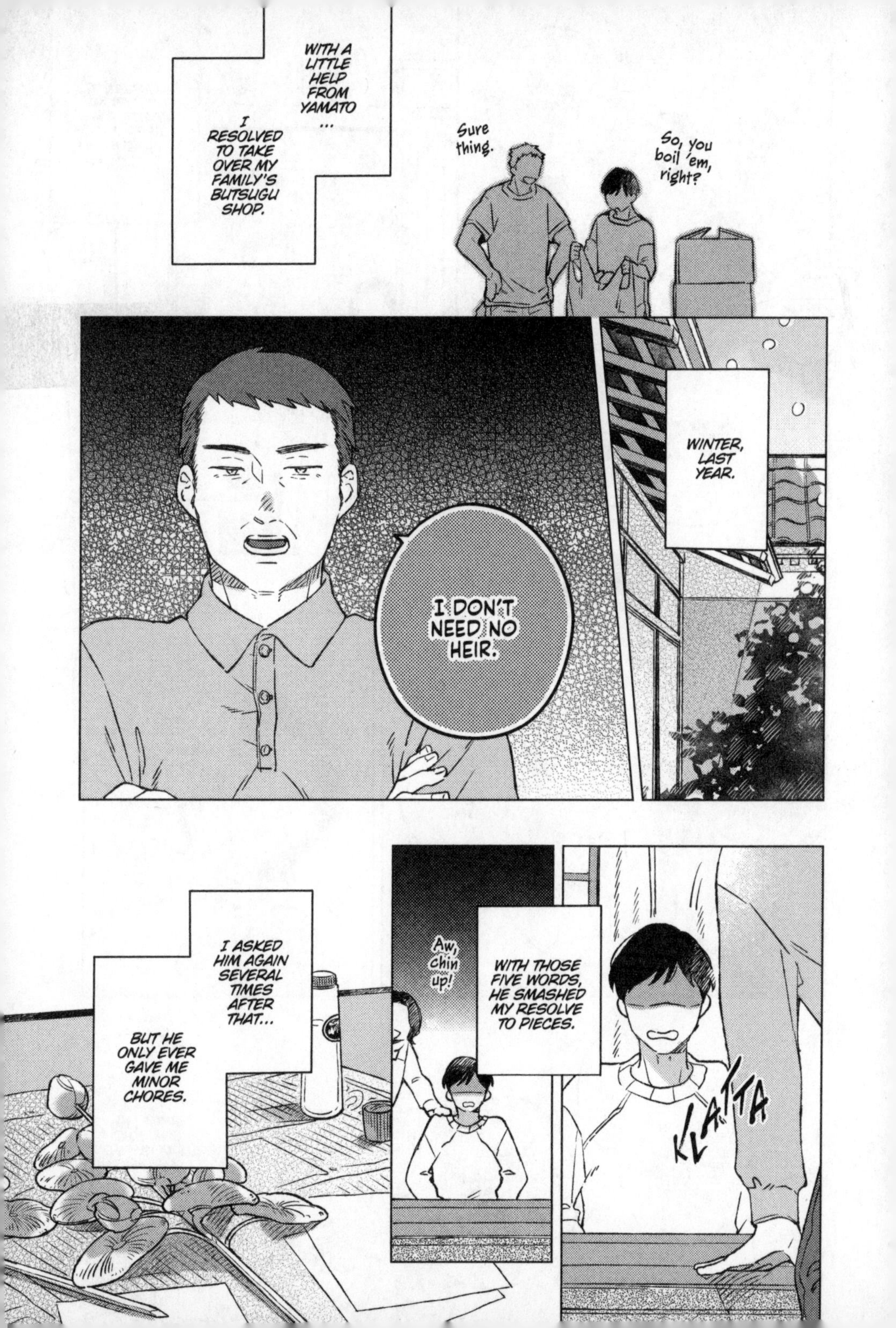
WITH A LITTLE HELP FROM YAMATO...
I RESOLVED TO TAKE OVER MY FAMILY'S BUTSUGU SHOP.
So, you boil 'em, right?
Sure thing.
WINTER, LAST YEAR.
I DON'T NEED NO HEIR.
WITH THOSE FIVE WORDS, HE SMASHED MY RESOLVE TO PIECES.
KLATTA
Aw, chin up!
I ASKED HIM AGAIN SEVERAL TIMES AFTER THAT...
BUT HE ONLY EVER GAVE ME MINOR CHORES.

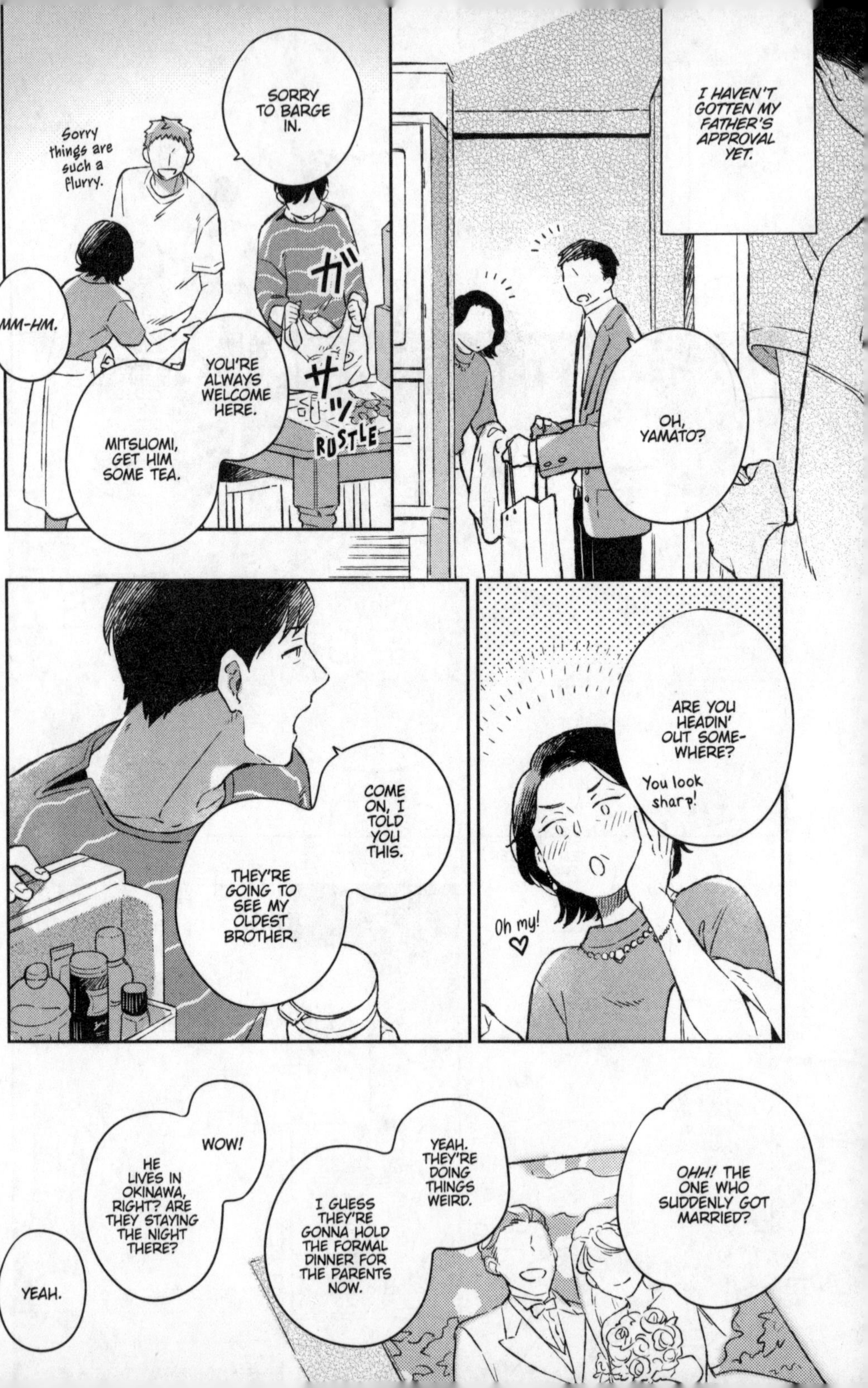
I HAVEN'T GOTTEN MY FATHER'S APPROVAL YET.
OH, YAMATO?
SORRY TO BARGE IN.
Sorry things are such a flurry.
ガ
ザッ
RUSTLE
YOU'RE ALWAYS WELCOME HERE.
MM-HM.
MITSUOMI, GET HIM SOME TEA.
ARE YOU HEADIN' OUT SOME-WHERE?
You look sharp!
Oh my! ♡
COME ON, I TOLD YOU THIS.
THEY'RE GOING TO SEE MY OLDEST BROTHER.
OHH! THE ONE WHO SUDDENLY GOT MARRIED?
YEAH. THEY'RE DOING THINGS WEIRD.
I GUESS THEY'RE GONNA HOLD THE FORMAL DINNER FOR THE PARENTS NOW.
WOW!
HE LIVES IN OKINAWA, RIGHT? ARE THEY STAYING THE NIGHT THERE?
YEAH.

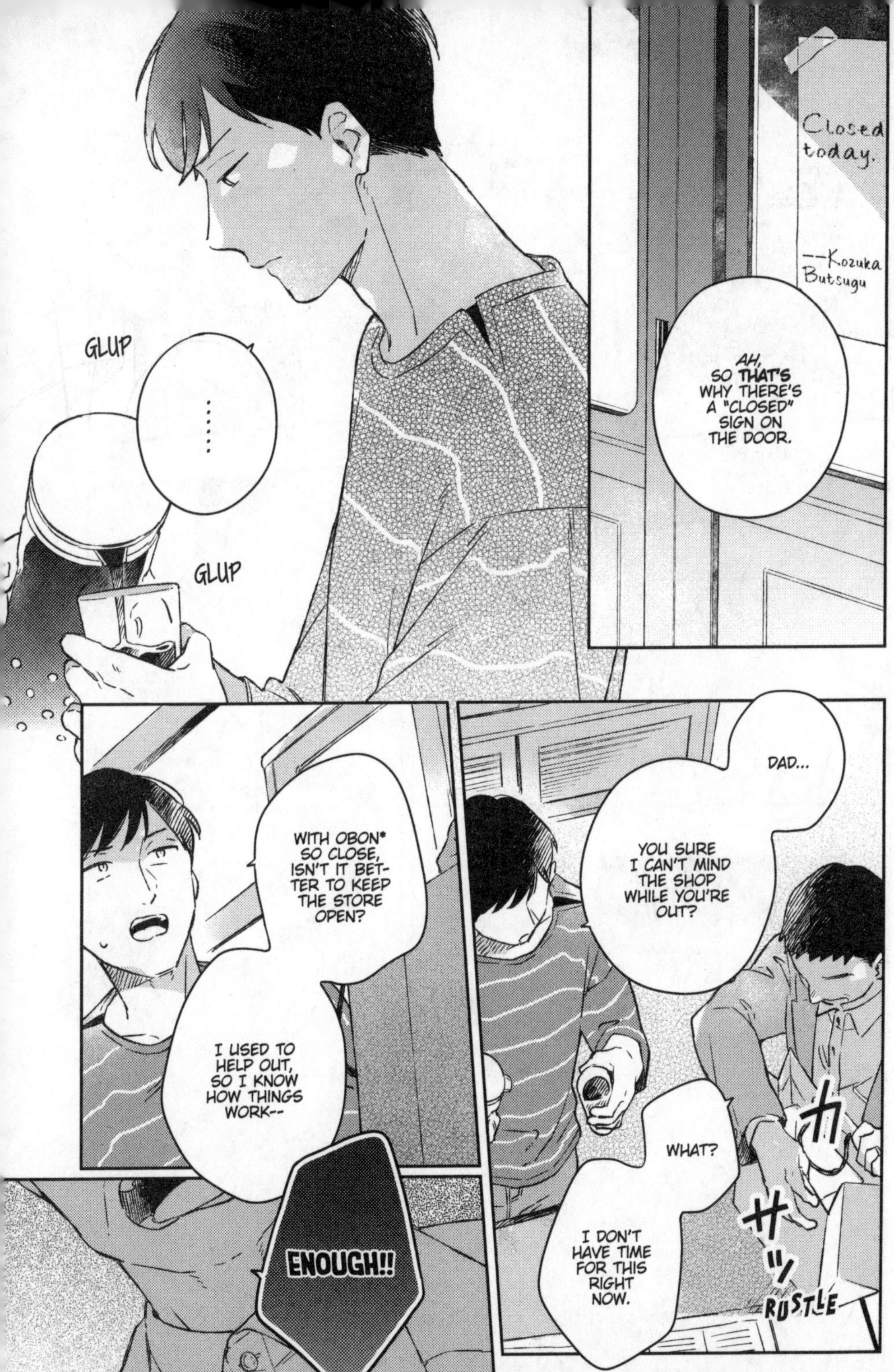
Closed today.
--Kozuka Butsugu
AH, SO THAT'S WHY THERE'S A "CLOSED" SIGN ON THE DOOR.
GLUP
......
GLUP
DAD...
YOU SURE I CAN'T MIND THE SHOP WHILE YOU'RE OUT?
WHAT?
I DON'T HAVE TIME FOR THIS RIGHT NOW.
RUSTLE
WITH OBON* SO CLOSE, ISN'T IT BETTER TO KEEP THE STORE OPEN?
I USED TO HELP OUT, SO I KNOW HOW THINGS WORK--
ENOUGH!!

*Obon is a Japanese festival held in August to commemorate one's ancestors.

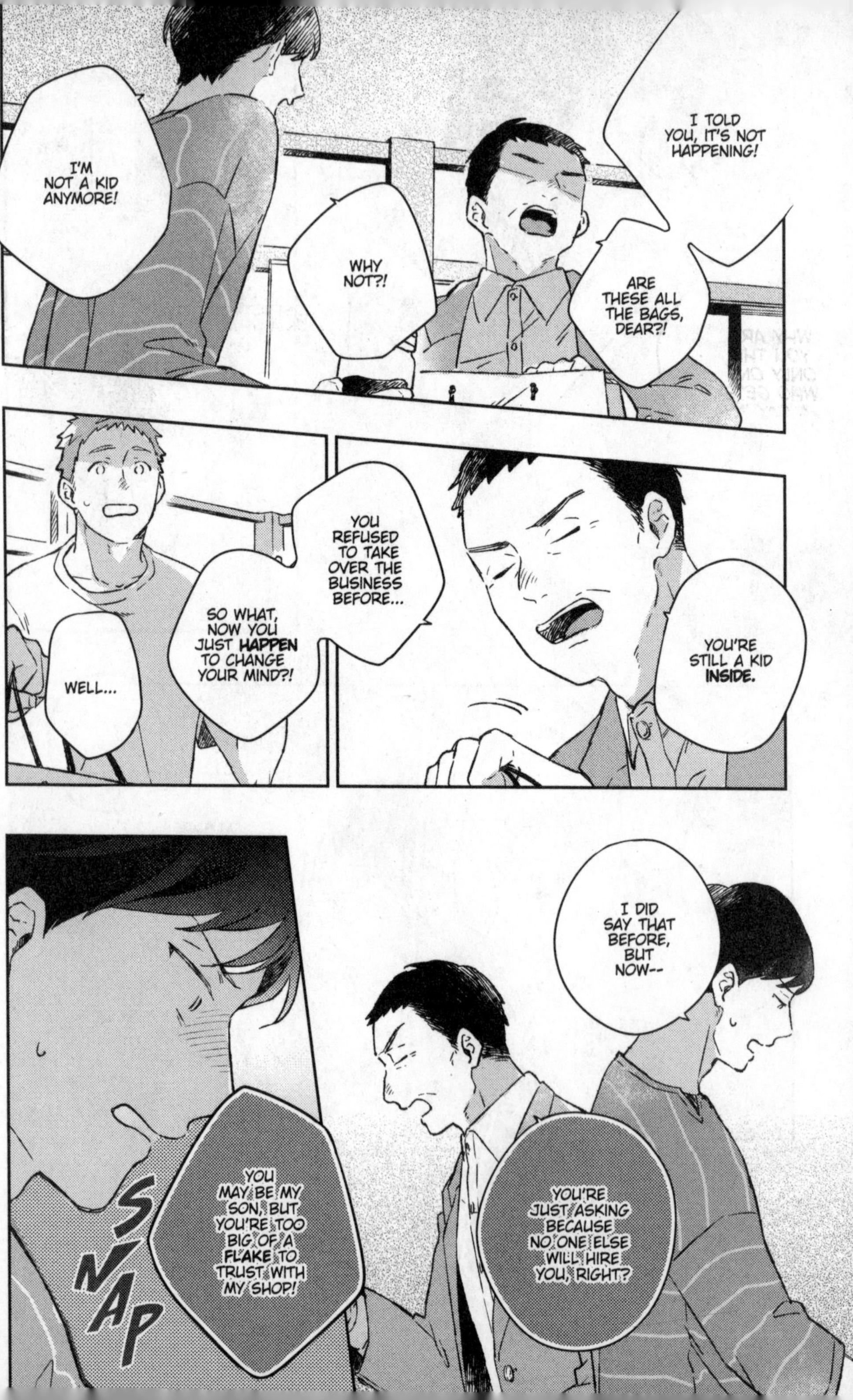
I TOLD YOU, IT'S NOT HAPPENING!
ARE THESE ALL THE BAGS, DEAR?!
WHY NOT?!
I'M NOT A KID ANYMORE!
YOU'RE STILL A KID **INSIDE.**
YOU REFUSED TO TAKE OVER THE BUSINESS BEFORE...
SO WHAT, NOW YOU JUST **HAPPEN** TO CHANGE YOUR MIND?!
WELL...
I DID SAY THAT BEFORE, BUT NOW--
YOU'RE JUST ASKING BECAUSE NO ONE ELSE WILL HIRE YOU, RIGHT?
YOU MAY BE MY SON, BUT YOU'RE TOO BIG OF A **FLAKE** TO TRUST WITH MY SHOP!
SNAP

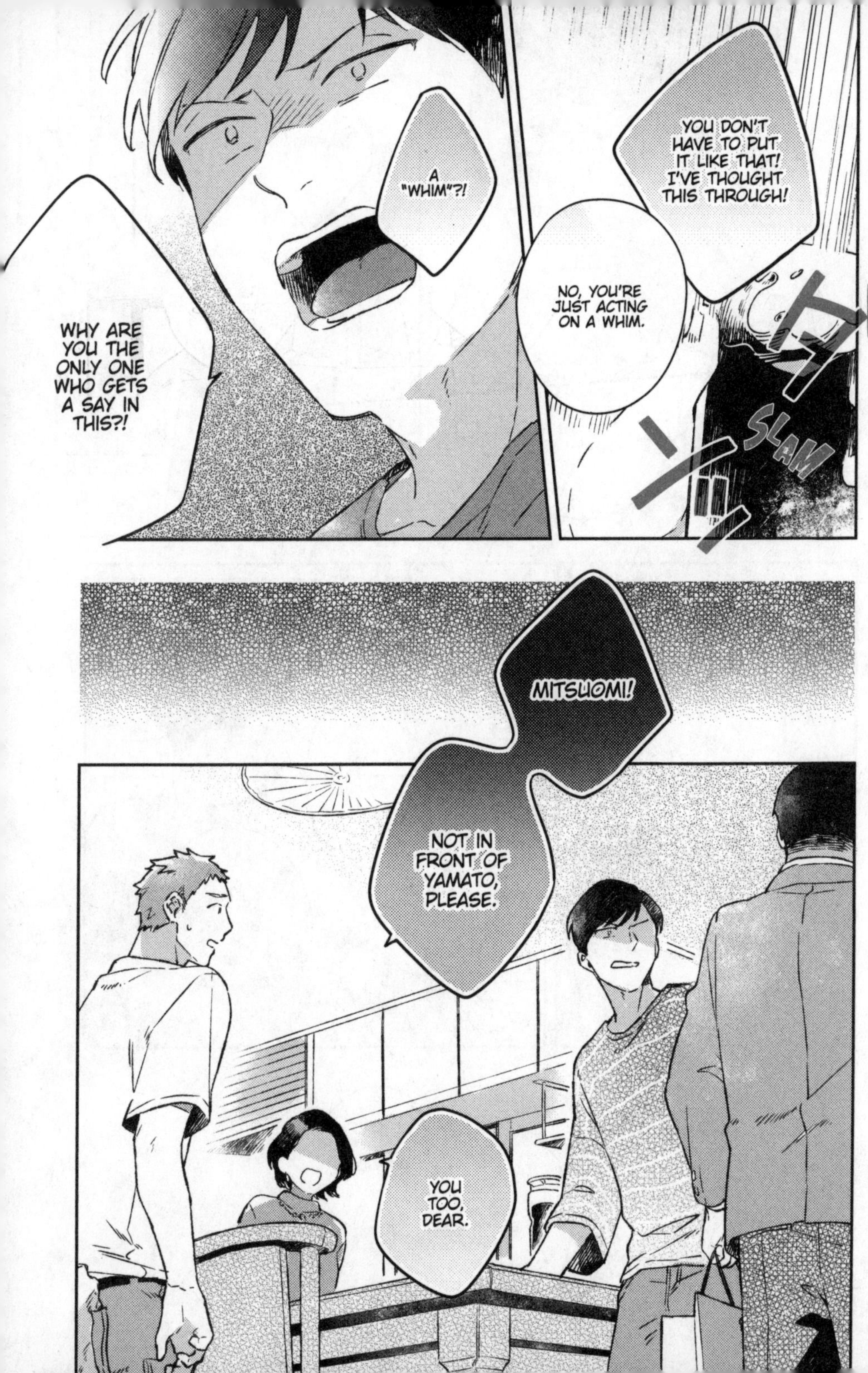
YOU DON'T HAVE TO PUT IT LIKE THAT! I'VE THOUGHT THIS THROUGH!
NO, YOU'RE JUST ACTING ON A WHIM.
SLAM
A "WHIM"?!
WHY ARE YOU THE ONLY ONE WHO GETS A SAY IN THIS?!
MITSUOMI!
NOT IN FRONT OF YAMATO, PLEASE.
YOU TOO, DEAR.

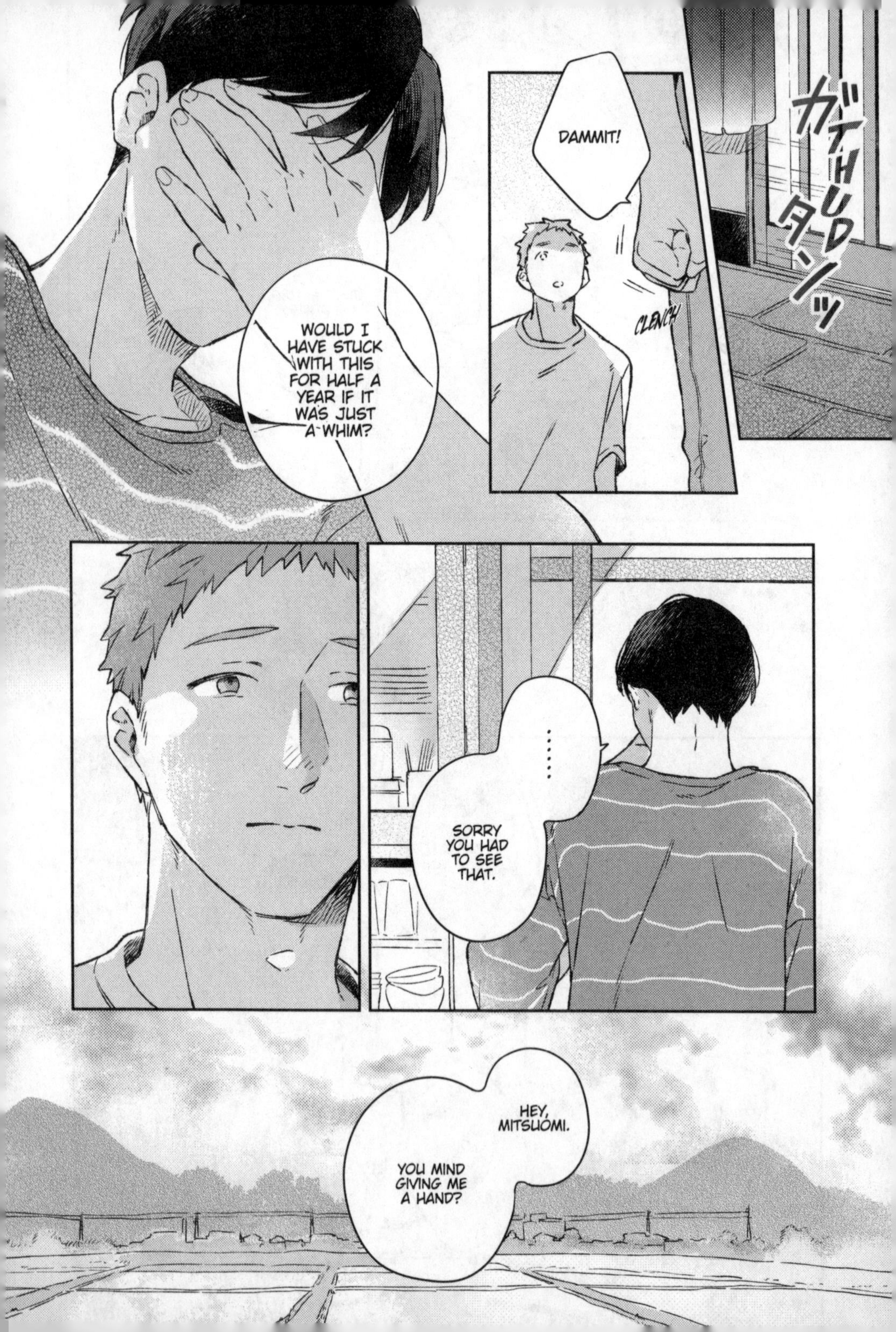

ガタンッ
THUD
DAMMIT!
CLENCH
WOULD I HAVE STUCK WITH THIS FOR HALF A YEAR IF IT WAS JUST A WHIM?
.....
SORRY YOU HAD TO SEE THAT.
HEY, MITSUOMI.
YOU MIND GIVING ME A HAND?

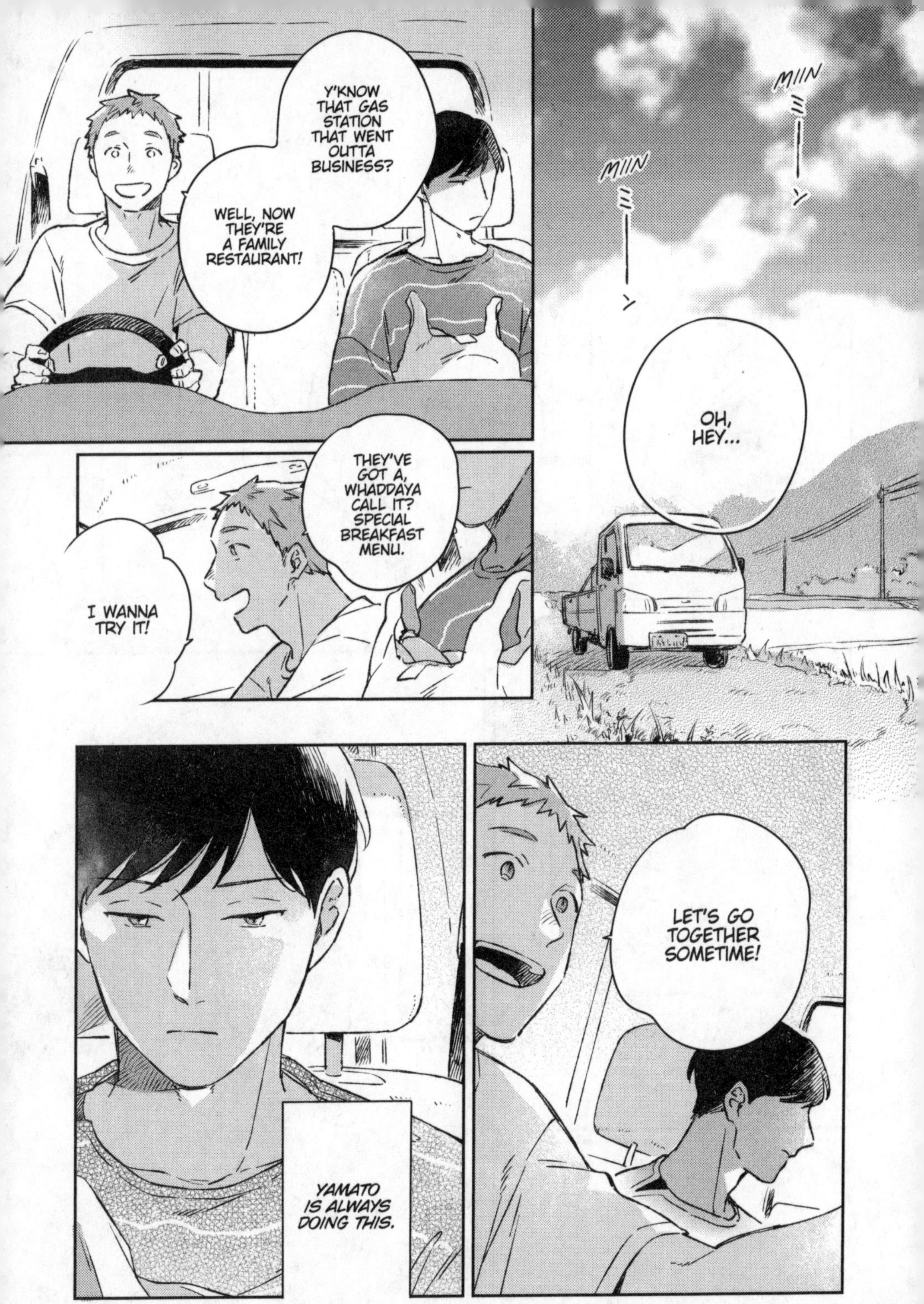
MIIN
MIIN
OH, HEY...
Y'KNOW THAT GAS STATION THAT WENT OUTTA BUSINESS?
WELL, NOW THEY'RE A FAMILY RESTAURANT!
THEY'VE GOT A, WHADDAYA CALL IT? SPECIAL BREAKFAST MENU.
I WANNA TRY IT!
LET'S GO TOGETHER SOMETIME!
YAMATO IS ALWAYS DOING THIS.

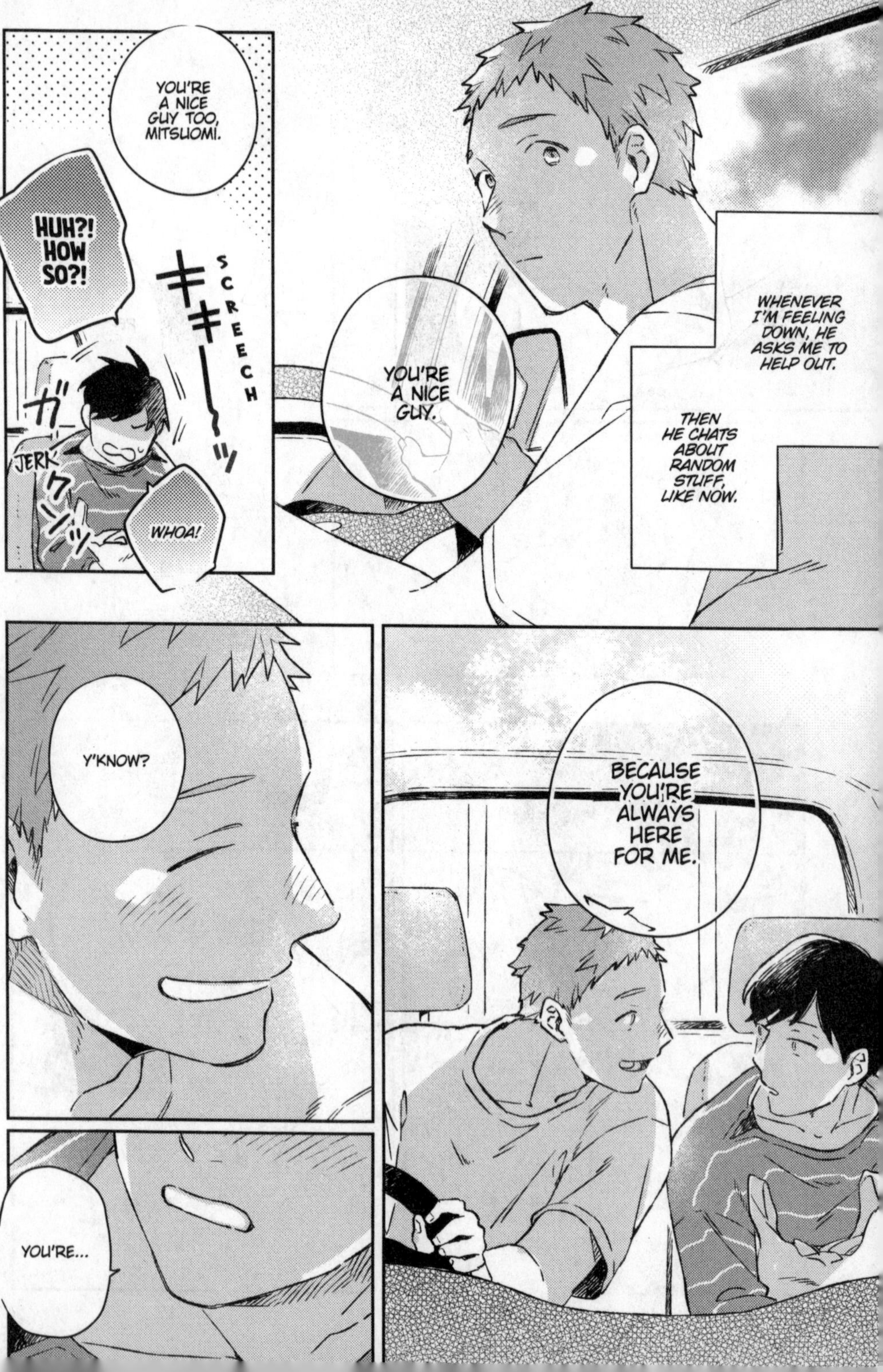
WHENEVER I'M FEELING DOWN, HE ASKS ME TO HELP OUT.
THEN HE CHATS ABOUT RANDOM STUFF, LIKE NOW.
YOU'RE A NICE GUY.
YOU'RE A NICE GUY TOO, MITSUOMI.
HUH?! HOW SO?!
キキーッ
SCREECH
ガクンッ
JERK
WHOA!
BECAUSE YOU'RE ALWAYS HERE FOR ME.
Y'KNOW?
YOU'RE...

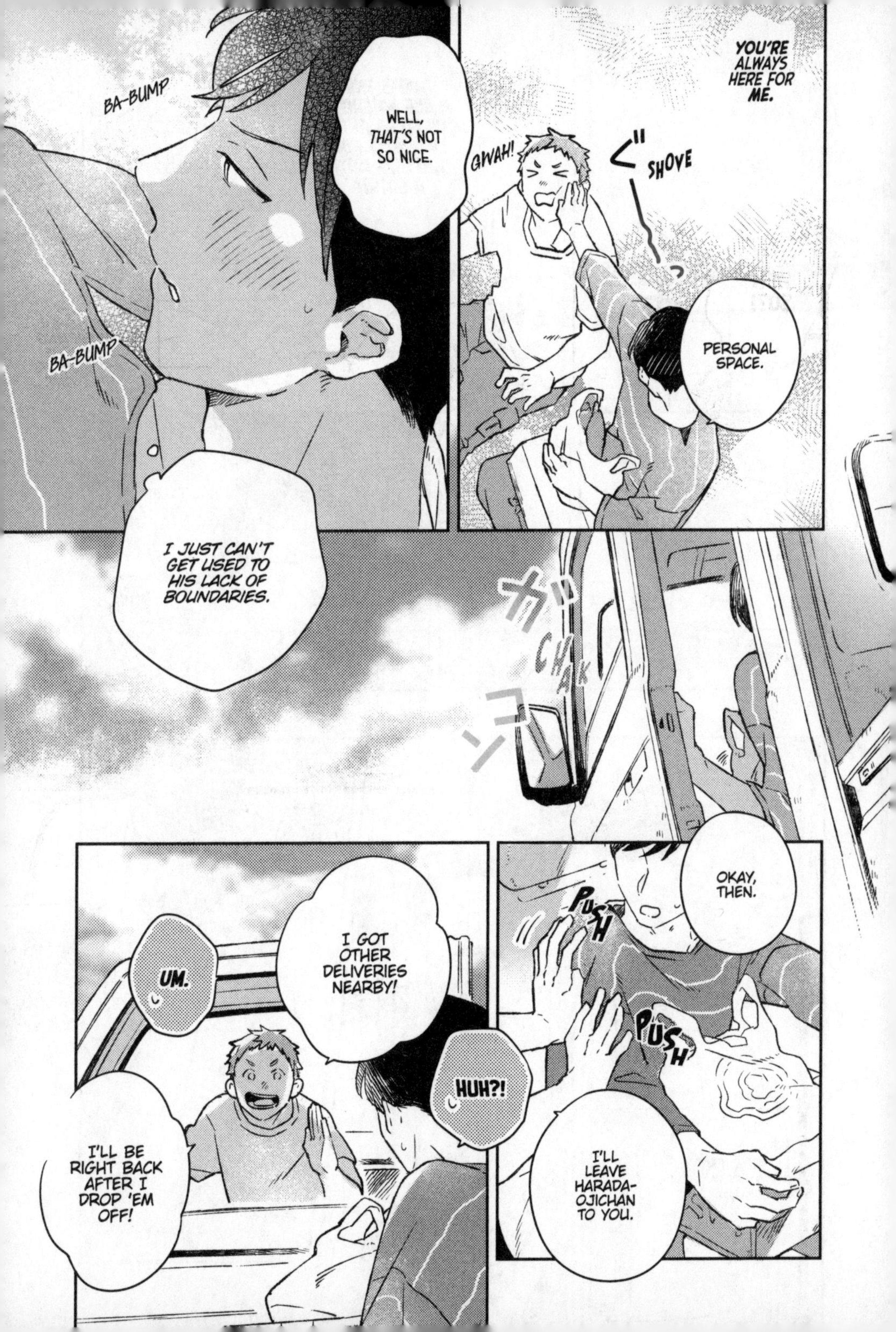
YOU'RE ALWAYS HERE FOR ME.
GWAH!
SHOVE
PERSONAL SPACE.
WELL, THAT'S NOT SO NICE.
BA-BUMP
BA-BUMP
I JUST CAN'T GET USED TO HIS LACK OF BOUNDARIES.
CHAK
OKAY, THEN.
PUSH
PUSH
I'LL LEAVE HARADA-OJICHAN TO YOU.
I GOT OTHER DELIVERIES NEARBY!
UM.
HUH?!
I'LL BE RIGHT BACK AFTER I DROP 'EM OFF!

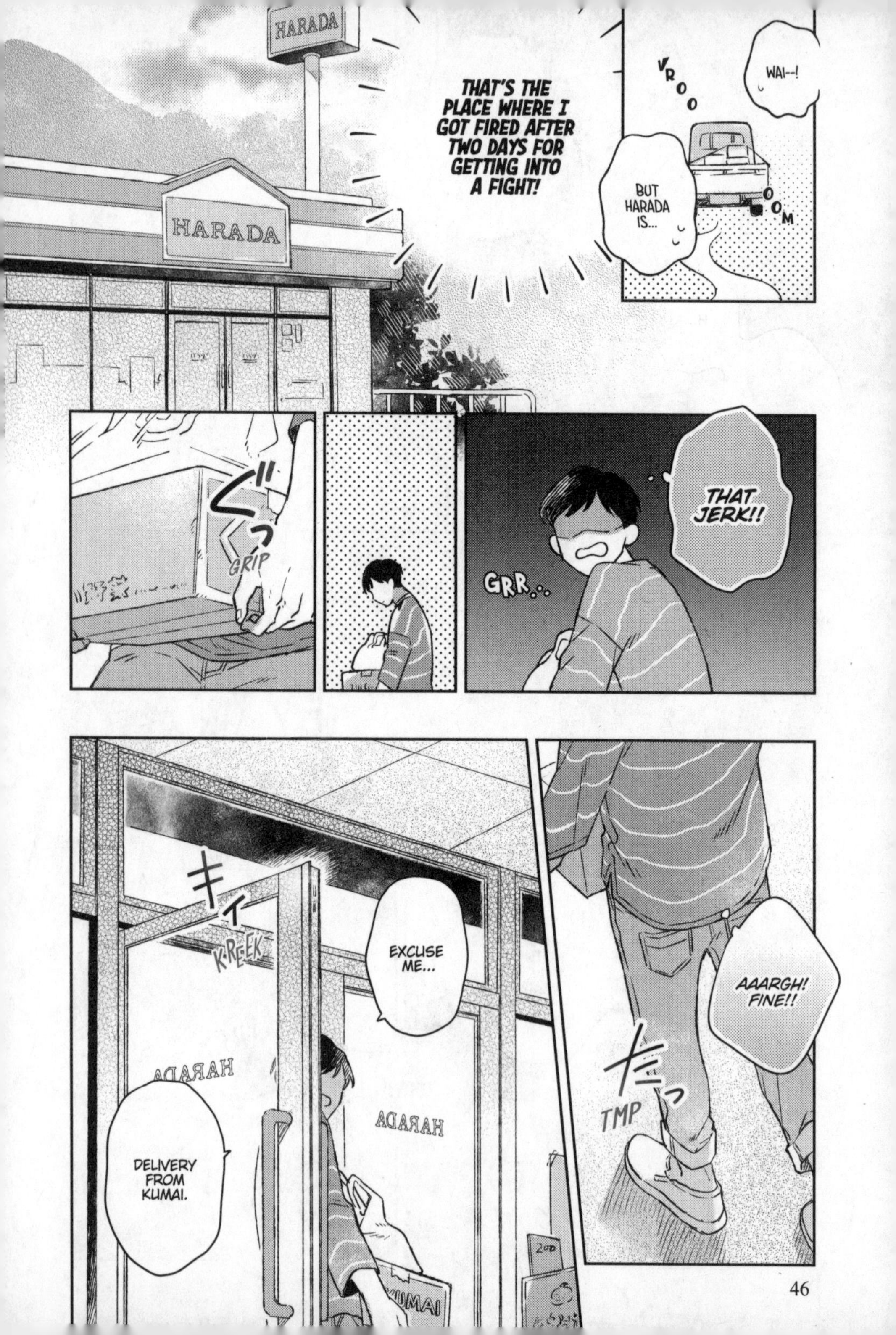
WAI--!
VROOOOM
BUT HARADA IS...
HARADA
HARADA
THAT'S THE PLACE WHERE I GOT FIRED AFTER TWO DAYS FOR GETTING INTO A FIGHT!
THAT JERK!!
GRR...
ぐっ
GRIP
AAARGH! FINE!!
だっ
TMP
キイ
KREEEK
EXCUSE ME...
HARADA
HARADA
DELIVERY FROM KUMAI.
KUMAI

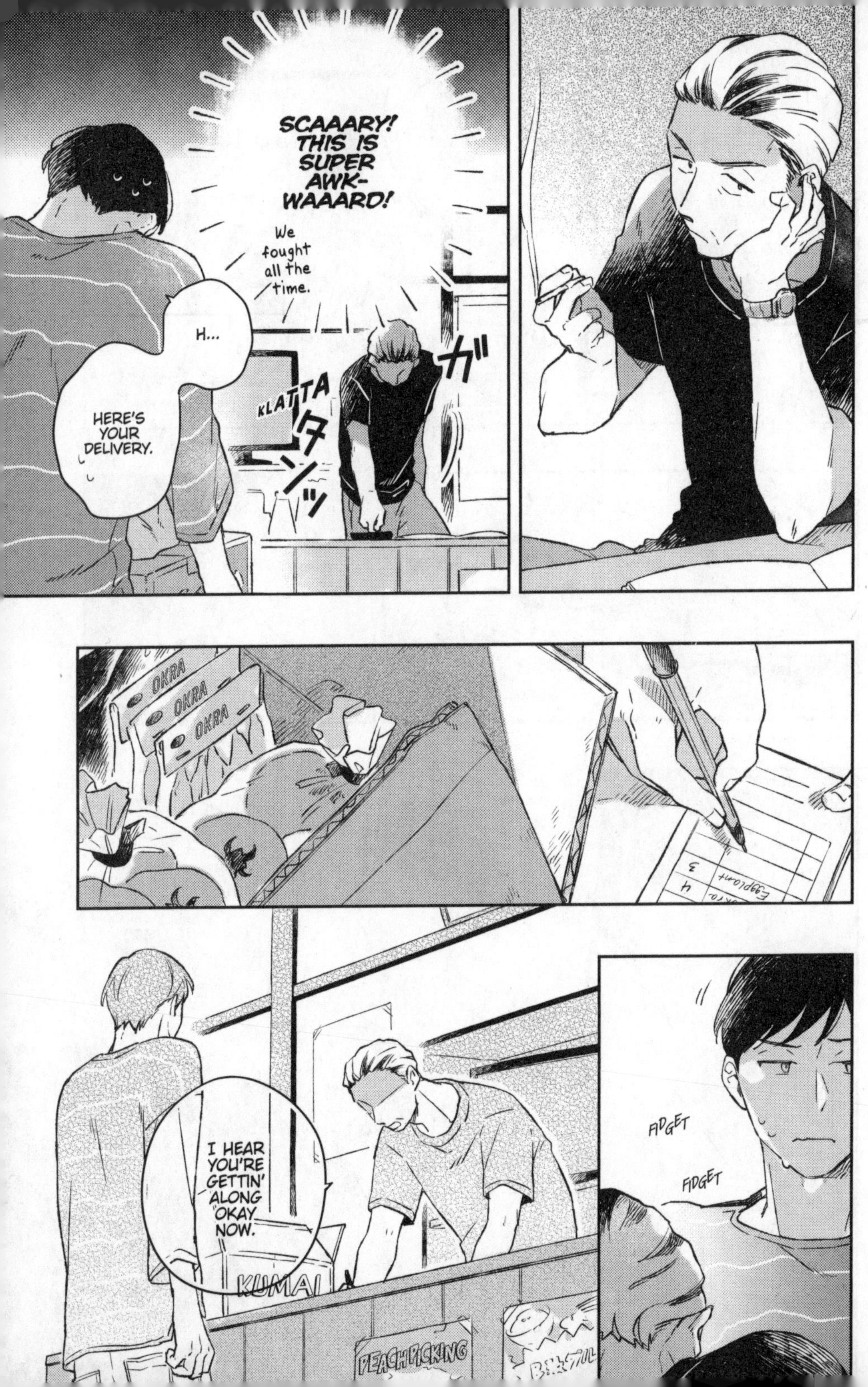
SCAAARY! THIS IS SUPER AWK-WAAARD!
We fought all the time.
ガタンッ
KLATTA
H...
HERE'S YOUR DELIVERY.
OKRA
OKRA
OKRA
Eggplant 3
Okra 4
FIDGET
FIDGET
I HEAR YOU'RE GETTIN' ALONG OKAY NOW.
KUMAI
PEACHPICKING

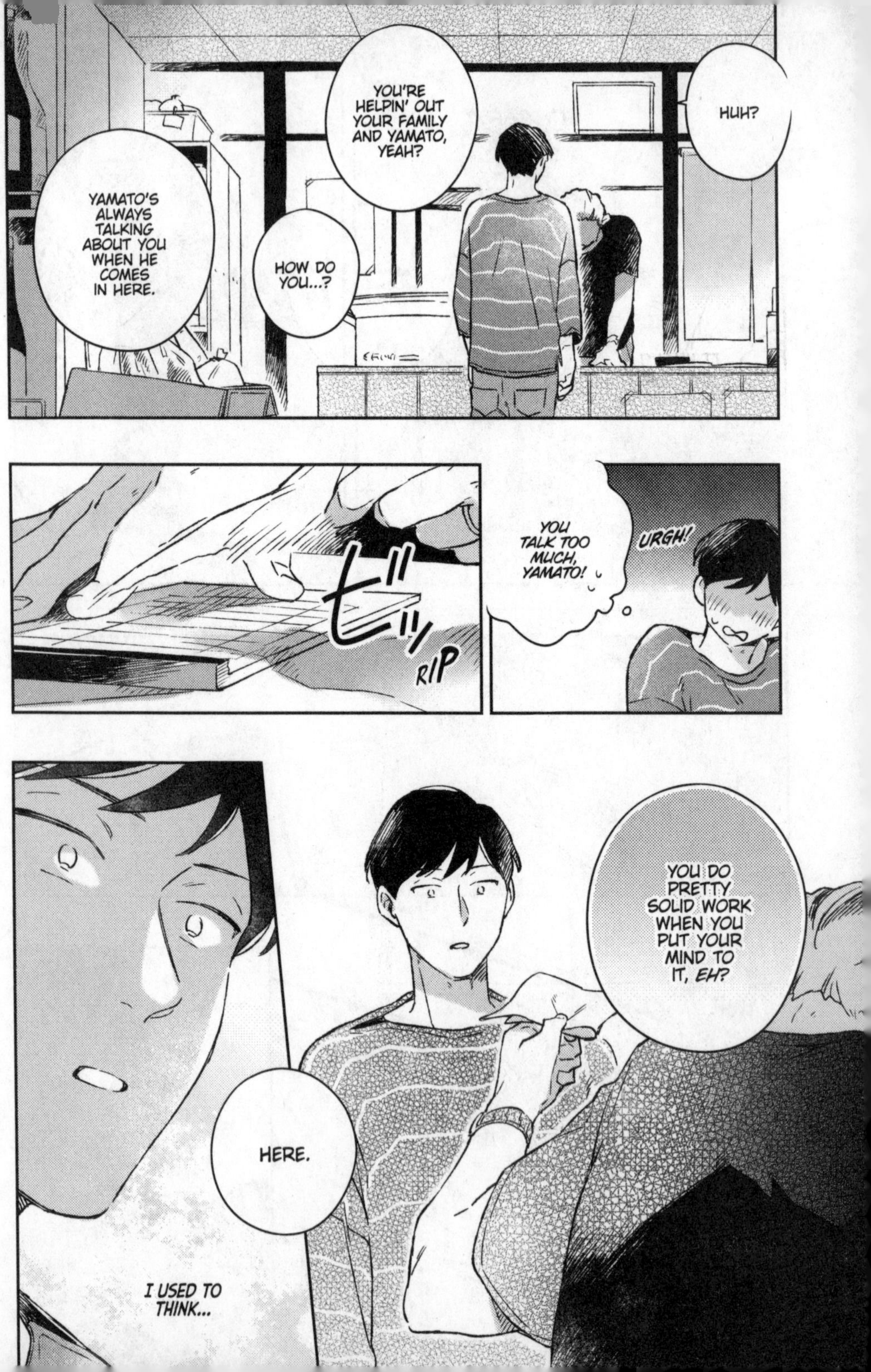
HUH?
YOU'RE HELPIN' OUT YOUR FAMILY AND YAMATO, YEAH?
HOW DO YOU...?
YAMATO'S ALWAYS TALKING ABOUT YOU WHEN HE COMES IN HERE.
URGH!
YOU TALK TOO MUCH, YAMATO!
ビッ
RIP
YOU DO PRETTY SOLID WORK WHEN YOU PUT YOUR MIND TO IT, *EH?*
HERE.
I USED TO THINK...

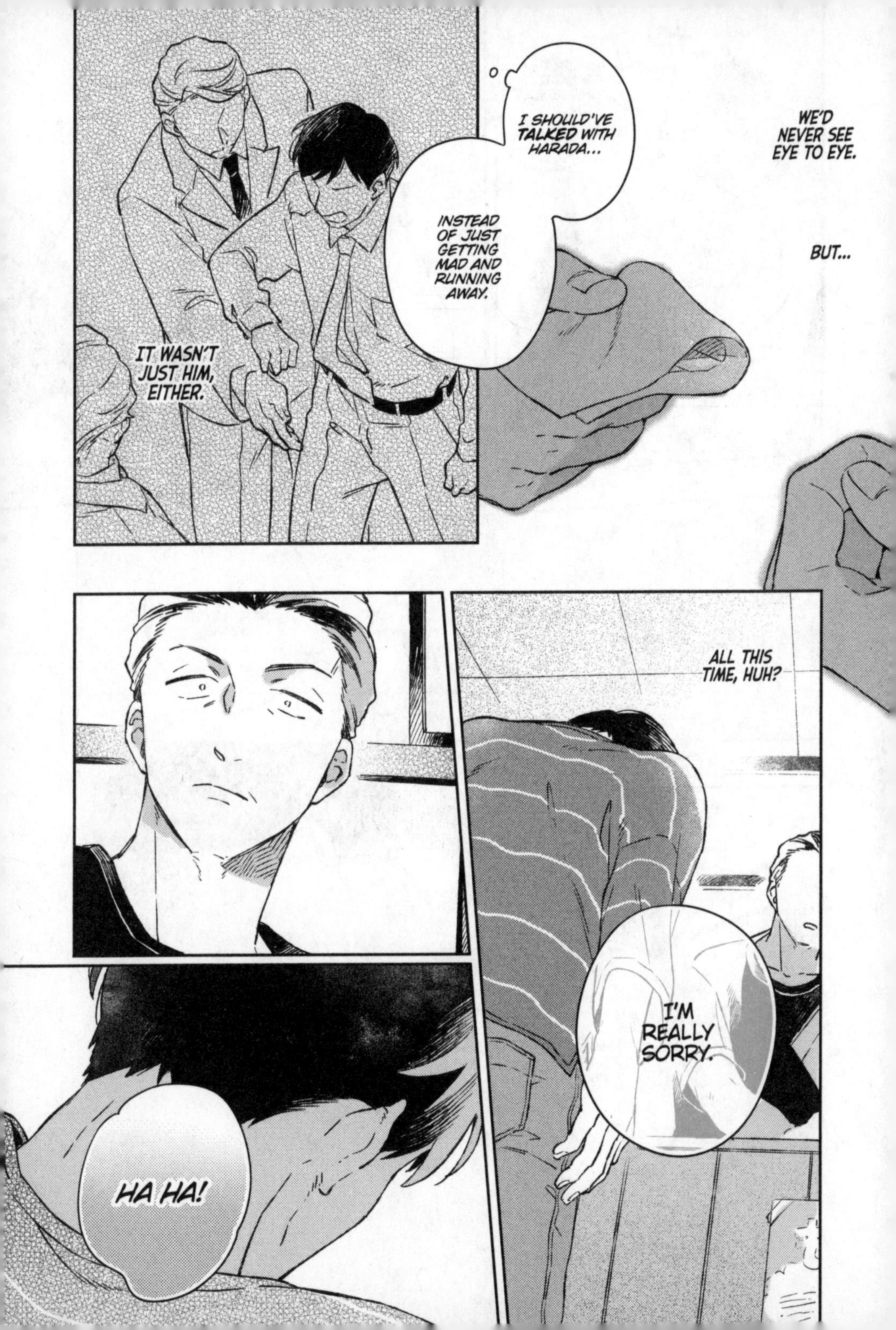
WE'D NEVER SEE EYE TO EYE.
BUT...
I SHOULD'VE TALKED WITH HARADA...
INSTEAD OF JUST GETTING MAD AND RUNNING AWAY.
IT WASN'T JUST HIM, EITHER.
ALL THIS TIME, HUH?
I'M REALLY SORRY.
HA HA!

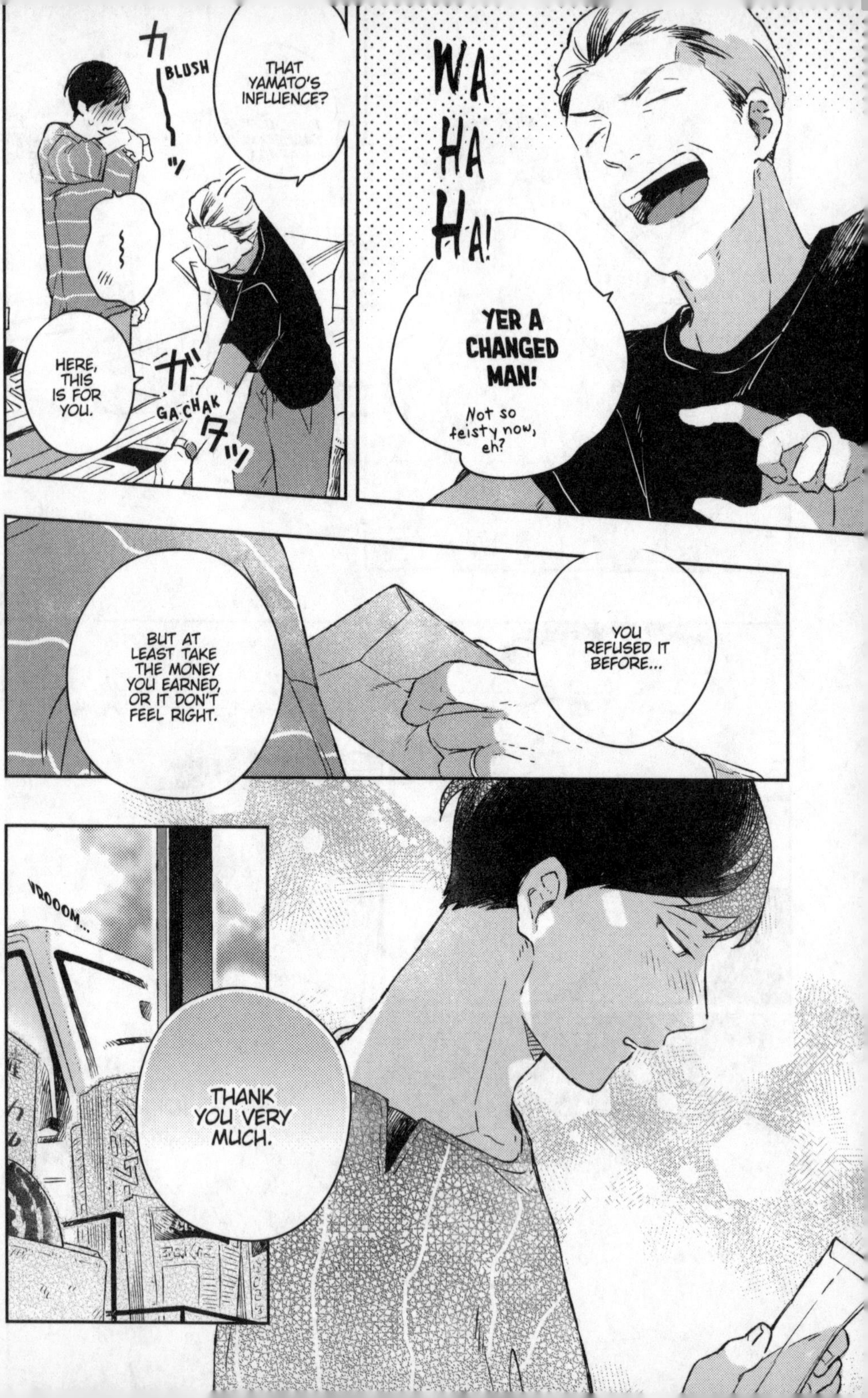
WA HA HA!
YER A CHANGED MAN!
Not so feisty now, eh?
THAT YAMATO'S INFLUENCE?
BLUSH
HERE, THIS IS FOR YOU.
GACHAK
YOU REFUSED IT BEFORE...
BUT AT LEAST TAKE THE MONEY YOU EARNED, OR IT DON'T FEEL RIGHT.
THANK YOU VERY MUCH.
VROOOM...

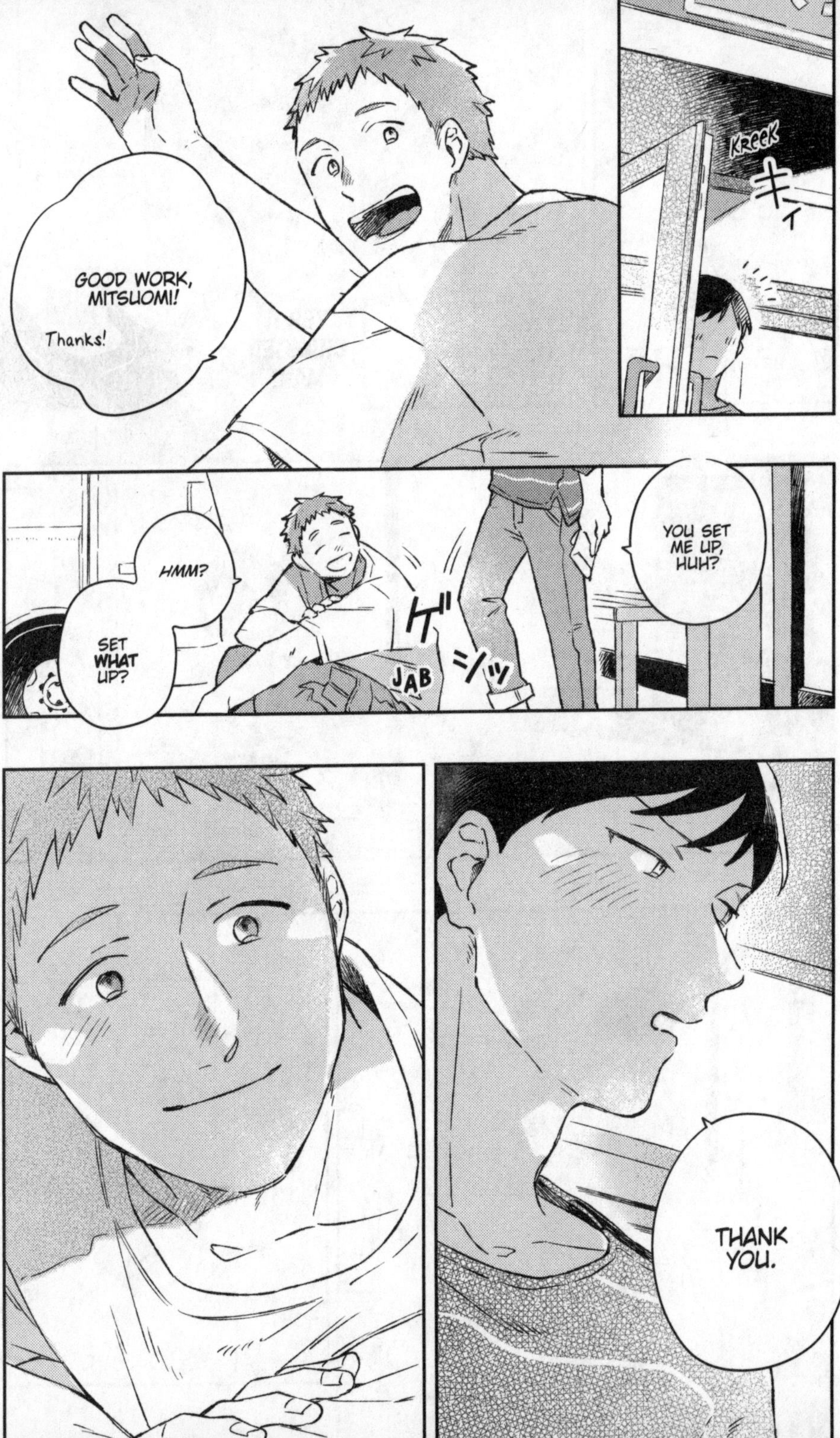
KREEK
キィ
GOOD WORK, MITSUOMI!
Thanks!
YOU SET ME UP, HUH?
ゲシッ
JAB
HMM?
SET WHAT UP?
THANK YOU.

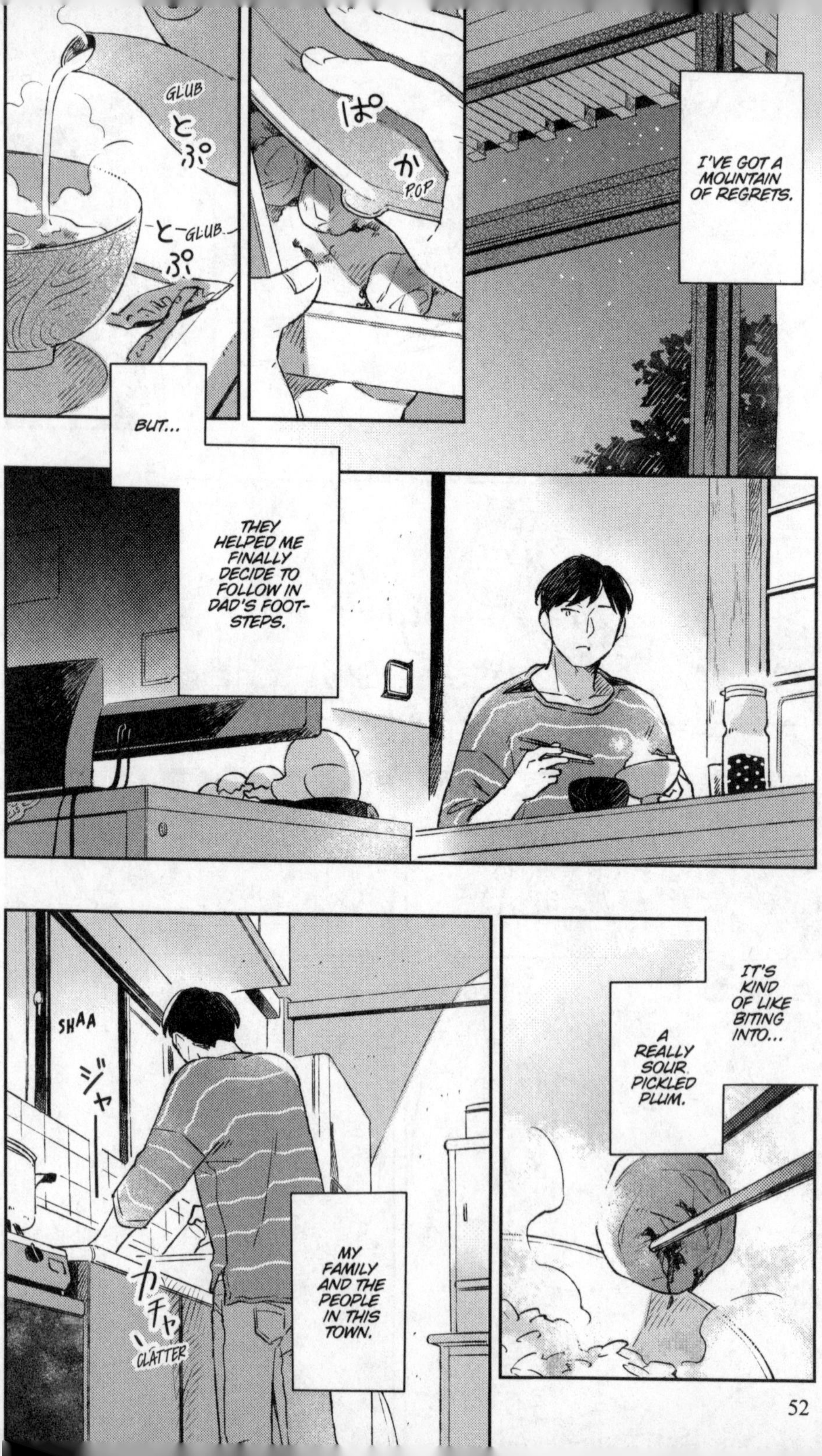
I'VE GOT A MOUNTAIN OF REGRETS.
ぱか
POP
GLUB
とぷ
とぷ
GLUB
BUT...
THEY HELPED ME FINALLY DECIDE TO FOLLOW IN DAD'S FOOT-STEPS.
IT'S KIND OF LIKE BITING INTO...
A REALLY SOUR PICKLED PLUM.
SHAA
ジャ
MY FAMILY AND THE PEOPLE IN THIS TOWN.
カチャ
CLATTER

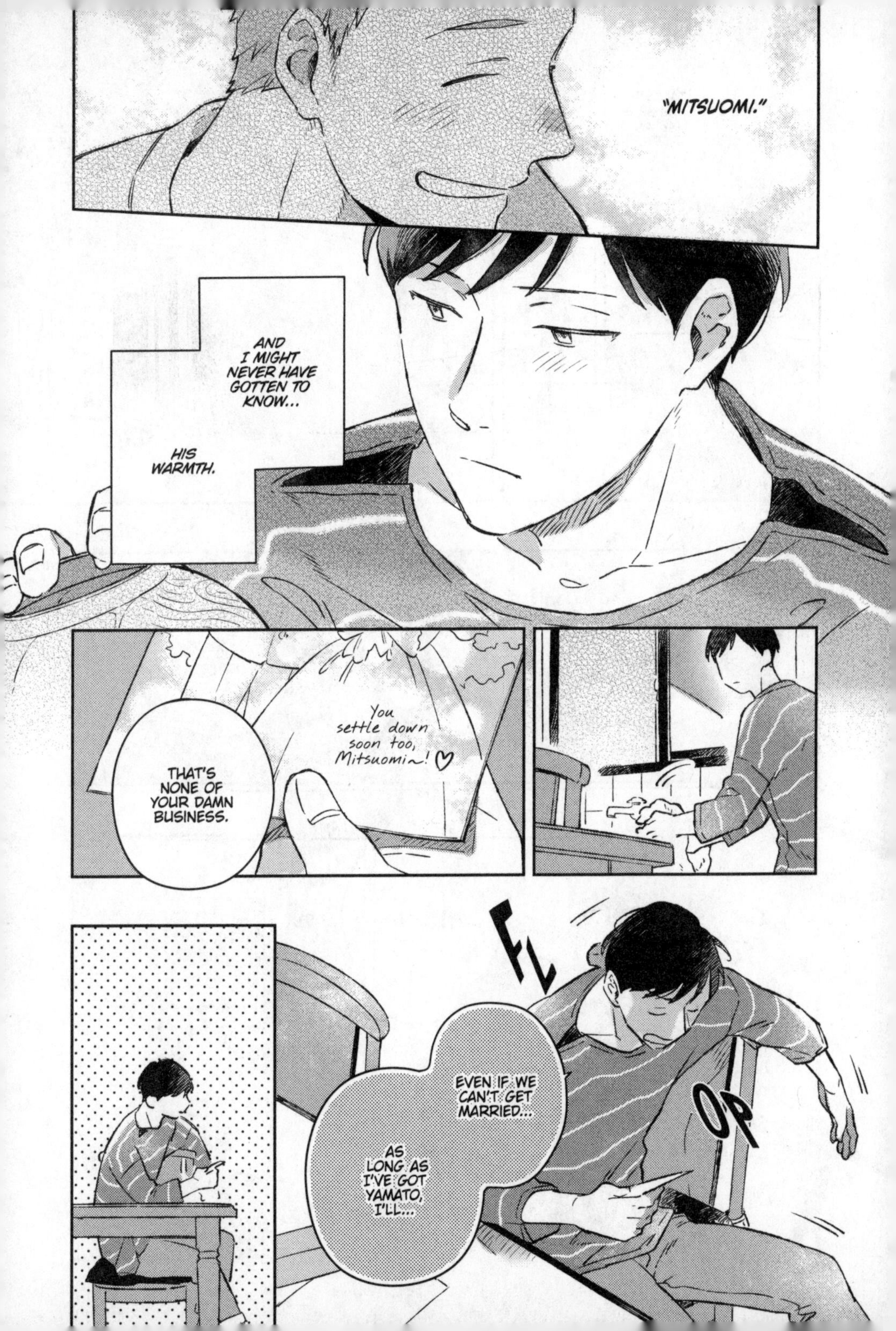
"MITSUOMI."
AND I MIGHT NEVER HAVE GOTTEN TO KNOW...
HIS WARMTH.
You settle down soon too, Mitsuomi~! ♡
THAT'S NONE OF YOUR DAMN BUSINESS.
FL
OP
EVEN IF WE CAN'T GET MARRIED...
AS LONG AS I'VE GOT YAMATO, I'LL...

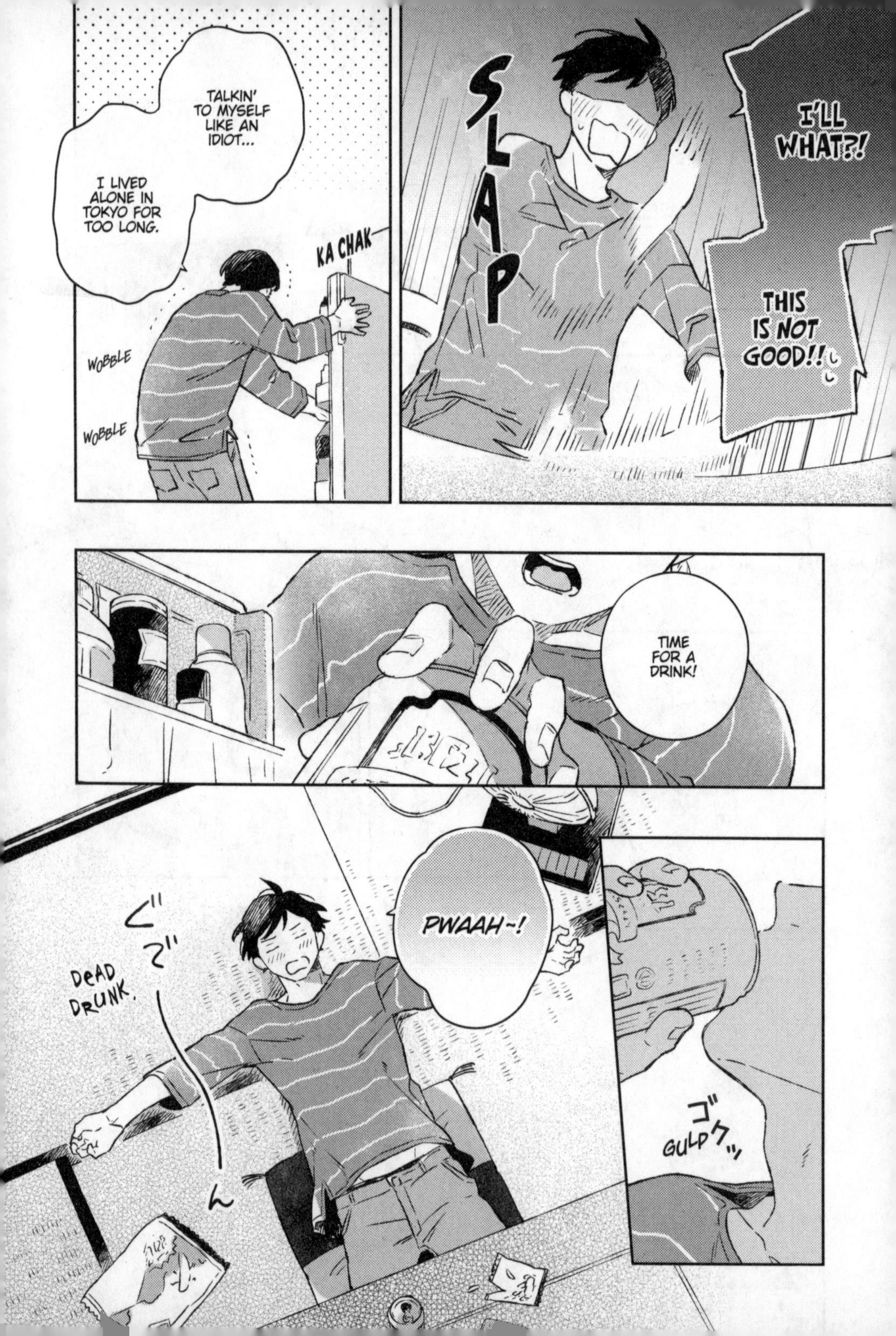
SLAP
I'LL WHAT?!
THIS IS NOT GOOD!!
TALKIN' TO MYSELF LIKE AN IDIOT...
I LIVED ALONE IN TOKYO FOR TOO LONG.
KA CHAK
WOBBLE
WOBBLE
TIME FOR A DRINK!
ゴクッ
GULP
PWAAH~!
DEAD DRUNK.

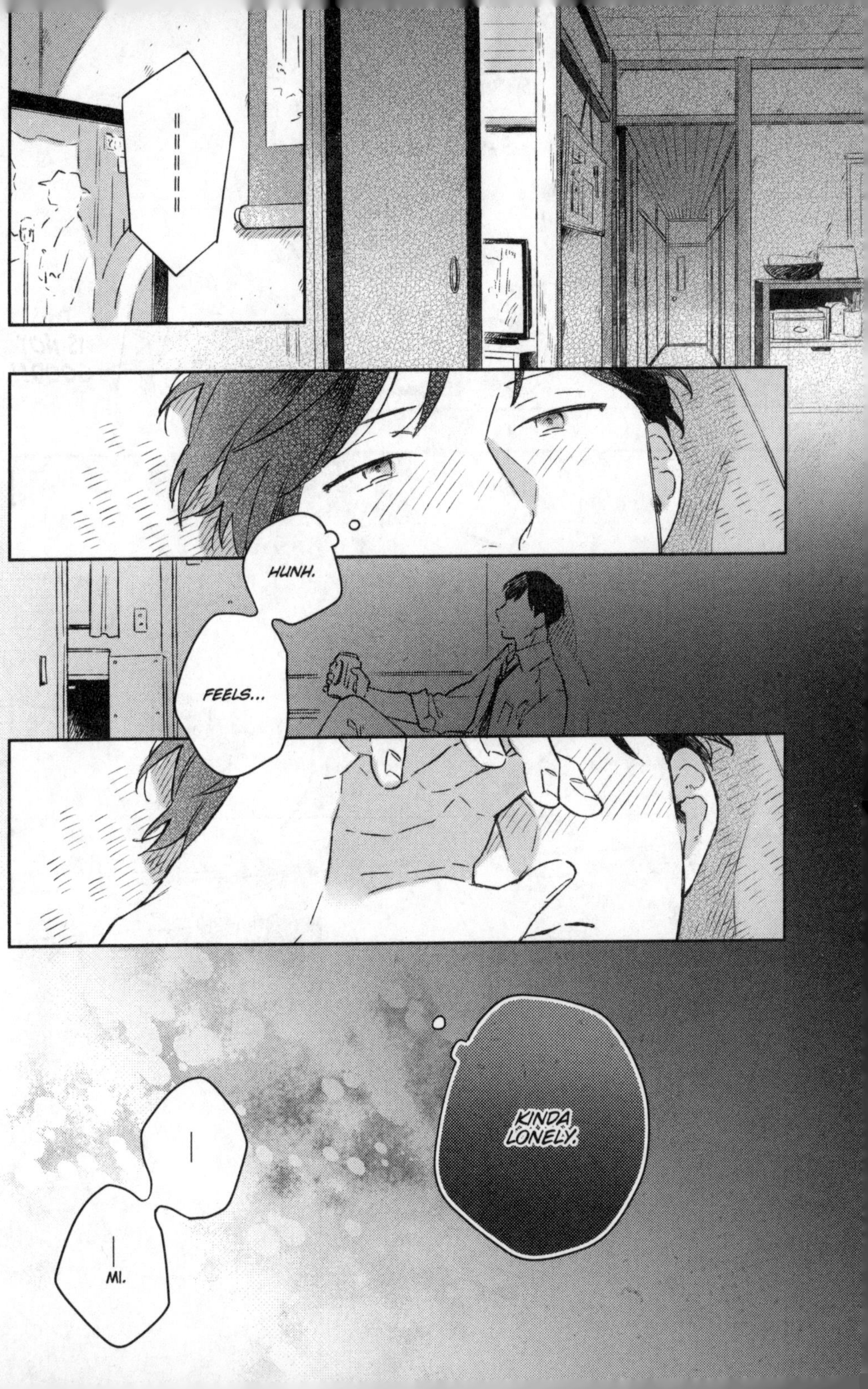
......
HUNH.
FEELS...
KINDA LONELY.
I
MI.

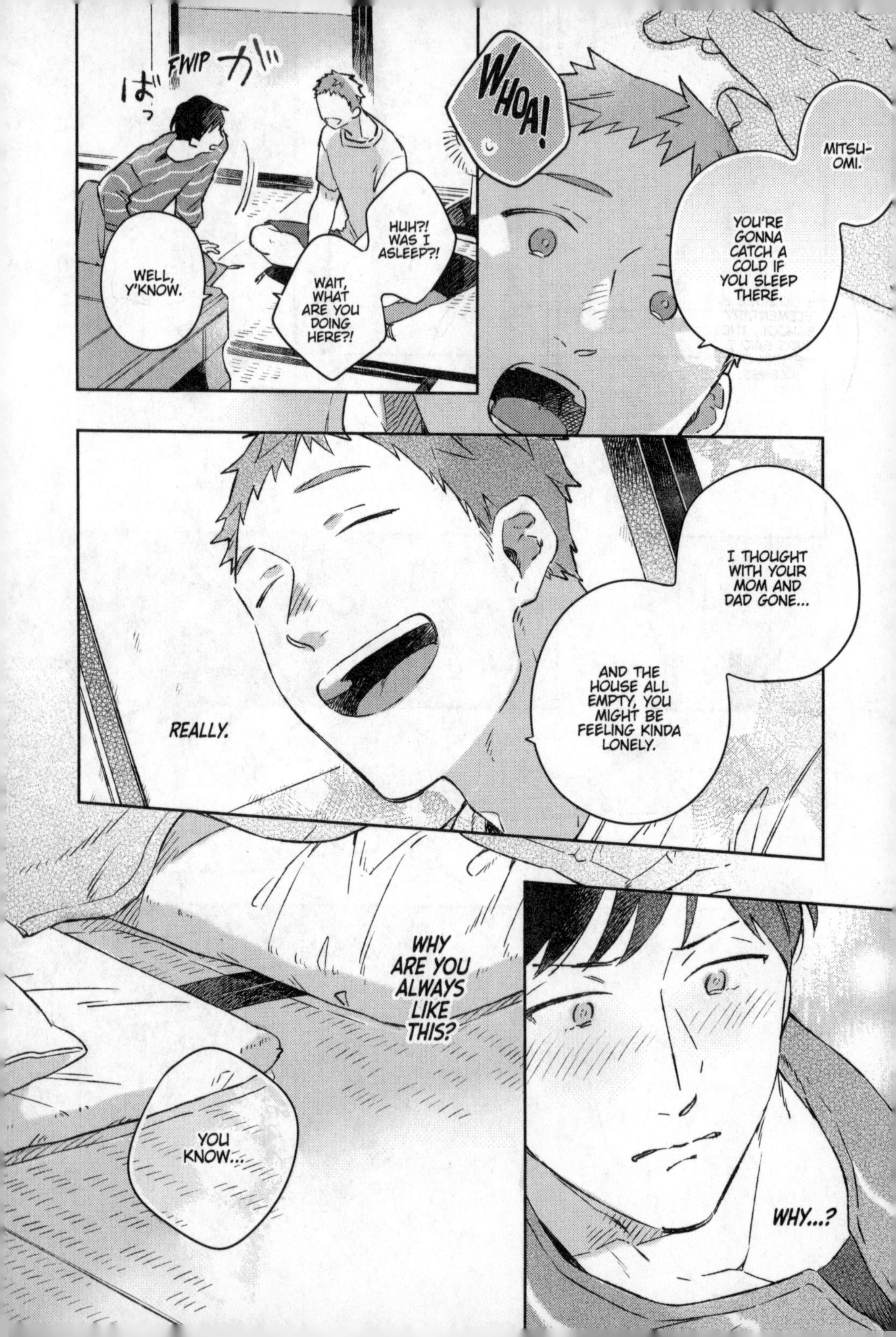
MITSU-OMI.
YOU'RE GONNA CATCH A COLD IF YOU SLEEP THERE.
WHOA!
がば
FWIP
ばっ
HUH?! WAS I ASLEEP?!
WAIT, WHAT ARE YOU DOING HERE?!
WELL, Y'KNOW.
I THOUGHT WITH YOUR MOM AND DAD GONE...
AND THE HOUSE ALL EMPTY, YOU MIGHT BE FEELING KINDA LONELY.
REALLY.
WHY...?
WHY ARE YOU ALWAYS LIKE THIS?
YOU KNOW...

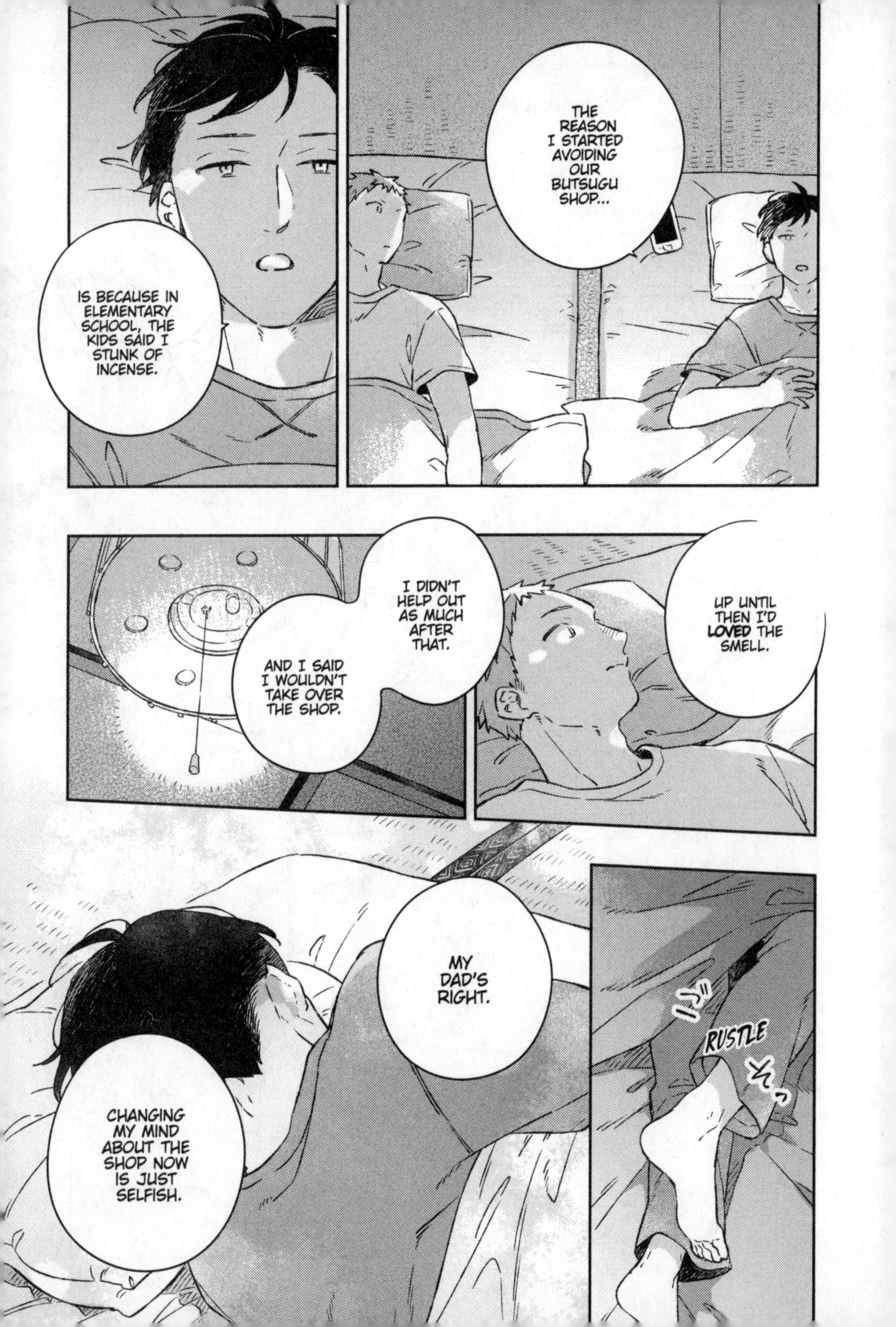
THE REASON I STARTED AVOIDING OUR BUTSUGU SHOP...
IS BECAUSE IN ELEMENTARY SCHOOL, THE KIDS SAID I STUNK OF INCENSE.
UP UNTIL THEN I'D **LOVED** THE SMELL.
I DIDN'T HELP OUT AS MUCH AFTER THAT.
AND I SAID I WOULDN'T TAKE OVER THE SHOP.
RUSTLE
MY DAD'S RIGHT.
CHANGING MY MIND ABOUT THE SHOP NOW IS JUST SELFISH.

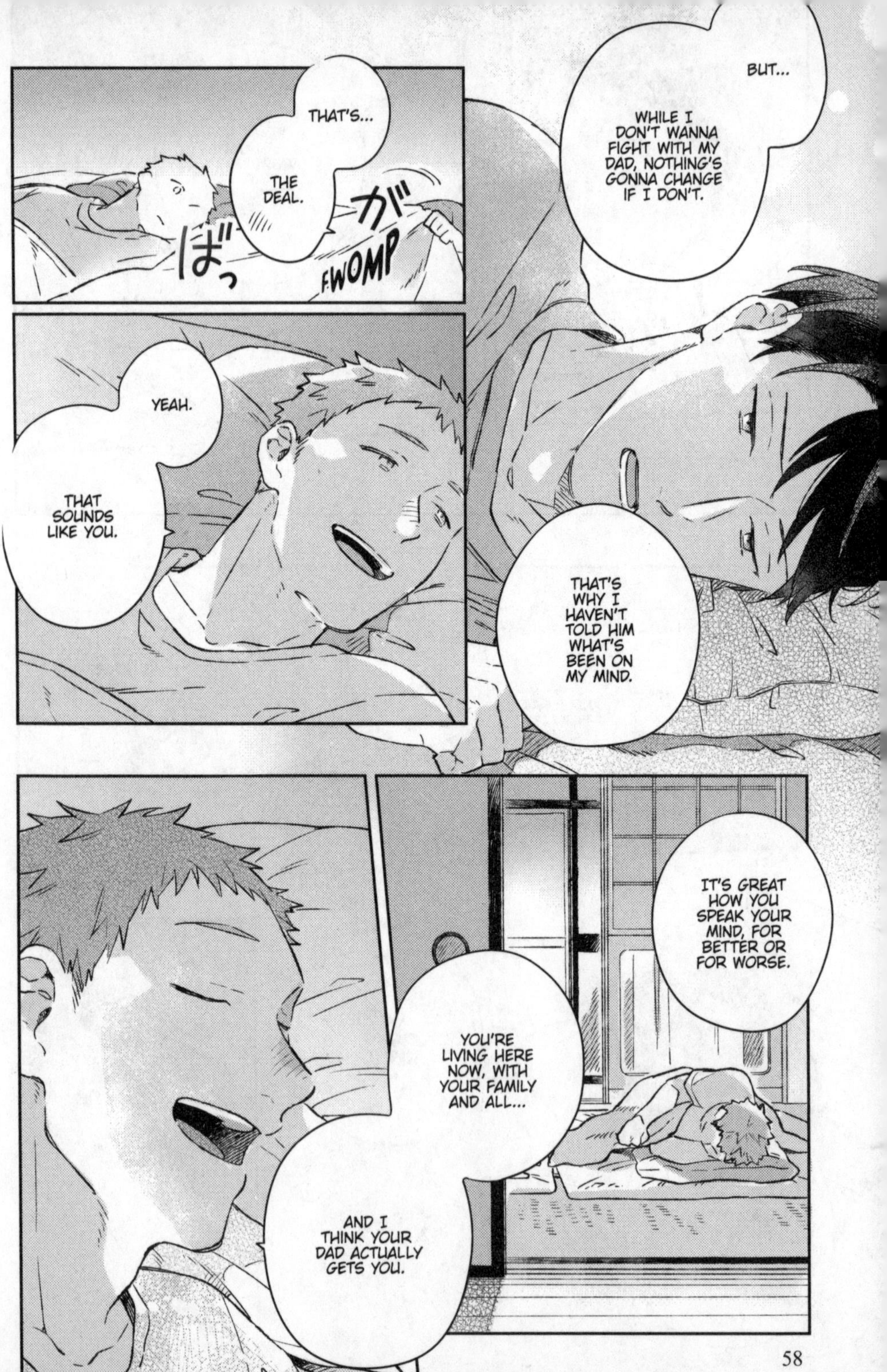
BUT...
WHILE I DON'T WANNA FIGHT WITH MY DAD, NOTHING'S GONNA CHANGE IF I DON'T.
THAT'S WHY I HAVEN'T TOLD HIM WHAT'S BEEN ON MY MIND.
THAT'S...
THE DEAL.
が
ばっ
FWOMP
YEAH.
THAT SOUNDS LIKE YOU.
IT'S GREAT HOW YOU SPEAK YOUR MIND, FOR BETTER OR FOR WORSE.
YOU'RE LIVING HERE NOW, WITH YOUR FAMILY AND ALL...
AND I THINK YOUR DAD ACTUALLY GETS YOU.

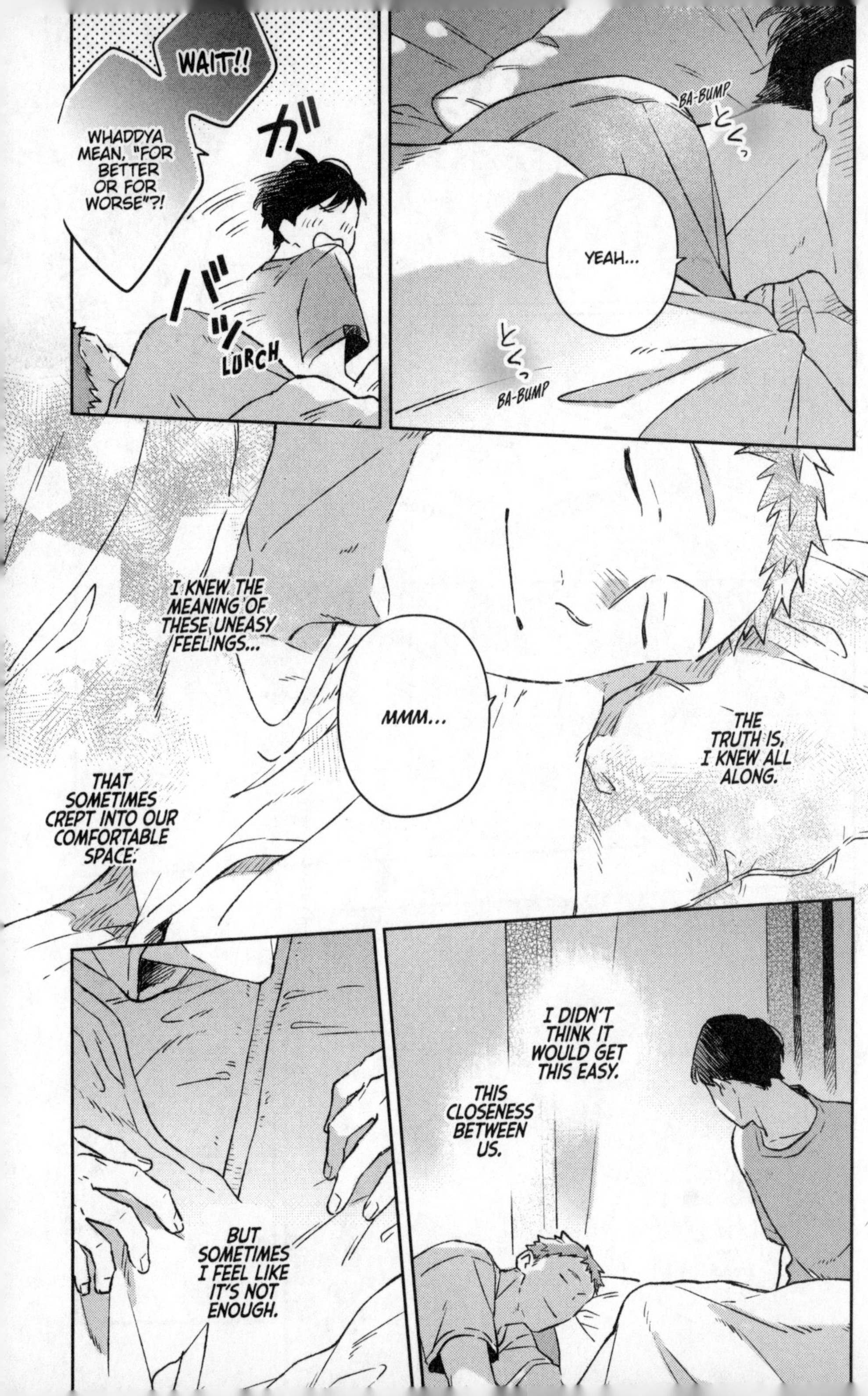
BA-BUMP
とくっ
YEAH...
とくっ
BA-BUMP
WAIT!!
WHADDYA MEAN, "FOR BETTER OR FOR WORSE"?!
ガッ
バッ
LURCH
THE TRUTH IS, I KNEW ALL ALONG.
I KNEW THE MEANING OF THESE UNEASY FEELINGS...
MMM...
THAT SOMETIMES CREPT INTO OUR COMFORTABLE SPACE.
I DIDN'T THINK IT WOULD GET THIS EASY.
THIS CLOSENESS BETWEEN US.
BUT SOMETIMES I FEEL LIKE IT'S NOT ENOUGH.

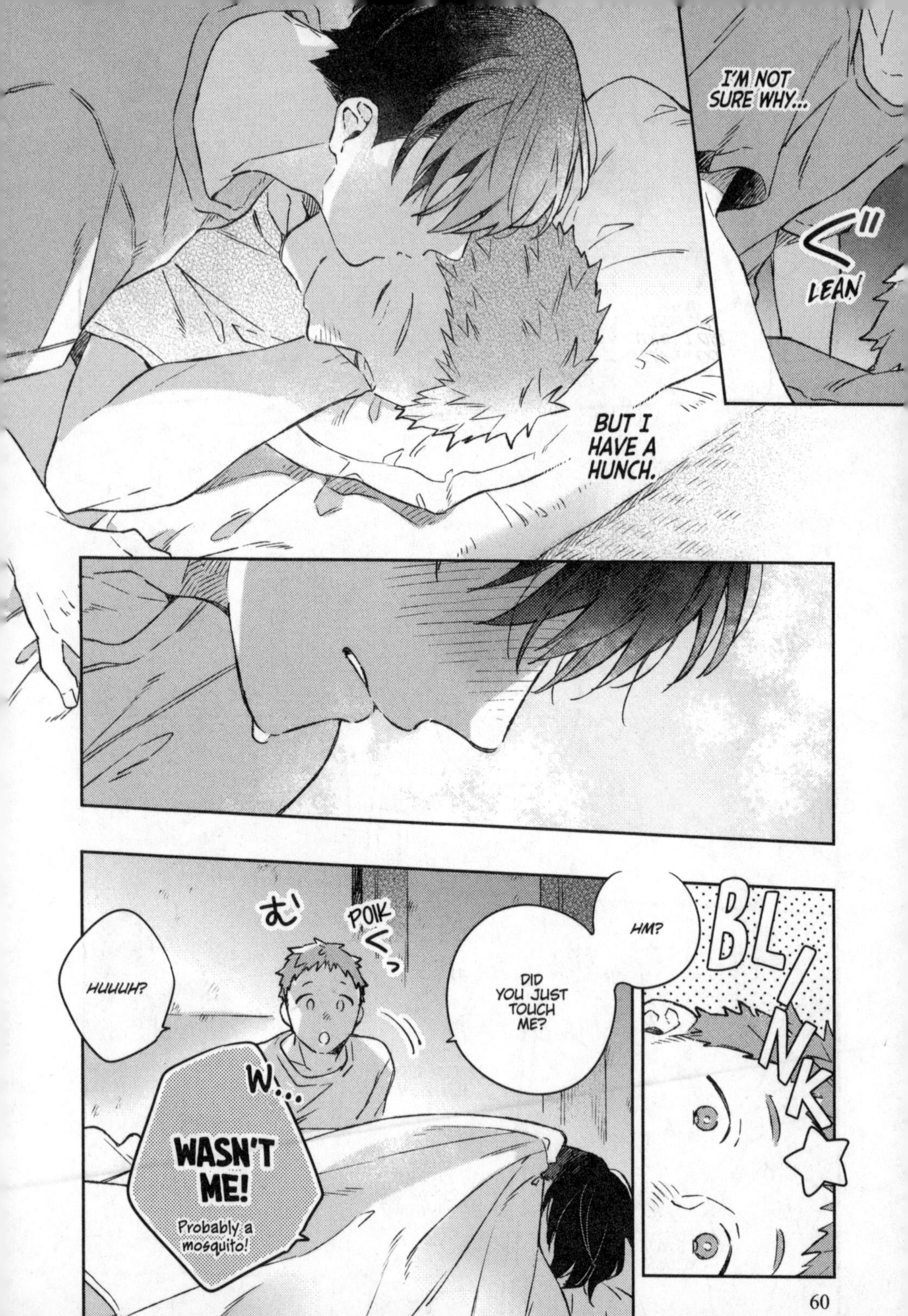
I'M NOT SURE WHY...
ぐ"
LEAN
BUT I HAVE A HUNCH.
BLINK
HM?
DID YOU JUST TOUCH ME?
む
POIK
くっ
HUUUH?
W...
WASN'T ME!
Probably a mosquito!

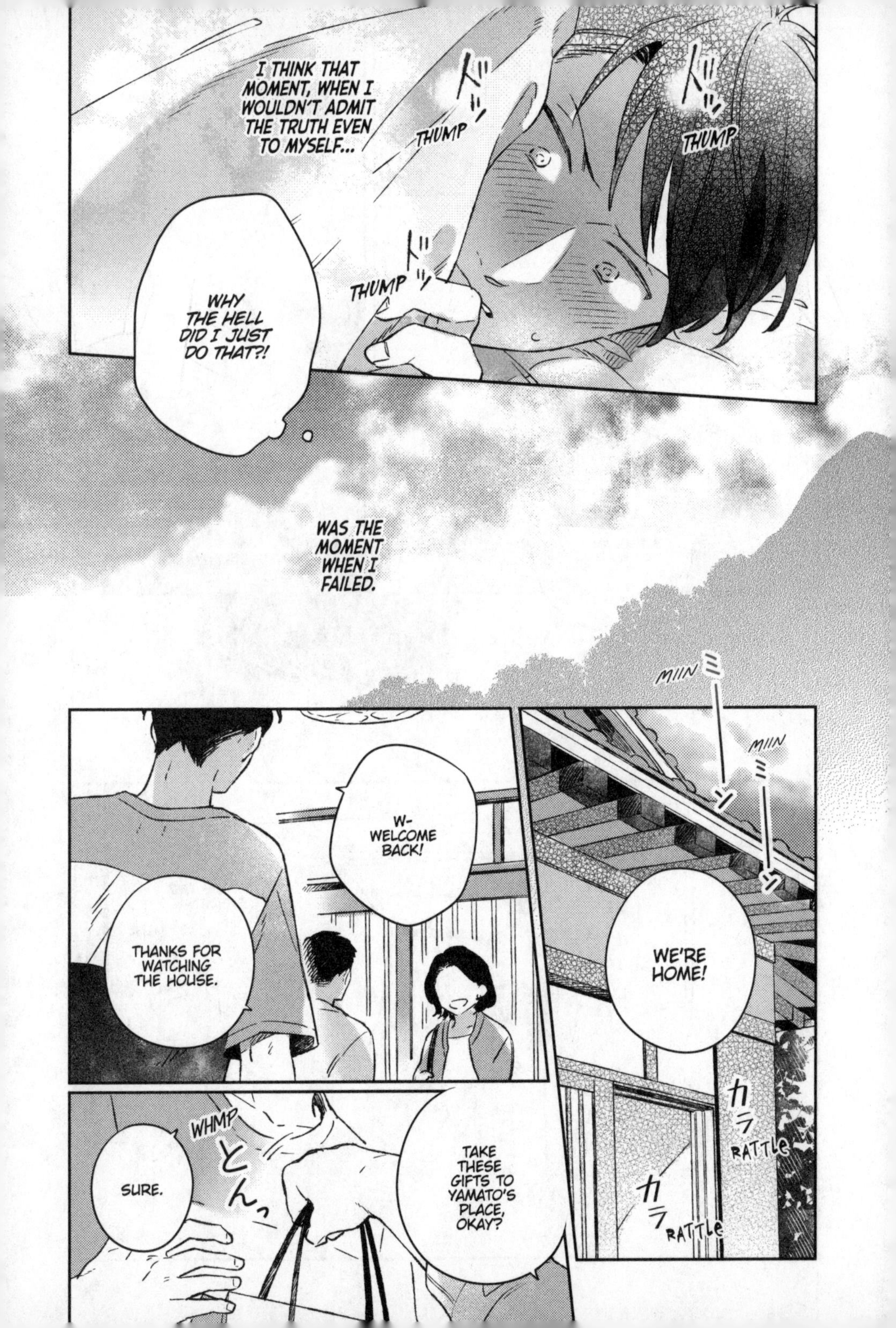
I THINK THAT MOMENT, WHEN I WOULDN'T ADMIT THE TRUTH EVEN TO MYSELF...
ドッ THUMP
ドッ THUMP
ドッ THUMP
WHY THE HELL DID I JUST DO THAT?!
WAS THE MOMENT WHEN I FAILED.
ミーン MIIN
ミーン MIIN
WE'RE HOME!
カラ RATTLE
カラ RATTLE
W-WELCOME BACK!
THANKS FOR WATCHING THE HOUSE.
TAKE THESE GIFTS TO YAMATO'S PLACE, OKAY?
とんっ WHMP
SURE.

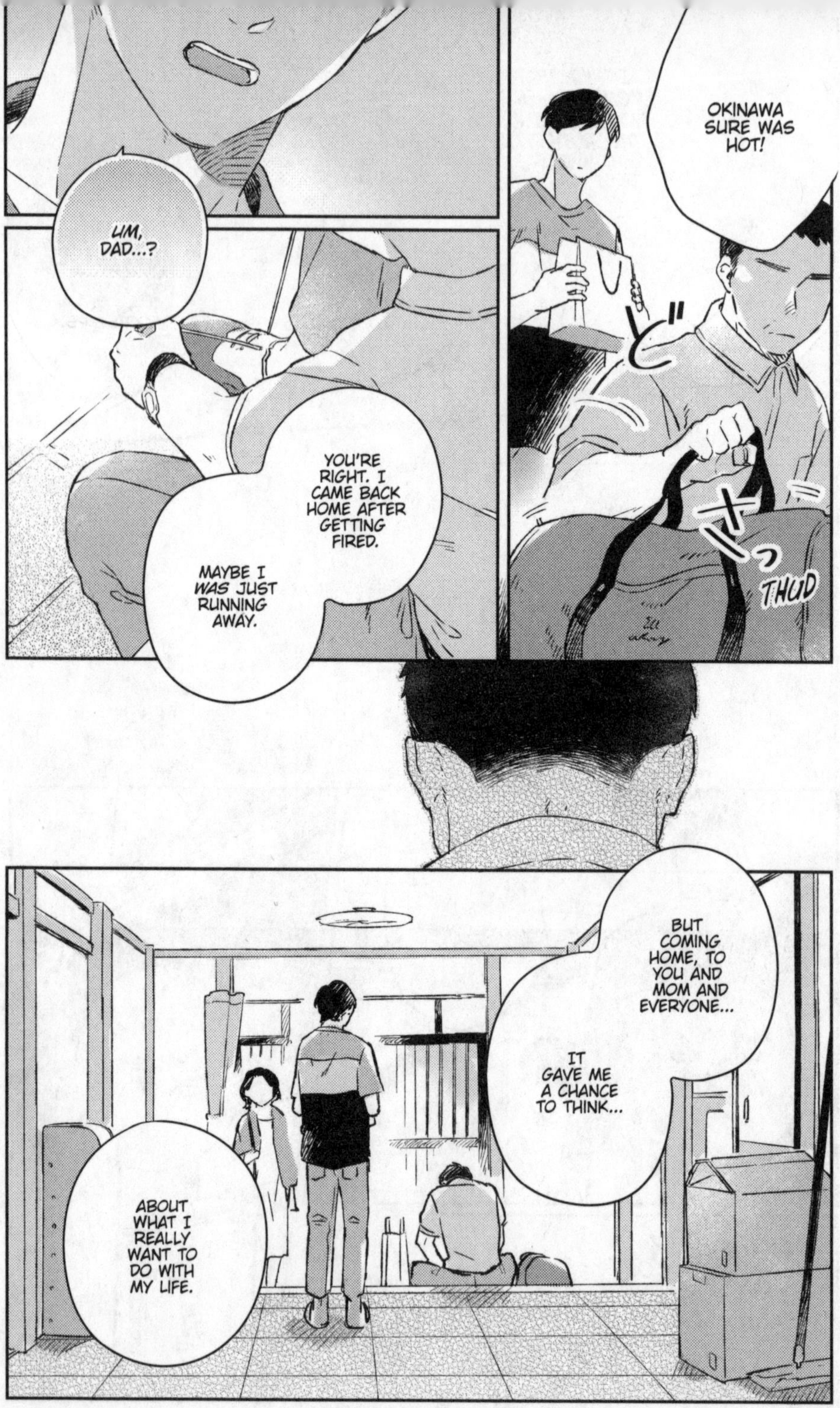
OKINAWA SURE WAS HOT!
THUD
UM, DAD...?
YOU'RE RIGHT. I CAME BACK HOME AFTER GETTING FIRED.
MAYBE I WAS JUST RUNNING AWAY.
BUT COMING HOME, TO YOU AND MOM AND EVERYONE...
IT GAVE ME A CHANCE TO THINK...
ABOUT WHAT I REALLY WANT TO DO WITH MY LIFE.

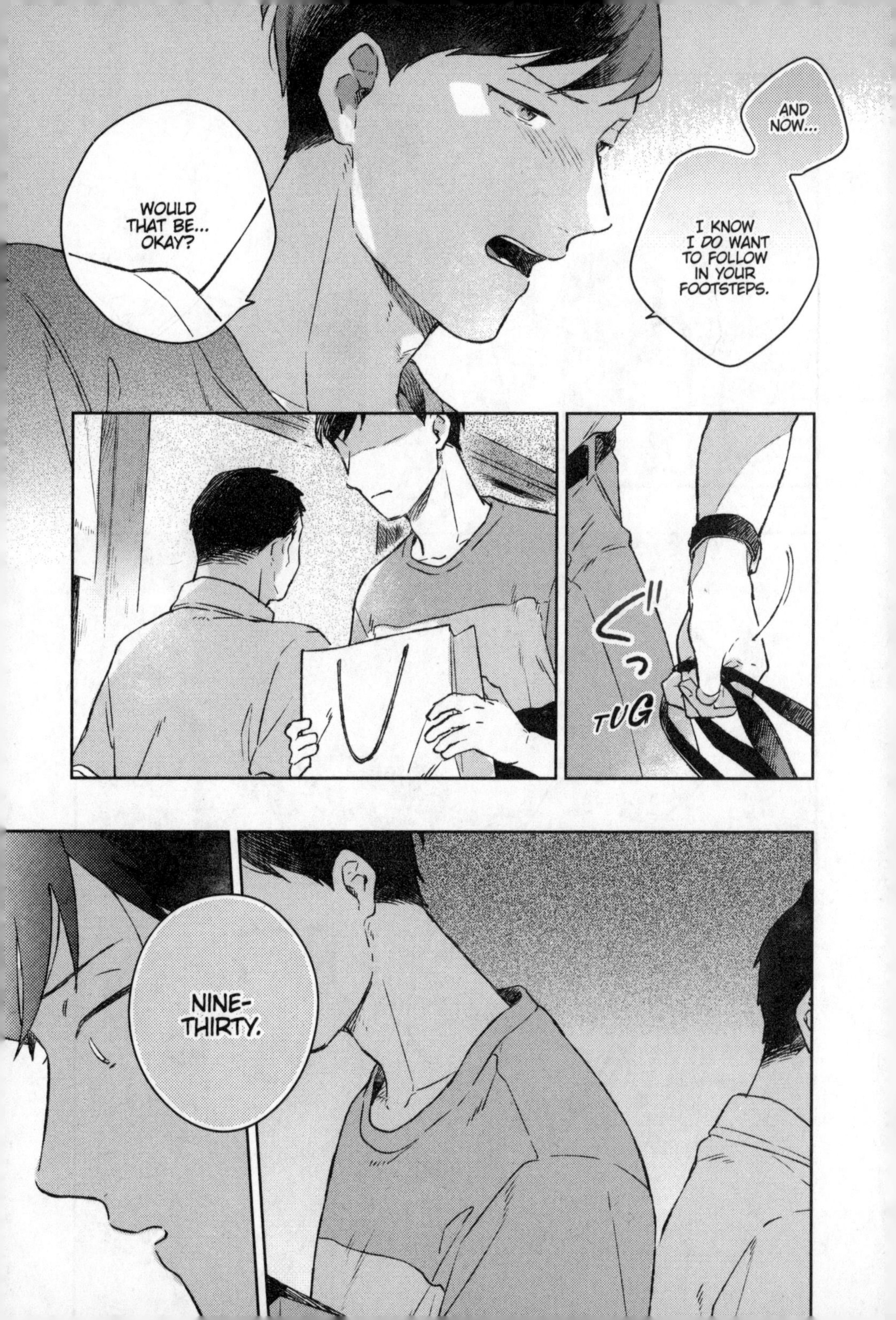
AND NOW...
I KNOW I DO WANT TO FOLLOW IN YOUR FOOTSTEPS.
WOULD THAT BE... OKAY?
ぐっ
TUG
NINE-THIRTY.

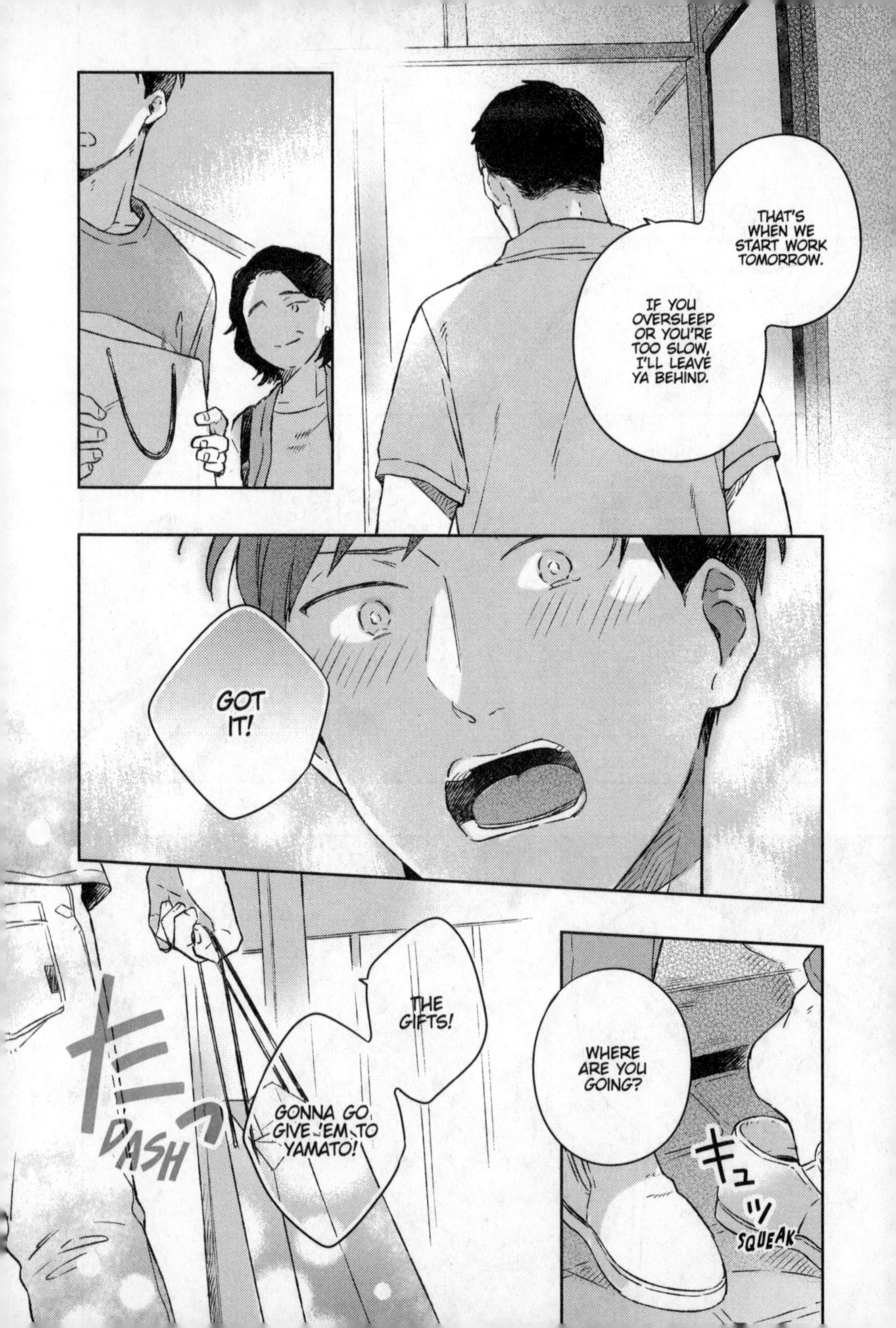
THAT'S WHEN WE START WORK TOMORROW.
IF YOU OVERSLEEP OR YOU'RE TOO SLOW, I'LL LEAVE YA BEHIND.
GOT IT!
WHERE ARE YOU GOING?
キュッ
SQUEAK
THE GIFTS!
GONNA GO GIVE 'EM TO YAMATO!
DASH

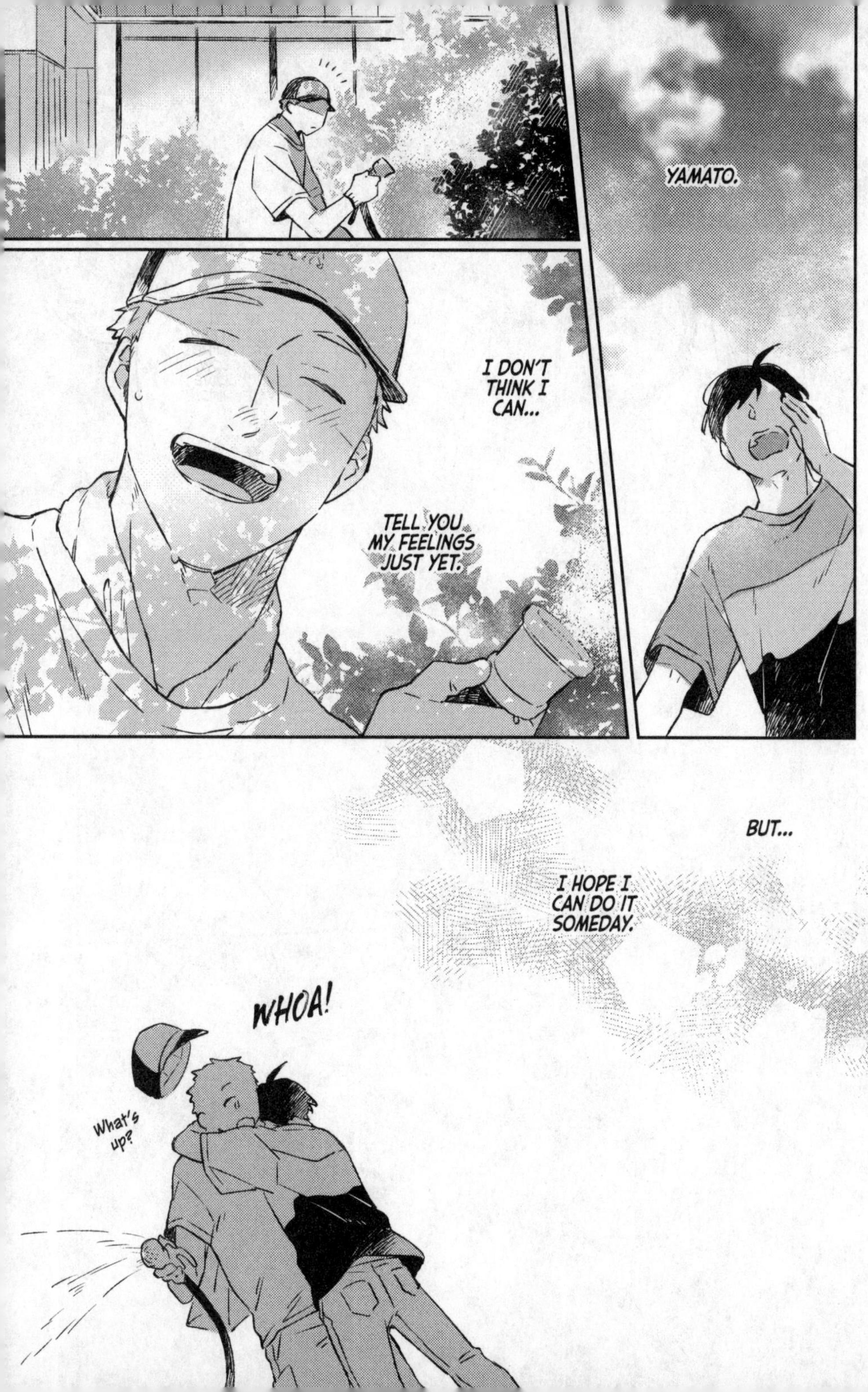
YAMATO.
I DON'T THINK I CAN...
TELL YOU MY FEELINGS JUST YET.
BUT...
I HOPE I CAN DO IT SOMEDAY.
WHOA!
What's up?

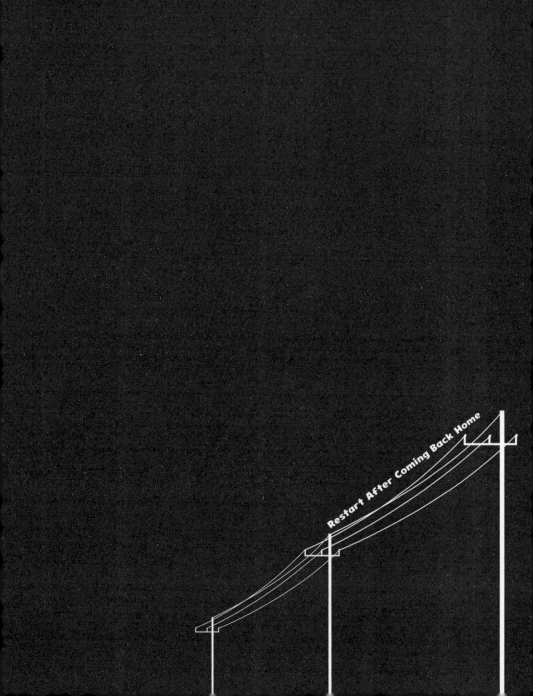

Restart After Coming Back Home

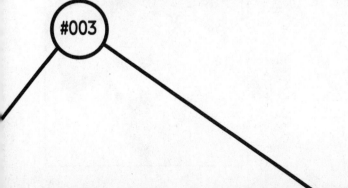

#003

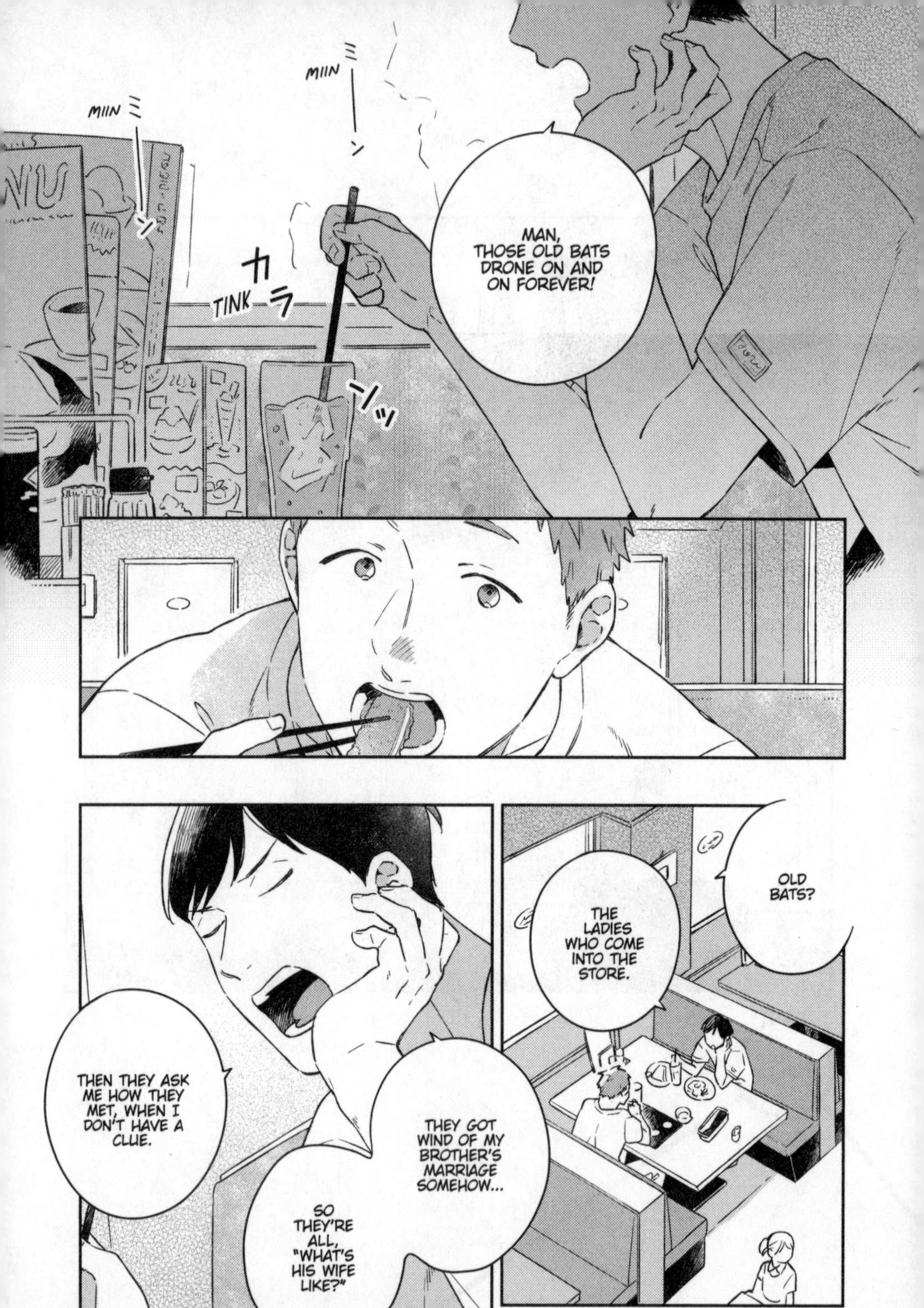
MIIN
MIIN
TINK
MAN, THOSE OLD BATS DRONE ON AND ON FOREVER!
OLD BATS?
THE LADIES WHO COME INTO THE STORE.
THEY GOT WIND OF MY BROTHER'S MARRIAGE SOMEHOW...
SO THEY'RE ALL, "WHAT'S HIS WIFE LIKE?"
THEN THEY ASK ME HOW THEY MET, WHEN I DON'T HAVE A CLUE.

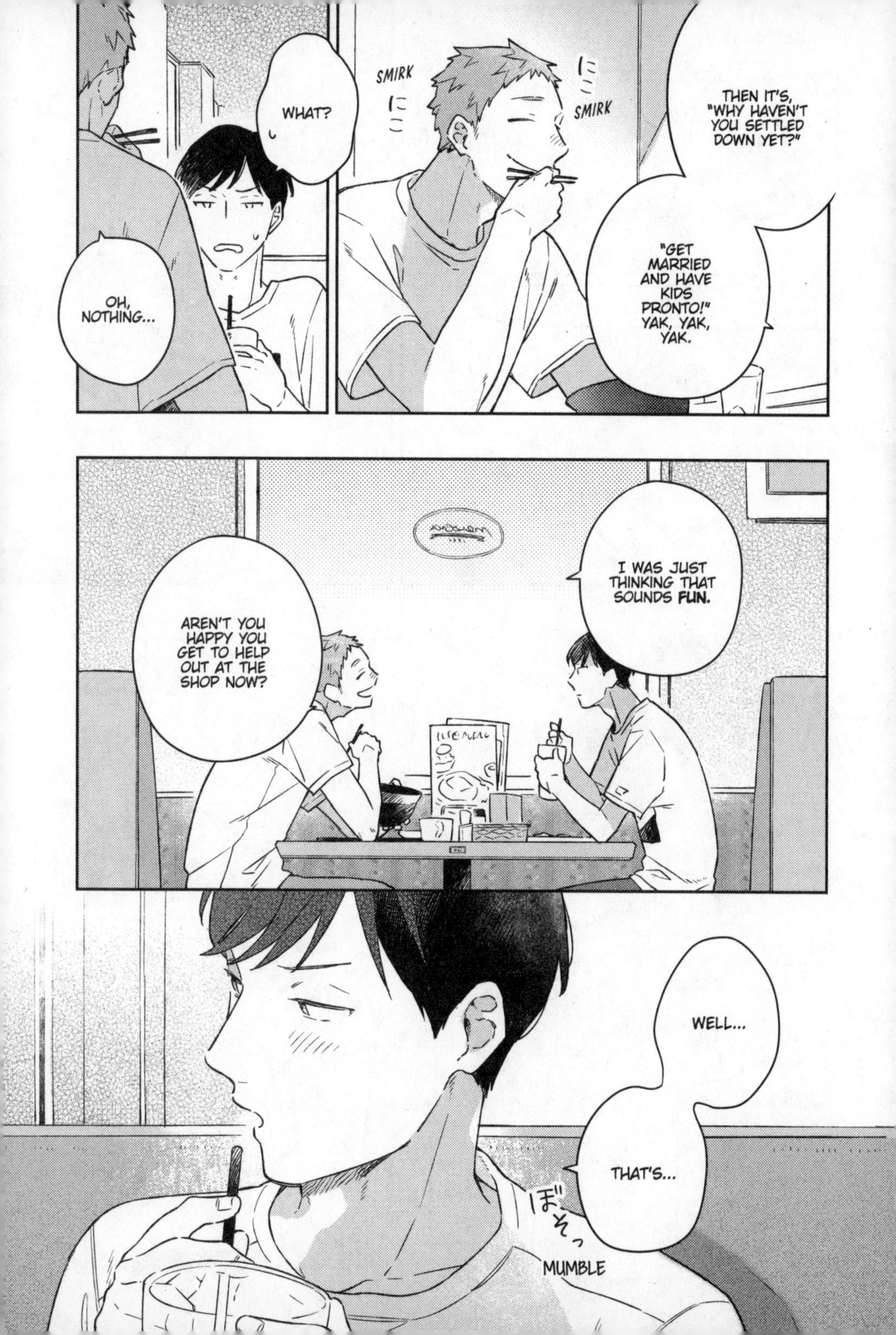
THEN IT'S, "WHY HAVEN'T YOU SETTLED DOWN YET?"
にこ
SMIRK
"GET MARRIED AND HAVE KIDS PRONTO!" YAK, YAK, YAK.
にこ
SMIRK
WHAT?
OH, NOTHING...
I WAS JUST THINKING THAT SOUNDS **FUN.**
AREN'T YOU HAPPY YOU GET TO HELP OUT AT THE SHOP NOW?
WELL...
THAT'S...
ぼそっ
MUMBLE

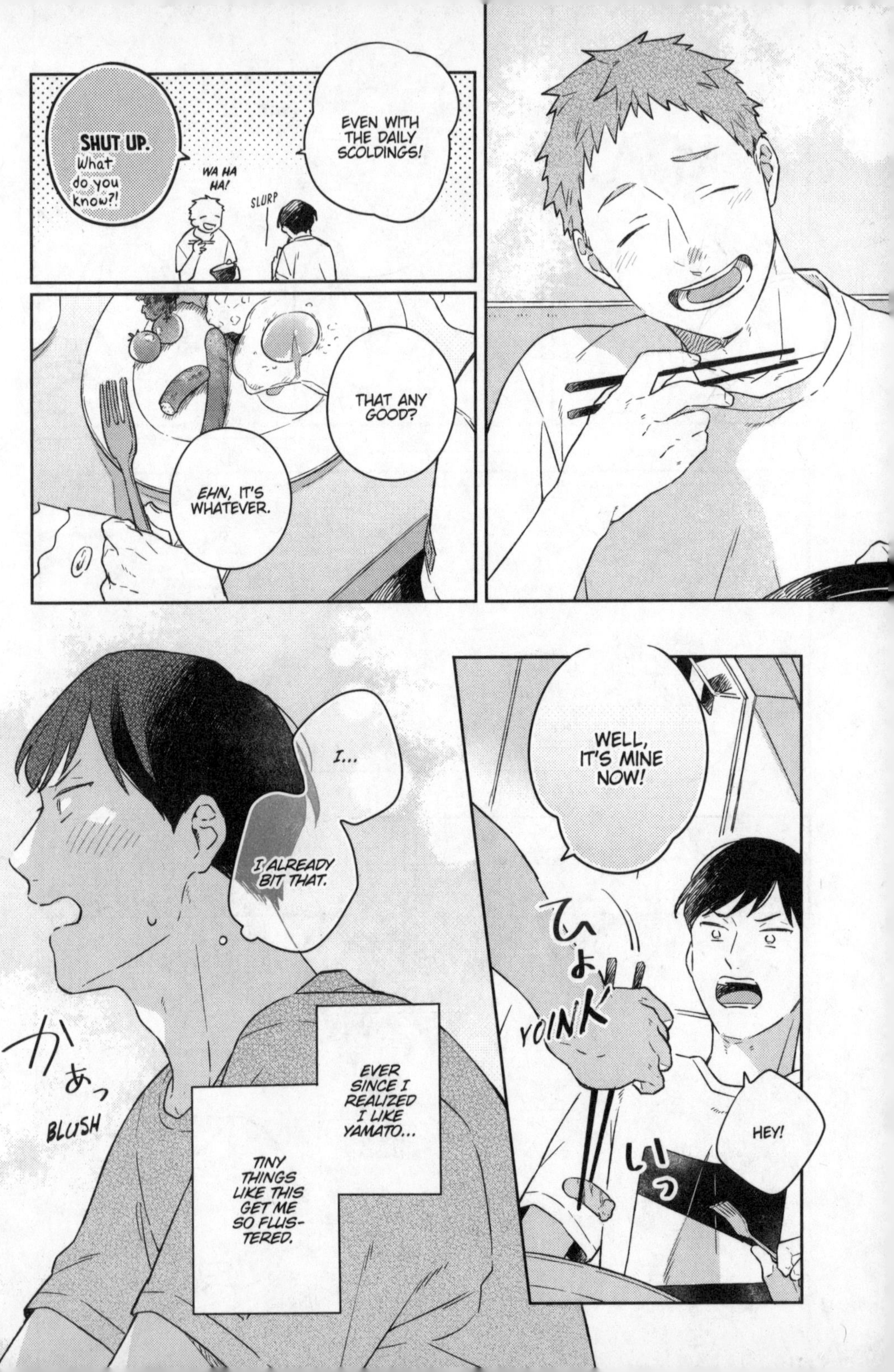
EVEN WITH THE DAILY SCOLDINGS!
WA HA HA!
SLURP
SHUT UP. What do you know?!
THAT ANY GOOD?
EHN, IT'S WHATEVER.
WELL, IT'S MINE NOW!
ひょい
YOINK
HEY!
いっ
I...
I ALREADY BIT THAT.
かあっ
BLUSH
EVER SINCE I REALIZED I LIKE YAMATO...
TINY THINGS LIKE THIS GET ME SO FLUS-TERED.

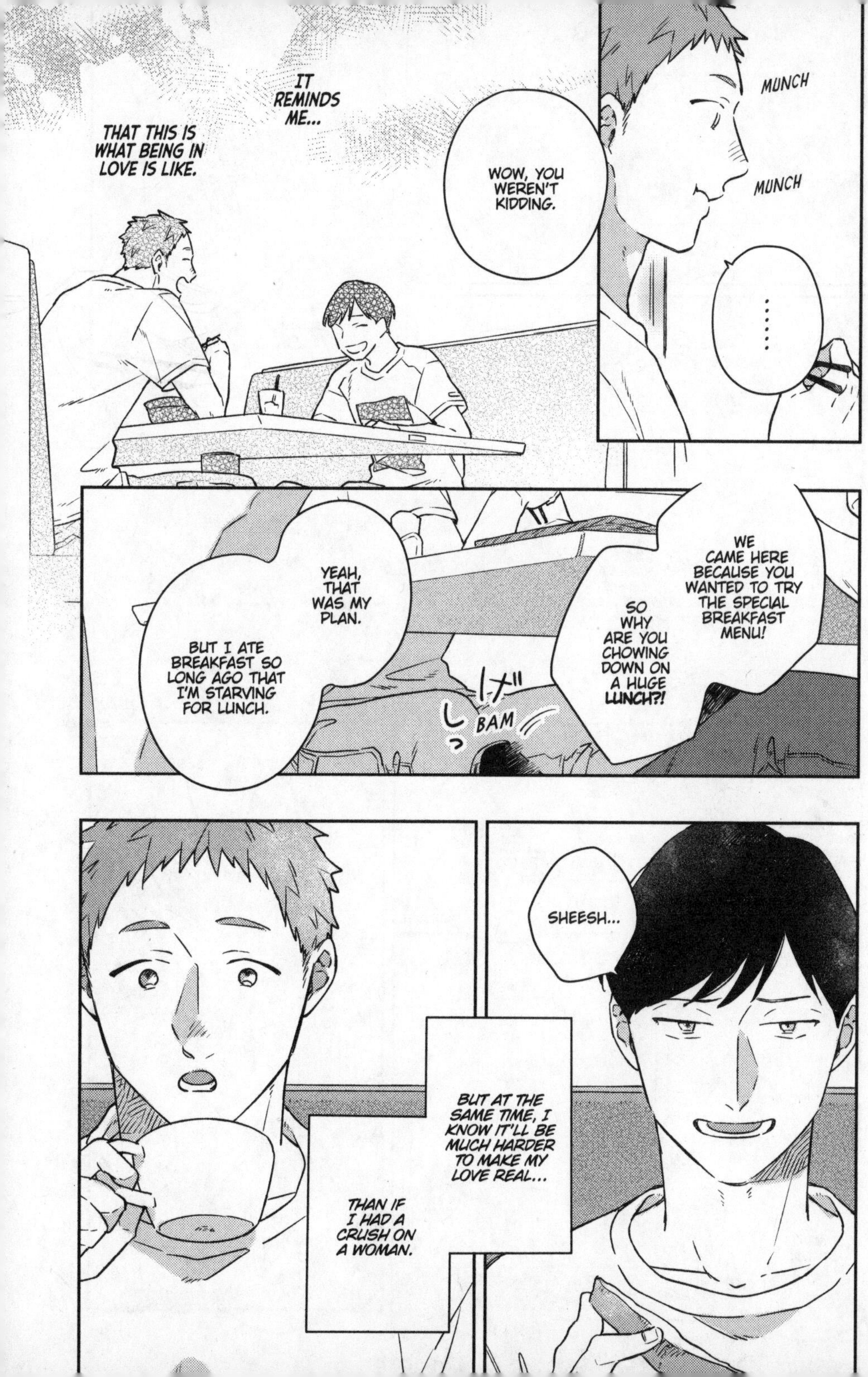
MUNCH
MUNCH
......
WOW, YOU WEREN'T KIDDING.
IT REMINDS ME...
THAT THIS IS WHAT BEING IN LOVE IS LIKE.
WE CAME HERE BECAUSE YOU WANTED TO TRY THE SPECIAL BREAKFAST MENU!
SO WHY ARE YOU CHOWING DOWN ON A HUGE **LUNCH**?!
BAM
YEAH, THAT WAS MY PLAN.
BUT I ATE BREAKFAST SO LONG AGO THAT I'M STARVING FOR LUNCH.
SHEESH...
BUT AT THE SAME TIME, I KNOW IT'LL BE MUCH HARDER TO MAKE MY LOVE REAL...
THAN IF I HAD A CRUSH ON A WOMAN.

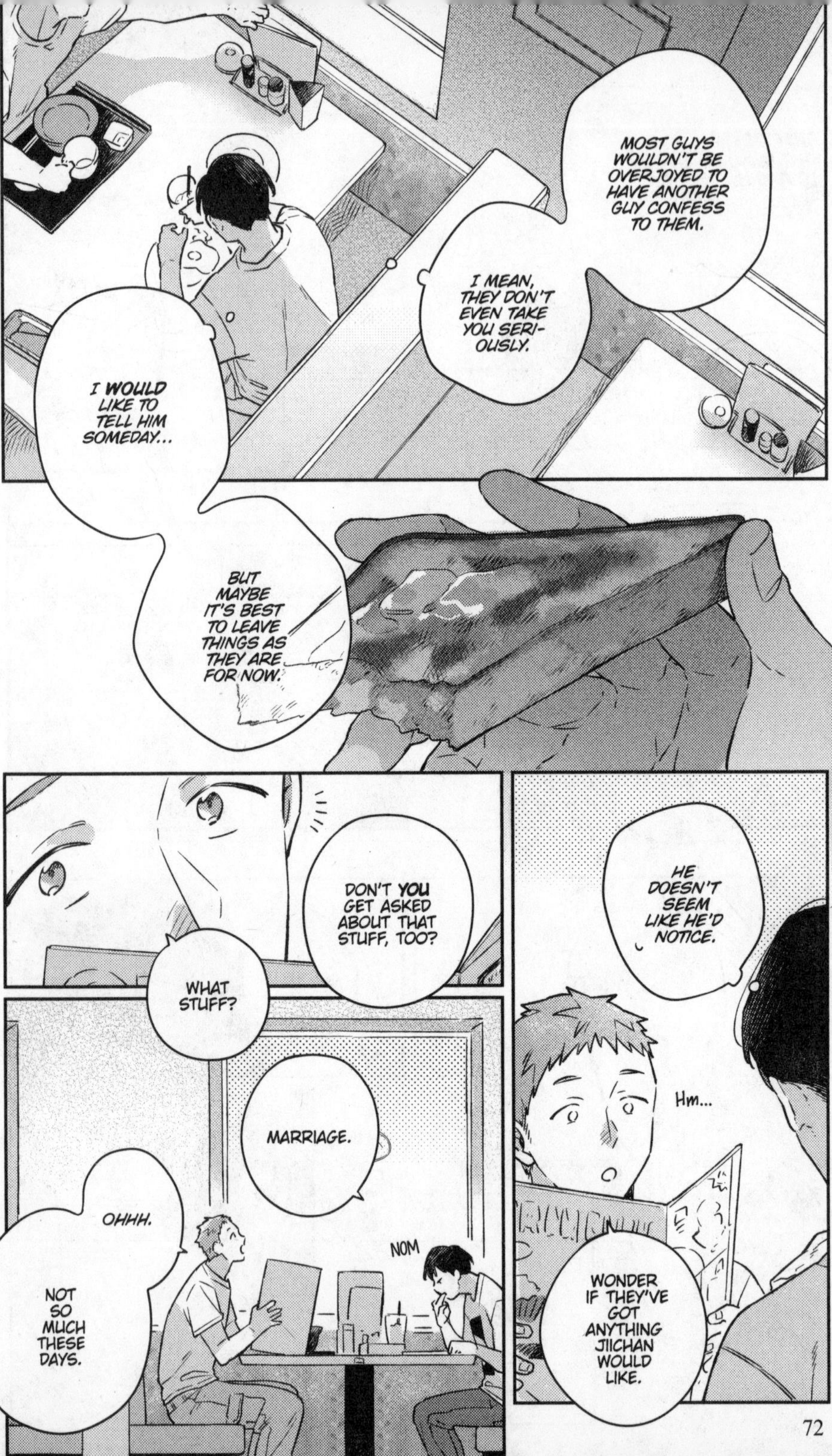
MOST GUYS WOULDN'T BE OVERJOYED TO HAVE ANOTHER GUY CONFESS TO THEM.
I MEAN, THEY DON'T EVEN TAKE YOU SERIOUSLY.
I **WOULD** LIKE TO TELL HIM SOMEDAY...
BUT MAYBE IT'S BEST TO LEAVE THINGS AS THEY ARE FOR NOW.
HE DOESN'T SEEM LIKE HE'D NOTICE.
Hm...
WONDER IF THEY'VE GOT ANYTHING JIICHAN WOULD LIKE.
DON'T **YOU** GET ASKED ABOUT THAT STUFF, TOO?
WHAT STUFF?
MARRIAGE.
NOM
OHHH.
NOT SO MUCH THESE DAYS.

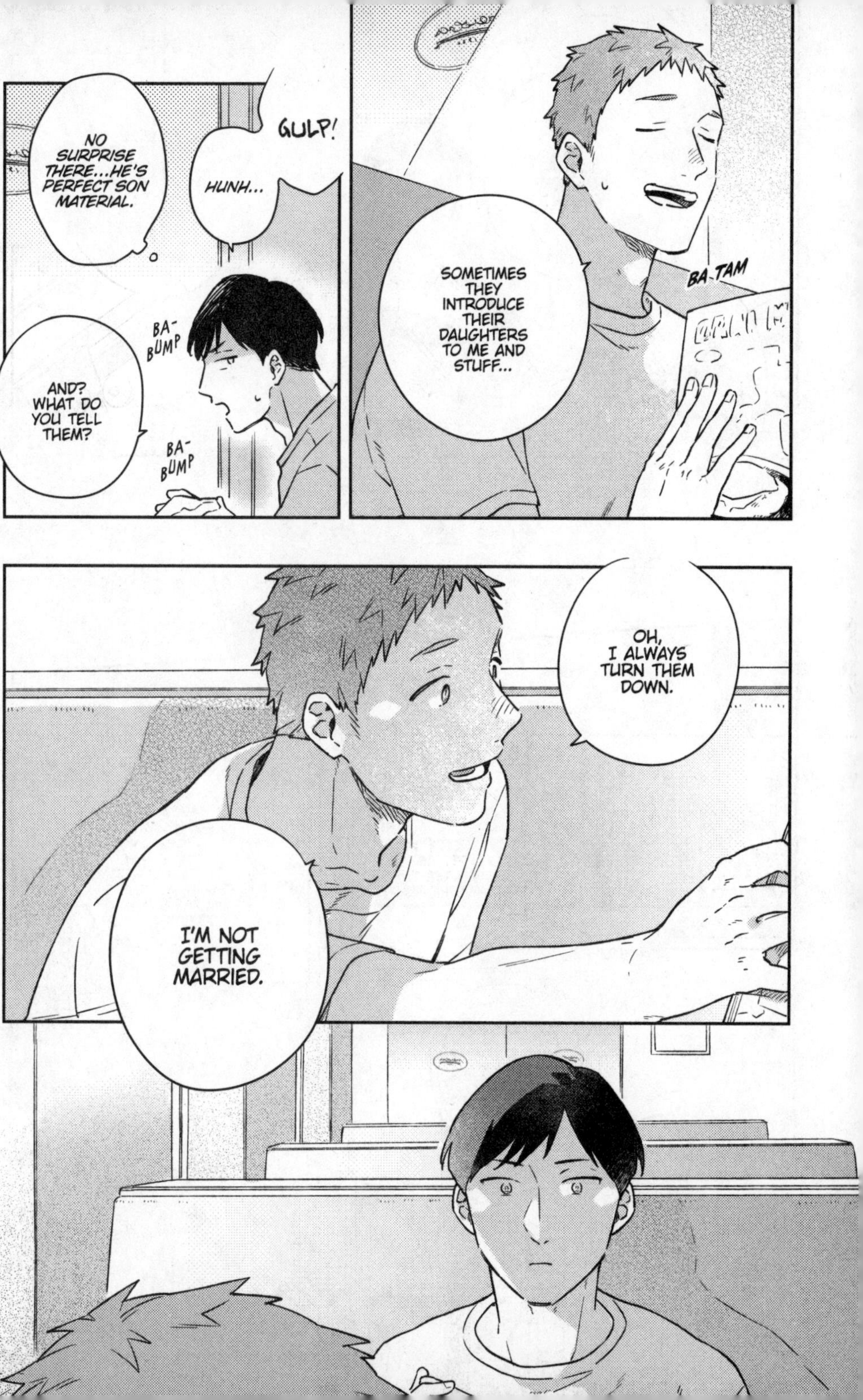
BA-TAM
SOMETIMES THEY INTRODUCE THEIR DAUGHTERS TO ME AND STUFF...
GULP!
HUNH...
NO SURPRISE THERE...HE'S PERFECT SON MATERIAL.
BA-BUMP
AND? WHAT DO YOU TELL THEM?
BA-BUMP
OH, I ALWAYS TURN THEM DOWN.
I'M NOT GETTING MARRIED.

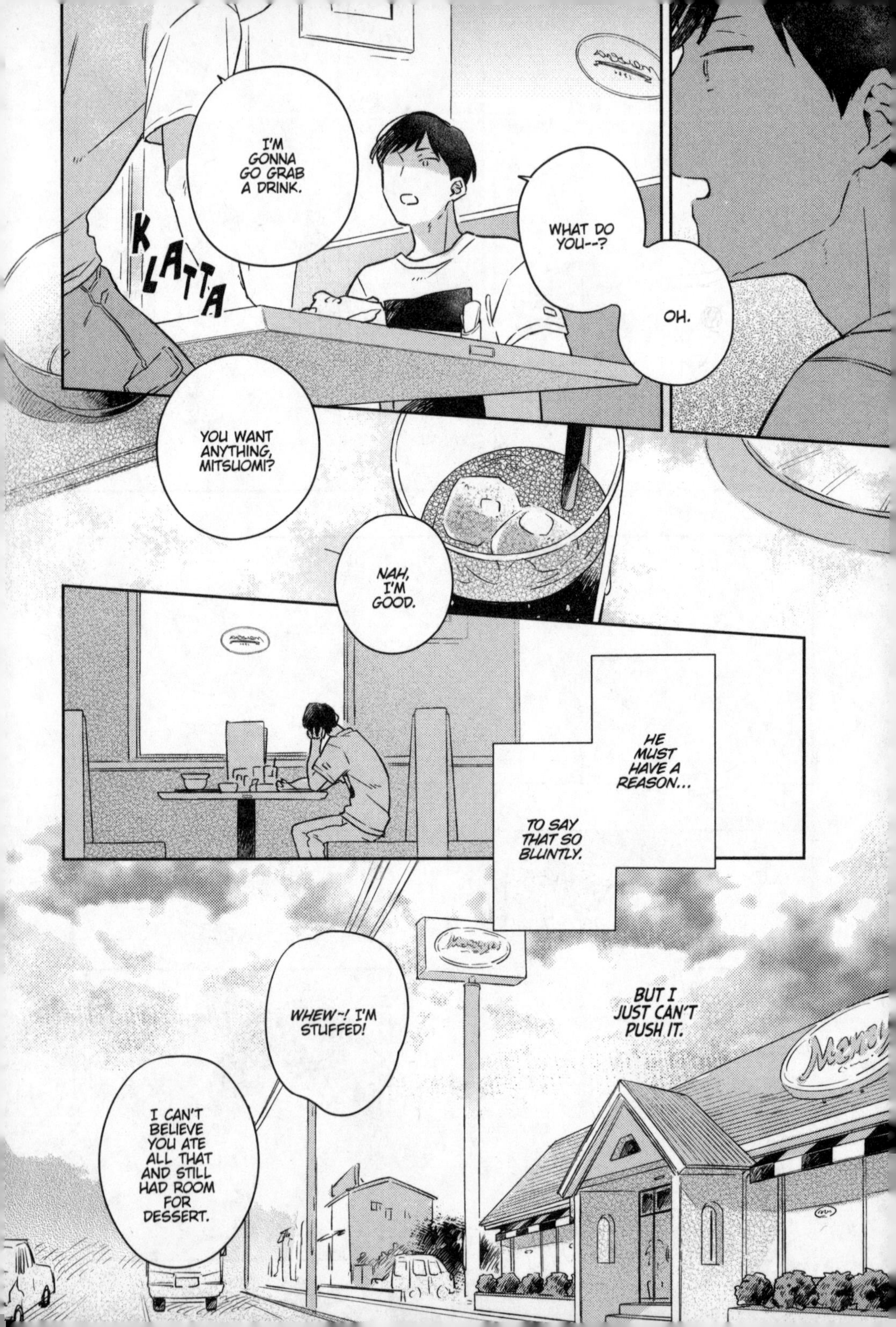
WHAT DO YOU--?
OH.
I'M GONNA GO GRAB A DRINK.
KLATTA
YOU WANT ANYTHING, MITSUOMI?
NAH, I'M GOOD.
HE MUST HAVE A REASON...
TO SAY THAT SO BLUNTLY.
BUT I JUST CAN'T PUSH IT.
WHEW~! I'M STUFFED!
I CAN'T BELIEVE YOU ATE ALL THAT AND STILL HAD ROOM FOR DESSERT.

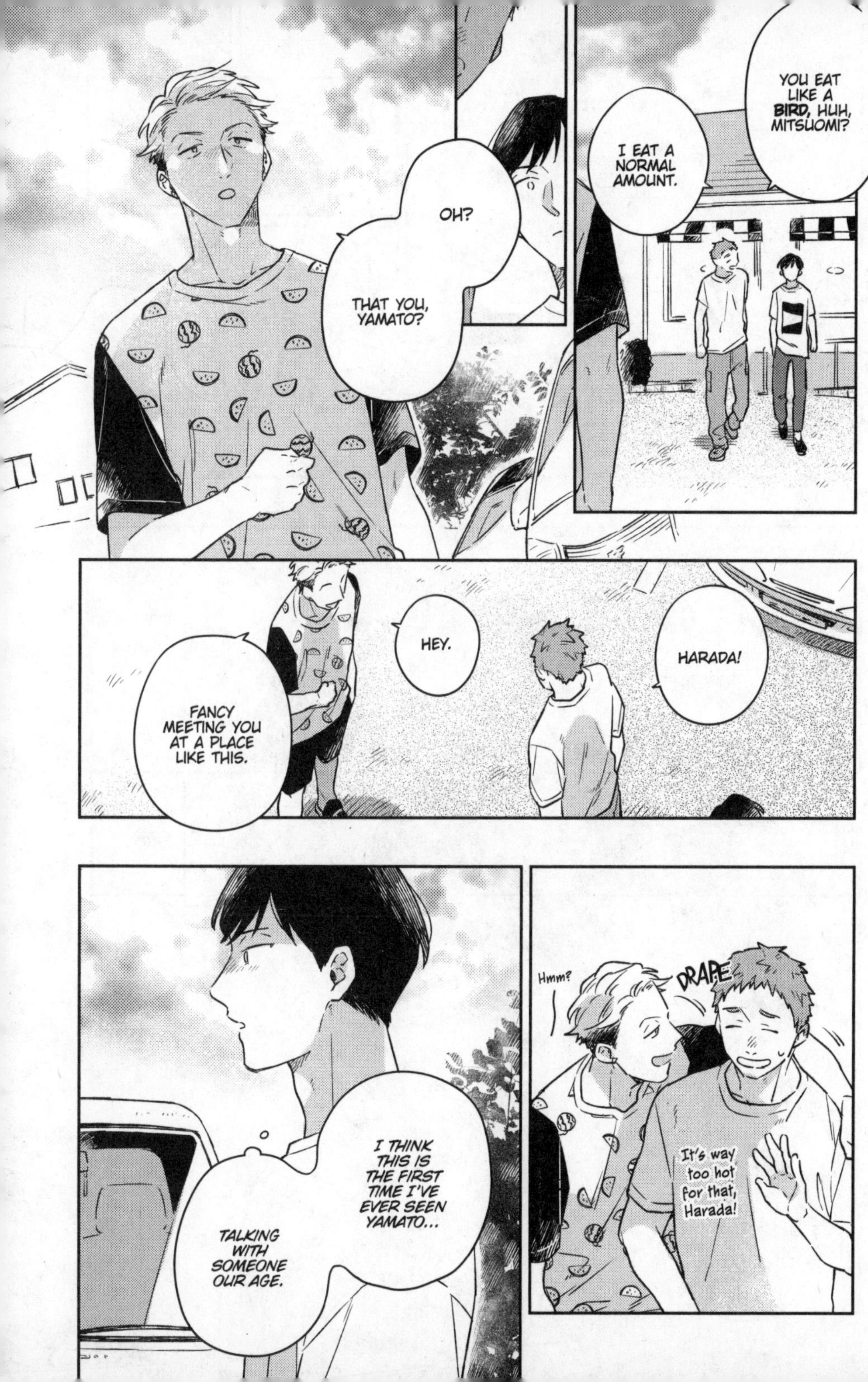
YOU EAT LIKE A BIRD, HUH, MITSUOMI?
I EAT A NORMAL AMOUNT.
OH?
THAT YOU, YAMATO?
HARADA!
HEY.
FANCY MEETING YOU AT A PLACE LIKE THIS.
Hmm?
DRAPE
It's way too hot for that, Harada!
I THINK THIS IS THE FIRST TIME I'VE EVER SEEN YAMATO...
TALKING WITH SOMEONE OUR AGE.

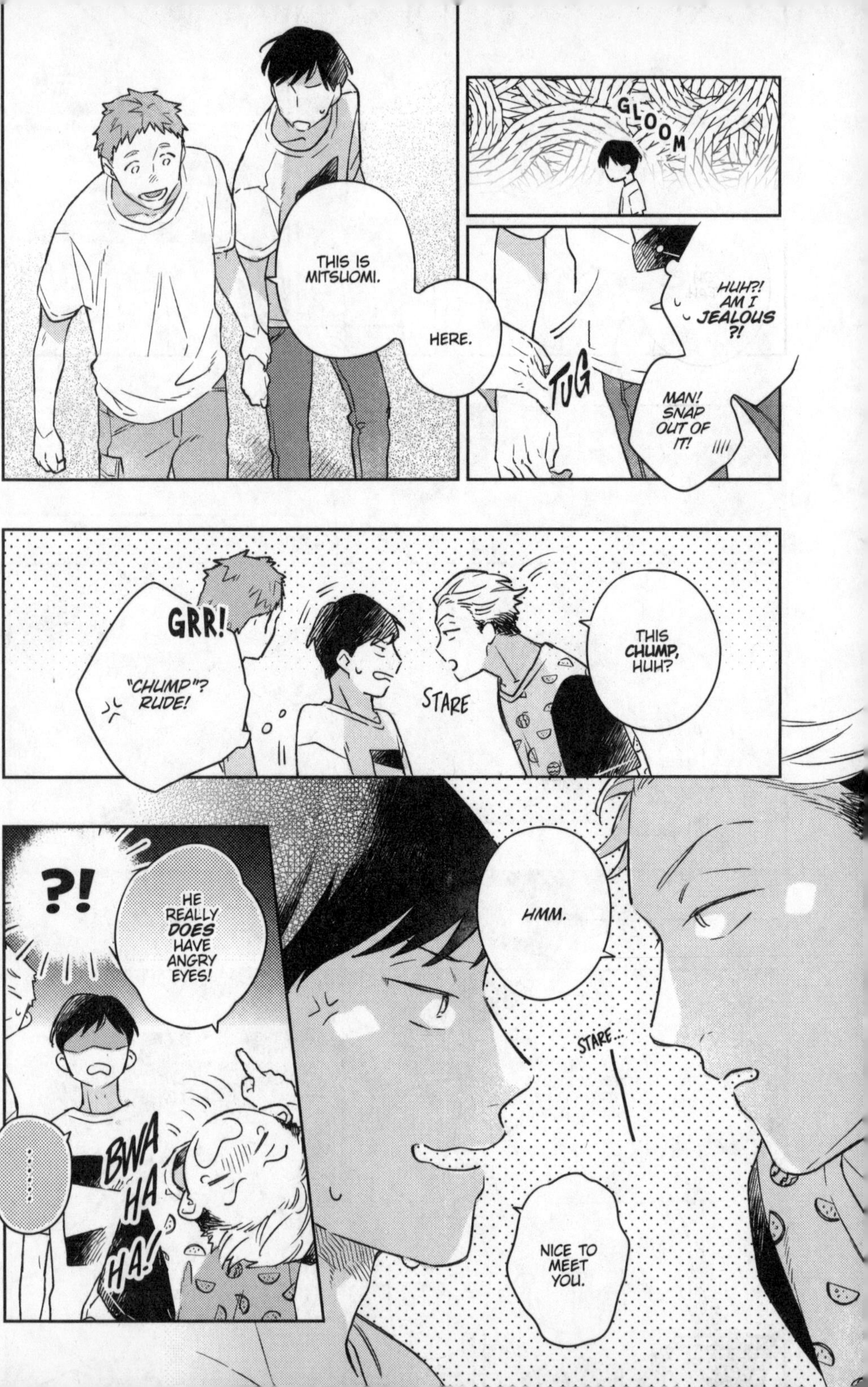
GLOOM
HUH?! AM I JEALOUS?!
TUG
MAN! SNAP OUT OF IT!
THIS IS MITSUOMI.
HERE.
THIS CHUMP, HUH?
STARE
"CHUMP"? RUDE!
GRR!
HMM.
STARE...
NICE TO MEET YOU.
?!
HE REALLY DOES HAVE ANGRY EYES!
BWA HA HA!
......

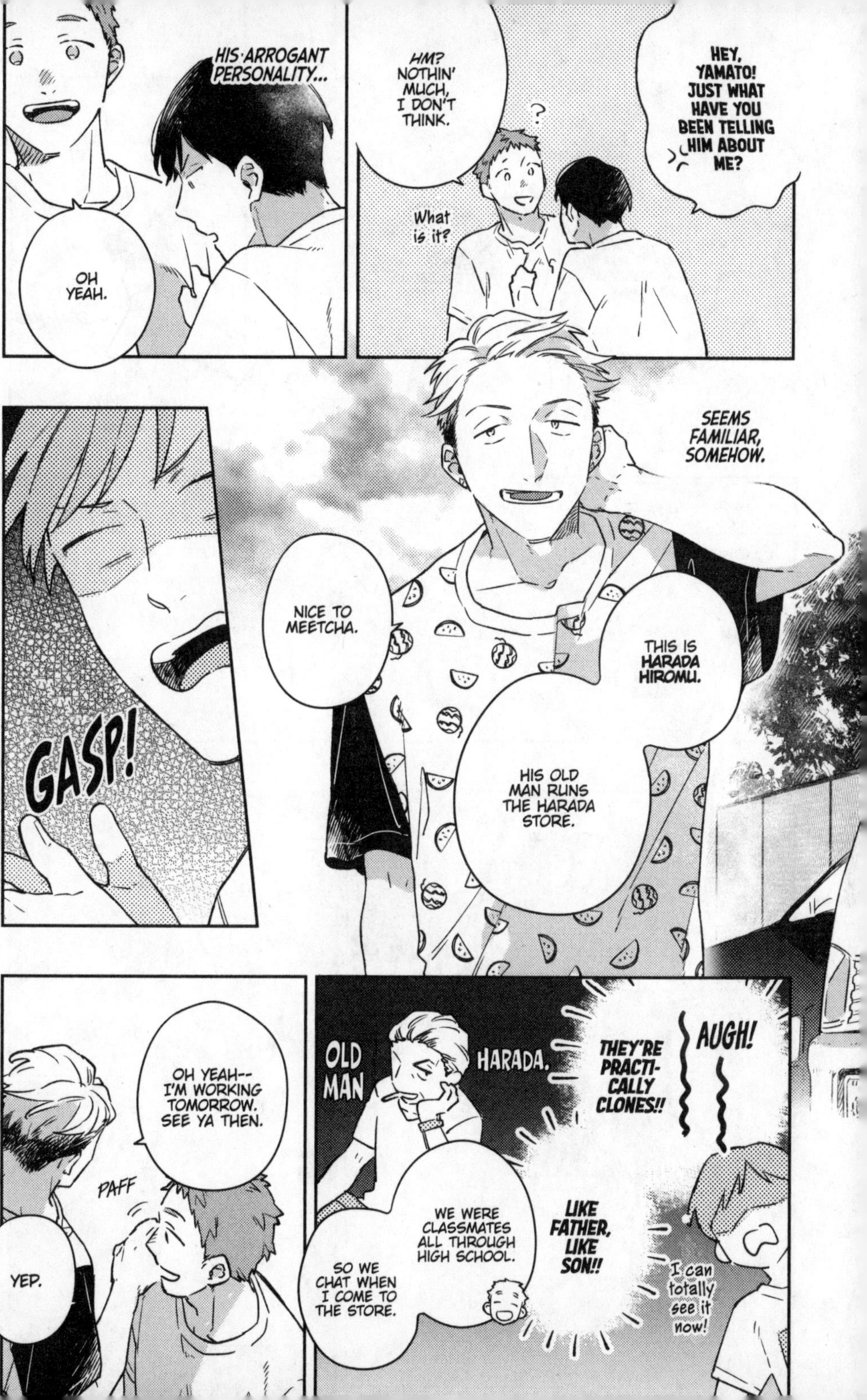
HEY, YAMATO! JUST WHAT HAVE YOU BEEN TELLING HIM ABOUT ME?
HM? NOTHIN' MUCH, I DON'T THINK.
What is it?
HIS ARROGANT PERSONALITY...
OH YEAH.
SEEMS FAMILIAR, SOMEHOW.
THIS IS HARADA HIROMU.
HIS OLD MAN RUNS THE HARADA STORE.
NICE TO MEETCHA.
GASP!
AUGH!
THEY'RE PRACTI-CALLY CLONES!!
HARADA.
OLD MAN
LIKE FATHER, LIKE SON!!
WE WERE CLASSMATES ALL THROUGH HIGH SCHOOL.
SO WE CHAT WHEN I COME TO THE STORE.
I can totally see it now!
OH YEAH-- I'M WORKING TOMORROW. SEE YA THEN.
PAFF
YEP.

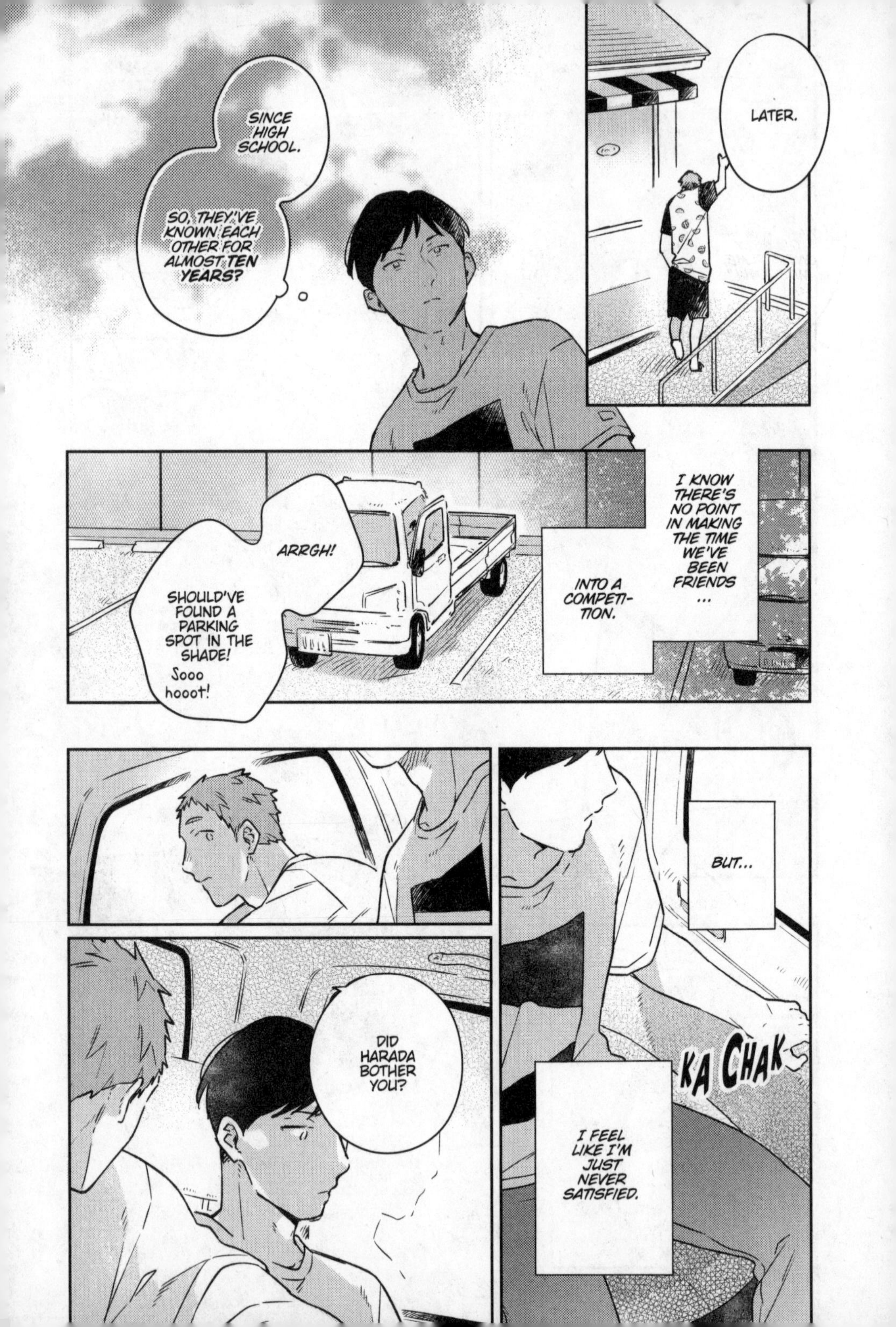
LATER.
SINCE HIGH SCHOOL.
SO, THEY'VE KNOWN EACH OTHER FOR ALMOST TEN YEARS?
I KNOW THERE'S NO POINT IN MAKING THE TIME WE'VE BEEN FRIENDS...
INTO A COMPETITION.
ARRGH!
SHOULD'VE FOUND A PARKING SPOT IN THE SHADE!
Sooo hooot!
BUT...
KA CHAK
I FEEL LIKE I'M JUST NEVER SATISFIED.
DID HARADA BOTHER YOU?

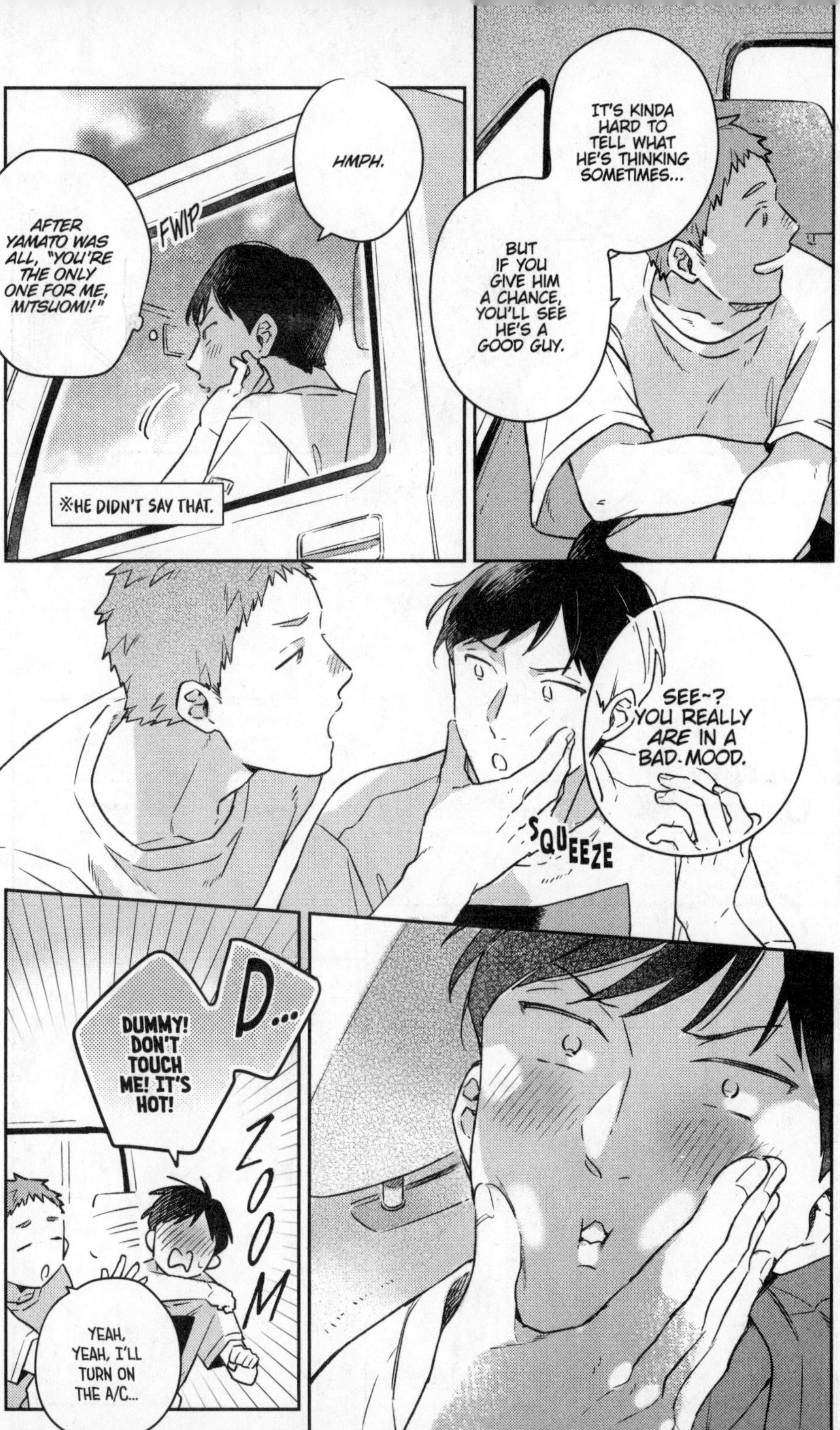
IT'S KINDA HARD TO TELL WHAT HE'S THINKING SOMETIMES...
BUT IF YOU GIVE HIM A CHANCE, YOU'LL SEE HE'S A GOOD GUY.
HMPH.
FWIP
AFTER YAMATO WAS ALL, "YOU'RE THE ONLY ONE FOR ME, MITSUOMI!"
※HE DIDN'T SAY THAT.
SEE~? YOU REALLY ARE IN A BAD MOOD.
SQUEEZE
D...
DUMMY! DON'T TOUCH ME! IT'S HOT!
ZOOOM
YEAH, YEAH, I'LL TURN ON THE A/C...

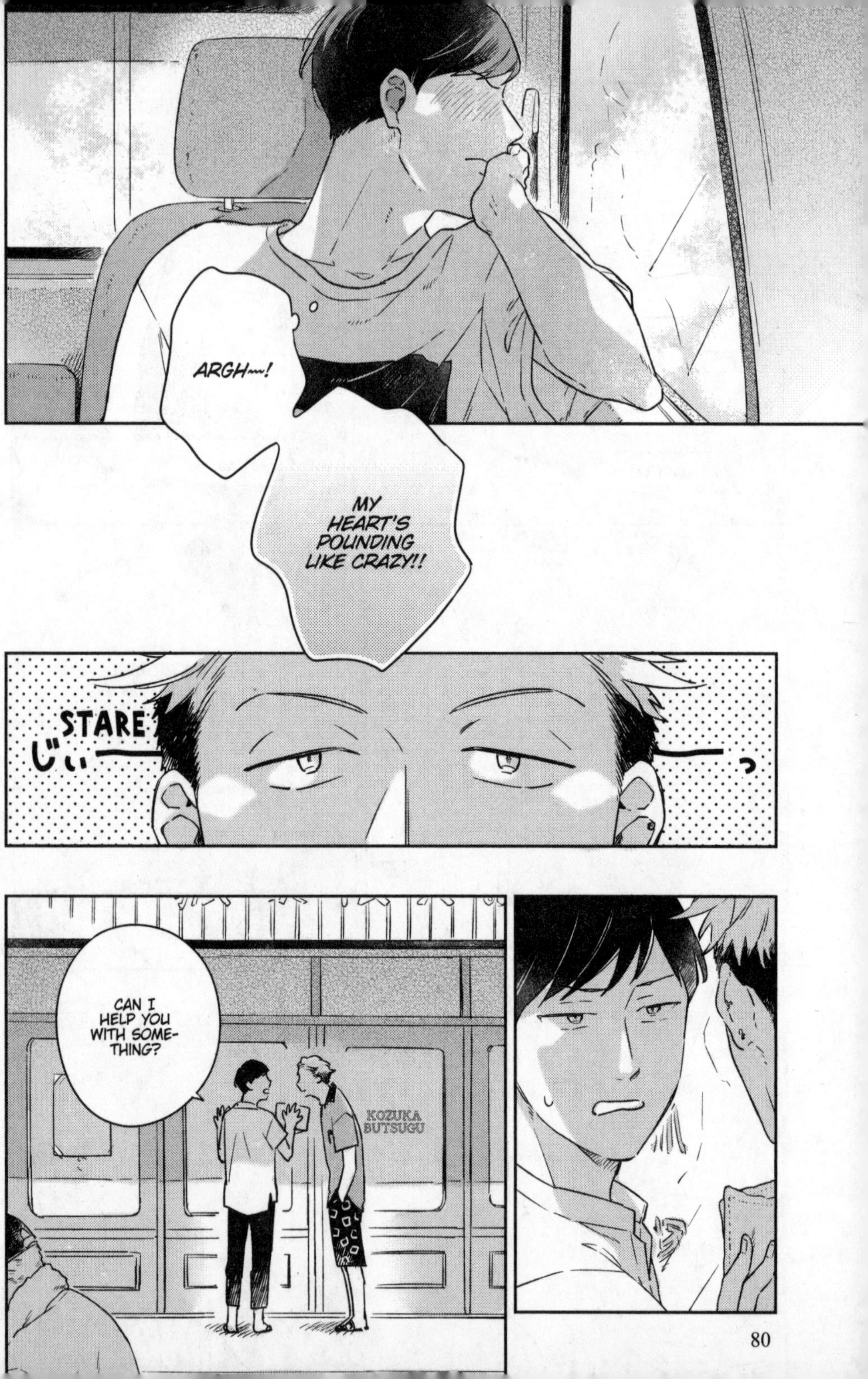
ARGH~~!
MY HEART'S POUNDING LIKE CRAZY!!
STARE
じぃーっ
CAN I HELP YOU WITH SOME-THING?
KOZUKA BUTSUGU

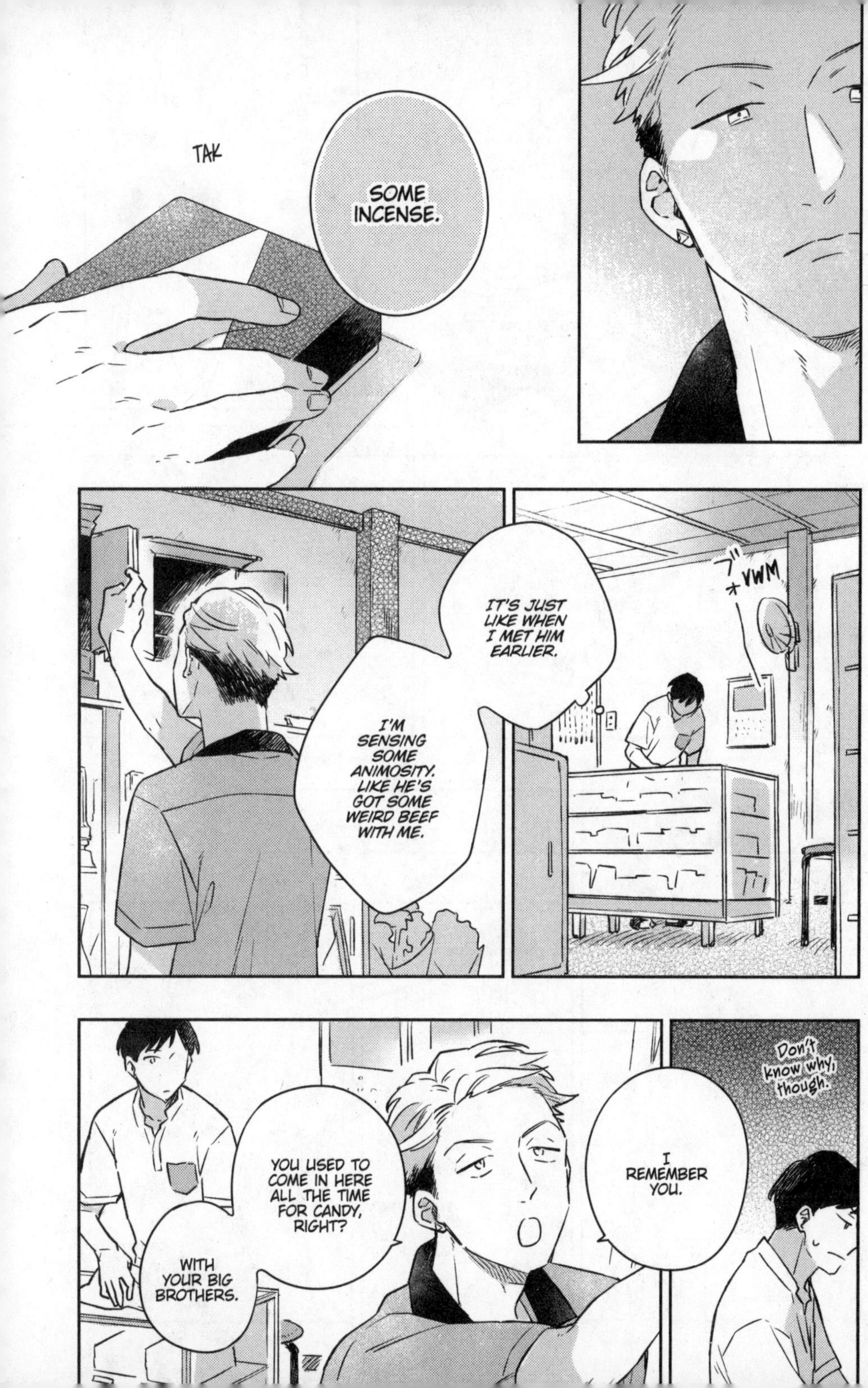
SOME INCENSE.
TAK
IT'S JUST LIKE WHEN I MET HIM EARLIER.
I'M SENSING SOME ANIMOSITY. LIKE HE'S GOT SOME WEIRD BEEF WITH ME.
ブ VWM
Don't know why, though.
I REMEMBER YOU.
YOU USED TO COME IN HERE ALL THE TIME FOR CANDY, RIGHT?
WITH YOUR BIG BROTHERS.

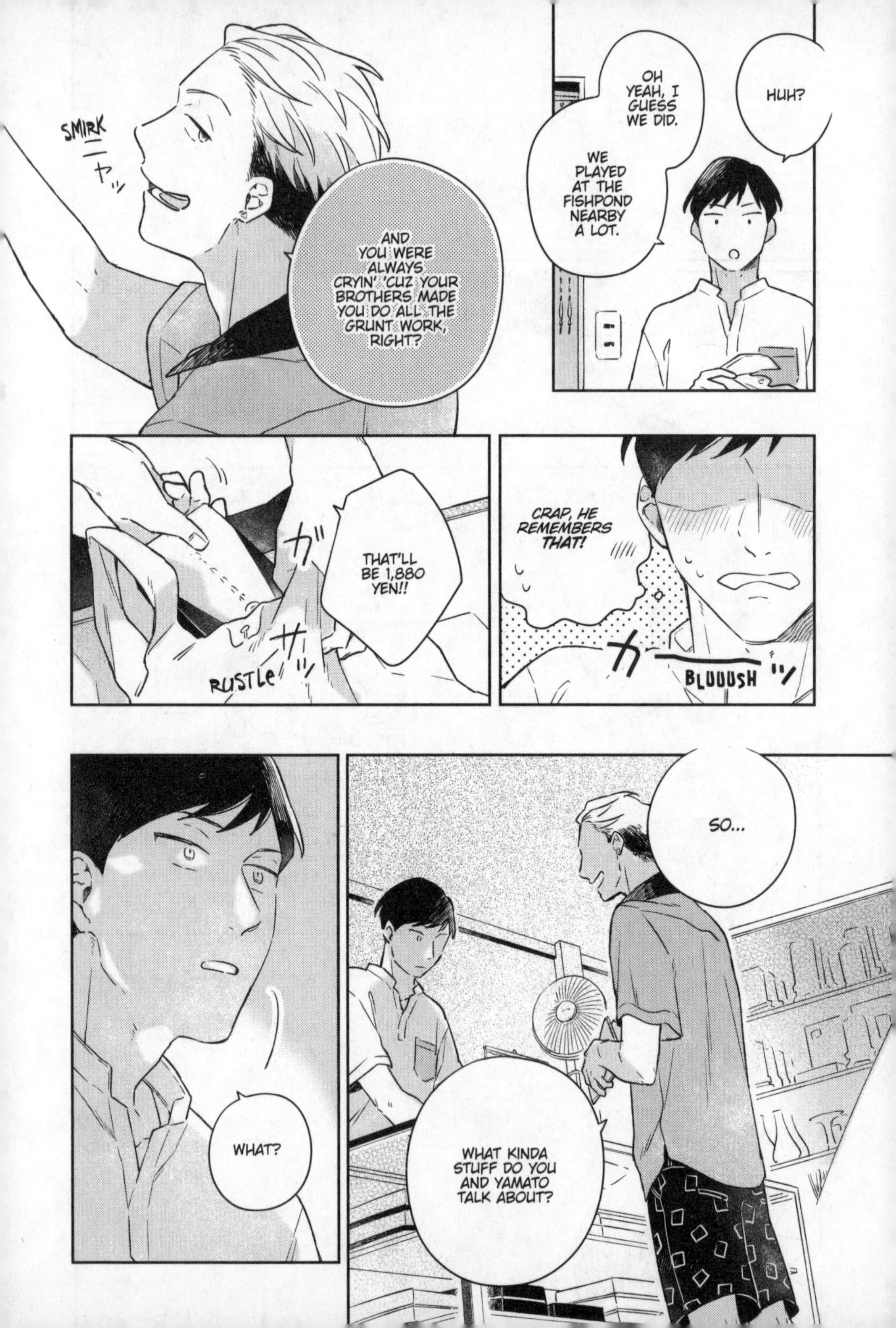
HUH?
OH YEAH, I GUESS WE DID.
WE PLAYED AT THE FISHPOND NEARBY A LOT.
SMIRK
ニヤッ
AND YOU WERE ALWAYS CRYIN' 'CUZ YOUR BROTHERS MADE YOU DO ALL THE GRUNT WORK, RIGHT?
CRAP, HE REMEMBERS THAT!
BLUUUSH
THAT'LL BE 1,880 YEN!!
RUSTLE
SO...
WHAT KINDA STUFF DO YOU AND YAMATO TALK ABOUT?
WHAT?

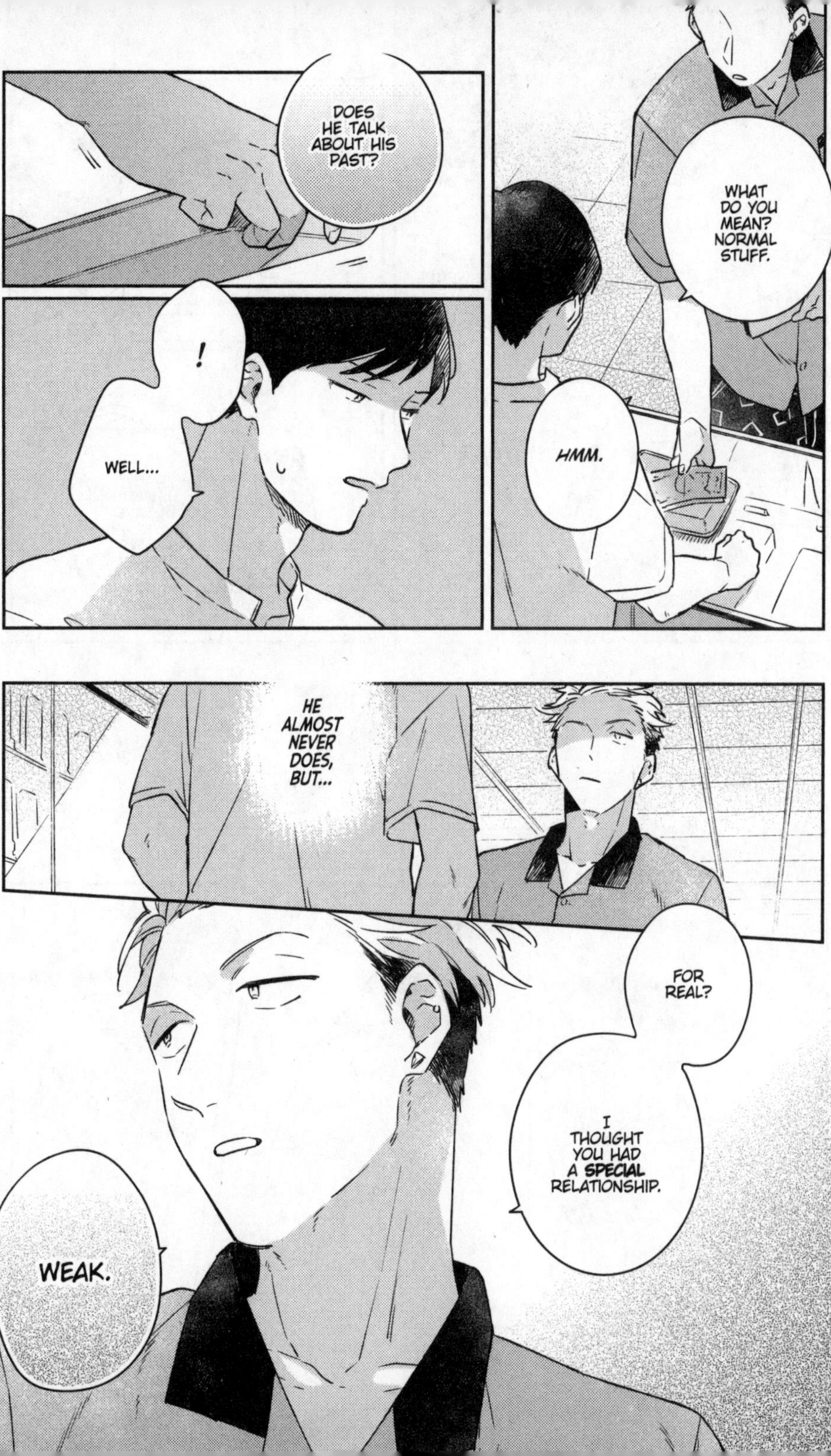
WHAT DO YOU MEAN? NORMAL STUFF.
HMM.
DOES HE TALK ABOUT HIS PAST?
!
WELL...
HE ALMOST NEVER DOES, BUT...
FOR REAL?
I THOUGHT YOU HAD A **SPECIAL** RELATIONSHIP.
WEAK.

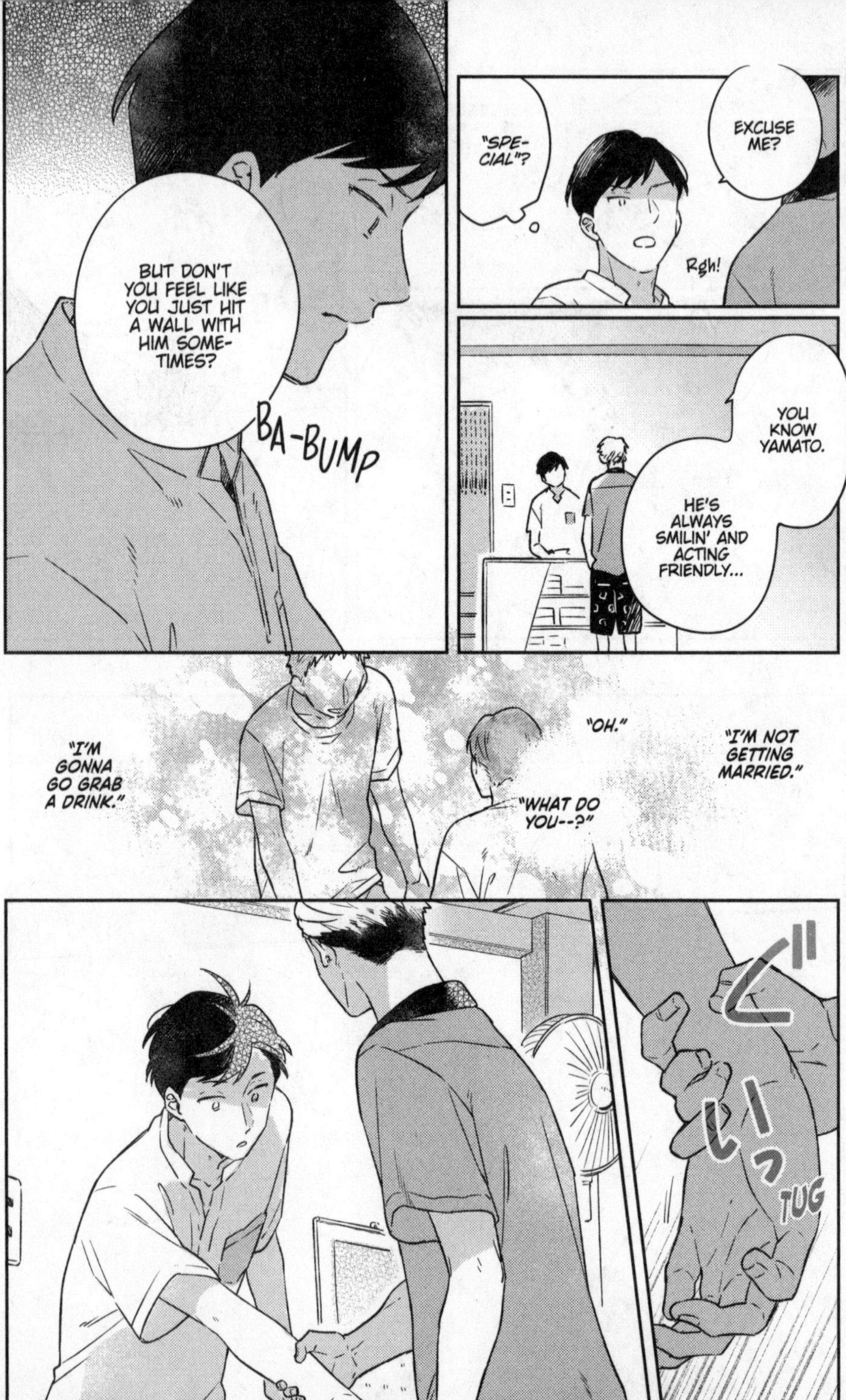
EXCUSE ME?
"SPE-CIAL"?
Rgh!
YOU KNOW YAMATO.
HE'S ALWAYS SMILIN' AND ACTING FRIENDLY...
BUT DON'T YOU FEEL LIKE YOU JUST HIT A WALL WITH HIM SOME-TIMES?
BA-BUMP
"I'M NOT GETTING MARRIED."
"OH."
"WHAT DO YOU--?"
"I'M GONNA GO GRAB A DRINK."
ぐいっ
TUG

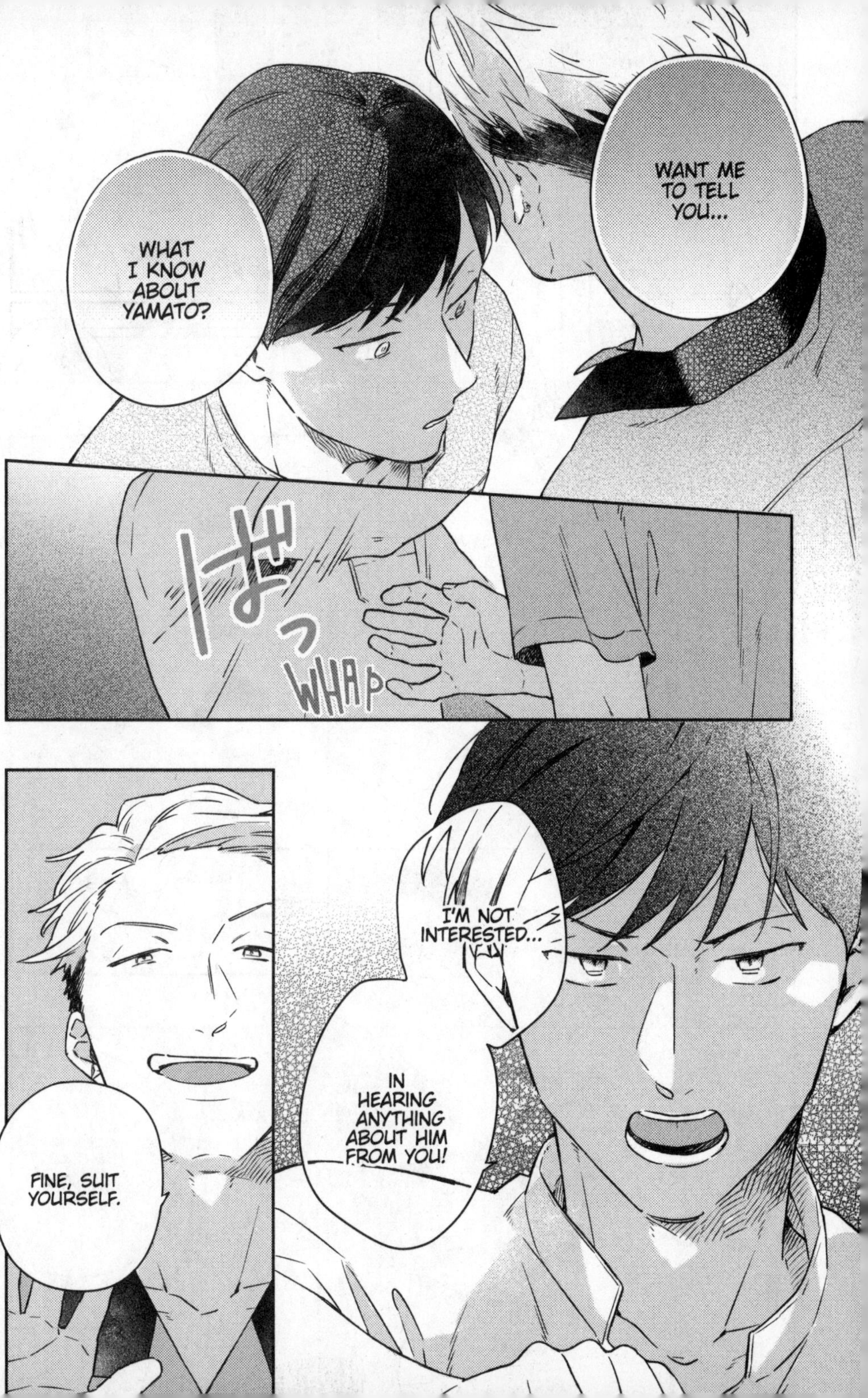
WANT ME TO TELL YOU...
WHAT I KNOW ABOUT YAMATO?
ぱっ
WHAP
I'M NOT INTERESTED...
IN HEARING ANYTHING ABOUT HIM FROM YOU!
FINE, SUIT YOURSELF.

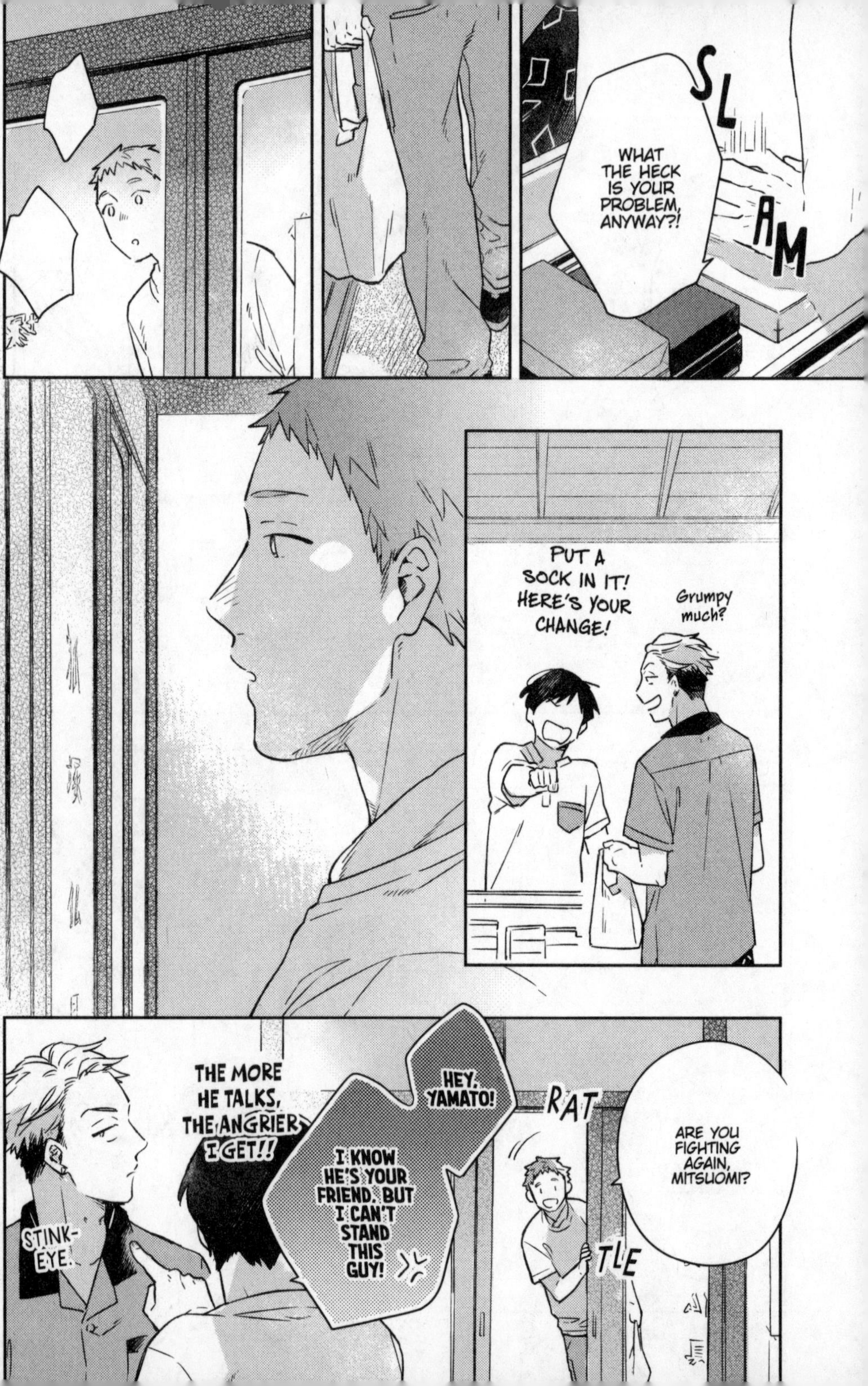
SLAM
WHAT THE HECK IS YOUR PROBLEM, ANYWAY?!
PUT A SOCK IN IT! HERE'S YOUR CHANGE!
Grumpy much?
RATTLE
ARE YOU FIGHTING AGAIN, MITSUOMI?
HEY, YAMATO!
I KNOW HE'S YOUR FRIEND, BUT I CAN'T STAND THIS GUY!
THE MORE HE TALKS, THE ANGRIER I GET!!
STINK-EYE.

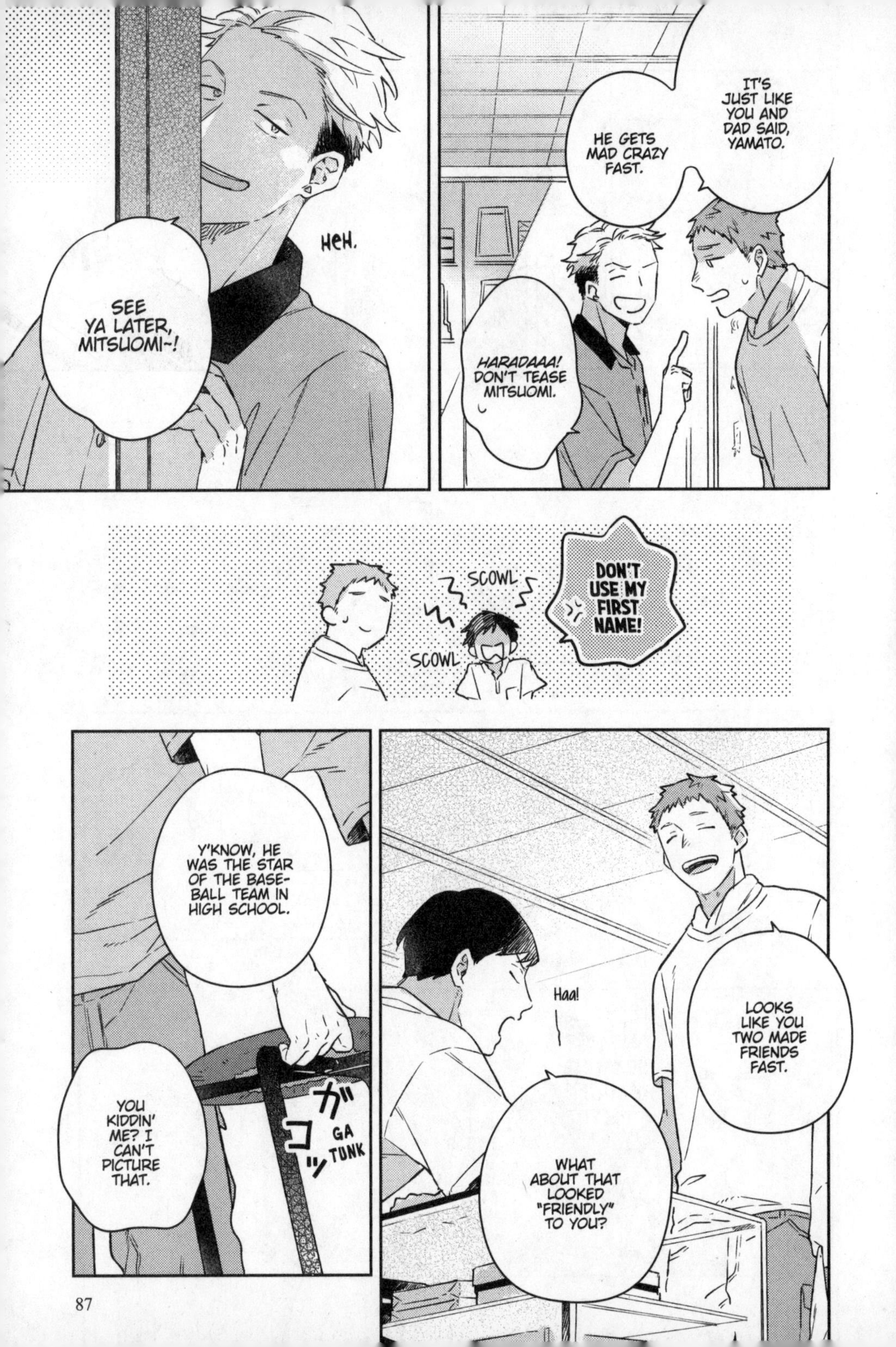
IT'S JUST LIKE YOU AND DAD SAID, YAMATO.
HE GETS MAD CRAZY FAST.
HARADAAA! DON'T TEASE MITSUOMI.
HEH.
SEE YA LATER, MITSUOMI~!
DON'T USE MY FIRST NAME!
SCOWL
SCOWL
LOOKS LIKE YOU TWO MADE FRIENDS FAST.
Haa!
WHAT ABOUT THAT LOOKED "FRIENDLY" TO YOU?
Y'KNOW, HE WAS THE STAR OF THE BASE-BALL TEAM IN HIGH SCHOOL.
ガコッ
GA TUNK
YOU KIDDIN' ME? I CAN'T PICTURE THAT.

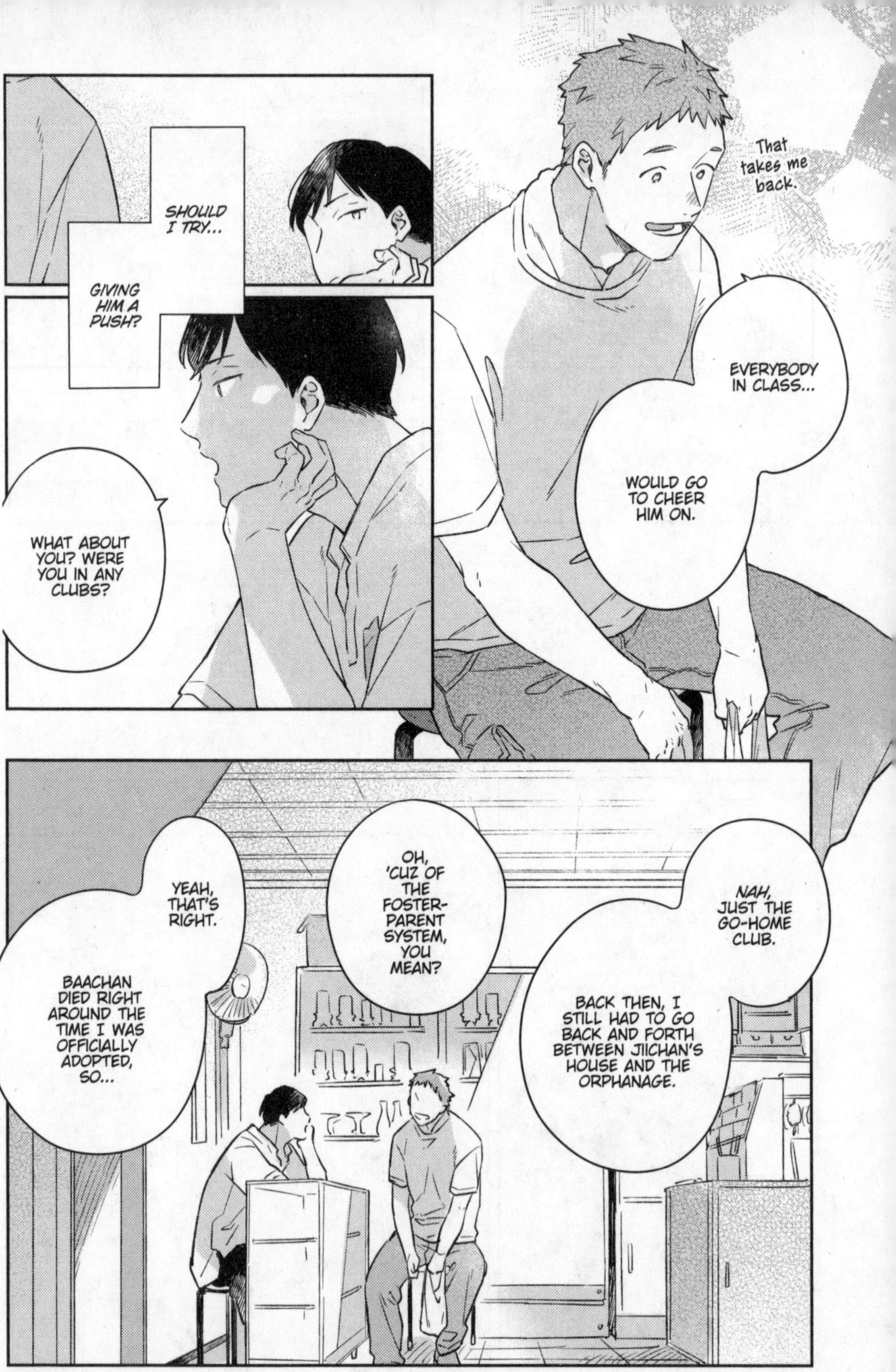
That takes me back.
EVERYBODY IN CLASS...
WOULD GO TO CHEER HIM ON.
SHOULD I TRY...
GIVING HIM A PUSH?
WHAT ABOUT YOU? WERE YOU IN ANY CLUBS?
NAH, JUST THE GO-HOME CLUB.
BACK THEN, I STILL HAD TO GO BACK AND FORTH BETWEEN JIICHAN'S HOUSE AND THE ORPHANAGE.
OH, 'CUZ OF THE FOSTER-PARENT SYSTEM, YOU MEAN?
YEAH, THAT'S RIGHT.
BAACHAN DIED RIGHT AROUND THE TIME I WAS OFFICIALLY ADOPTED, SO...

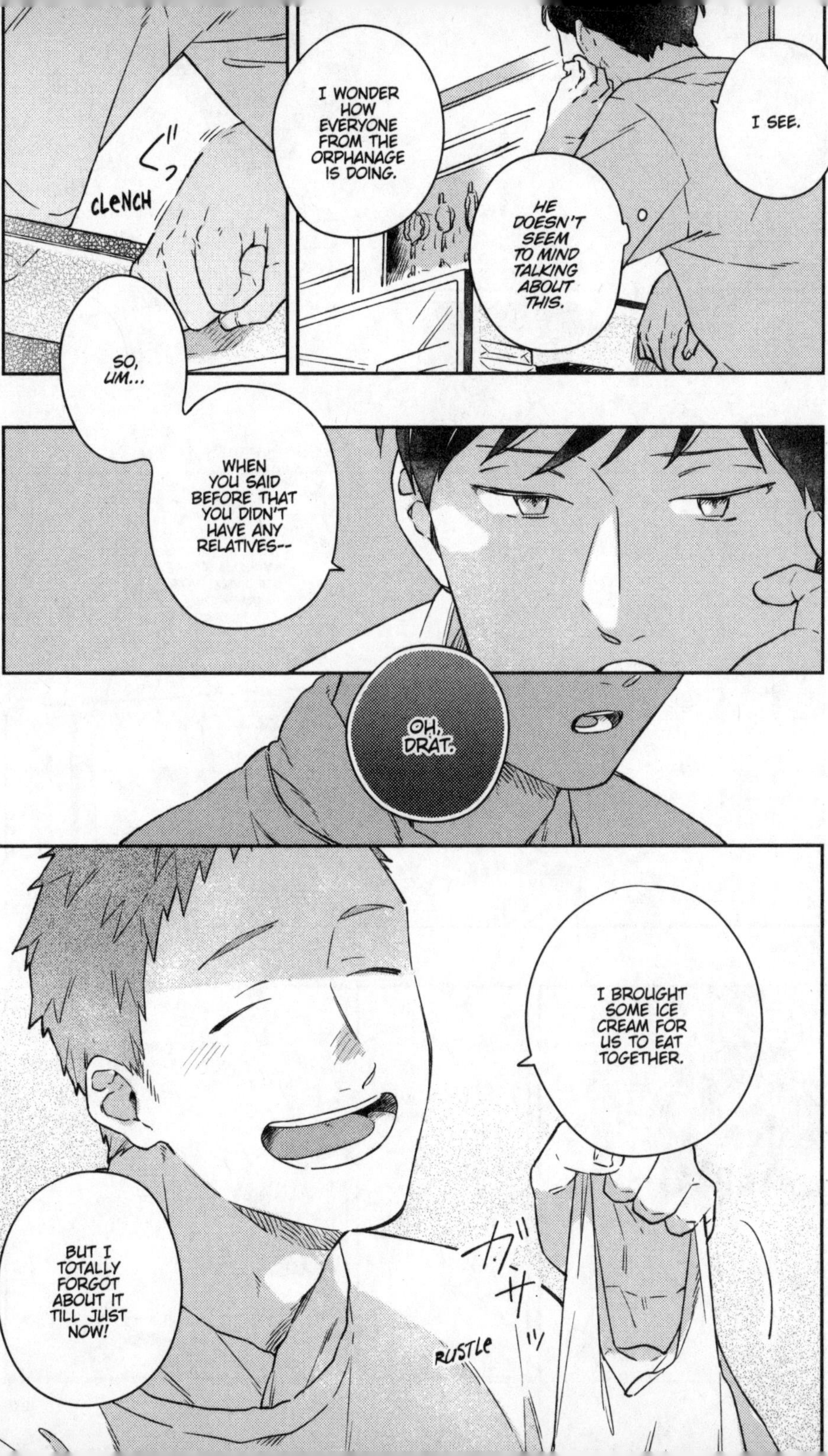
I SEE.
I WONDER HOW EVERYONE FROM THE ORPHANAGE IS DOING.
HE DOESN'T SEEM TO MIND TALKING ABOUT THIS.
CLENCH
SO, UM...
WHEN YOU SAID BEFORE THAT YOU DIDN'T HAVE ANY RELATIVES--
OH, DRAT.
I BROUGHT SOME ICE CREAM FOR US TO EAT TOGETHER.
RUSTLE
BUT I TOTALLY FORGOT ABOUT IT TILL JUST NOW!

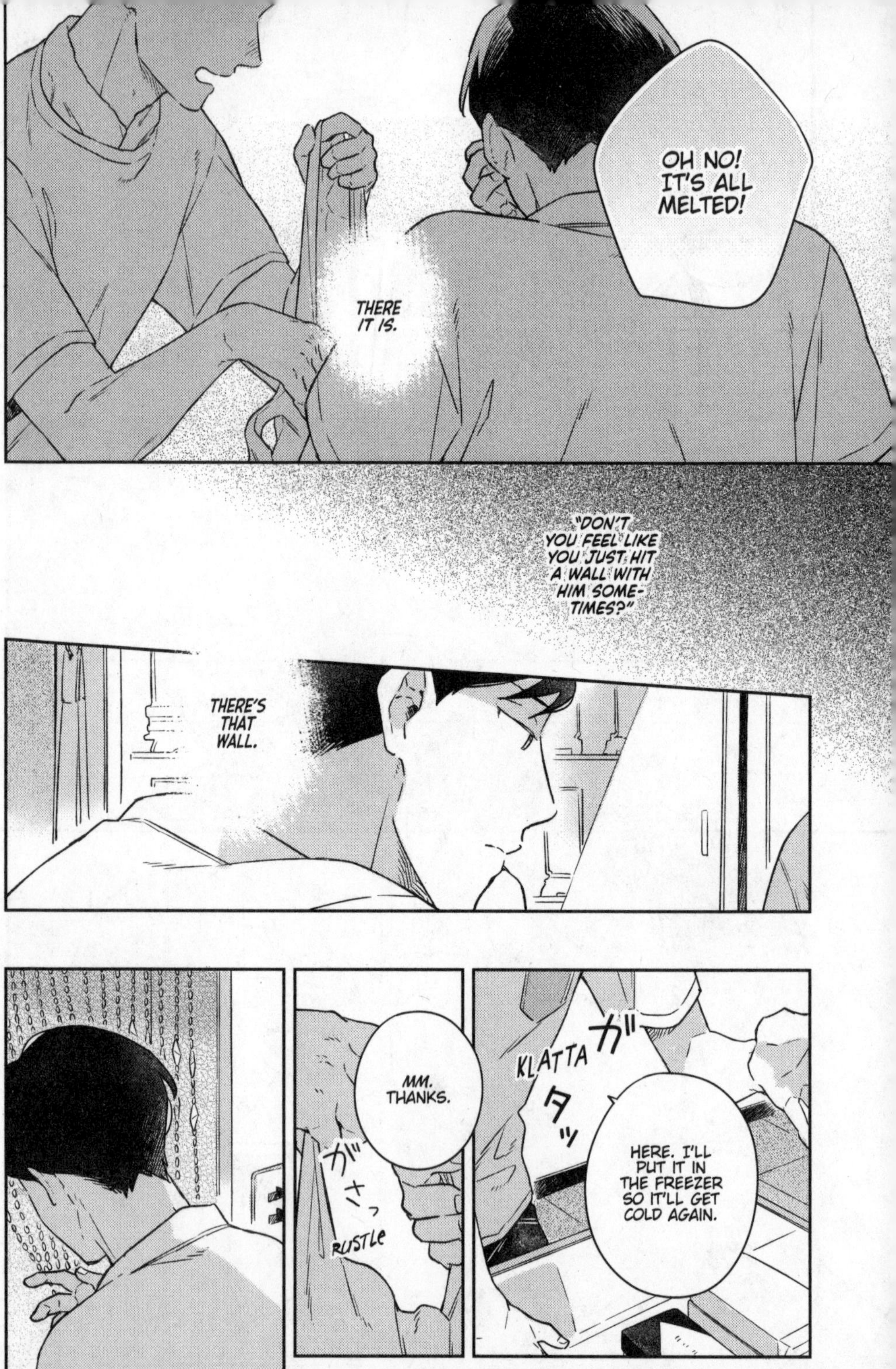
OH NO! IT'S ALL MELTED!
THERE IT IS.
"DON'T YOU FEEL LIKE YOU JUST HIT A WALL WITH HIM SOME-TIMES?"
THERE'S THAT WALL.
ガ
KLATTA
タッ
HERE. I'LL PUT IT IN THE FREEZER SO IT'LL GET COLD AGAIN.
MM. THANKS.
がさっ
RUSTLE

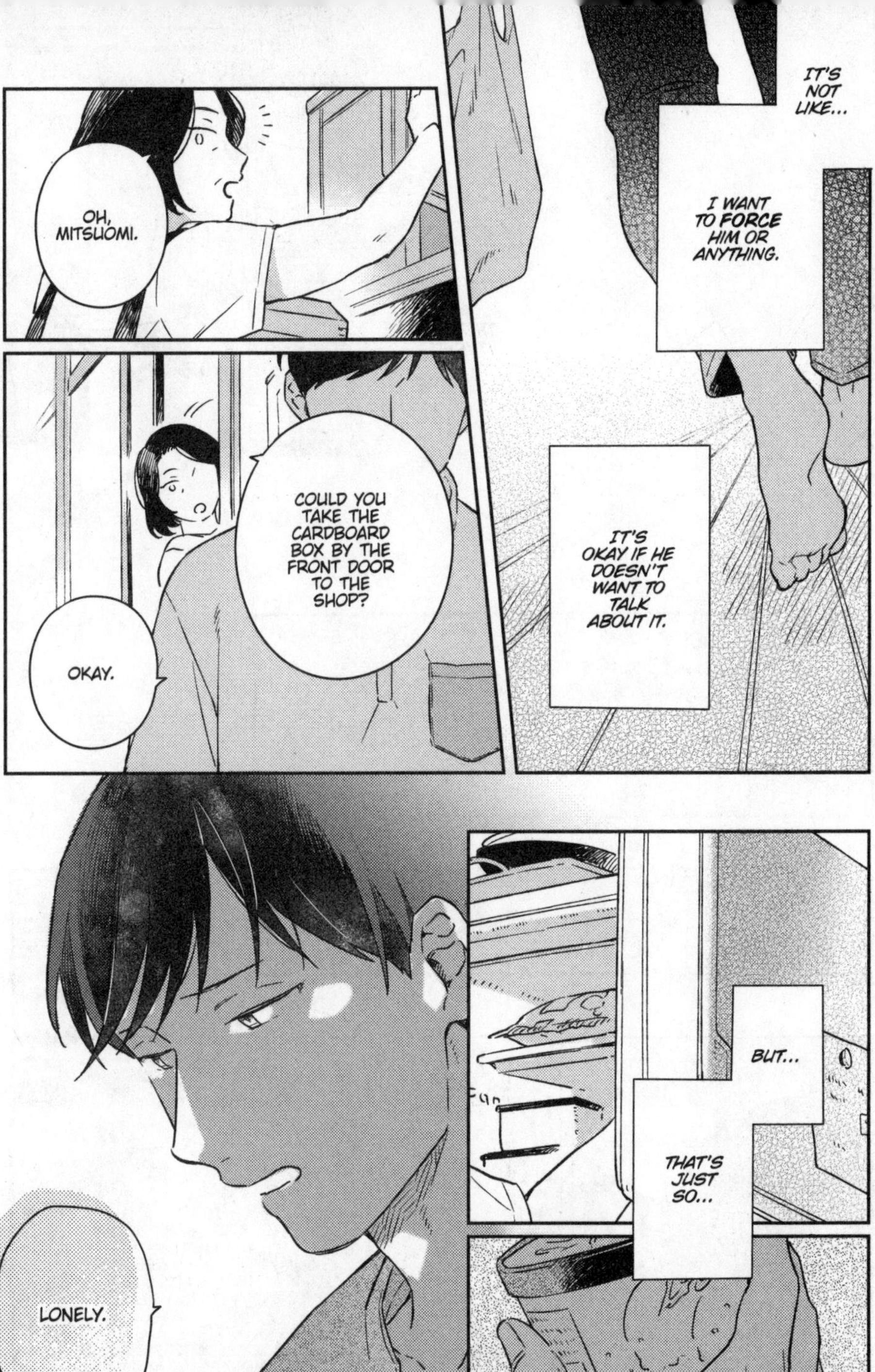
IT'S NOT LIKE...
I WANT TO FORCE HIM OR ANYTHING.
IT'S OKAY IF HE DOESN'T WANT TO TALK ABOUT IT.
OH, MITSUOMI.
COULD YOU TAKE THE CARDBOARD BOX BY THE FRONT DOOR TO THE SHOP?
OKAY.
BUT...
THAT'S JUST SO...
LONELY.

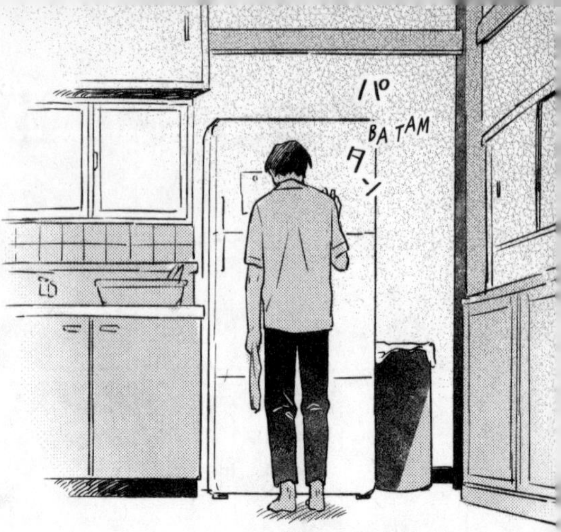
パ
BATAM
タン

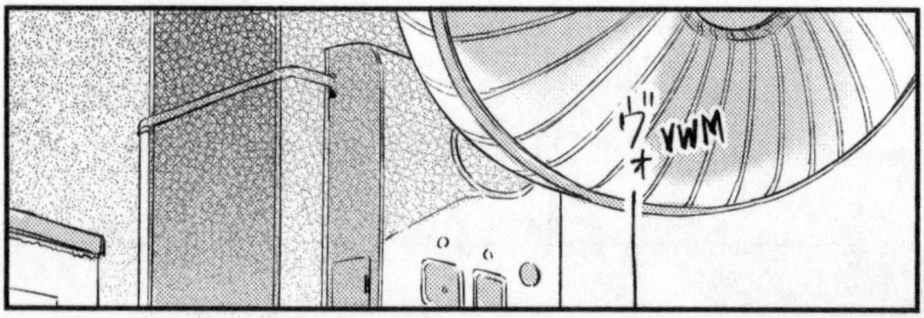
ヴォ
VWM

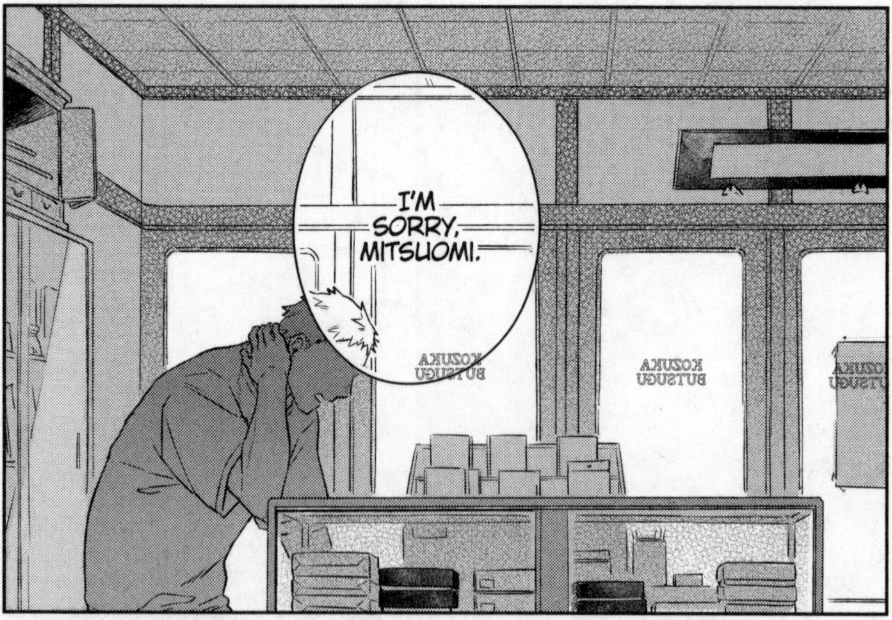
I'M SORRY, MITSUOMI.
KOZUKA BUTSUGU

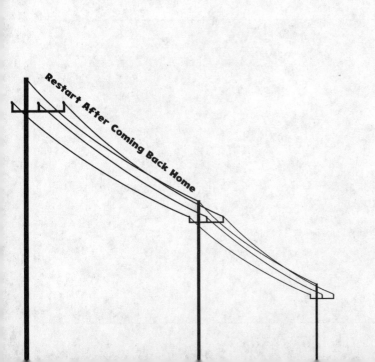
Restart After Coming Back Home

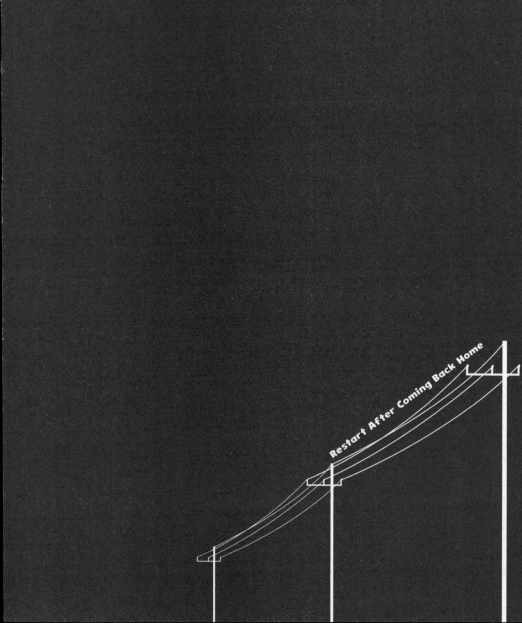

Restart After Coming Back Home

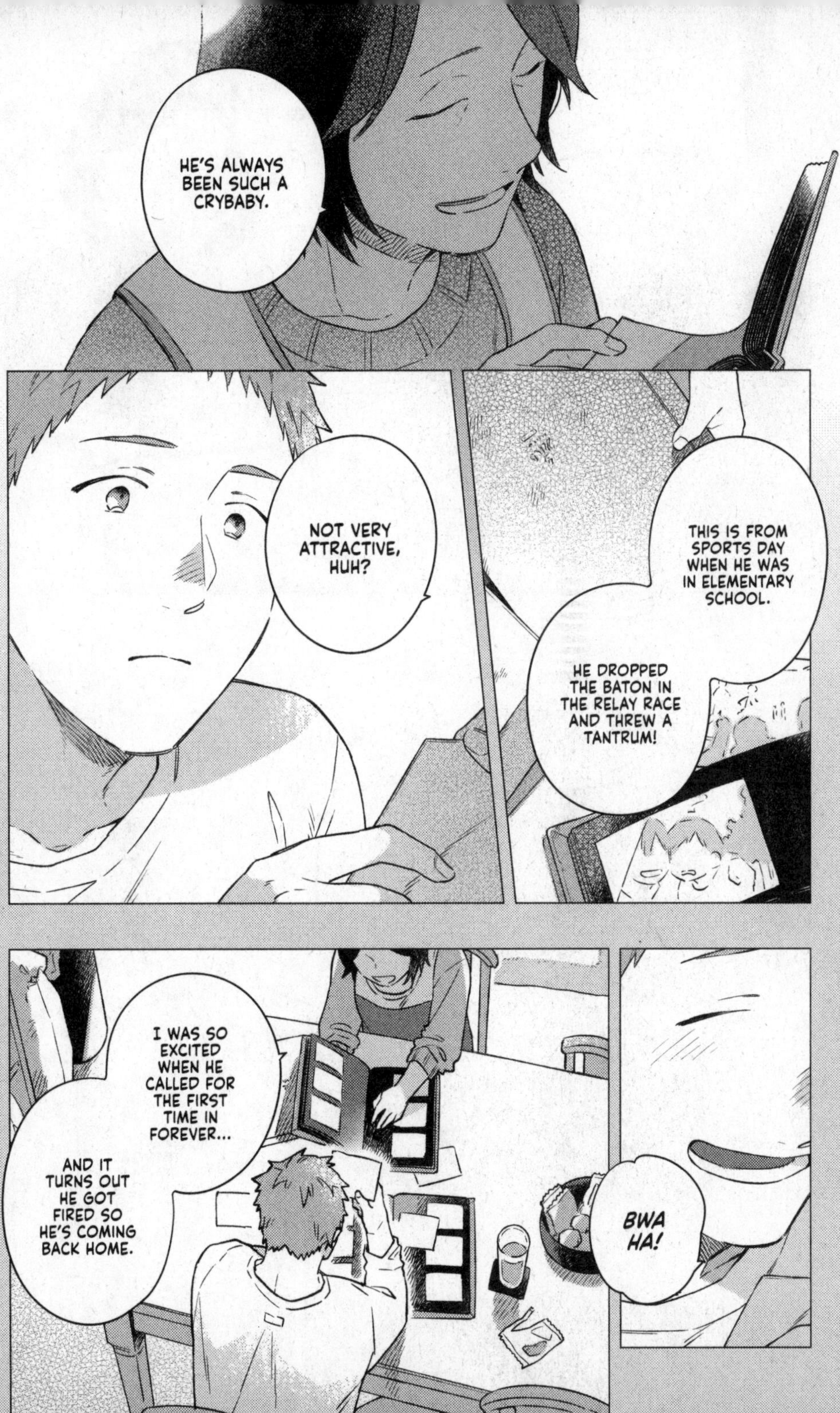
HE'S ALWAYS BEEN SUCH A CRYBABY.
THIS IS FROM SPORTS DAY WHEN HE WAS IN ELEMENTARY SCHOOL.
HE DROPPED THE BATON IN THE RELAY RACE AND THREW A TANTRUM!
NOT VERY ATTRACTIVE, HUH?
BWA HA!
I WAS SO EXCITED WHEN HE CALLED FOR THE FIRST TIME IN FOREVER...
AND IT TURNS OUT HE GOT FIRED SO HE'S COMING BACK HOME.

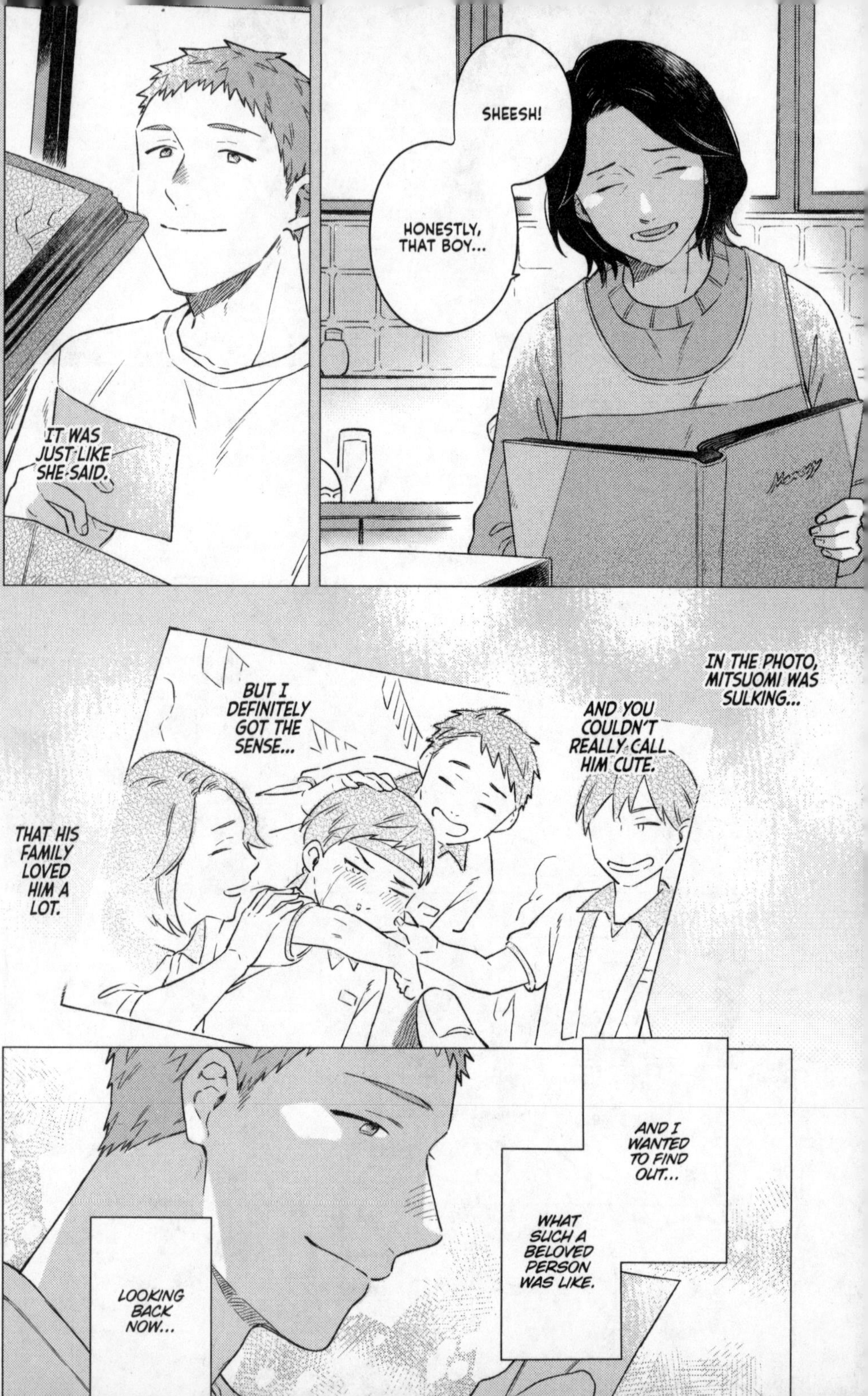
SHEESH!
HONESTLY, THAT BOY...
IT WAS JUST LIKE SHE SAID.
IN THE PHOTO, MITSUOMI WAS SULKING...
AND YOU COULDN'T REALLY CALL HIM CUTE.
BUT I DEFINITELY GOT THE SENSE...
THAT HIS FAMILY LOVED HIM A LOT.
AND I WANTED TO FIND OUT...
WHAT SUCH A BELOVED PERSON WAS LIKE.
LOOKING BACK NOW...

#004

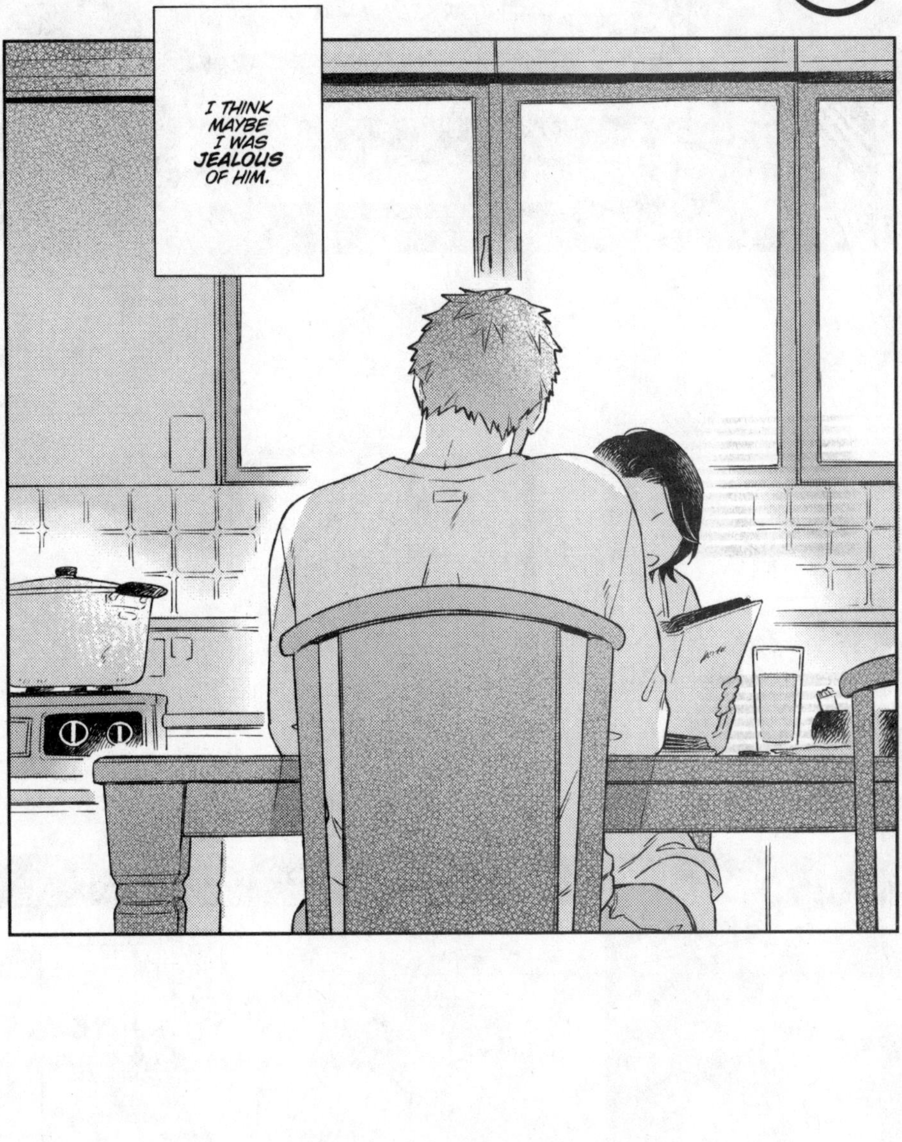
I THINK MAYBE I WAS JEALOUS OF HIM.

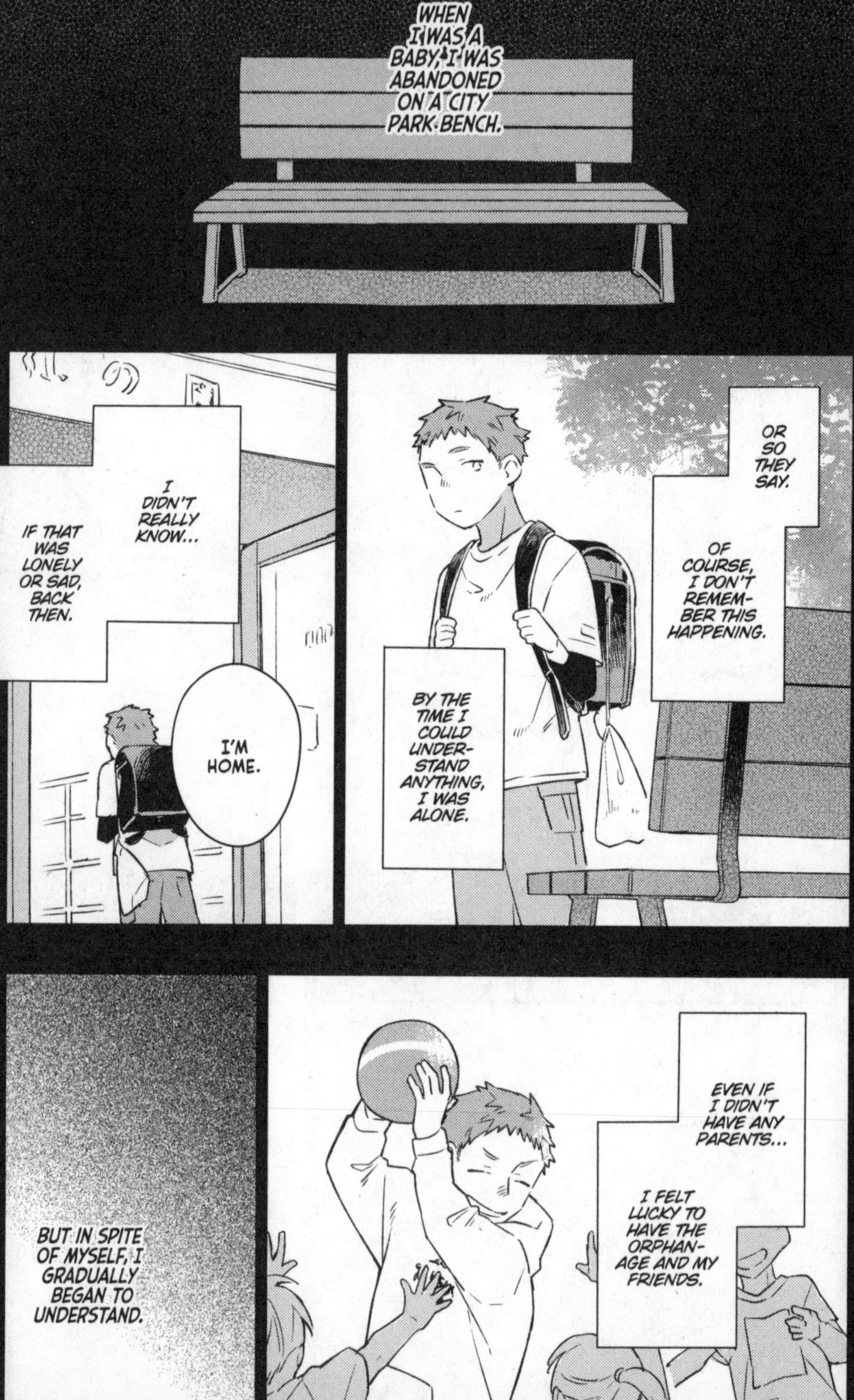
WHEN I WAS A BABY, I WAS ABANDONED ON A CITY PARK BENCH.
OR SO THEY SAY.
OF COURSE, I DON'T REMEMBER THIS HAPPENING.
BY THE TIME I COULD UNDERSTAND ANYTHING, I WAS ALONE.
I DIDN'T REALLY KNOW...
IF THAT WAS LONELY OR SAD, BACK THEN.
I'M HOME.
EVEN IF I DIDN'T HAVE ANY PARENTS...
I FELT LUCKY TO HAVE THE ORPHANAGE AND MY FRIENDS.
BUT IN SPITE OF MYSELF, I GRADUALLY BEGAN TO UNDERSTAND.

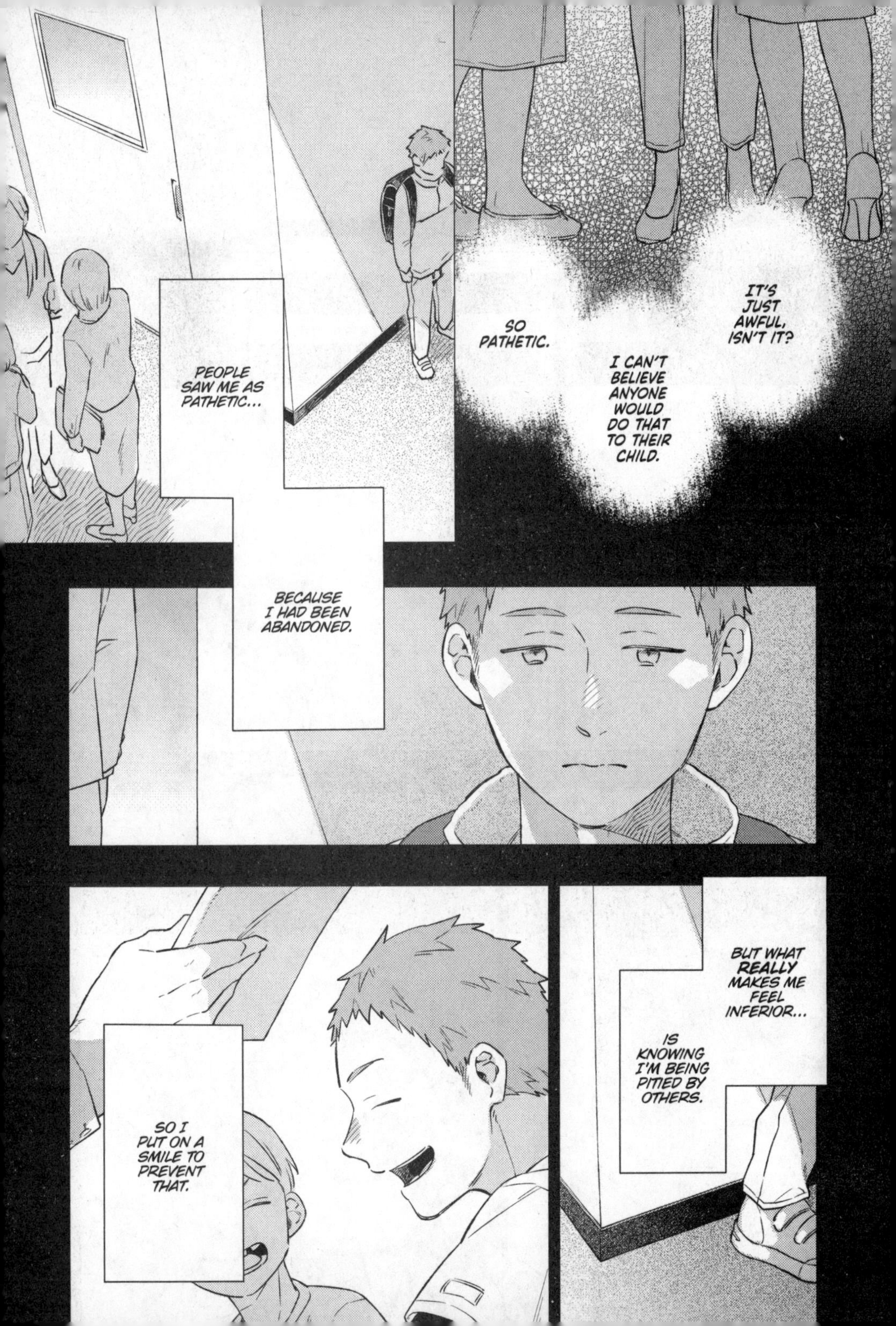
IT'S JUST AWFUL, ISN'T IT?
SO PATHETIC.
I CAN'T BELIEVE ANYONE WOULD DO THAT TO THEIR CHILD.
PEOPLE SAW ME AS PATHETIC...
BECAUSE I HAD BEEN ABANDONED.
BUT WHAT REALLY MAKES ME FEEL INFERIOR...
IS KNOWING I'M BEING PITIED BY OTHERS.
SO I PUT ON A SMILE TO PREVENT THAT.

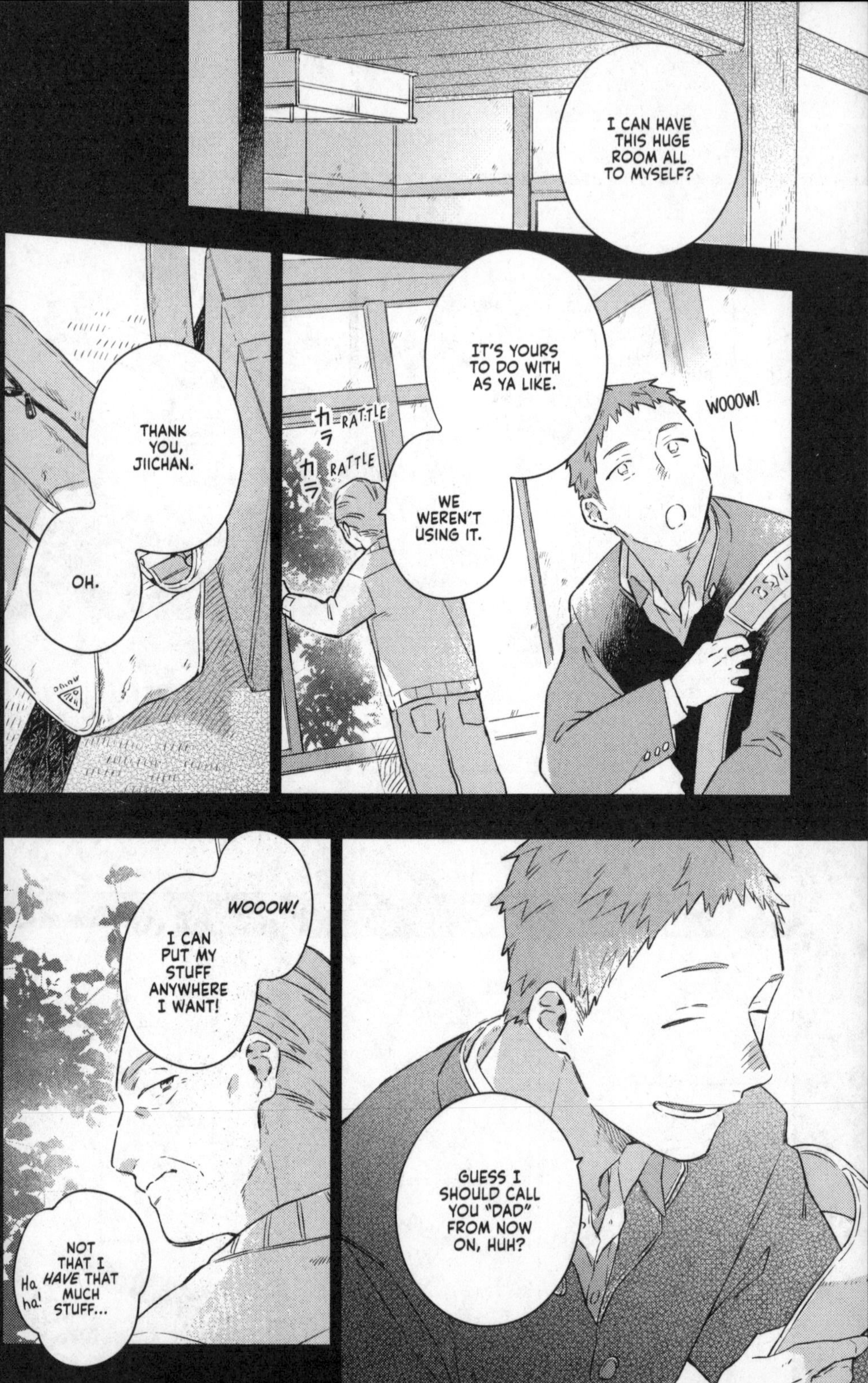
I CAN HAVE THIS HUGE ROOM ALL TO MYSELF?
WOOOW!
IT'S YOURS TO DO WITH AS YA LIKE.
カラ RATTLE
カラ RATTLE
WE WEREN'T USING IT.
THANK YOU, JIICHAN.
OH.
GUESS I SHOULD CALL YOU "DAD" FROM NOW ON, HUH?
WOOOW!
I CAN PUT MY STUFF ANYWHERE I WANT!
NOT THAT I *HAVE* THAT MUCH STUFF...
Ha ha!

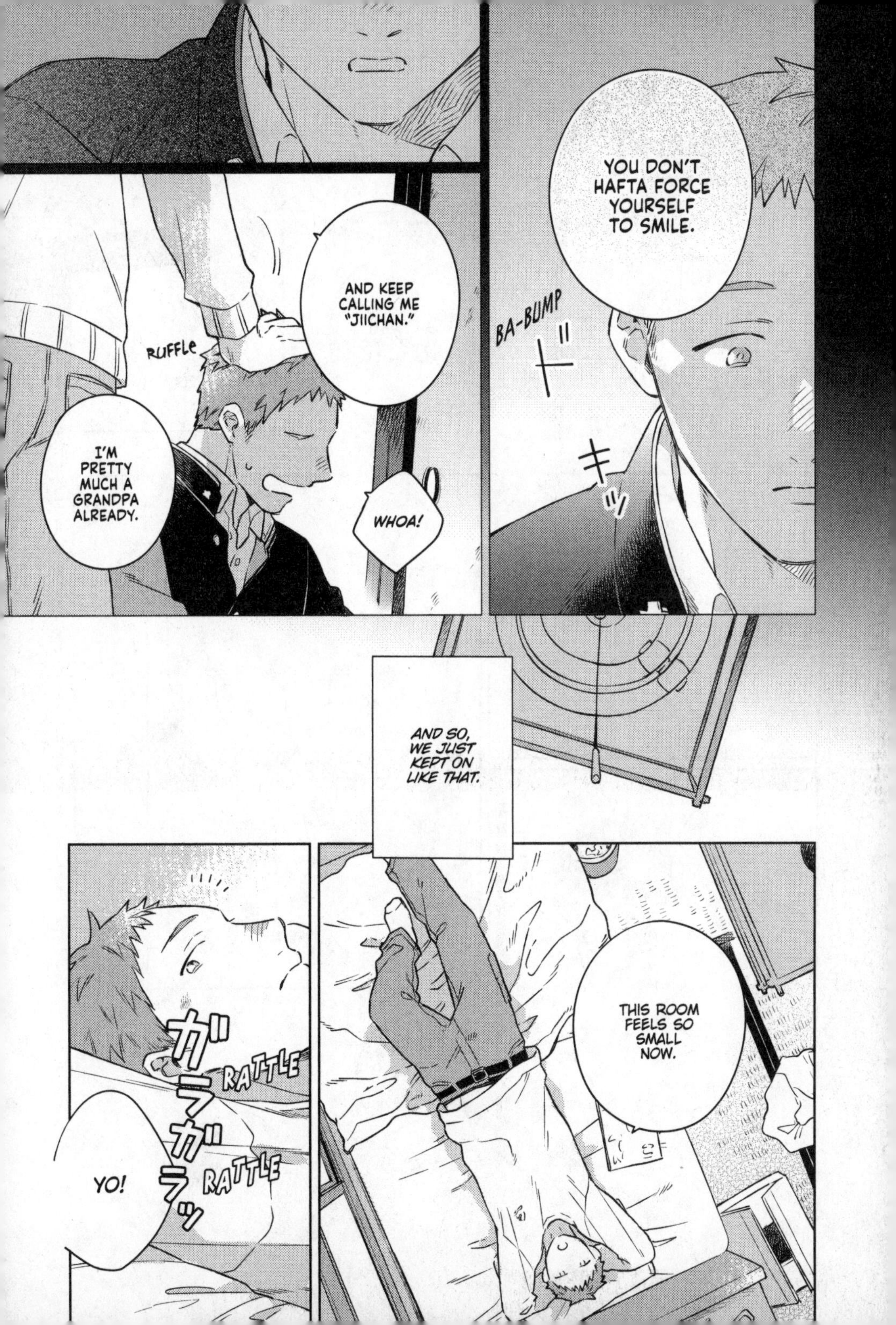
YOU DON'T HAFTA FORCE YOURSELF TO SMILE.
BA-BUMP
ドキッ
AND KEEP CALLING ME "JIICHAN."
WHOA!
RUFFLE
I'M PRETTY MUCH A GRANDPA ALREADY.
AND SO, WE JUST KEPT ON LIKE THAT.
THIS ROOM FEELS SO SMALL NOW.
ガラガラッ
RATTLE
RATTLE
YO!

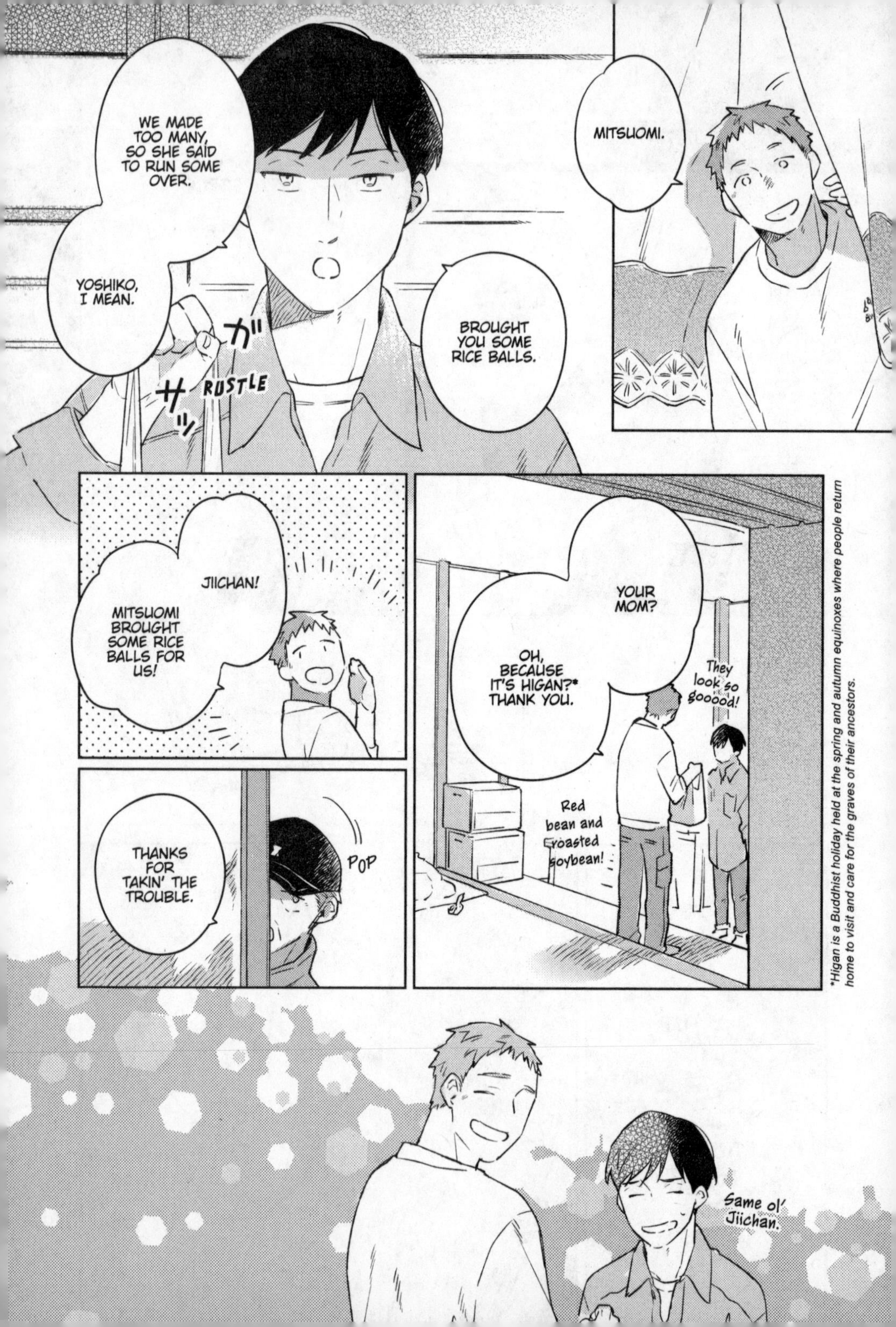
MITSUOMI.
BROUGHT YOU SOME RICE BALLS.
WE MADE TOO MANY, SO SHE SAID TO RUN SOME OVER.
ガサッ RUSTLE
YOSHIKO, I MEAN.
YOUR MOM?
OH, BECAUSE IT'S HIGAN?* THANK YOU.
They look so gooood!
Red bean and roasted soybean!
JIICHAN!
MITSUOMI BROUGHT SOME RICE BALLS FOR US!
POP
THANKS FOR TAKIN' THE TROUBLE.
Same ol' Jiichan.

*Higan is a Buddhist holiday held at the spring and autumn equinoxes where people return home to visit and care for the graves of their ancestors.

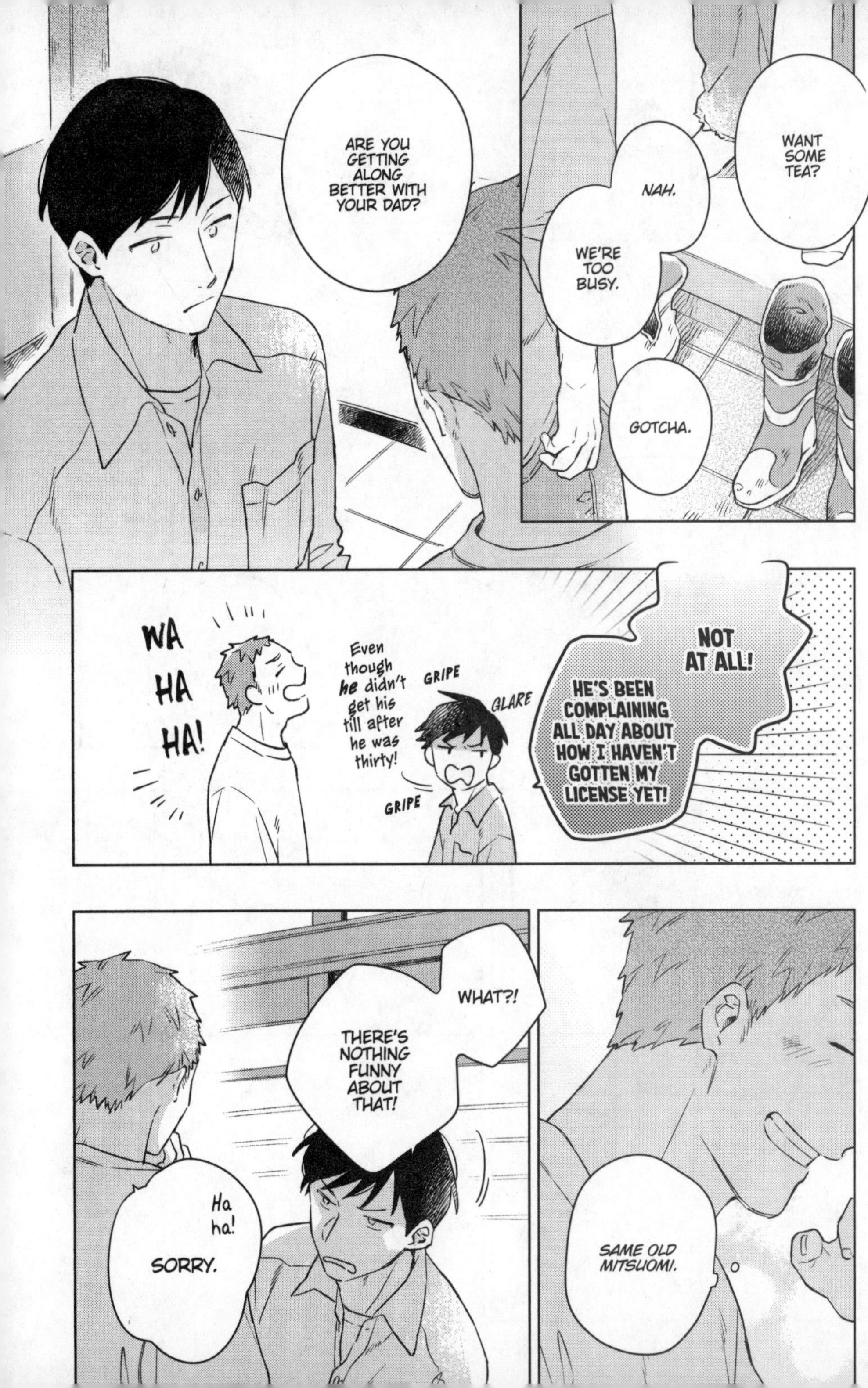
WANT SOME TEA?
NAH.
WE'RE TOO BUSY.
GOTCHA.
ARE YOU GETTING ALONG BETTER WITH YOUR DAD?
NOT AT ALL!
HE'S BEEN COMPLAINING ALL DAY ABOUT HOW I HAVEN'T GOTTEN MY LICENSE YET!
GLARE
GRIPE
Even though he didn't get his till after he was thirty!
GRIPE
WA HA HA!
SAME OLD MITSUOMI.
WHAT?!
THERE'S NOTHING FUNNY ABOUT THAT!
Ha ha!
SORRY.

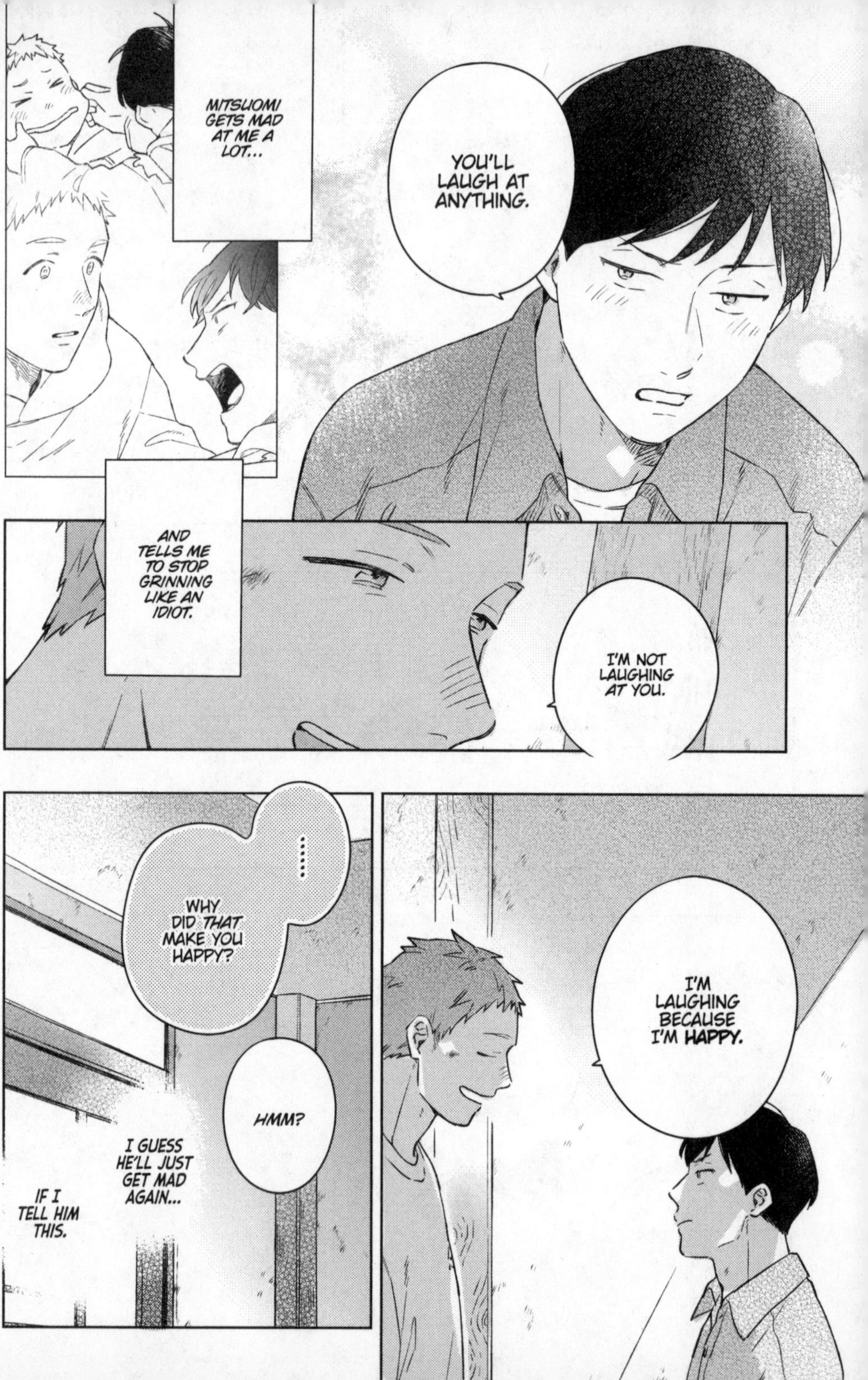
YOU'LL LAUGH AT ANYTHING.
MITSUOMI GETS MAD AT ME A LOT...
AND TELLS ME TO STOP GRINNING LIKE AN IDIOT.
I'M NOT LAUGHING AT YOU.
I'M LAUGHING BECAUSE I'M **HAPPY.**
......
WHY DID THAT MAKE YOU HAPPY?
HMM?
I GUESS HE'LL JUST GET MAD AGAIN...
IF I TELL HIM THIS.

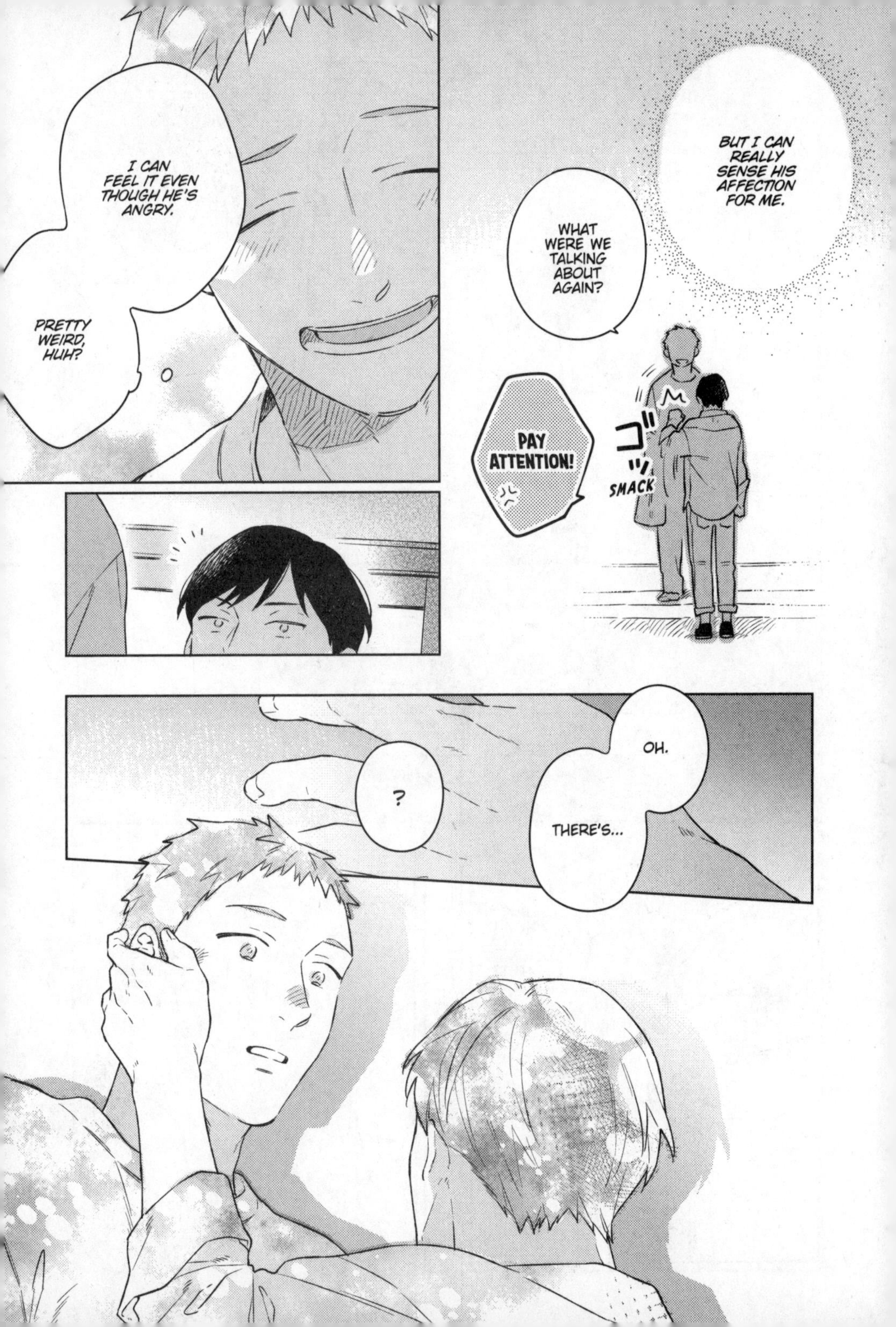
BUT I CAN REALLY SENSE HIS AFFECTION FOR ME.
WHAT WERE WE TALKING ABOUT AGAIN?
PAY ATTENTION!
SMACK
I CAN FEEL IT EVEN THOUGH HE'S ANGRY.
PRETTY WEIRD, HUH?
OH.
THERE'S...
?

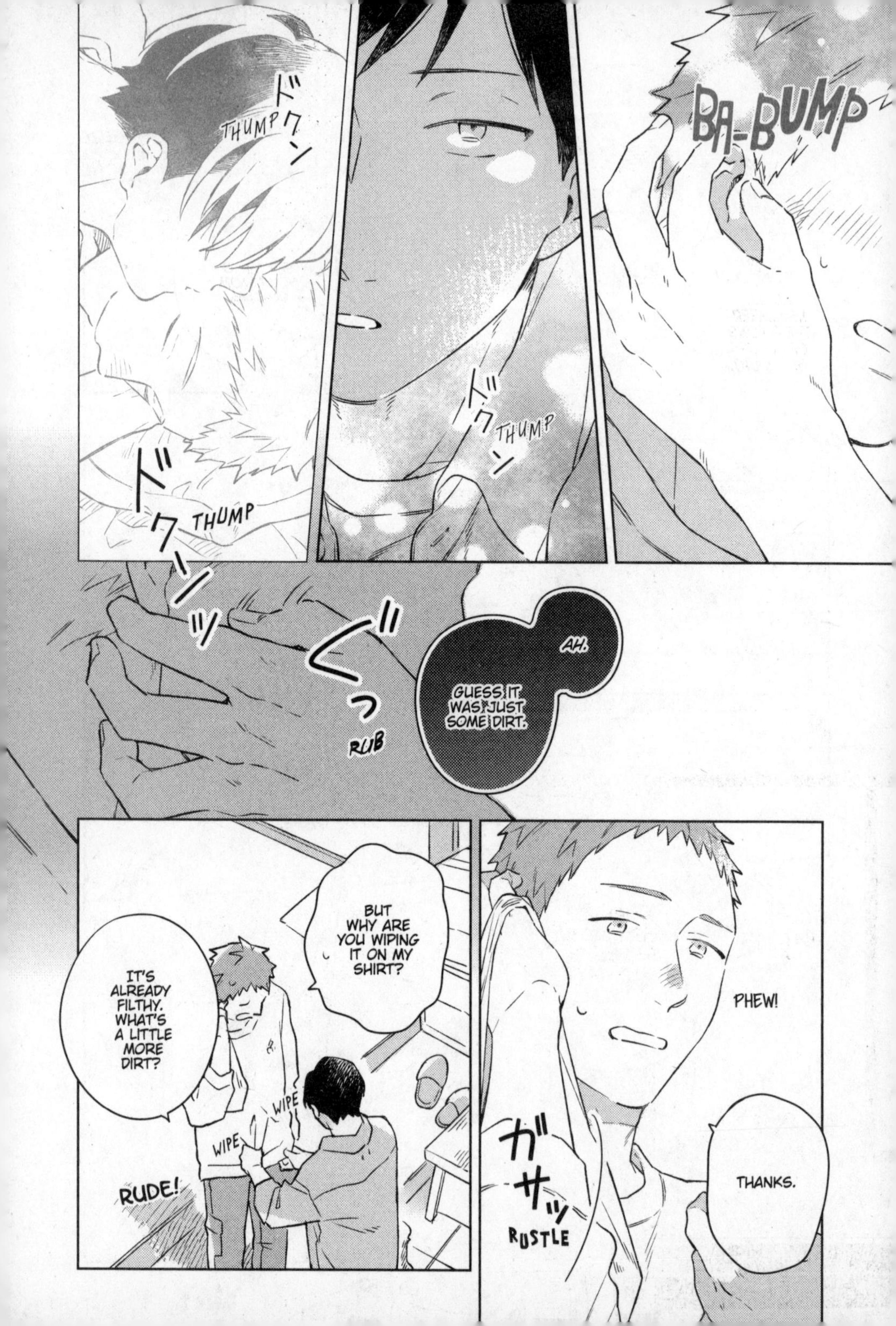
BA-BUMP
ドクン
THUMP
ドクン
THUMP
ドクーンッ
THUMP
AH.
GUESS IT WAS JUST SOME DIRT.
ぐっ
RUB
PHEW!
THANKS.
ガサッ
RUSTLE
BUT WHY ARE YOU WIPING IT ON MY SHIRT?
IT'S ALREADY FILTHY. WHAT'S A LITTLE MORE DIRT?
WIPE
WIPE
RUDE!

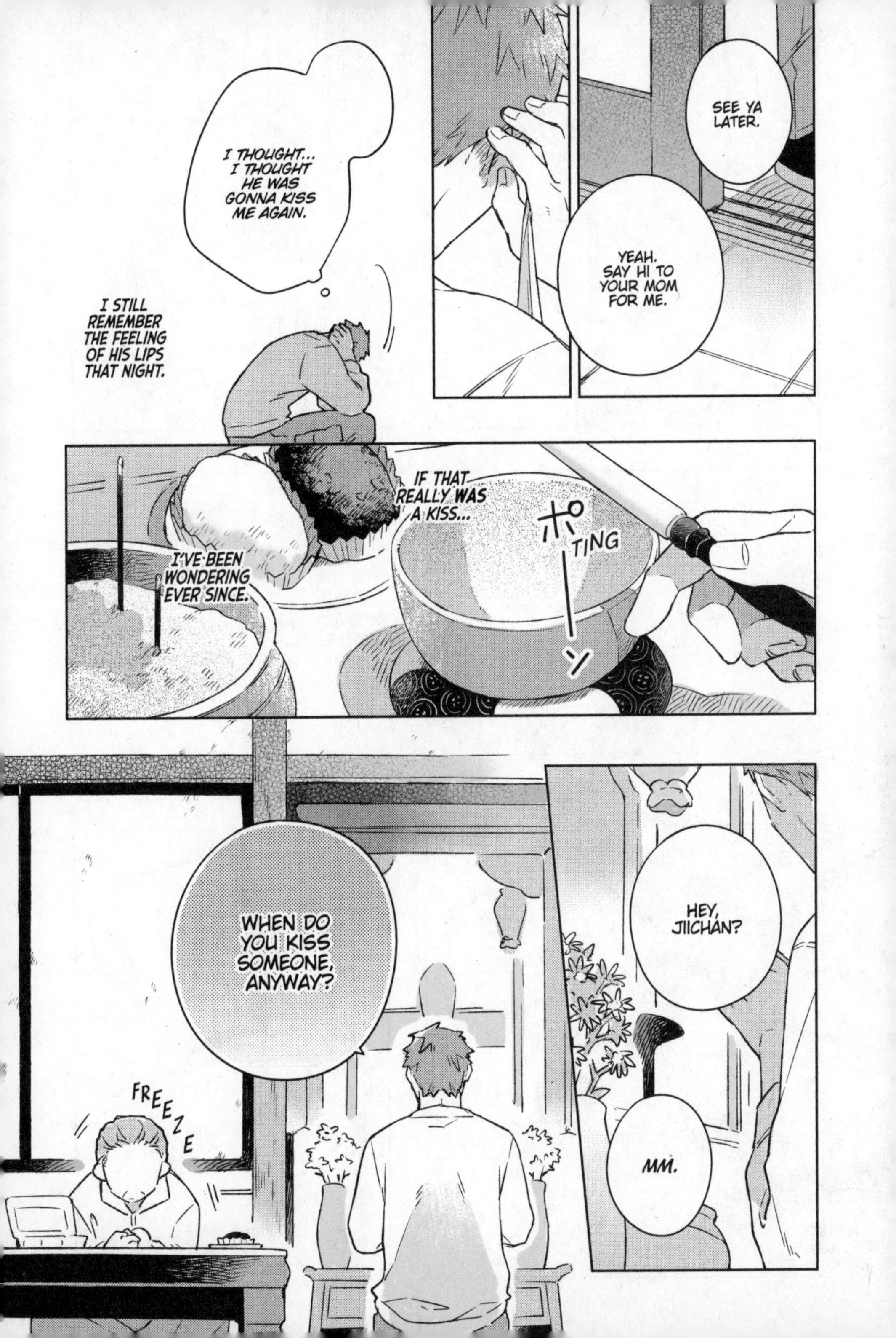
SEE YA LATER.
YEAH. SAY HI TO YOUR MOM FOR ME.
I THOUGHT... I THOUGHT HE WAS GONNA KISS ME AGAIN.
I STILL REMEMBER THE FEELING OF HIS LIPS THAT NIGHT.
ポーン
TING
IF THAT REALLY WAS A KISS...
I'VE BEEN WONDERING EVER SINCE.
HEY, JIICHAN?
MM.
WHEN DO YOU KISS SOMEONE, ANYWAY?
FREEZE

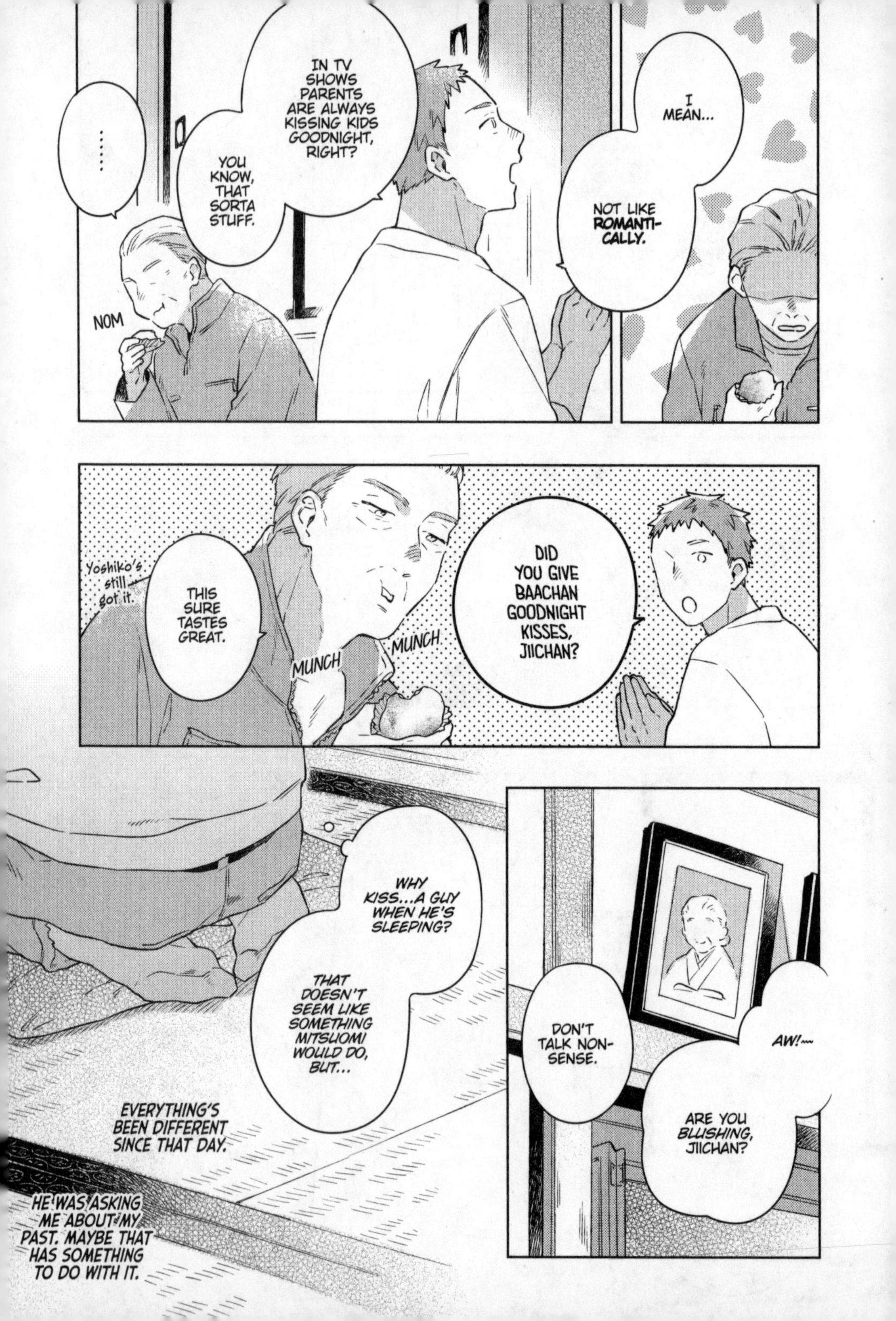
I MEAN...
NOT LIKE ROMANTICALLY.
IN TV SHOWS PARENTS ARE ALWAYS KISSING KIDS GOODNIGHT, RIGHT?
YOU KNOW, THAT SORTA STUFF.
......
NOM
DID YOU GIVE BAACHAN GOODNIGHT KISSES, JIICHAN?
MUNCH
MUNCH
THIS SURE TASTES GREAT.
Yoshiko's still got it.
AW!~
ARE YOU BLUSHING, JIICHAN?
DON'T TALK NONSENSE.
WHY KISS...A GUY WHEN HE'S SLEEPING?
THAT DOESN'T SEEM LIKE SOMETHING MITSUOMI WOULD DO, BUT...
EVERYTHING'S BEEN DIFFERENT SINCE THAT DAY.
HE WAS ASKING ME ABOUT MY PAST. MAYBE THAT HAS SOMETHING TO DO WITH IT.

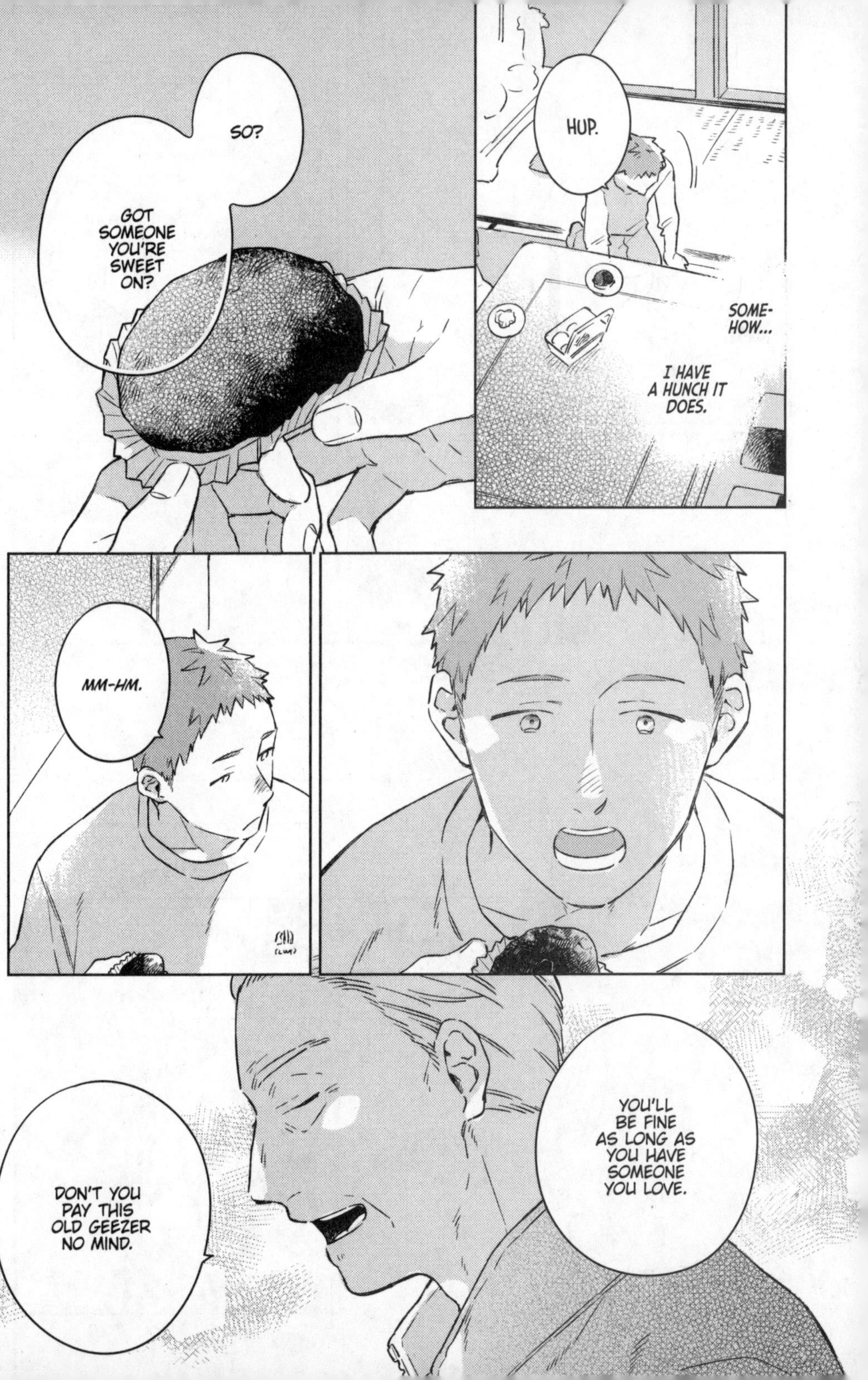
HUP.
SOME-HOW...
I HAVE A HUNCH IT DOES.
SO?
GOT SOMEONE YOU'RE SWEET ON?
MM-HM.
YOU'LL BE FINE AS LONG AS YOU HAVE SOMEONE YOU LOVE.
DON'T YOU PAY THIS OLD GEEZER NO MIND.

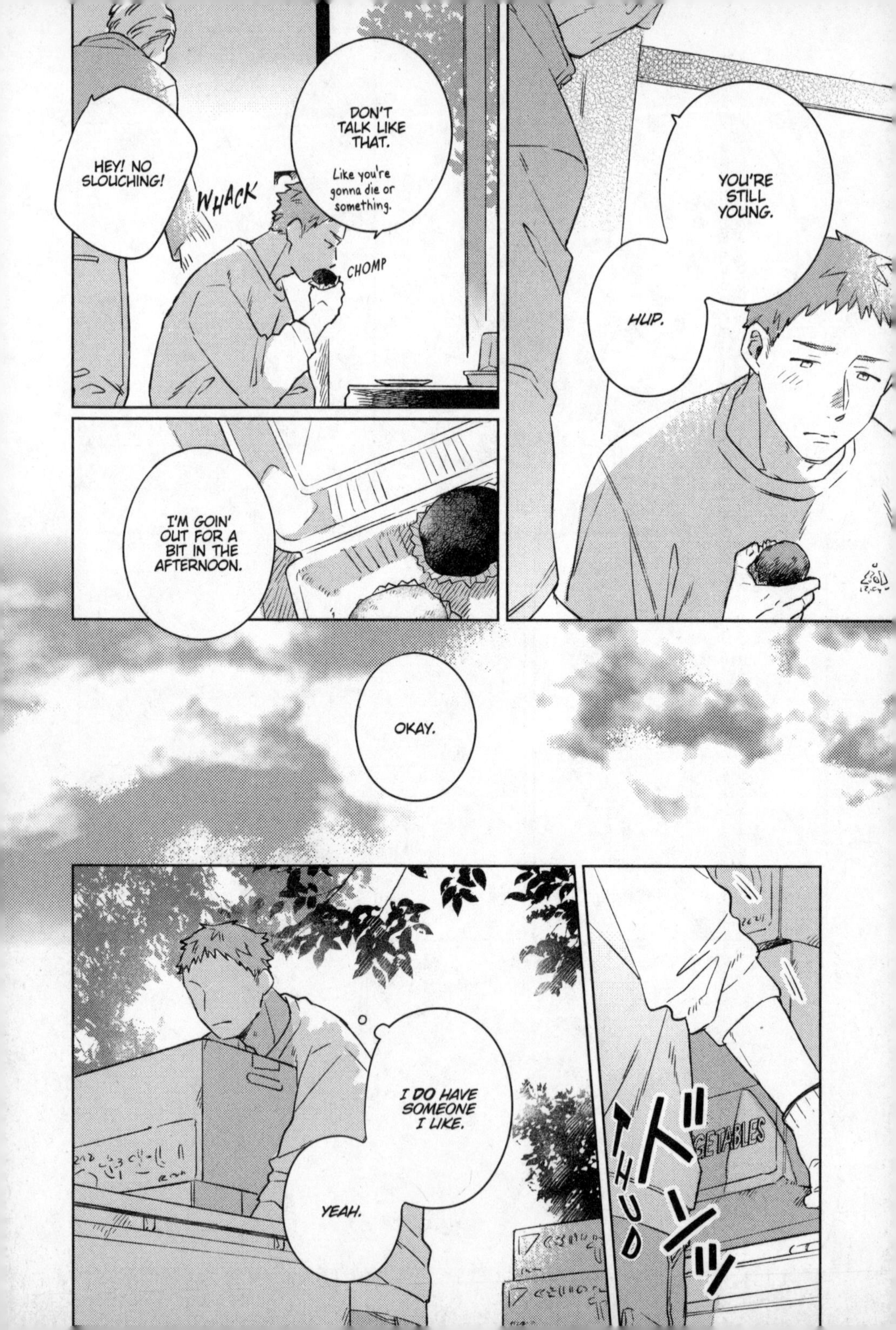
YOU'RE STILL YOUNG.
HUP.
DON'T TALK LIKE THAT.
Like you're gonna die or something.
HEY! NO SLOUCHING!
WHACK
CHOMP
I'M GOIN' OUT FOR A BIT IN THE AFTERNOON.
OKAY.
THUD
GETABLES
I DO HAVE SOMEONE I LIKE.
YEAH.

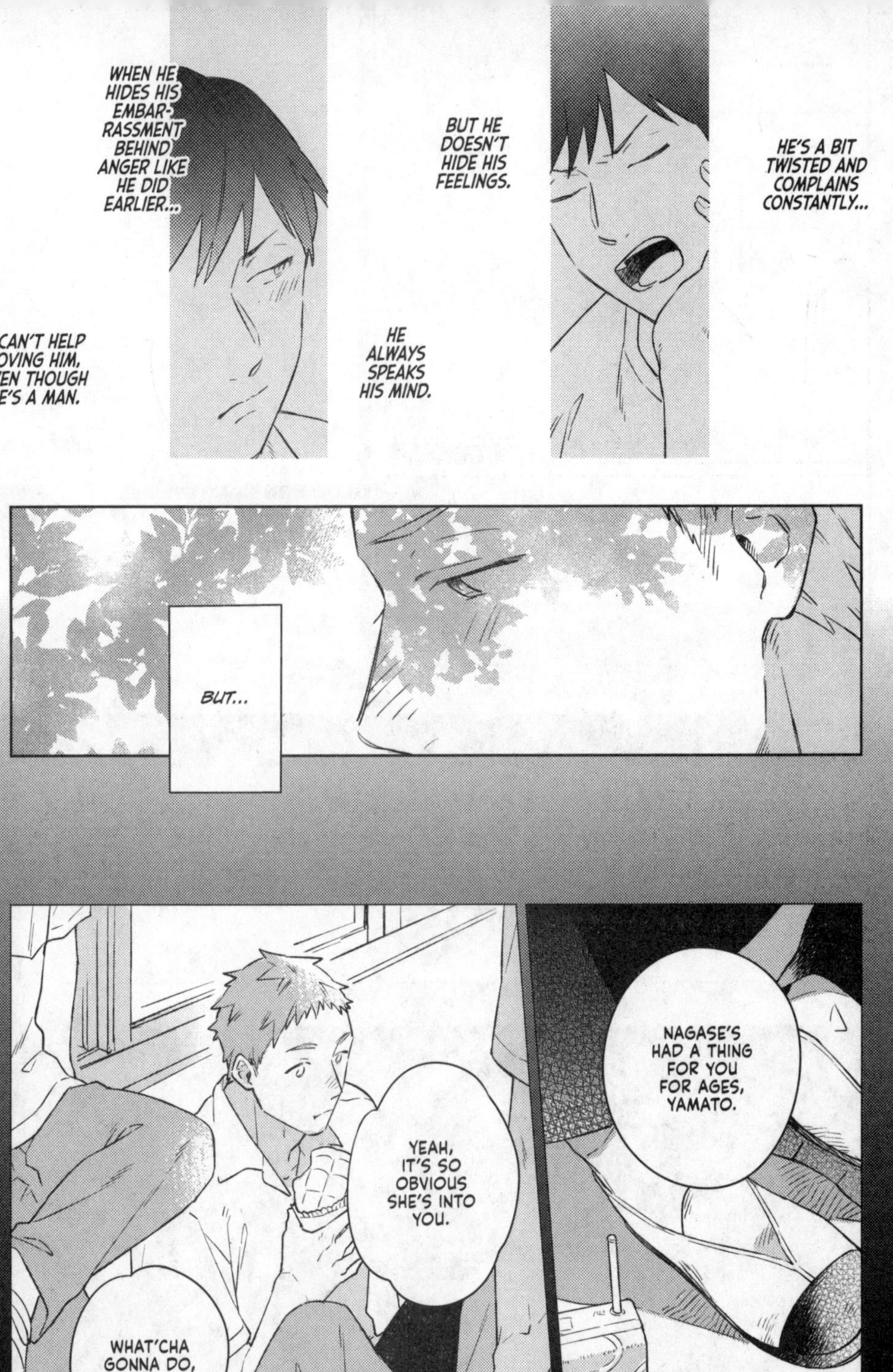
HE'S A BIT TWISTED AND COMPLAINS CONSTANTLY...
BUT HE DOESN'T HIDE HIS FEELINGS.
HE ALWAYS SPEAKS HIS MIND.
WHEN HE HIDES HIS EMBAR-RASSMENT BEHIND ANGER LIKE HE DID EARLIER...
I CAN'T HELP LOVING HIM, EVEN THOUGH HE'S A MAN.
BUT...
NAGASE'S HAD A THING FOR YOU FOR AGES, YAMATO.
YEAH, IT'S SO OBVIOUS SHE'S INTO YOU.
WHAT'CHA GONNA DO, YAMATO?

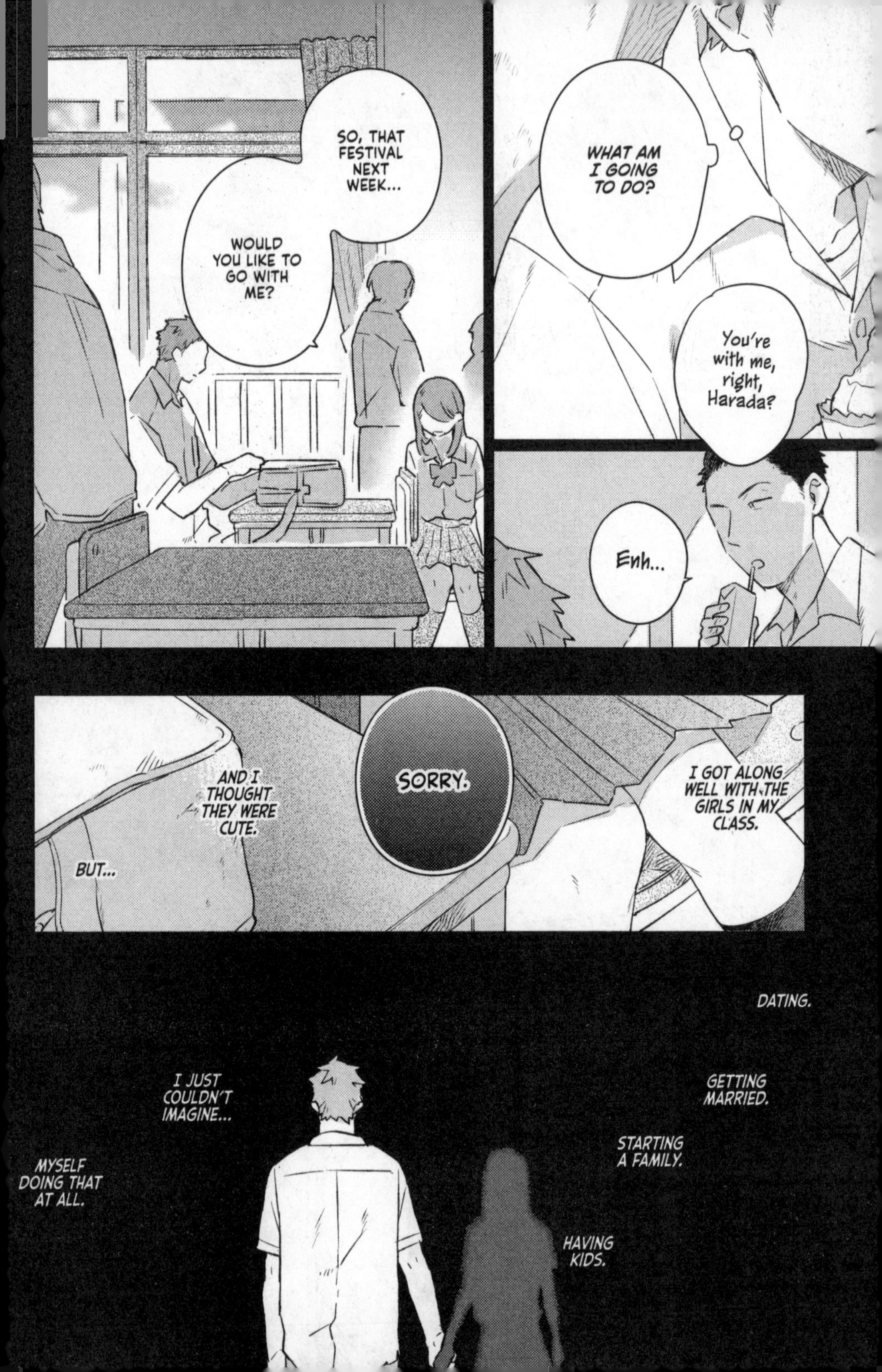
WHAT AM I GOING TO DO?
You're with me, right, Harada?
Enh...
SO, THAT FESTIVAL NEXT WEEK...
WOULD YOU LIKE TO GO WITH ME?
I GOT ALONG WELL WITH THE GIRLS IN MY CLASS.
SORRY.
AND I THOUGHT THEY WERE CUTE.
BUT...
DATING.
GETTING MARRIED.
STARTING A FAMILY.
HAVING KIDS.
I JUST COULDN'T IMAGINE...
MYSELF DOING THAT AT ALL.

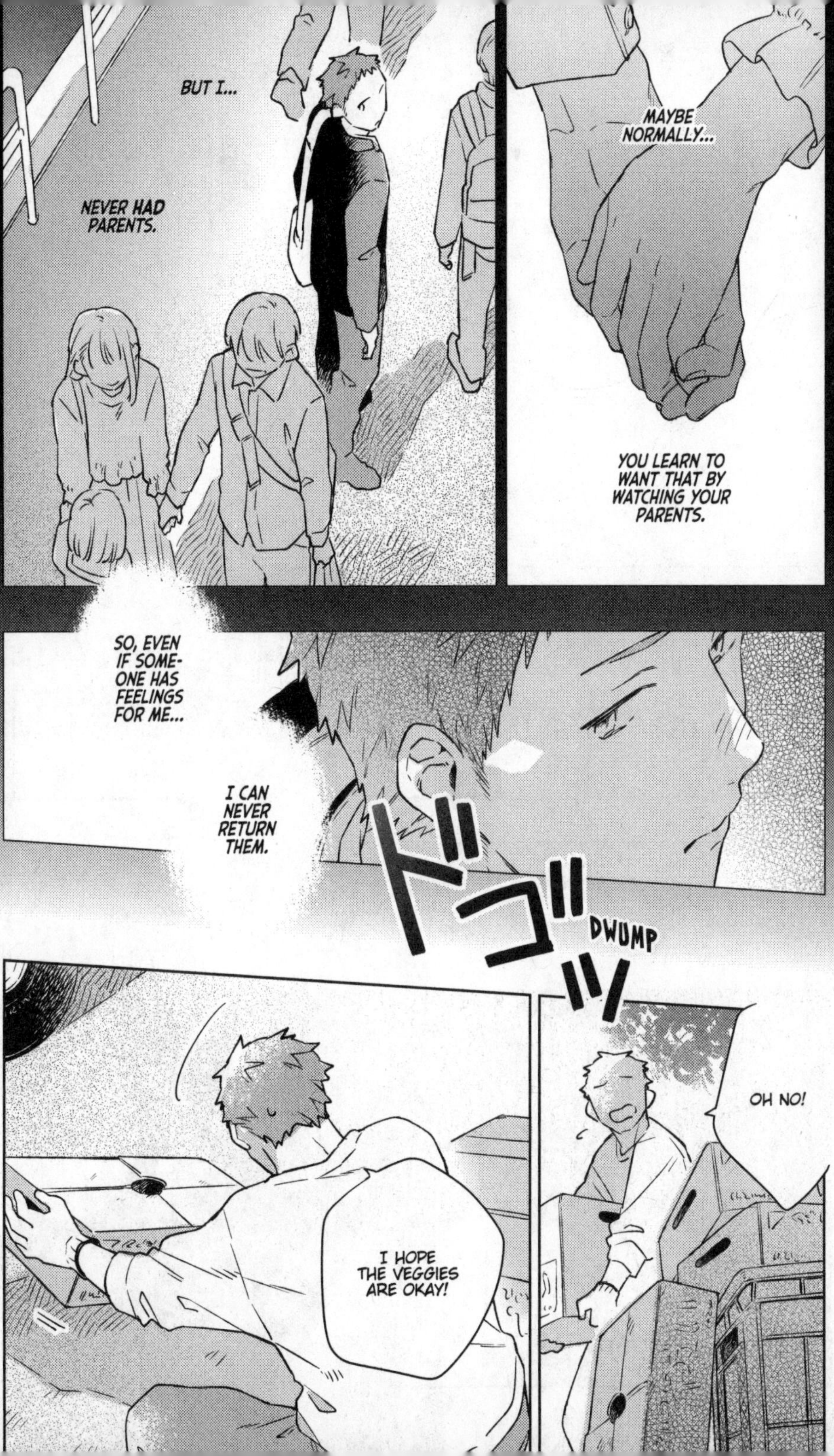
MAYBE NORMALLY...
YOU LEARN TO WANT THAT BY WATCHING YOUR PARENTS.
BUT I...
NEVER HAD PARENTS.
SO, EVEN IF SOME-ONE HAS FEELINGS FOR ME...
I CAN NEVER RETURN THEM.
ドゴッ
DWUMP
OH NO!
I HOPE THE VEGGIES ARE OKAY!

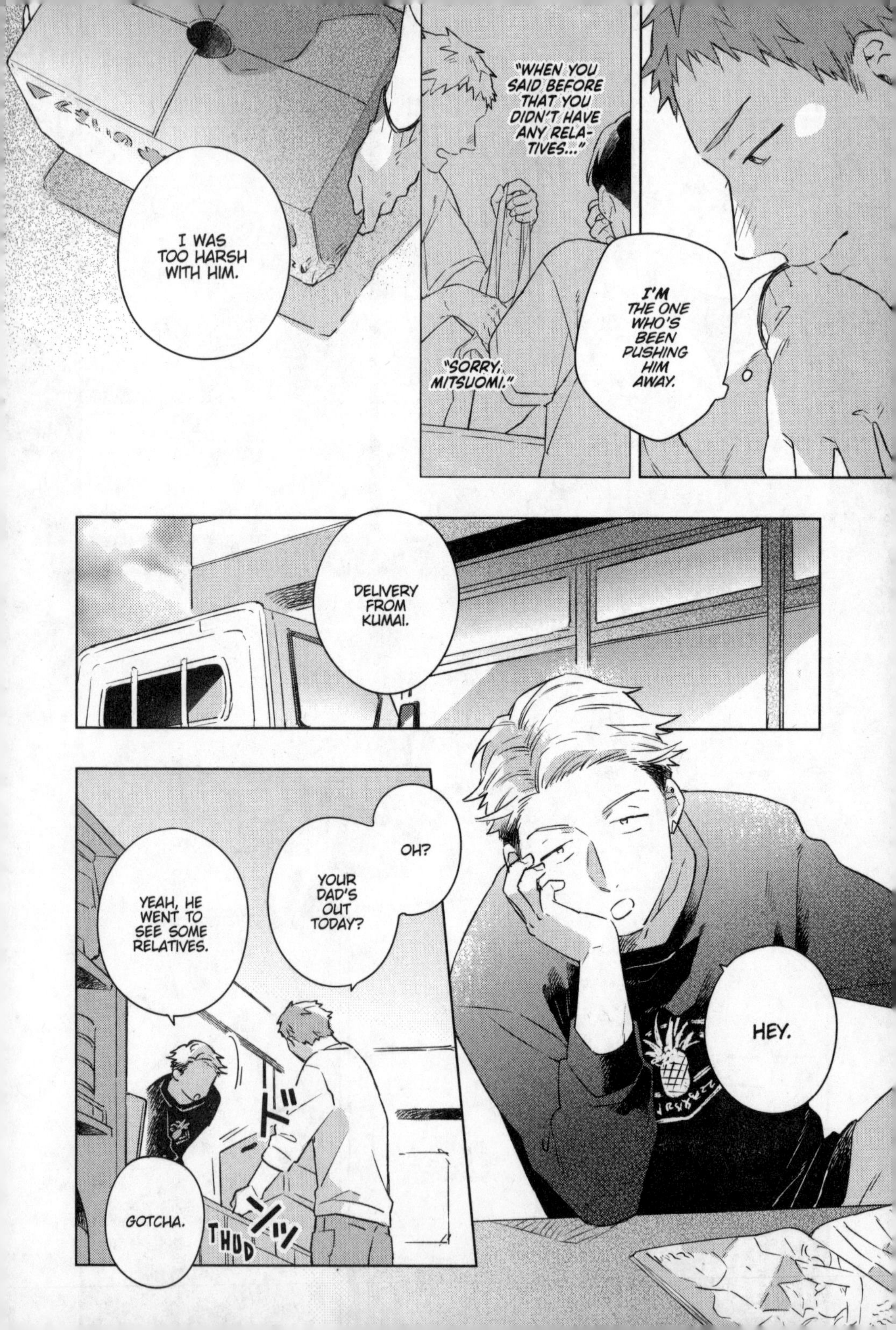
I'M THE ONE WHO'S BEEN PUSHING HIM AWAY.
"WHEN YOU SAID BEFORE THAT YOU DIDN'T HAVE ANY RELA-TIVES..."
"SORRY, MITSUOMI."
I WAS TOO HARSH WITH HIM.
DELIVERY FROM KUMAI.
HEY.
OH?
YOUR DAD'S OUT TODAY?
YEAH, HE WENT TO SEE SOME RELATIVES.
THUD
GOTCHA.

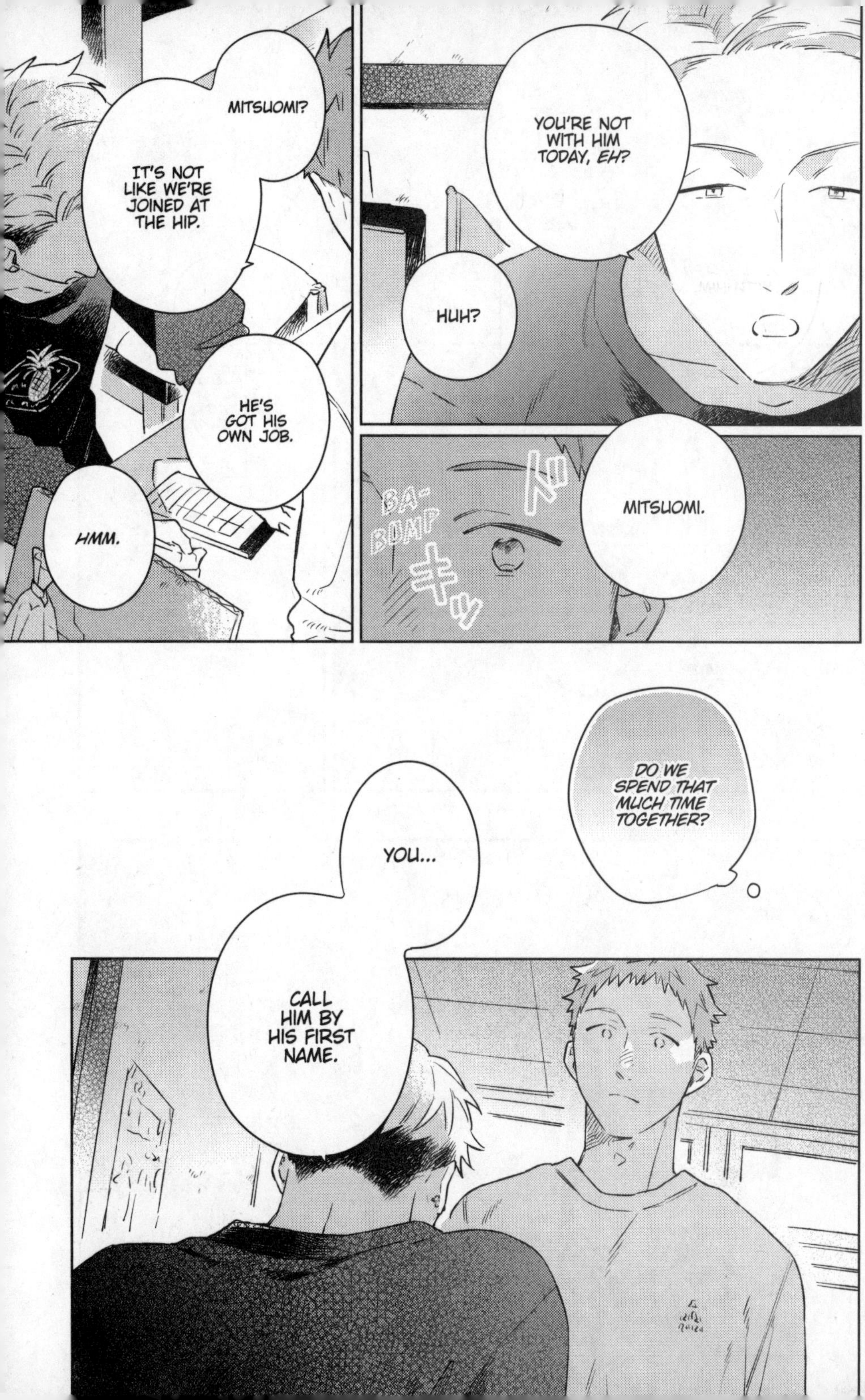
YOU'RE NOT WITH HIM TODAY, EH?
HUH?
MITSUOMI.
BA-BUMP
ドキッ
MITSUOMI?
IT'S NOT LIKE WE'RE JOINED AT THE HIP.
HE'S GOT HIS OWN JOB.
HMM.
DO WE SPEND THAT MUCH TIME TOGETHER?
YOU...
CALL HIM BY HIS FIRST NAME.

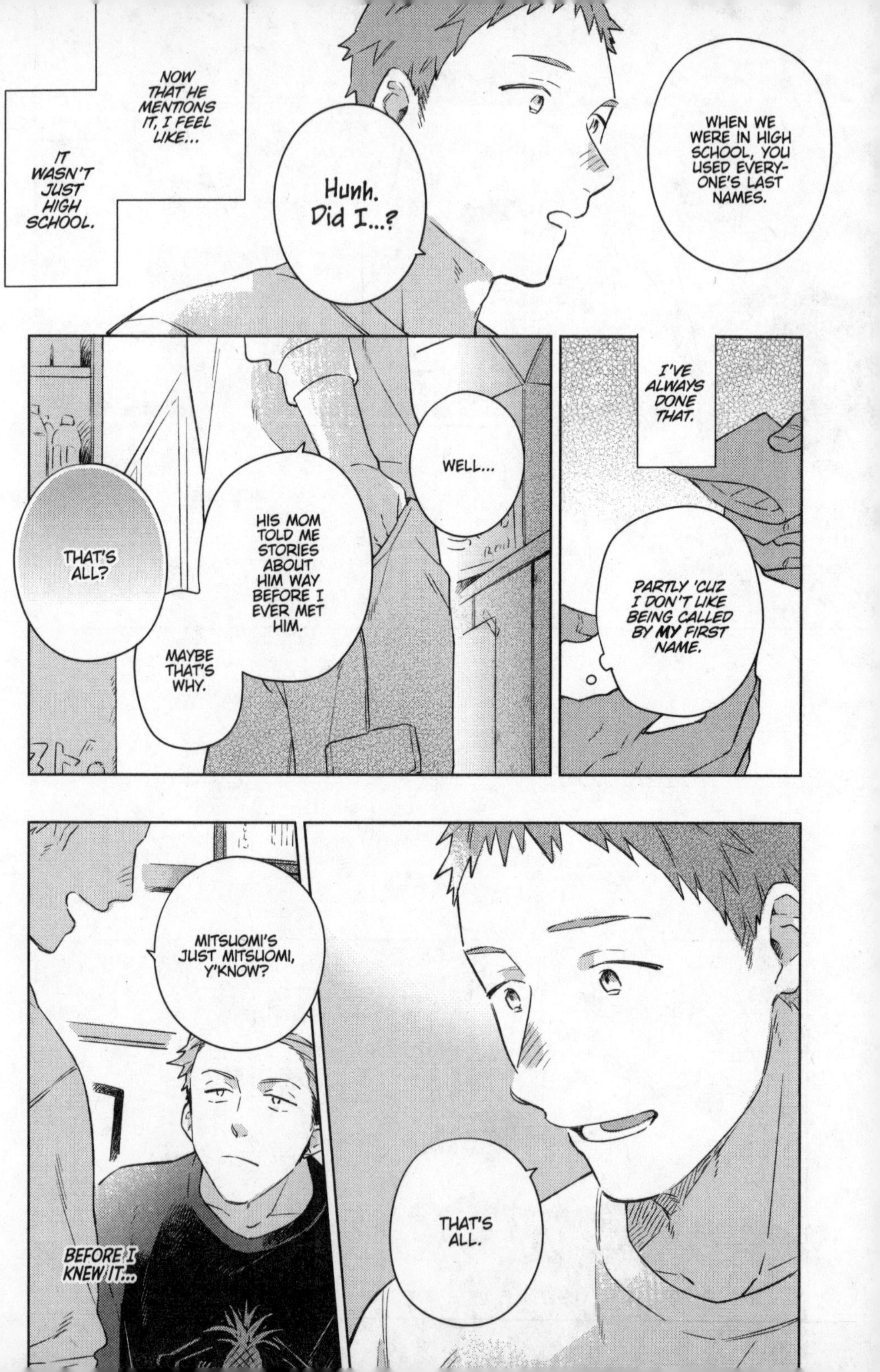
WHEN WE WERE IN HIGH SCHOOL, YOU USED EVERYONE'S LAST NAMES.
Hunh. Did I...?
NOW THAT HE MENTIONS IT, I FEEL LIKE...
IT WASN'T JUST HIGH SCHOOL.
I'VE ALWAYS DONE THAT.
PARTLY 'CUZ I DON'T LIKE BEING CALLED BY MY FIRST NAME.
WELL...
HIS MOM TOLD ME STORIES ABOUT HIM WAY BEFORE I EVER MET HIM.
THAT'S ALL?
MAYBE THAT'S WHY.
THAT'S ALL.
MITSUOMI'S JUST MITSUOMI, Y'KNOW?
BEFORE I KNEW IT...

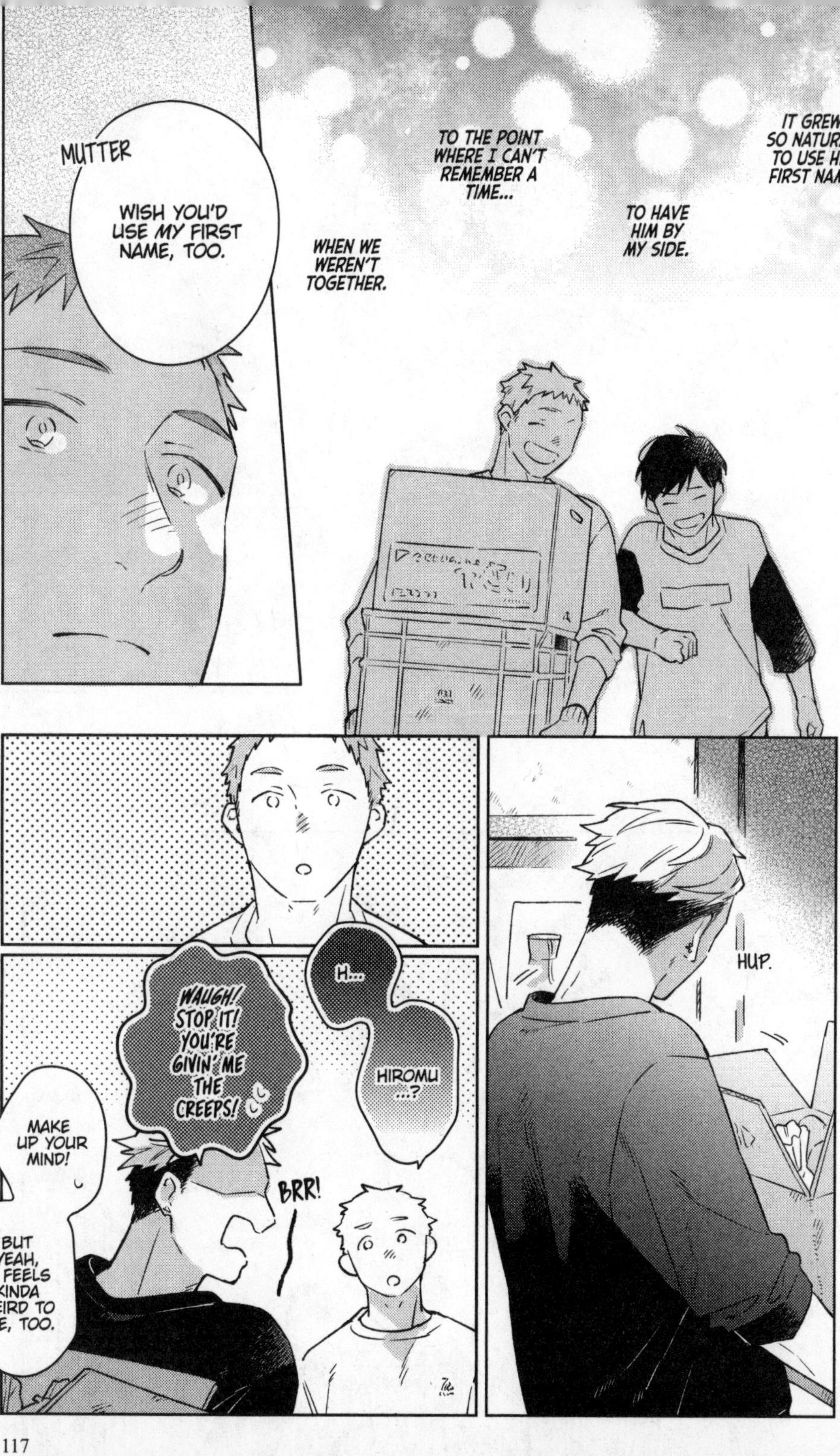
IT GREW SO NATURAL TO USE HIS FIRST NAME.
TO HAVE HIM BY MY SIDE.
TO THE POINT WHERE I CAN'T REMEMBER A TIME...
WHEN WE WEREN'T TOGETHER.
MUTTER
WISH YOU'D USE MY FIRST NAME, TOO.
HUP.
H...
HIROMU ...?
WAUGH! STOP IT! YOU'RE GIVIN' ME THE CREEPS!
BRR!
MAKE UP YOUR MIND!
BUT YEAH, IT FEELS KINDA WEIRD TO ME, TOO.

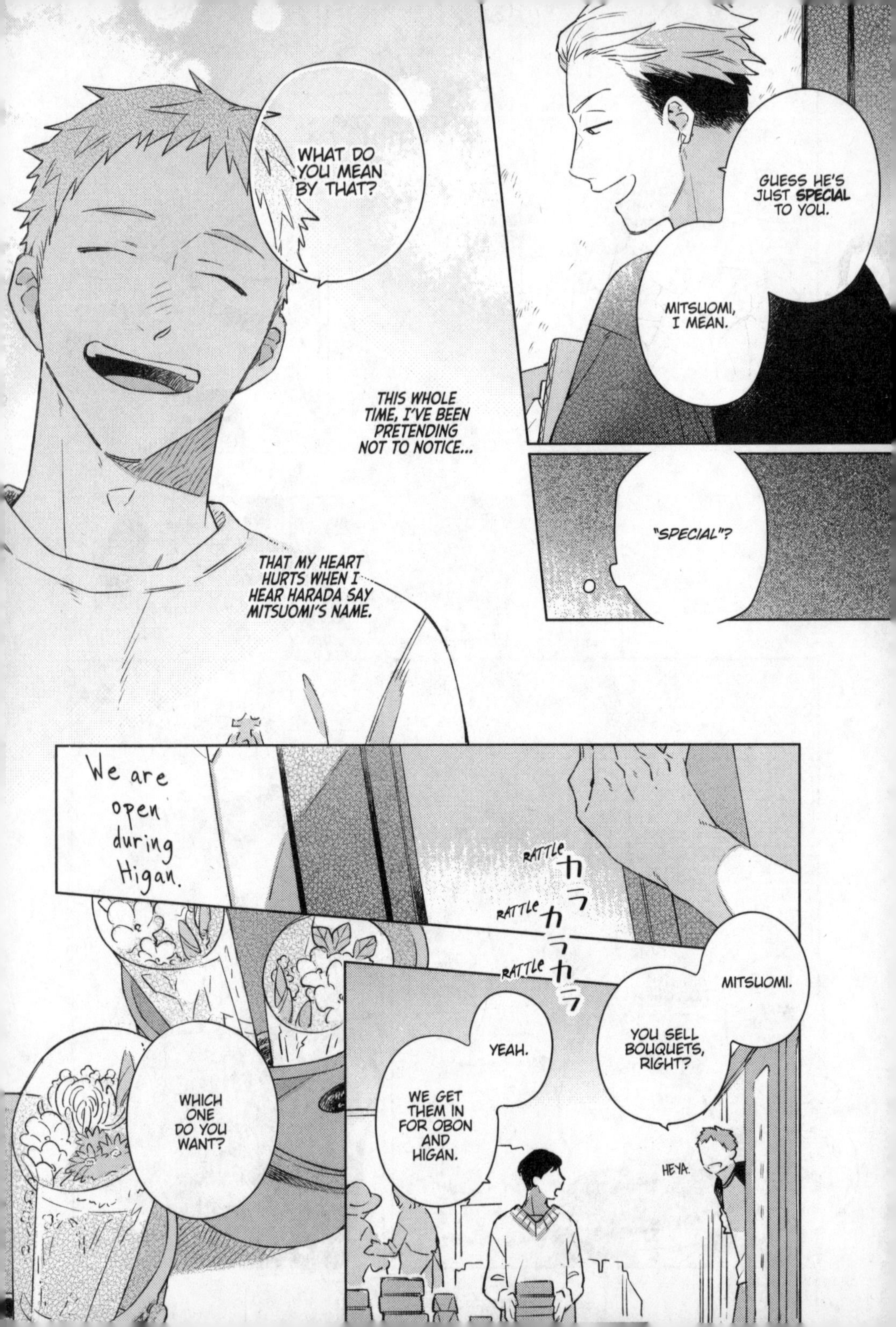
GUESS HE'S JUST **SPECIAL** TO YOU.
MITSUOMI, I MEAN.
"SPECIAL"?
WHAT DO YOU MEAN BY THAT?
THIS WHOLE TIME, I'VE BEEN PRETENDING NOT TO NOTICE...
THAT MY HEART HURTS WHEN I HEAR HARADA SAY MITSUOMI'S NAME.
RATTLE カラ
RATTLE カラ
RATTLE カラ
We are open during Higan.
HEYA.
MITSUOMI.
YOU SELL BOUQUETS, RIGHT?
YEAH.
WE GET THEM IN FOR OBON AND HIGAN.
WHICH ONE DO YOU WANT?

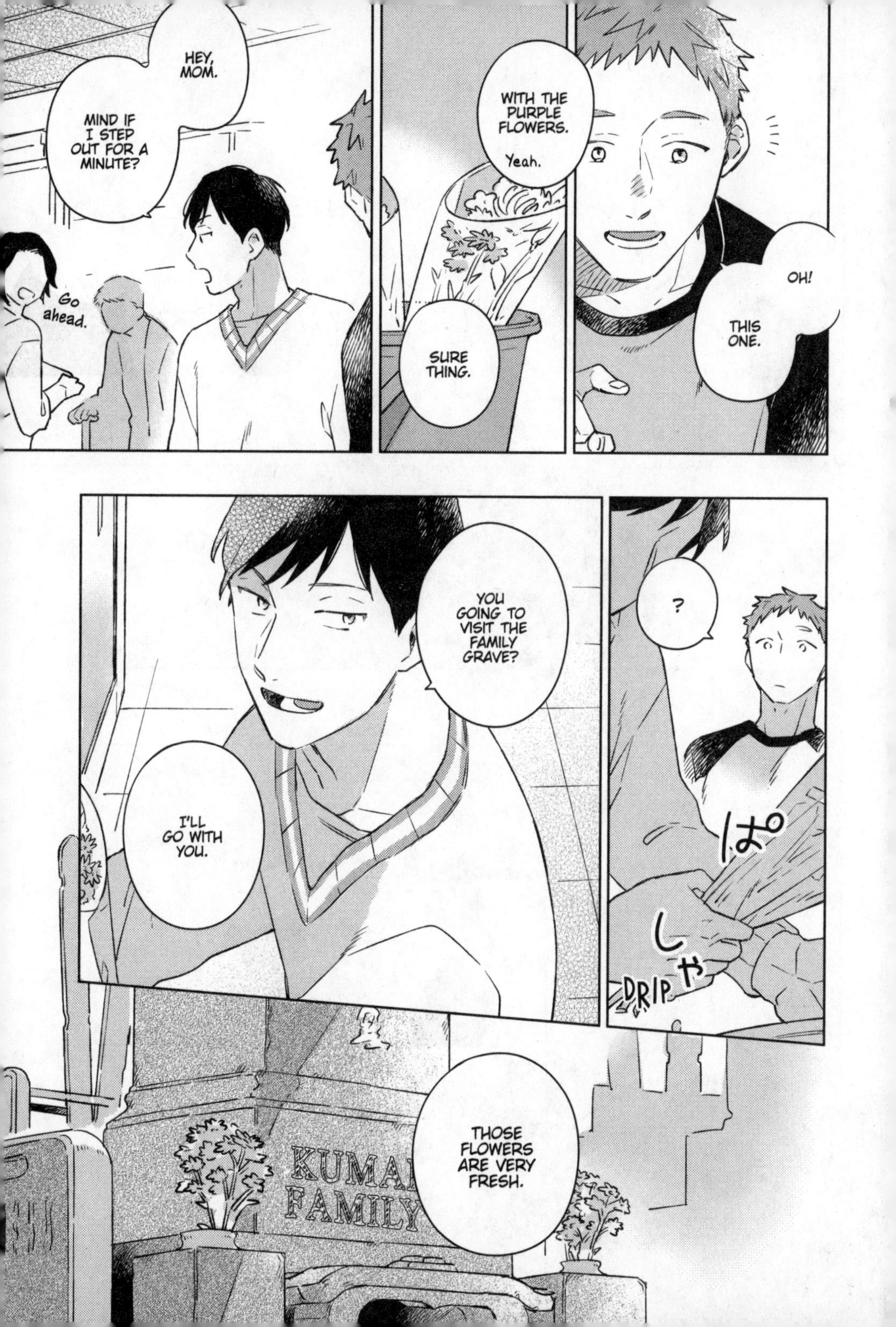
OH!
THIS ONE.
WITH THE PURPLE FLOWERS.
Yeah.
SURE THING.
HEY, MOM.
MIND IF I STEP OUT FOR A MINUTE?
Go ahead.
?
ぱ
しゃ
DRIP
YOU GOING TO VISIT THE FAMILY GRAVE?
I'LL GO WITH YOU.
THOSE FLOWERS ARE VERY FRESH.

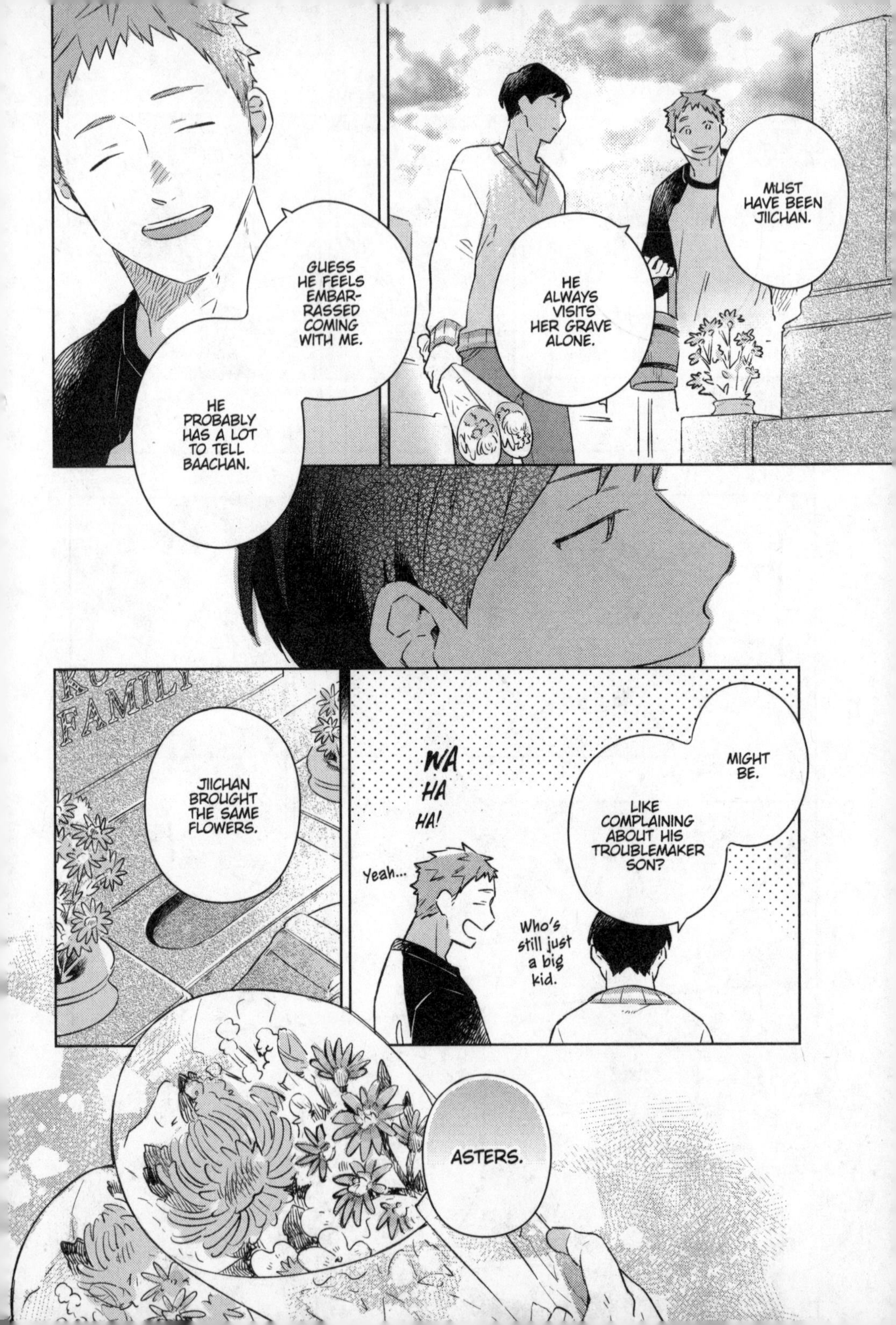
MUST HAVE BEEN JIICHAN.
HE ALWAYS VISITS HER GRAVE ALONE.
GUESS HE FEELS EMBARRASSED COMING WITH ME.
HE PROBABLY HAS A LOT TO TELL BAACHAN.
MIGHT BE.
LIKE COMPLAINING ABOUT HIS TROUBLEMAKER SON?
WA HA HA!
Yeah...
Who's still just a big kid.
FAMILY
JIICHAN BROUGHT THE SAME FLOWERS.
ASTERS.

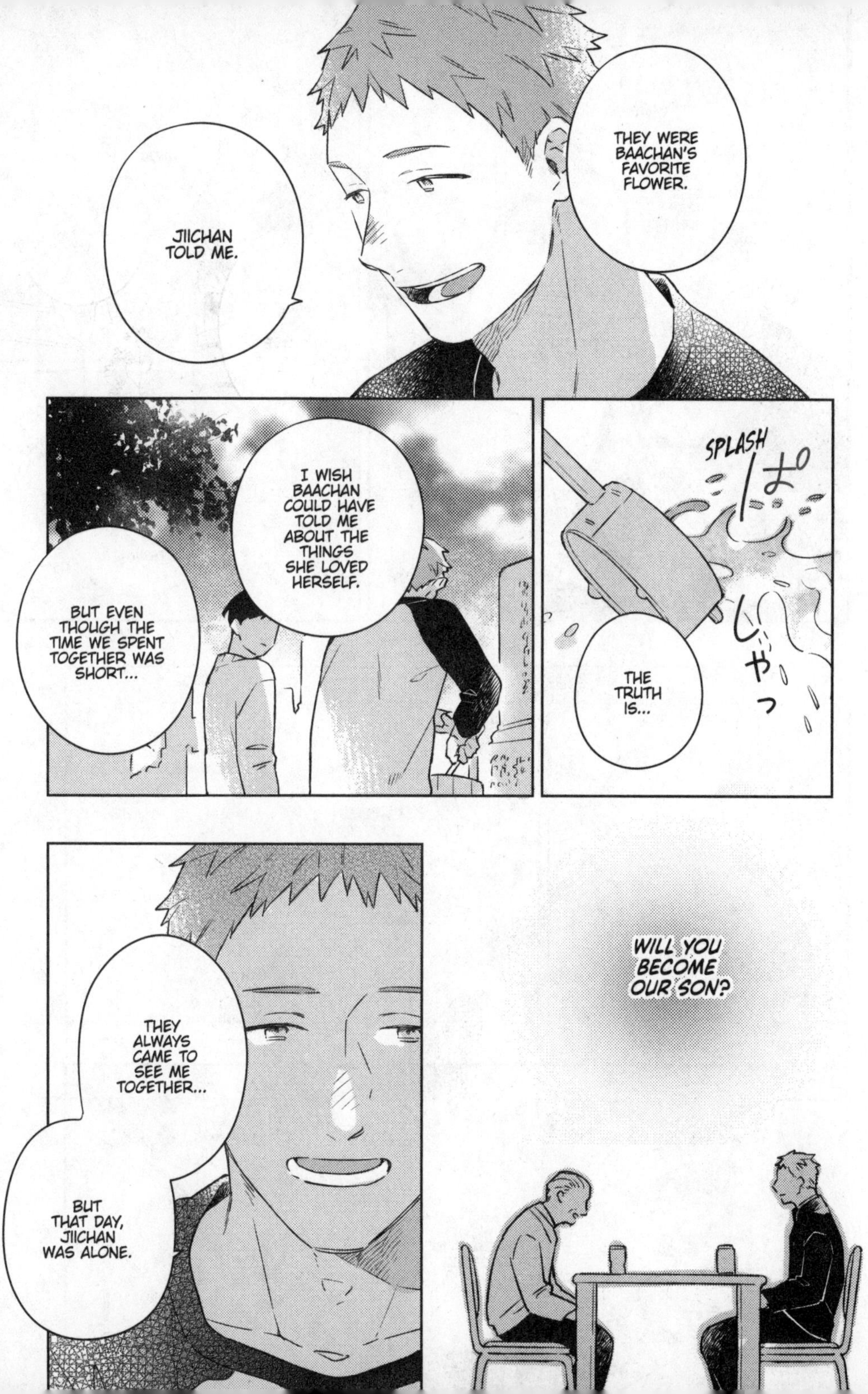
THEY WERE BAACHAN'S FAVORITE FLOWER.
JIICHAN TOLD ME.
SPLASH
THE TRUTH IS...
I WISH BAACHAN COULD HAVE TOLD ME ABOUT THE THINGS SHE LOVED HERSELF.
BUT EVEN THOUGH THE TIME WE SPENT TOGETHER WAS SHORT...
WILL YOU BECOME OUR SON?
THEY ALWAYS CAME TO SEE ME TOGETHER...
BUT THAT DAY, JIICHAN WAS ALONE.

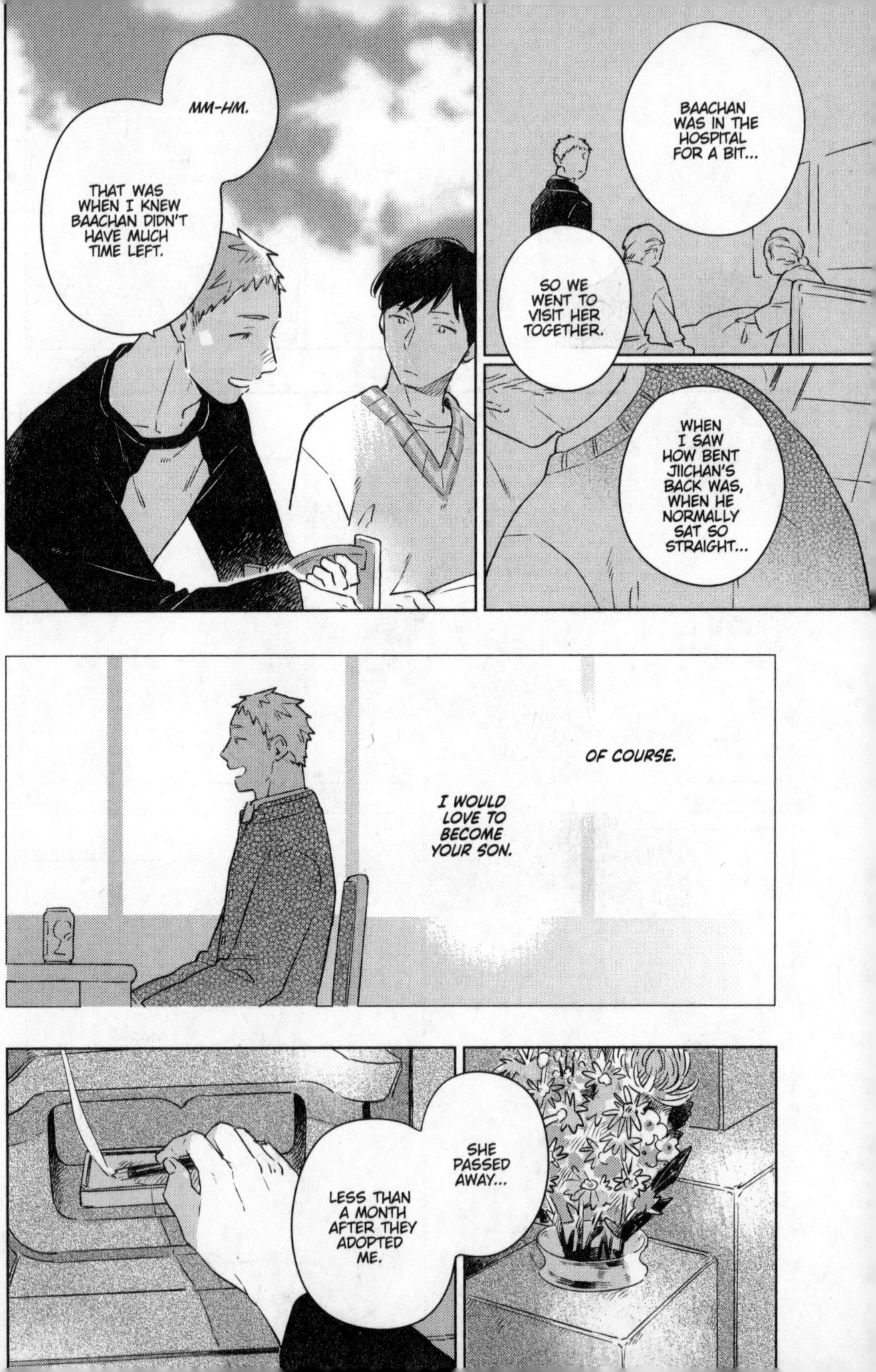
BAACHAN WAS IN THE HOSPITAL FOR A BIT...
SO WE WENT TO VISIT HER TOGETHER.
WHEN I SAW HOW BENT JIICHAN'S BACK WAS, WHEN HE NORMALLY SAT SO STRAIGHT...
MM-HM.
THAT WAS WHEN I KNEW BAACHAN DIDN'T HAVE MUCH TIME LEFT.
OF COURSE.
I WOULD LOVE TO BECOME YOUR SON.
SHE PASSED AWAY...
LESS THAN A MONTH AFTER THEY ADOPTED ME.

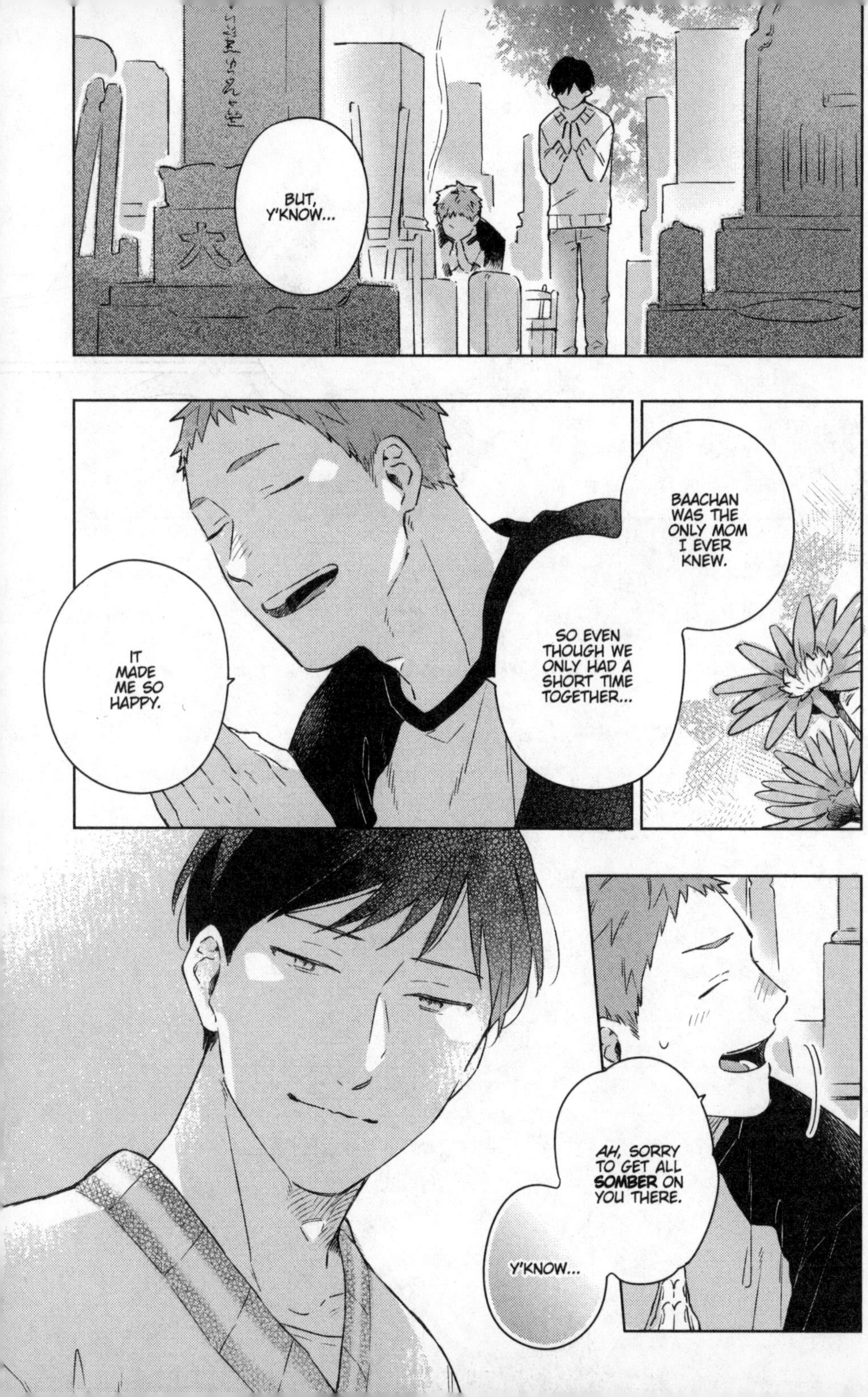
BUT, Y'KNOW...
BAACHAN WAS THE ONLY MOM I EVER KNEW.
SO EVEN THOUGH WE ONLY HAD A SHORT TIME TOGETHER...
IT MADE ME SO HAPPY.
AH, SORRY TO GET ALL SOMBER ON YOU THERE.
Y'KNOW...

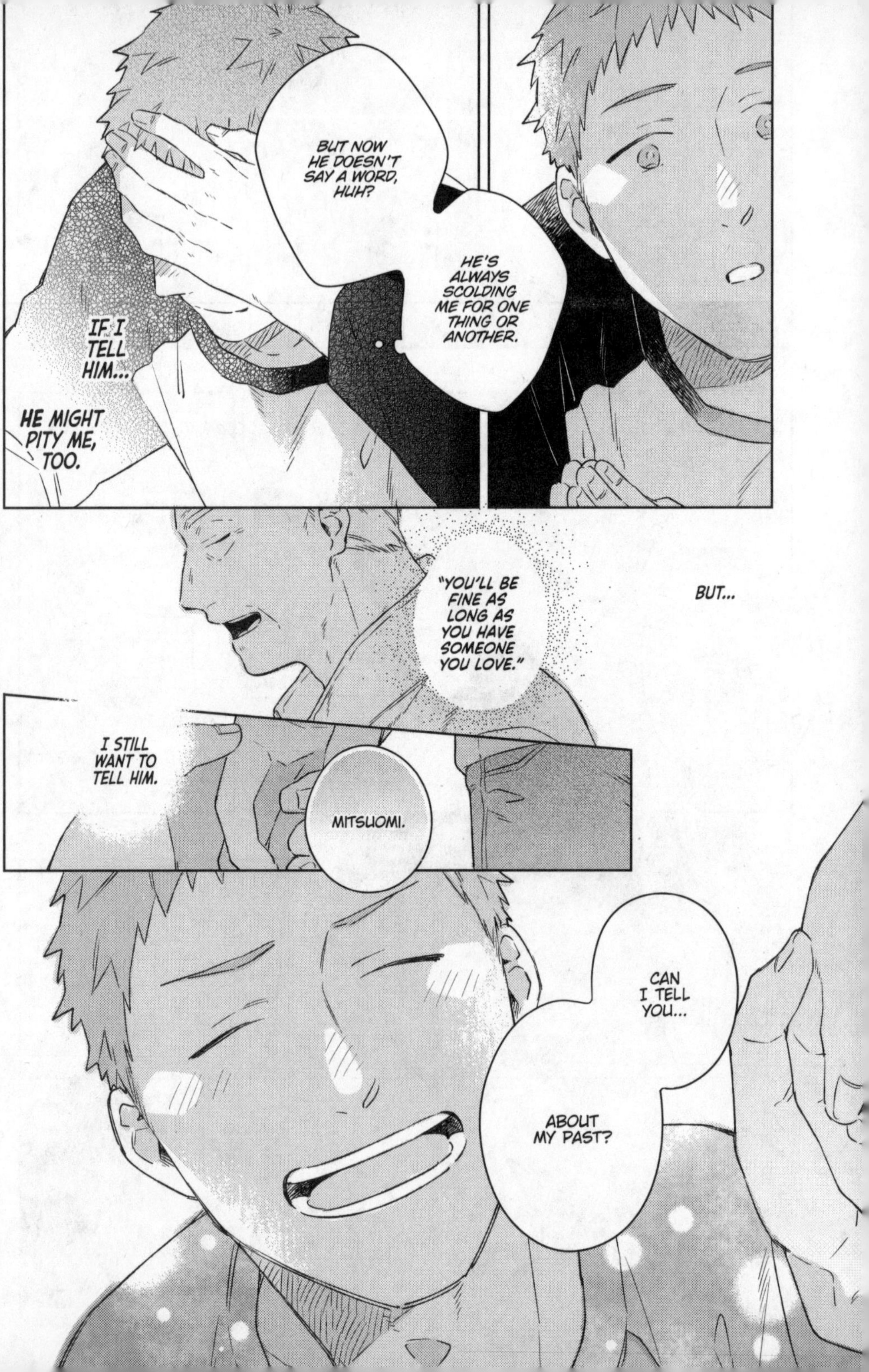
HE'S ALWAYS SCOLDING ME FOR ONE THING OR ANOTHER.
BUT NOW HE DOESN'T SAY A WORD, HUH?
IF I TELL HIM...
HE MIGHT PITY ME, TOO.
BUT...
"YOU'LL BE FINE AS LONG AS YOU HAVE SOMEONE YOU LOVE."
I STILL WANT TO TELL HIM.
MITSUOMI.
CAN I TELL YOU...
ABOUT MY PAST?

#005

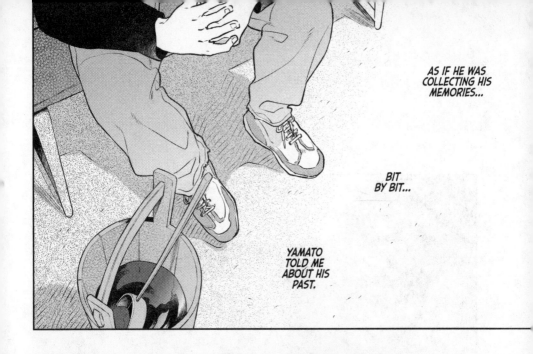

AS IF HE WAS COLLECTING HIS MEMORIES...

BIT BY BIT...

YAMATO TOLD ME ABOUT HIS PAST.

HOW HE WAS BORN IN TOKYO, ABANDONED ON A PARK BENCH...

AND RAISED IN SEVERAL DIFFERENT ORPHANAGES.

HE TOLD ME ABOUT THE OTHER ORPHANAGE KIDS, TOO.

BUT NO MATTER HOW MUCH HE SAID...

HE NEVER TOLD ME HOW HE FELT ABOUT IT ALL.

I TRIED TO READ IT FROM HIS EXPRESSION.

BUT ME, I HAD PARENTS THAT WERE THERE WHEN I WENT HOME.

SIBLINGS I SOMETIMES FOUGHT WITH.

THAT FELT SO NATURAL TO ME, I COULDN'T IMAGINE ANYTHING DIFFERENT.

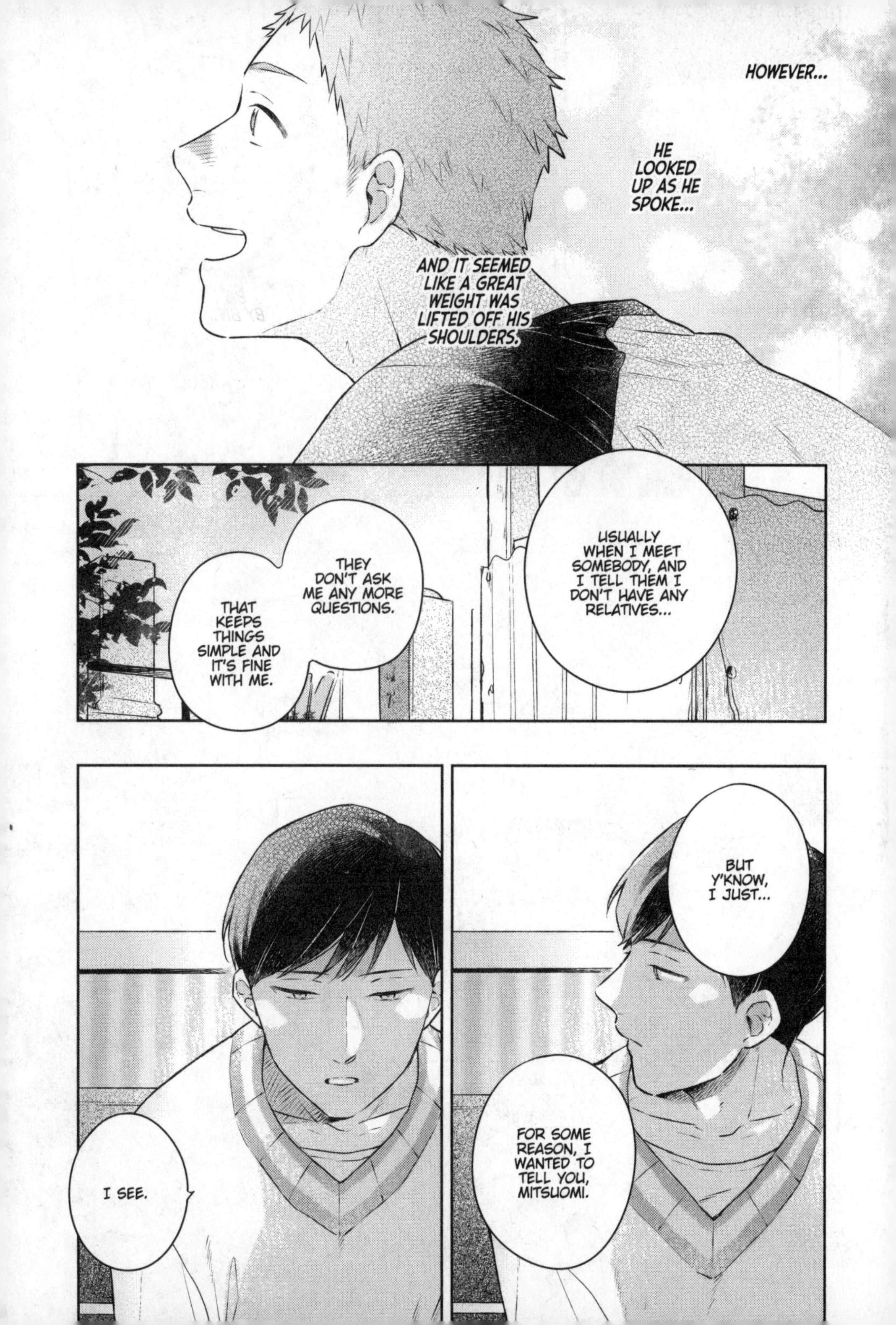
HOWEVER...
HE LOOKED UP AS HE SPOKE...
AND IT SEEMED LIKE A GREAT WEIGHT WAS LIFTED OFF HIS SHOULDERS.
USUALLY WHEN I MEET SOMEBODY, AND I TELL THEM I DON'T HAVE ANY RELATIVES...
THEY DON'T ASK ME ANY MORE QUESTIONS.
THAT KEEPS THINGS SIMPLE AND IT'S FINE WITH ME.
BUT Y'KNOW, I JUST...
FOR SOME REASON, I WANTED TO TELL YOU, MITSUOMI.
I SEE.

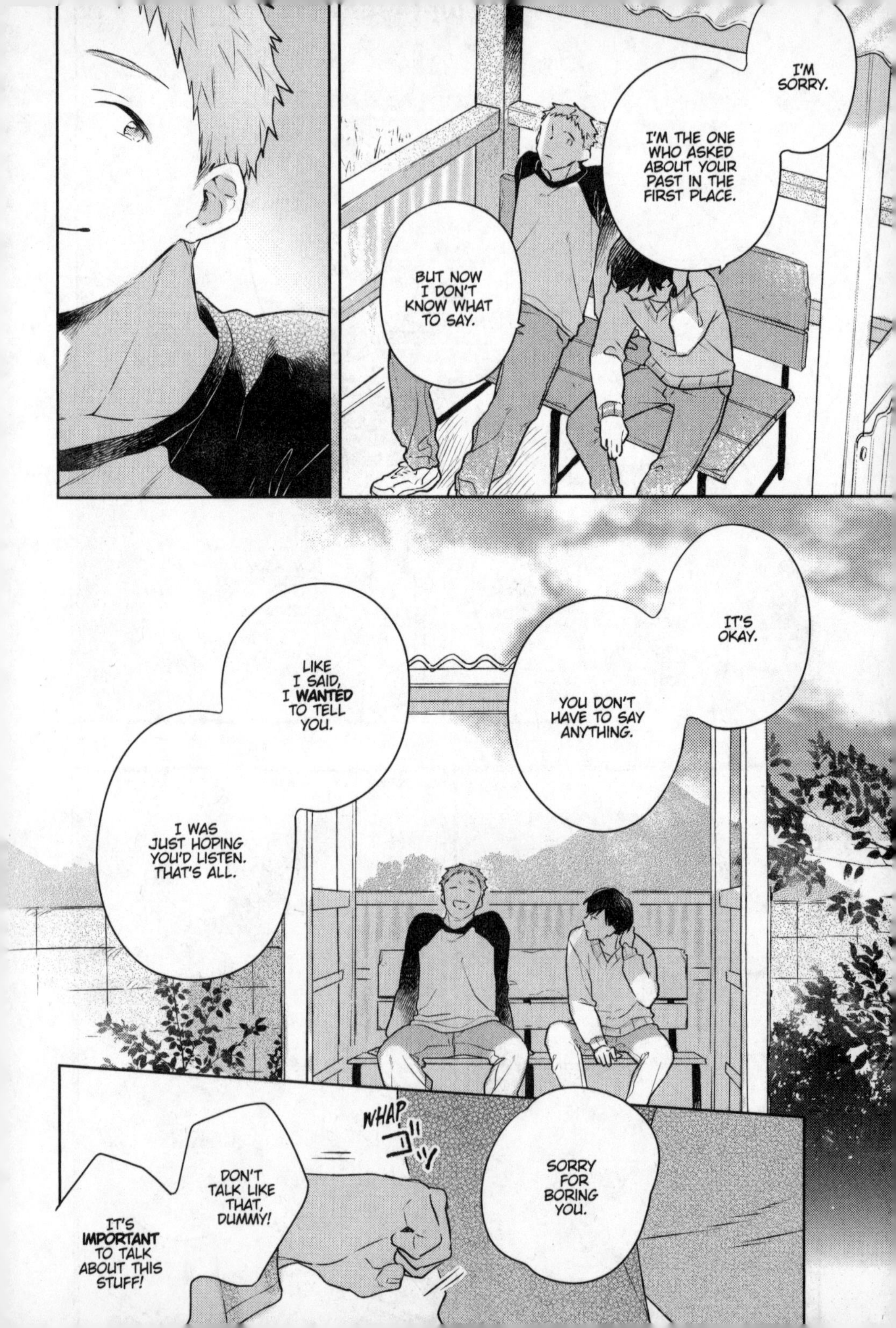
I'M SORRY.
I'M THE ONE WHO ASKED ABOUT YOUR PAST IN THE FIRST PLACE.
BUT NOW I DON'T KNOW WHAT TO SAY.
IT'S OKAY.
YOU DON'T HAVE TO SAY ANYTHING.
LIKE I SAID, I **WANTED** TO TELL YOU.
I WAS JUST HOPING YOU'D LISTEN. THAT'S ALL.
SORRY FOR BORING YOU.
WHAP
ゴッ
DON'T TALK LIKE THAT, DUMMY!
IT'S **IMPORTANT** TO TALK ABOUT THIS STUFF!

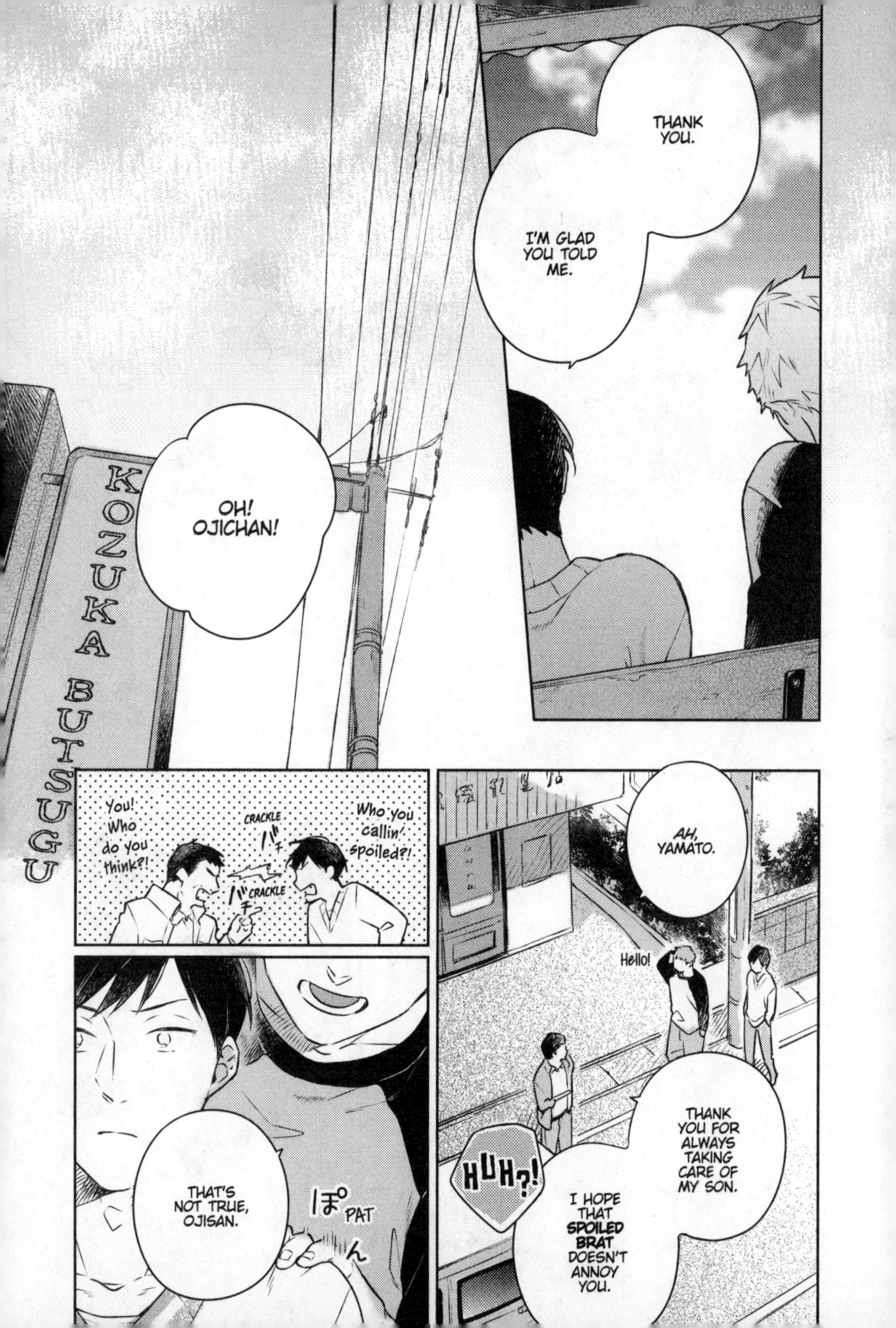
THANK YOU.
I'M GLAD YOU TOLD ME.
KOZUKA BUTSUGU
OH! OJICHAN!
AH, YAMATO.
Hello!
THANK YOU FOR ALWAYS TAKING CARE OF MY SON.
I HOPE THAT **SPOILED BRAT** DOESN'T ANNOY YOU.
HUH?!
Who you callin' spoiled?!
CRACKLE
バチ
You! Who do you think?!
バチ
CRACKLE
THAT'S NOT TRUE, OJISAN.
ぽん
PAT

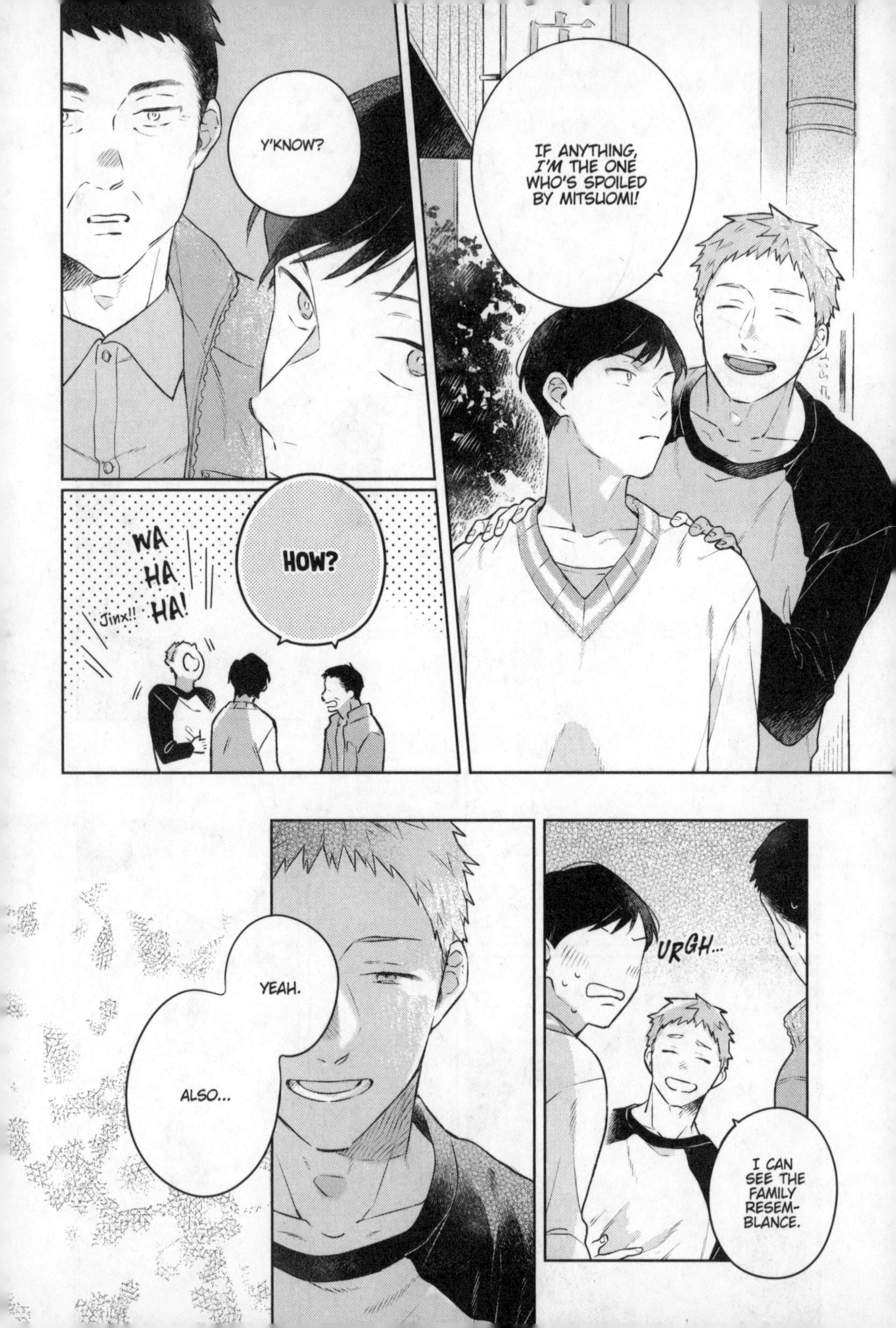
IF ANYTHING, I'M THE ONE WHO'S SPOILED BY MITSUOMI!
Y'KNOW?
HOW?
WA HA HA!
Jinx!!
URGH...
I CAN SEE THE FAMILY RESEM-BLANCE.
YEAH.
ALSO...

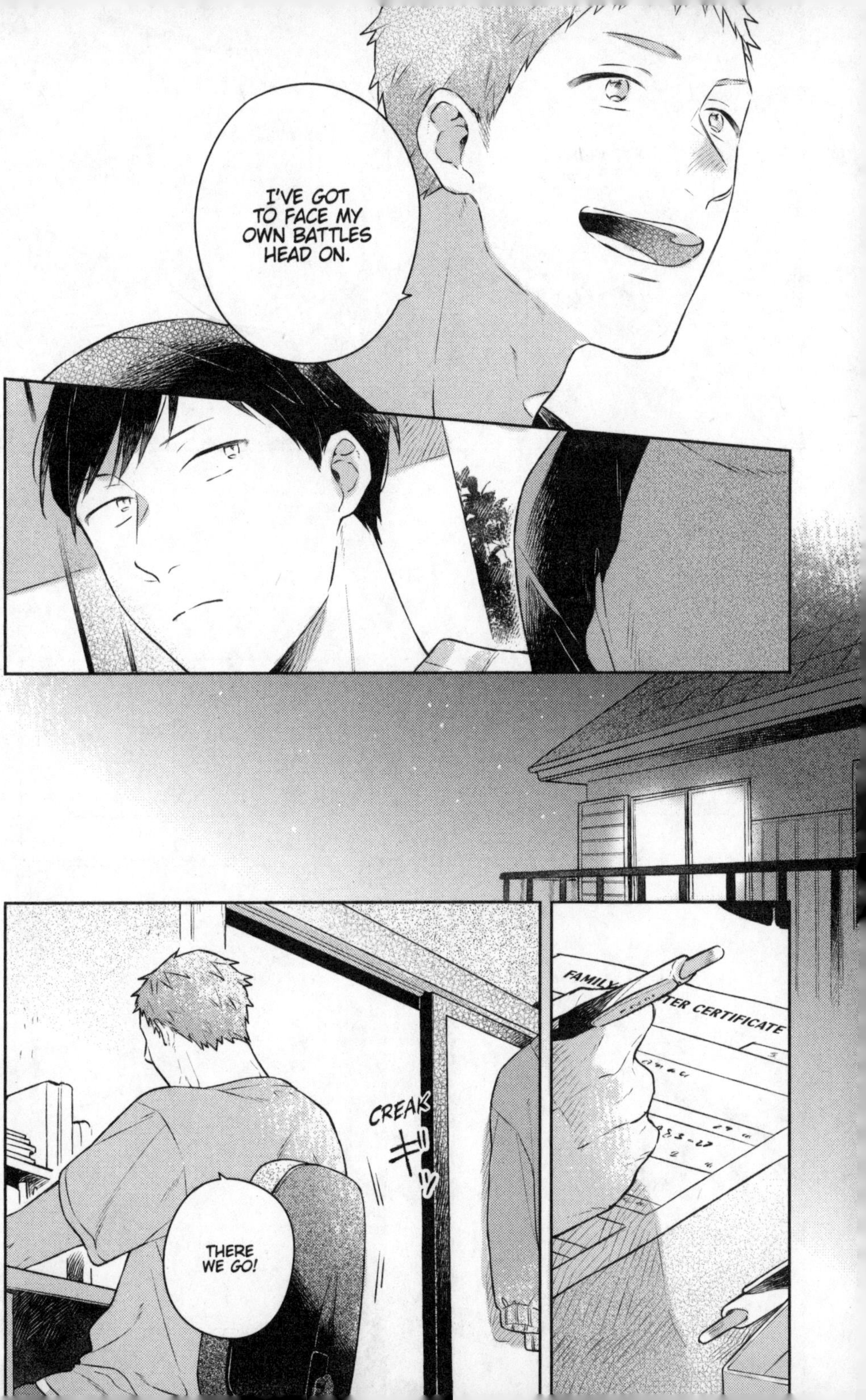
I'VE GOT TO FACE MY OWN BATTLES HEAD ON.
CREAK
THERE WE GO!

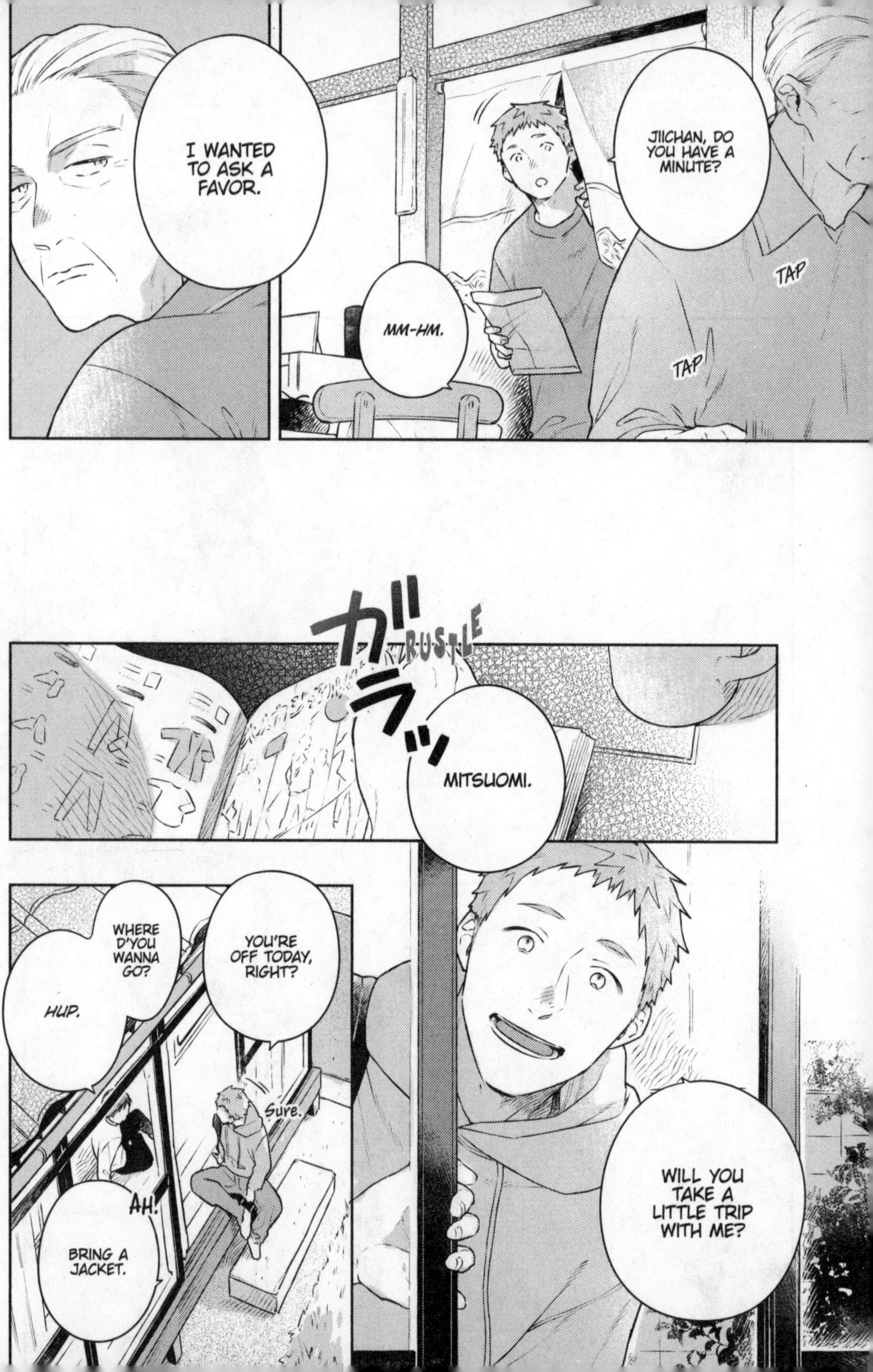
JIICHAN, DO YOU HAVE A MINUTE?
TAP
TAP
MM-HM.
I WANTED TO ASK A FAVOR.
ガラッ
RUSTLE
MITSUOMI.
WILL YOU TAKE A LITTLE TRIP WITH ME?
YOU'RE OFF TODAY, RIGHT?
WHERE D'YOU WANNA GO?
HUP.
Sure.
AH!
BRING A JACKET.

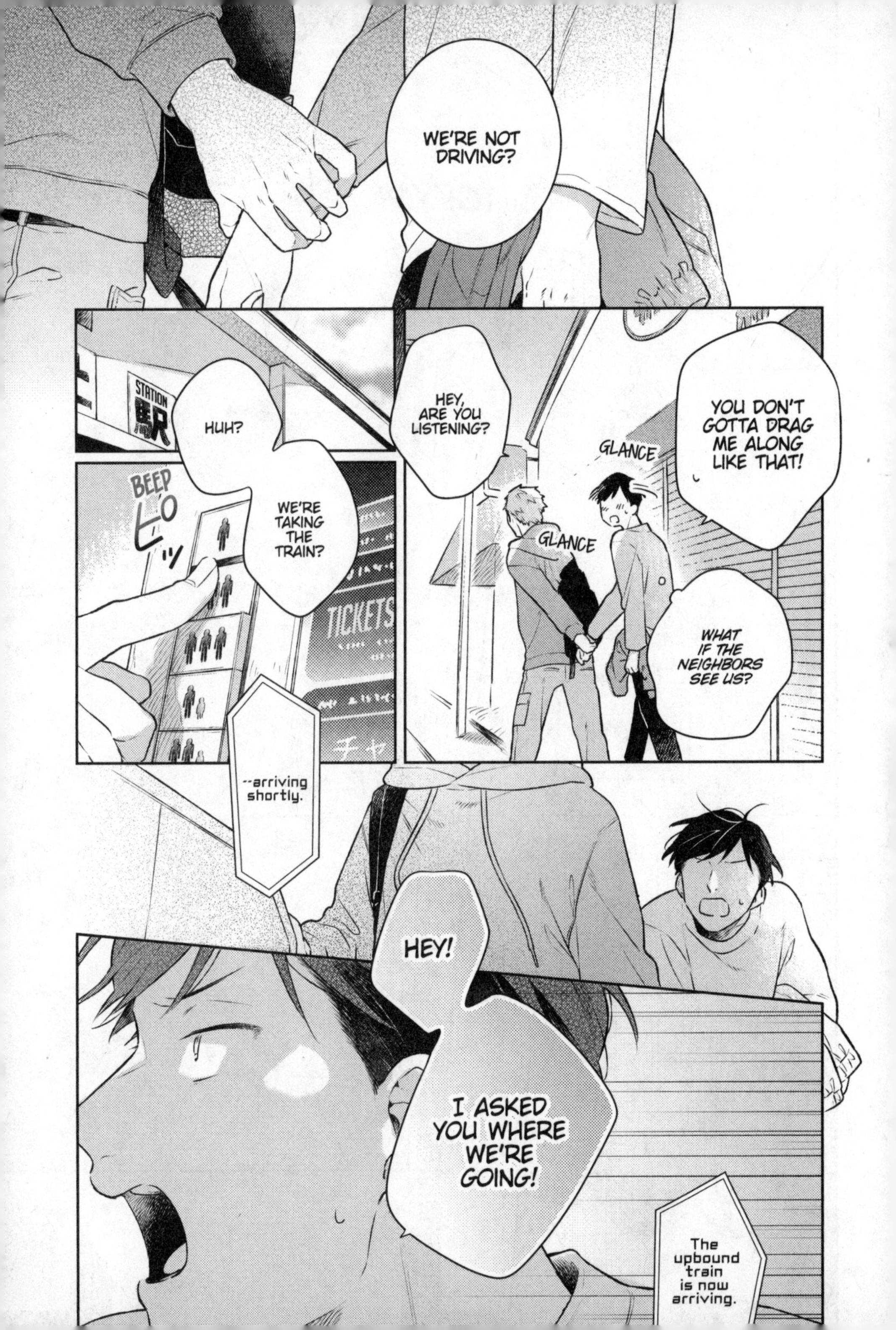
WE'RE NOT DRIVING?
YOU DON'T GOTTA DRAG ME ALONG LIKE THAT!
HEY, ARE YOU LISTENING?
GLANCE
GLANCE
WHAT IF THE NEIGHBORS SEE US?
STATION 駅
HUH?
BEEP ピッ
WE'RE TAKING THE TRAIN?
TICKETS
--arriving shortly.
HEY!
I ASKED YOU WHERE WE'RE GOING!
The upbound train is now arriving.

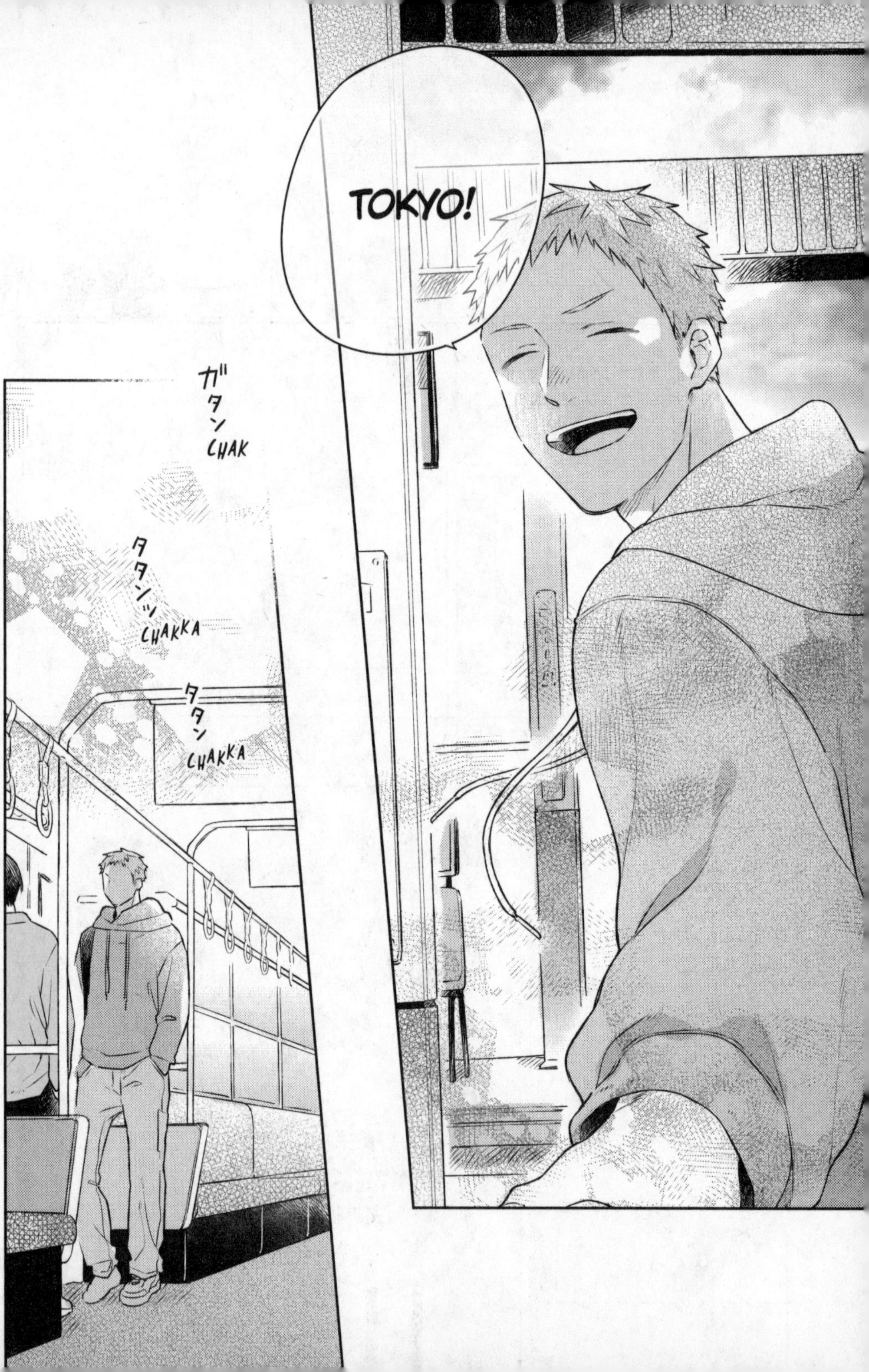
TOKYO!
ガタン
CHAK
タタンッ
CHAKKA
タタン
CHAKKA

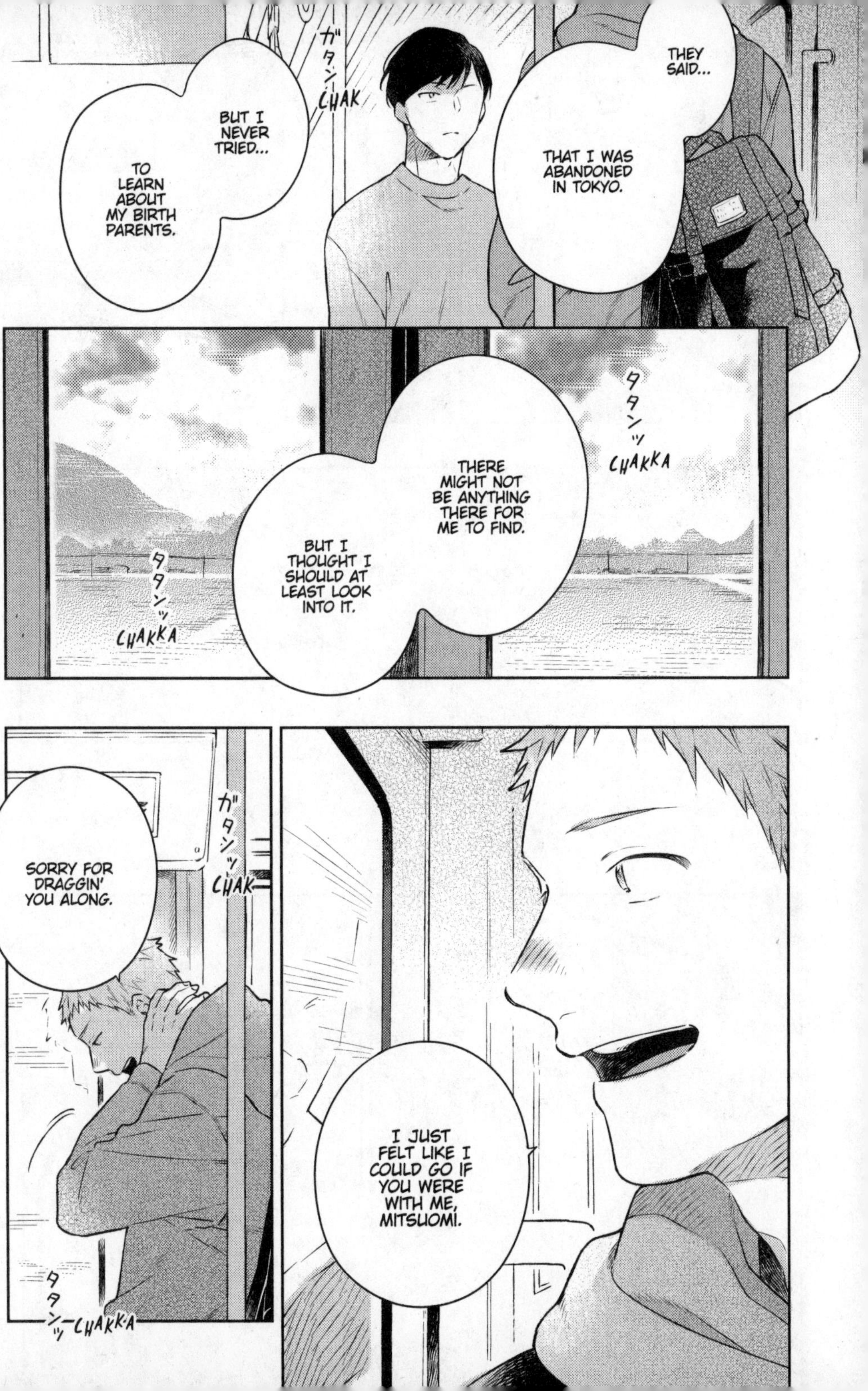
THEY SAID...
THAT I WAS ABANDONED IN TOKYO.
ガタン CHAK
BUT I NEVER TRIED...
TO LEARN ABOUT MY BIRTH PARENTS.
タタンッ CHAKKA
THERE MIGHT NOT BE ANYTHING THERE FOR ME TO FIND.
BUT I THOUGHT I SHOULD AT LEAST LOOK INTO IT.
タタンッ CHAKKA
I JUST FELT LIKE I COULD GO IF YOU WERE WITH ME, MITSUOMI.
ガタンッ CHAK
SORRY FOR DRAGGIN' YOU ALONG.
タタンッ CHAKKA

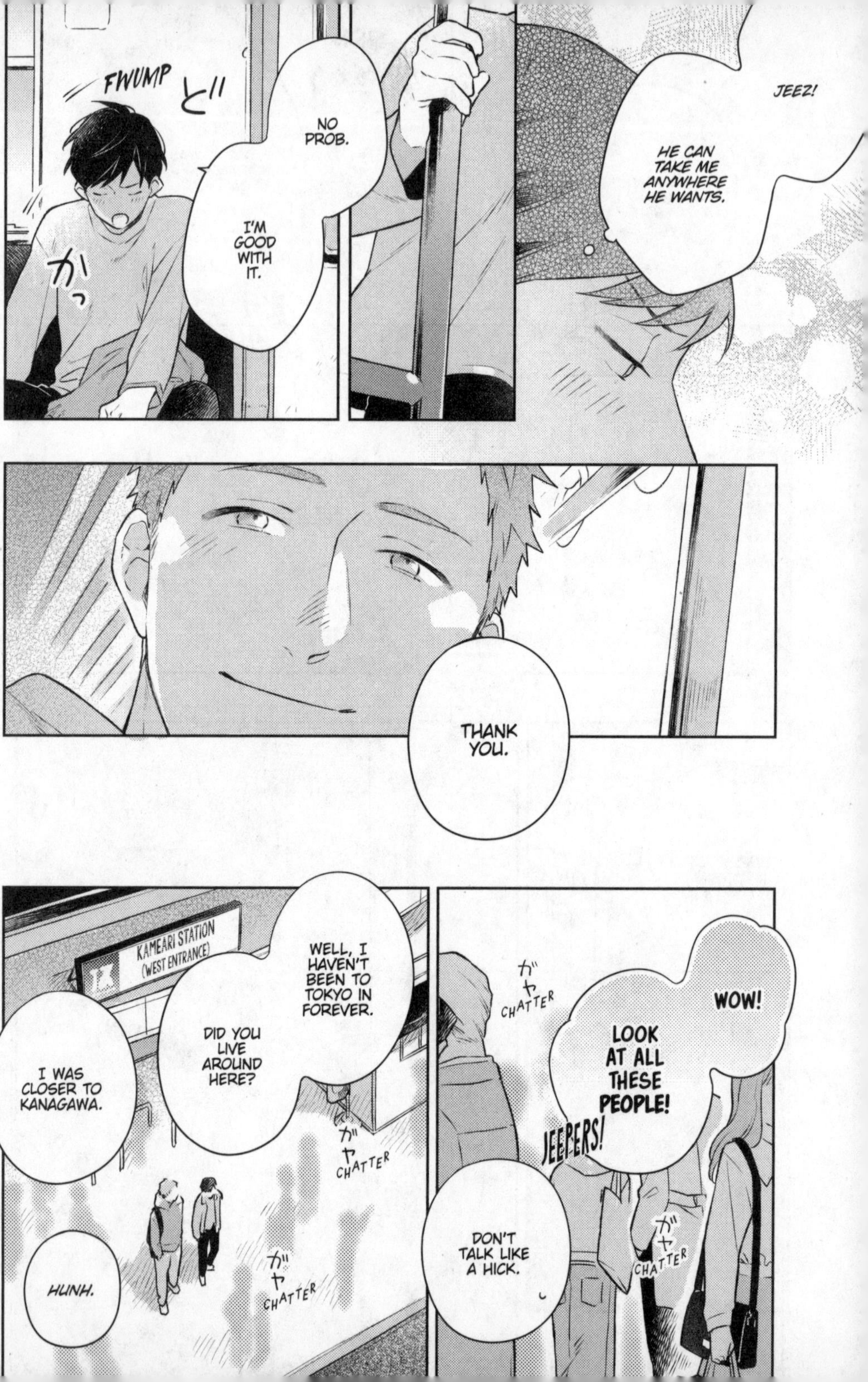
JEEZ!
HE CAN TAKE ME ANYWHERE HE WANTS.
NO PROB.
I'M GOOD WITH IT.
FWUMP
THANK YOU.
WOW!
LOOK AT ALL THESE PEOPLE!
JEEPERS!
ガヤ CHATTER
DON'T TALK LIKE A HICK.
ガヤ CHATTER
KAMEARI STATION (WEST ENTRANCE)
WELL, I HAVEN'T BEEN TO TOKYO IN FOREVER.
DID YOU LIVE AROUND HERE?
I WAS CLOSER TO KANAGAWA.
ガヤ CHATTER
ガヤ CHATTER
HUNH.

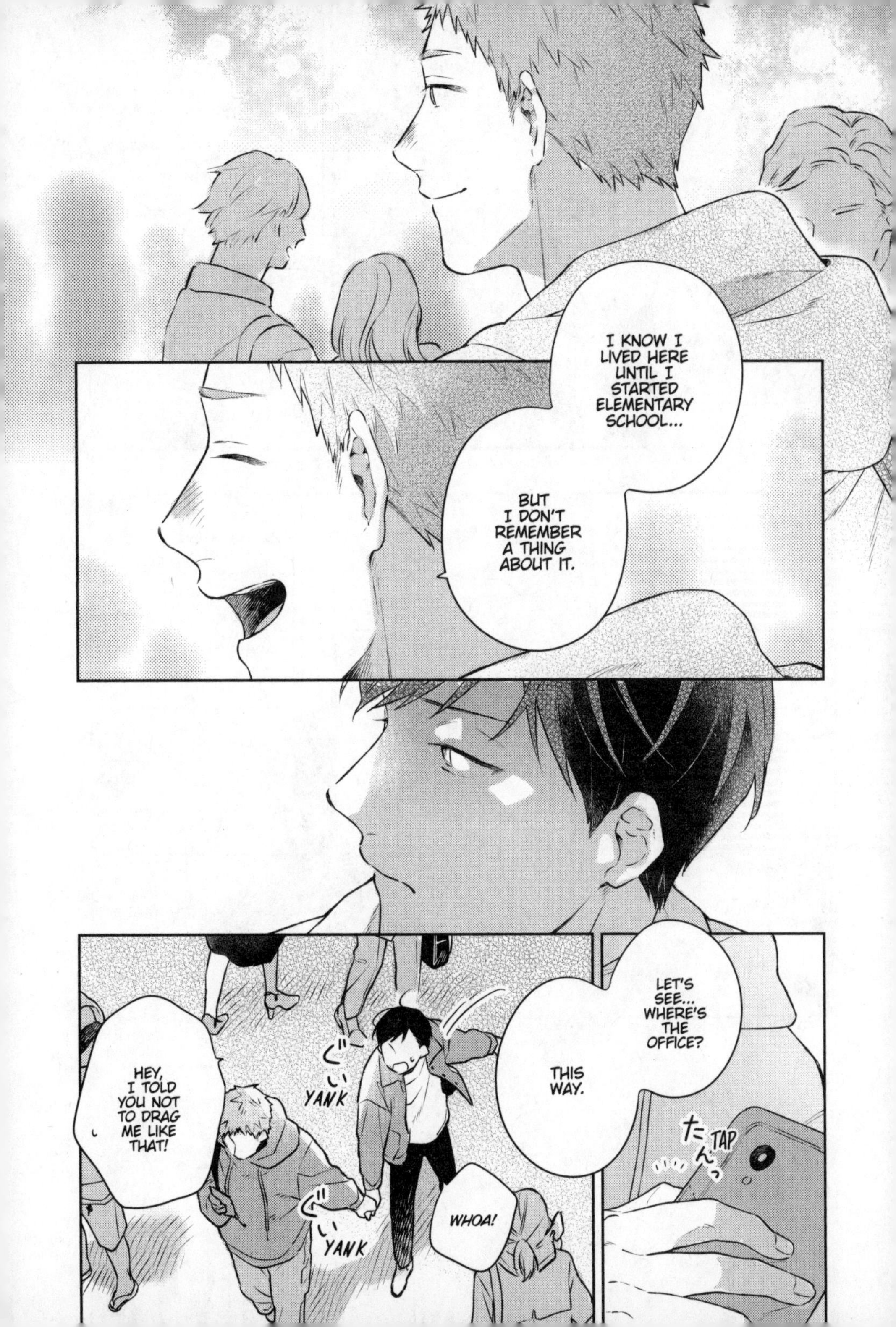
I KNOW I LIVED HERE UNTIL I STARTED ELEMENTARY SCHOOL...
BUT I DON'T REMEMBER A THING ABOUT IT.
LET'S SEE... WHERE'S THE OFFICE?
THIS WAY.
たんっ TAP
ぐい YANK
ぐい YANK
WHOA!
HEY, I TOLD YOU NOT TO DRAG ME LIKE THAT!

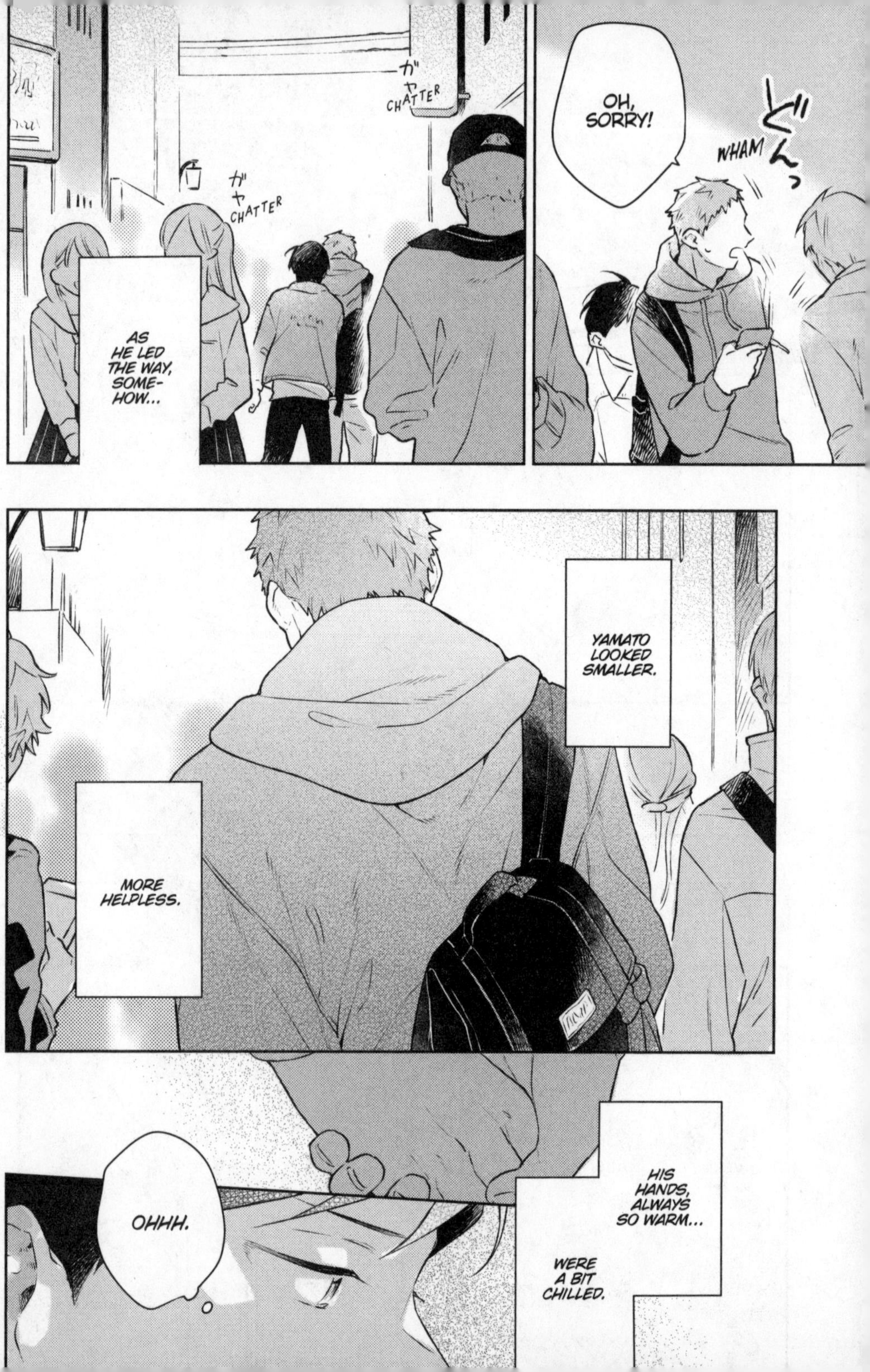

どんっ
WHAM
OH, SORRY!
ガヤ
CHATTER
ガヤ
CHATTER
AS HE LED THE WAY, SOME-HOW...
YAMATO LOOKED SMALLER.
MORE HELPLESS.
HIS HANDS, ALWAYS SO WARM...
WERE A BIT CHILLED.
OHHH.

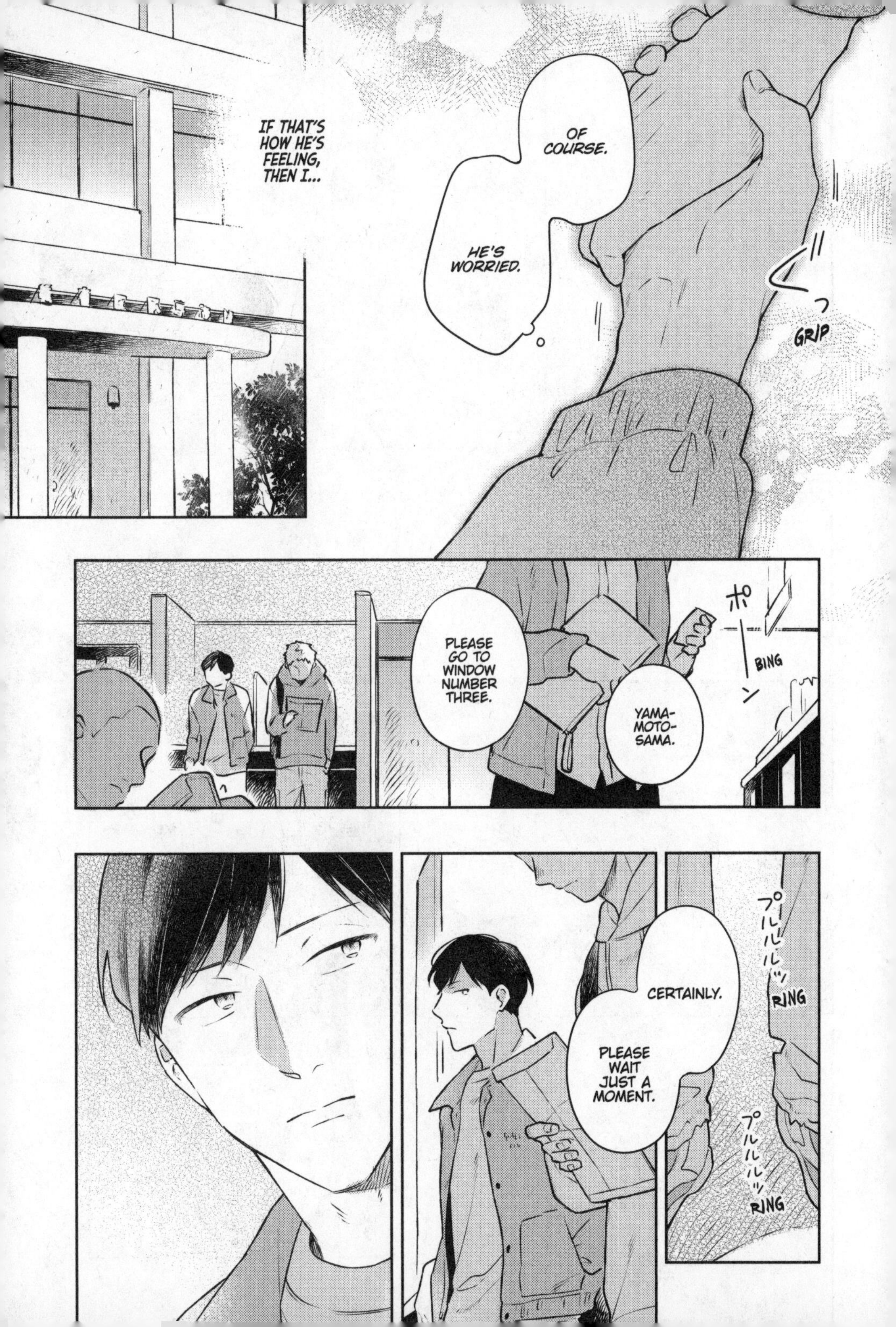
OF COURSE.
HE'S WORRIED.
ぐっ
GRIP
IF THAT'S HOW HE'S FEELING, THEN I...
ポーン
BING
YAMA-MOTO-SAMA.
PLEASE GO TO WINDOW NUMBER THREE.
プルルルッ
RING
プルルルッ
RING
CERTAINLY.
PLEASE WAIT JUST A MOMENT.

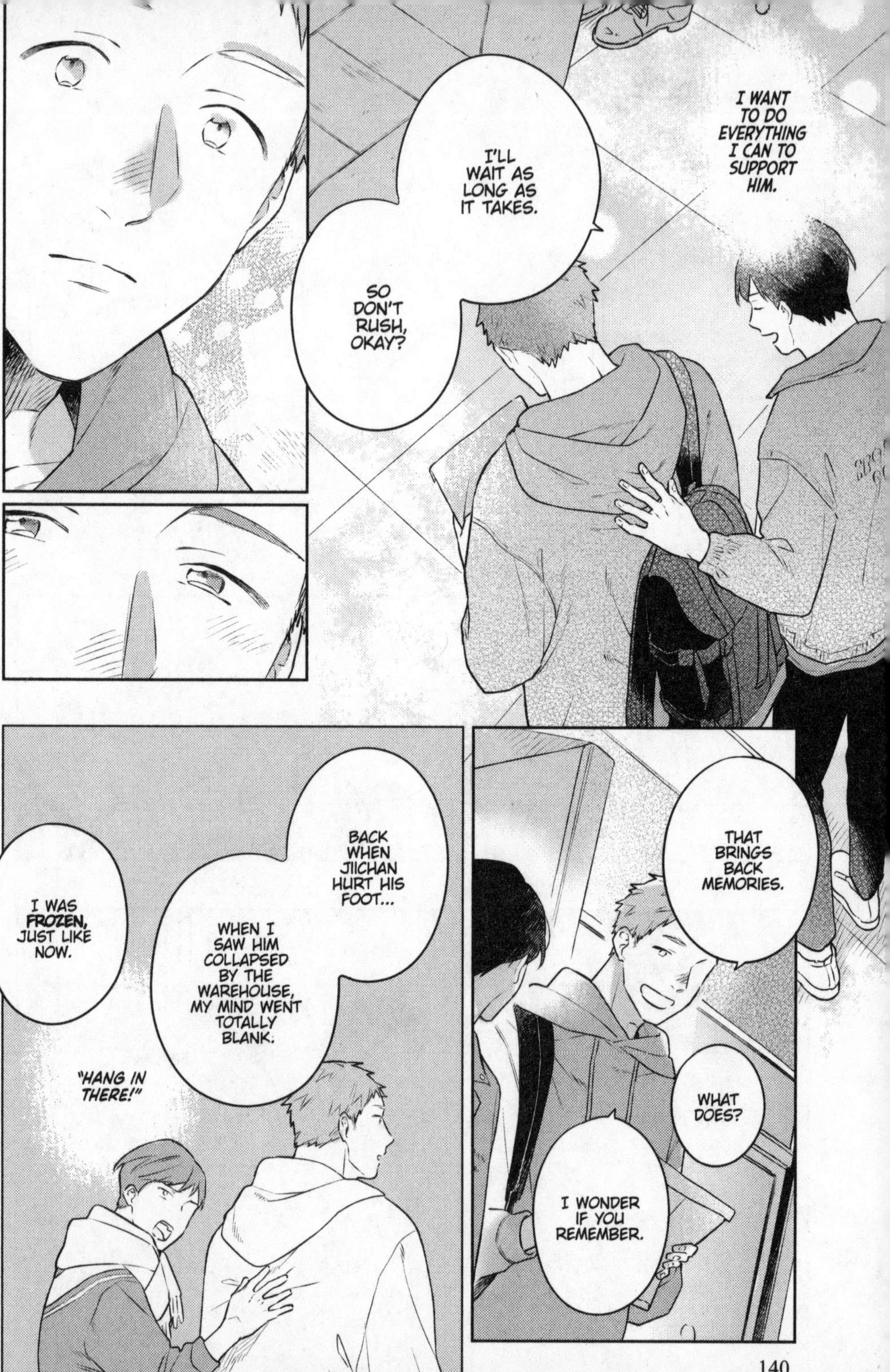
I WANT TO DO EVERYTHING I CAN TO SUPPORT HIM.
I'LL WAIT AS LONG AS IT TAKES.
SO DON'T RUSH, OKAY?
THAT BRINGS BACK MEMORIES.
WHAT DOES?
I WONDER IF YOU REMEMBER.
BACK WHEN JIICHAN HURT HIS FOOT...
WHEN I SAW HIM COLLAPSED BY THE WAREHOUSE, MY MIND WENT TOTALLY BLANK.
I WAS **FROZEN**, JUST LIKE NOW.
"HANG IN THERE!"

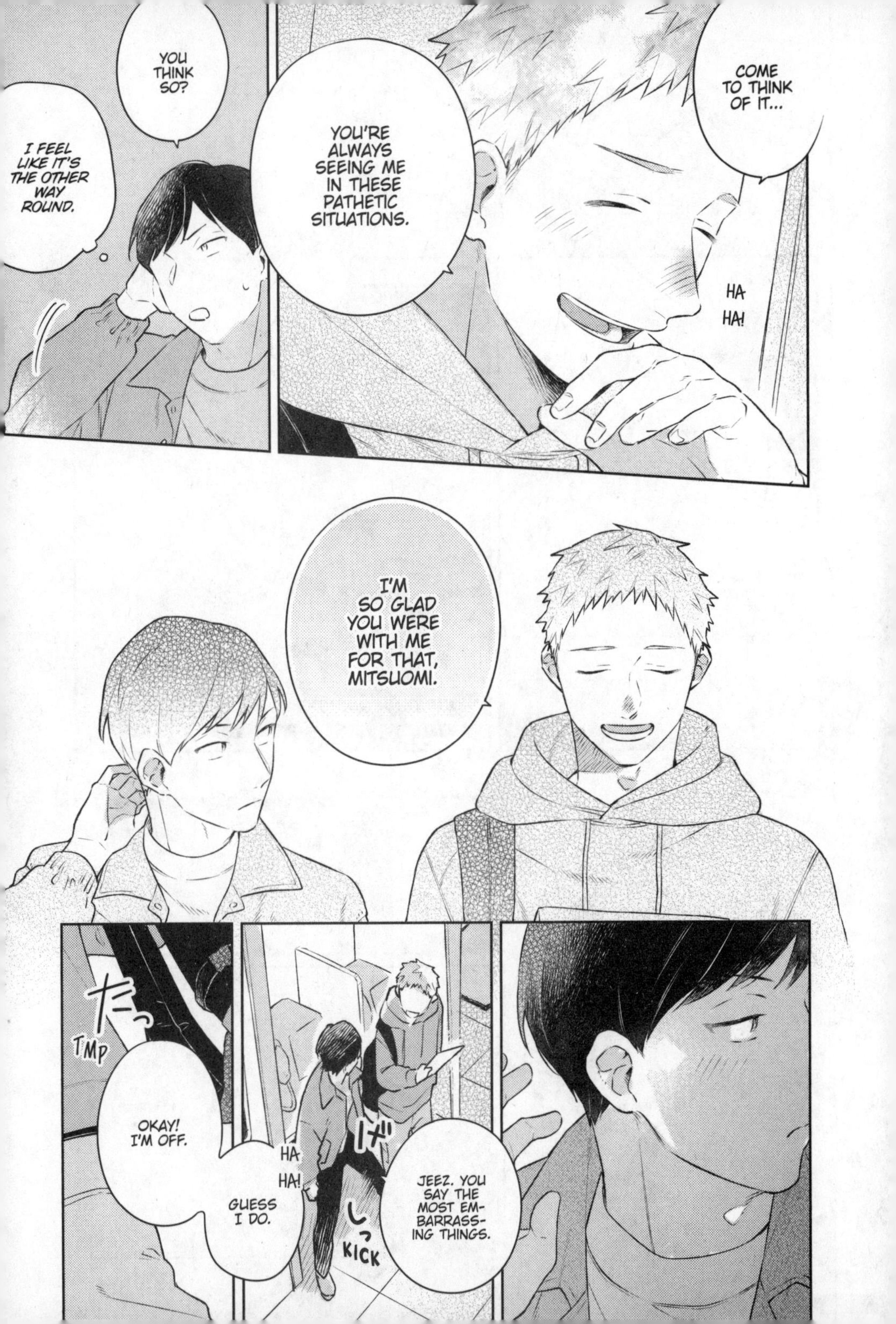

COME TO THINK OF IT...
YOU'RE ALWAYS SEEING ME IN THESE PATHETIC SITUATIONS.
HA HA!
YOU THINK SO?
I FEEL LIKE IT'S THE OTHER WAY ROUND.
I'M SO GLAD YOU WERE WITH ME FOR THAT, MITSUOMI.
JEEZ. YOU SAY THE MOST EM-BARRASS-ING THINGS.
KICK
HA HA! GUESS I DO.
TMP
OKAY! I'M OFF.

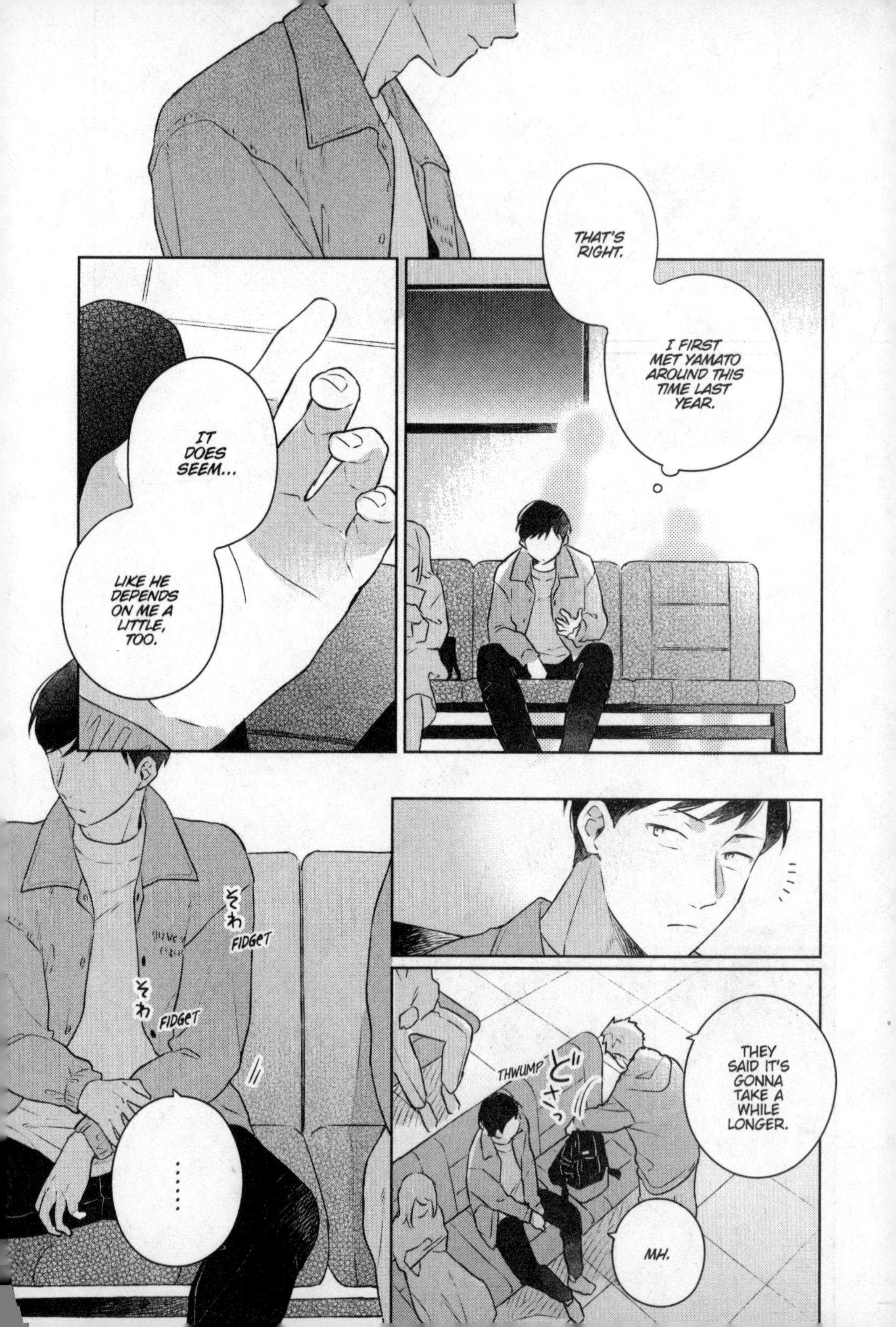
THAT'S RIGHT.
I FIRST MET YAMATO AROUND THIS TIME LAST YEAR.
IT DOES SEEM...
LIKE HE DEPENDS ON ME A LITTLE, TOO.
THEY SAID IT'S GONNA TAKE A WHILE LONGER.
THWUMP
MH.
そわ FIDGET
そわ FIDGET
......

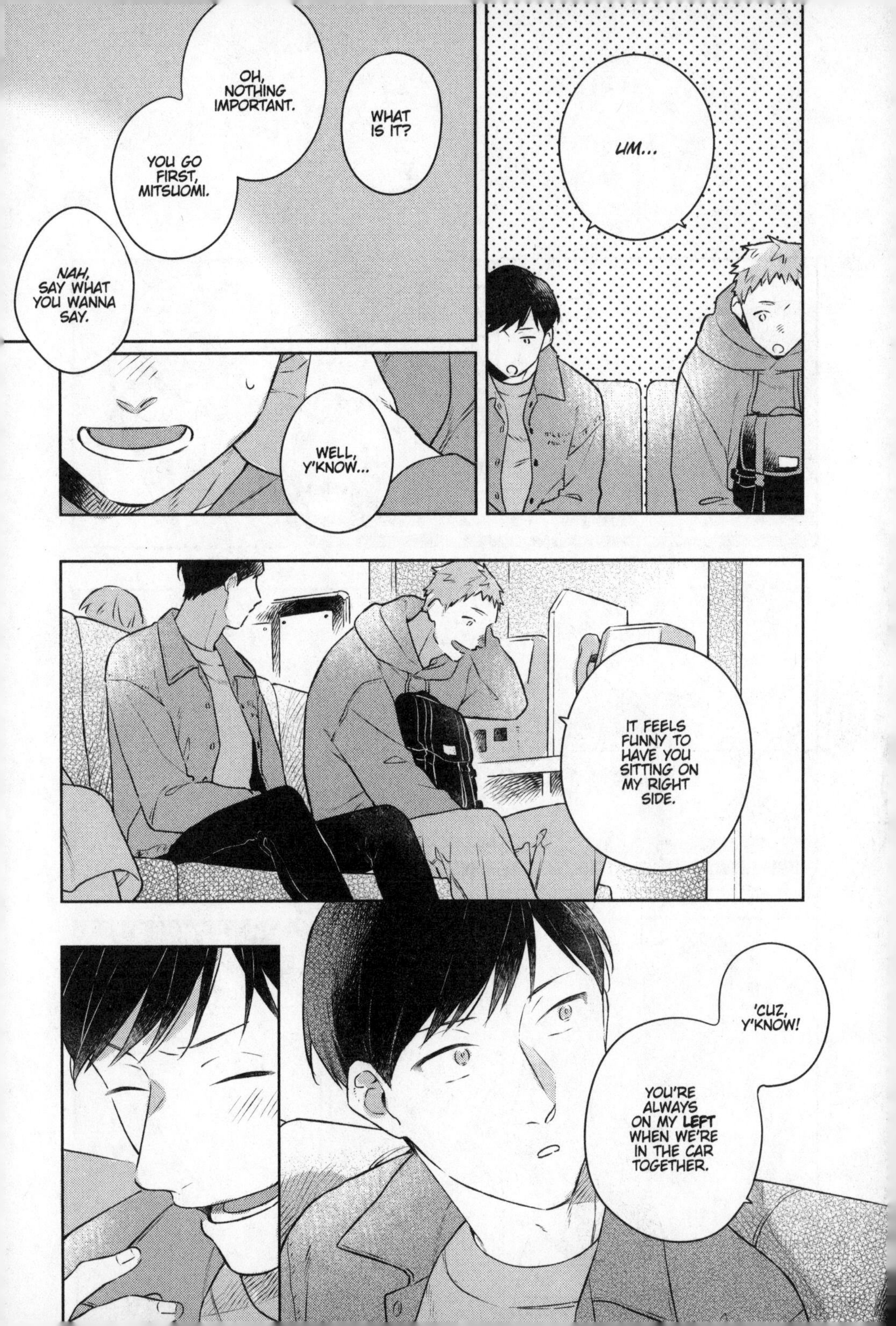
UM...
WHAT IS IT?
OH, NOTHING IMPORTANT.
YOU GO FIRST, MITSUOMI.
NAH, SAY WHAT YOU WANNA SAY.
WELL, Y'KNOW...
IT FEELS FUNNY TO HAVE YOU SITTING ON MY RIGHT SIDE.
'CUZ, Y'KNOW!
YOU'RE ALWAYS ON MY **LEFT** WHEN WE'RE IN THE CAR TOGETHER.

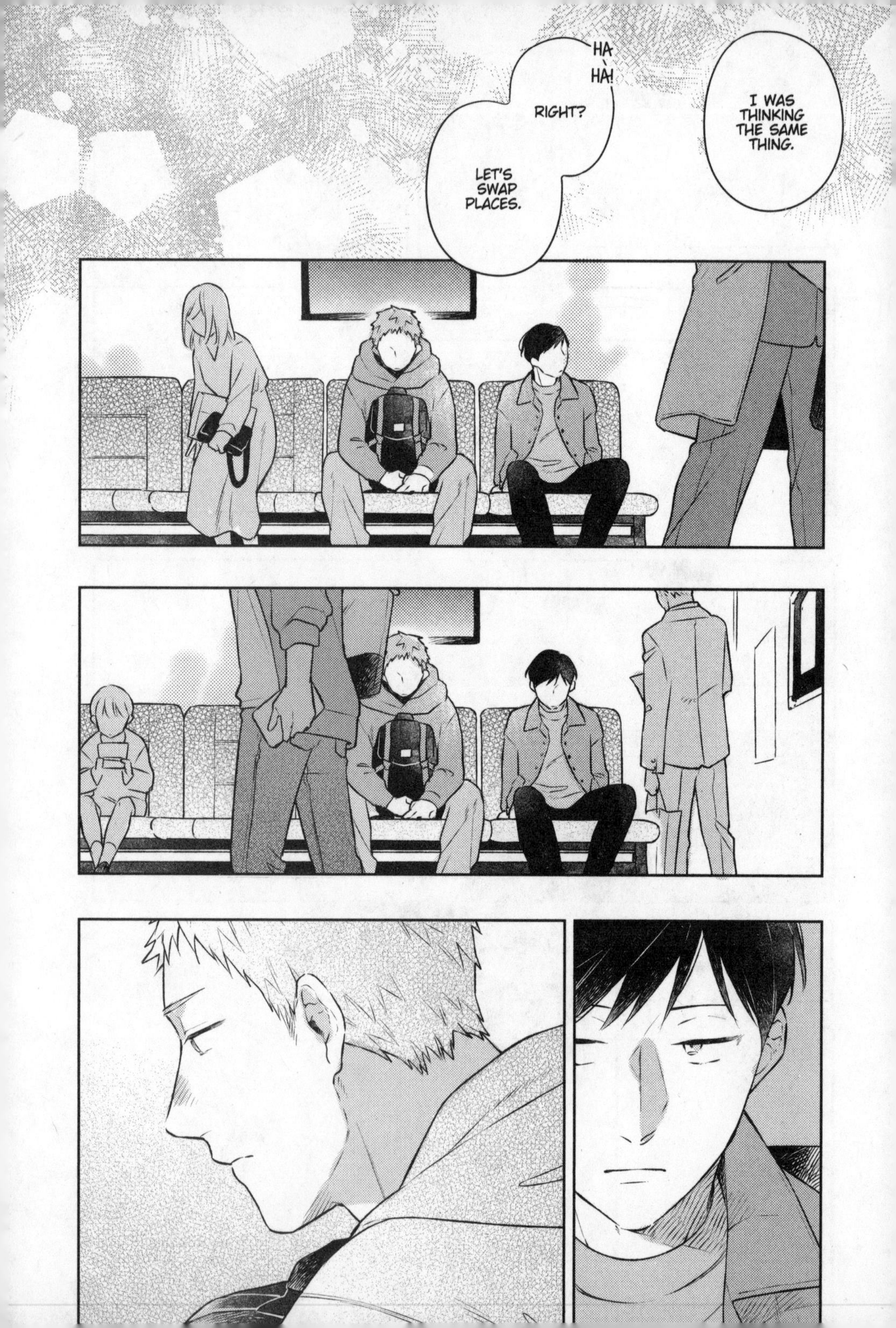
I WAS THINKING THE SAME THING.
HA HA!
RIGHT?
LET'S SWAP PLACES.

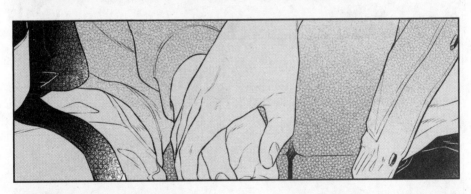

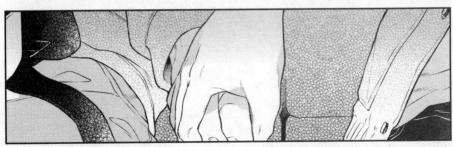

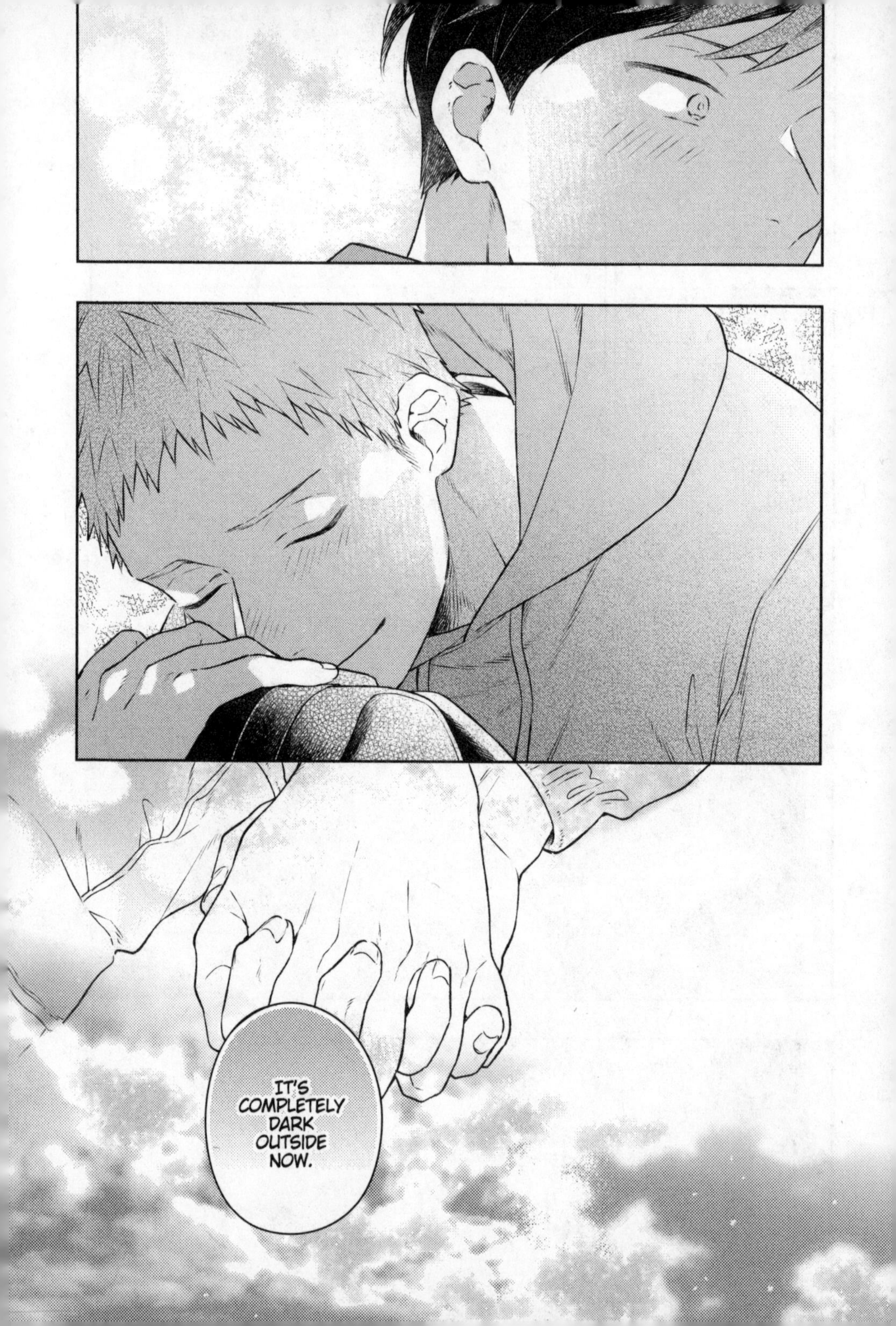
IT'S COMPLETELY DARK OUTSIDE NOW.

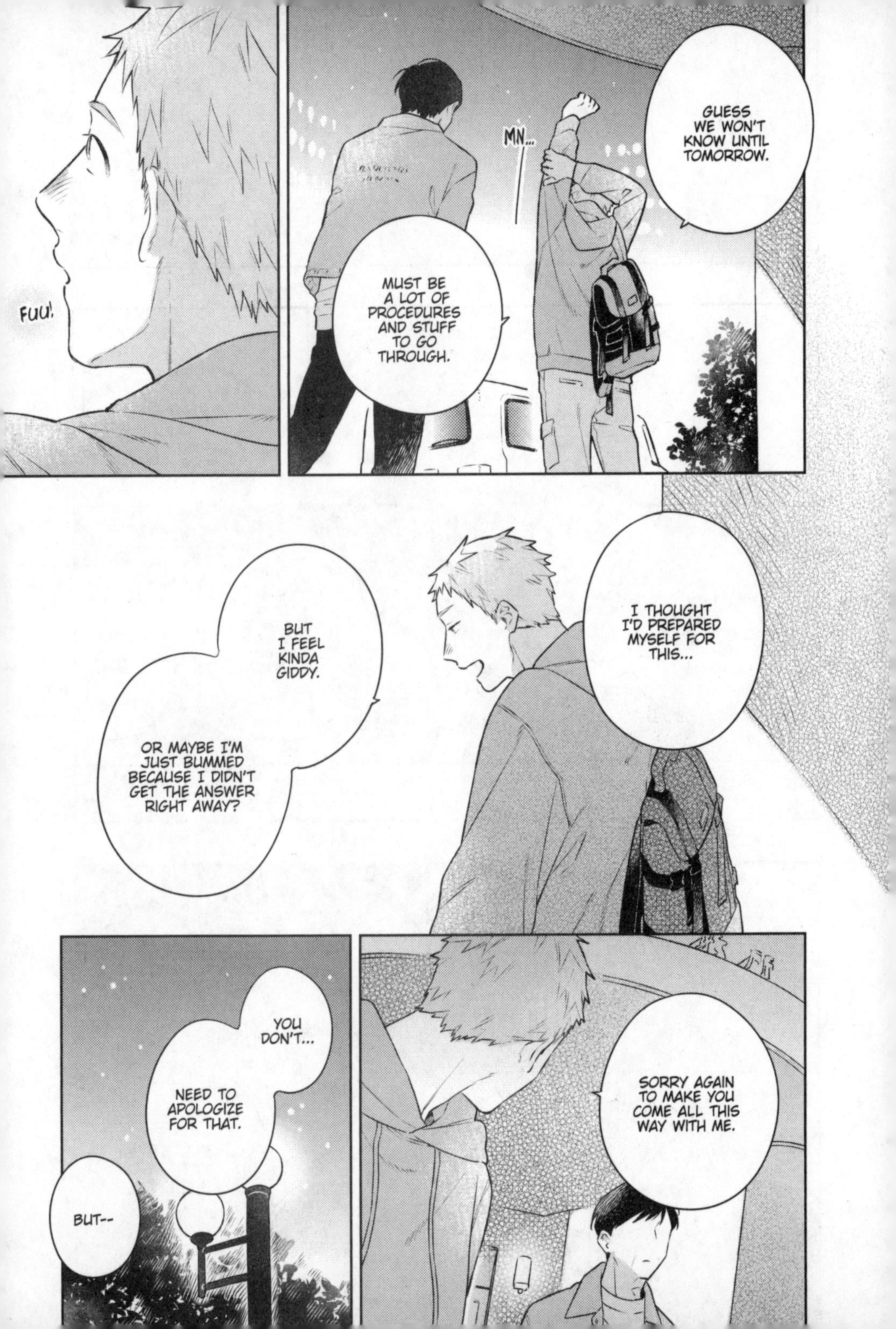
GUESS WE WON'T KNOW UNTIL TOMORROW.
MN...
MUST BE A LOT OF PROCEDURES AND STUFF TO GO THROUGH.
FUU!
I THOUGHT I'D PREPARED MYSELF FOR THIS...
BUT I FEEL KINDA GIDDY.
OR MAYBE I'M JUST BUMMED BECAUSE I DIDN'T GET THE ANSWER RIGHT AWAY?
SORRY AGAIN TO MAKE YOU COME ALL THIS WAY WITH ME.
YOU DON'T...
NEED TO APOLOGIZE FOR THAT.
BUT--

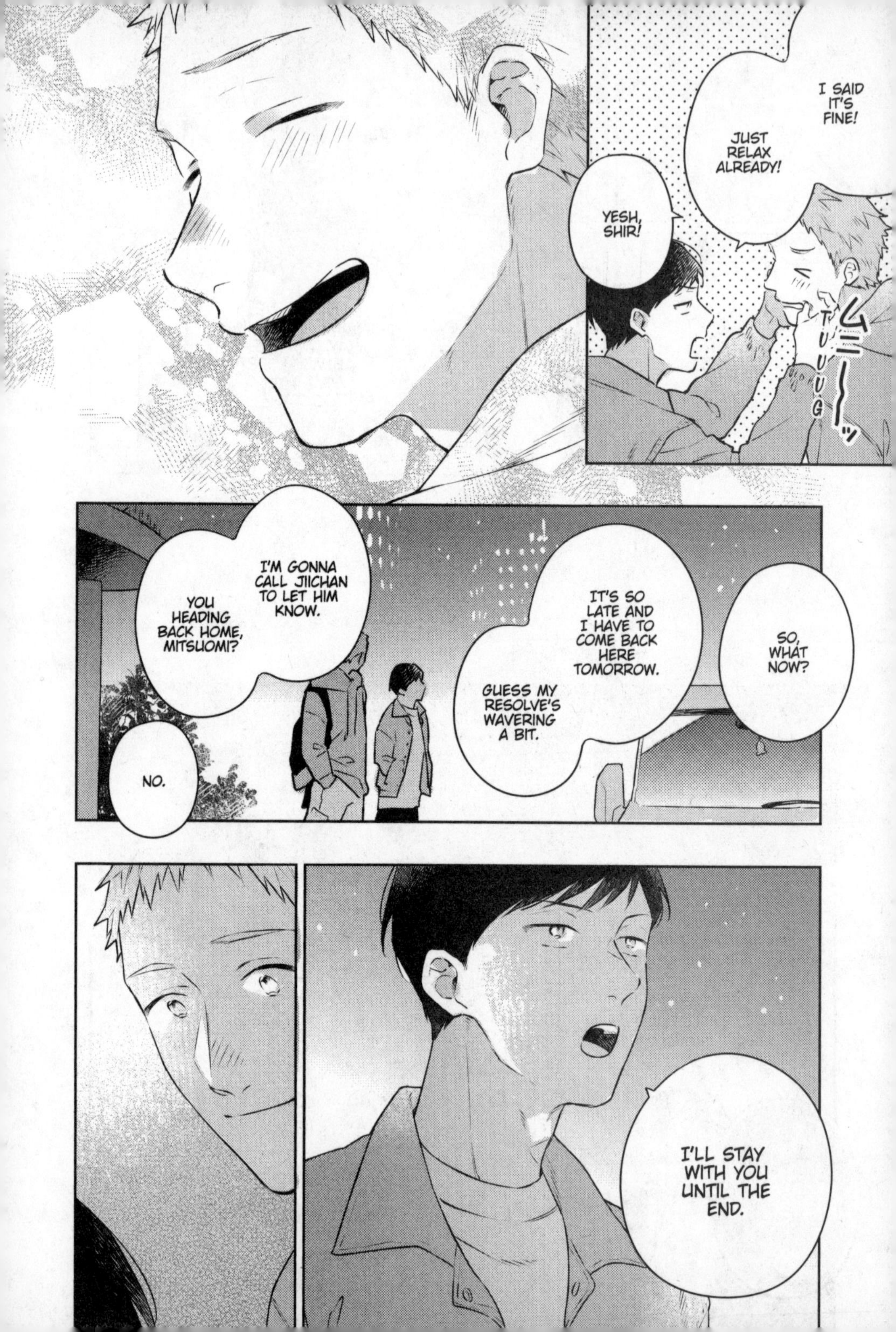
I SAID IT'S FINE!
JUST RELAX ALREADY!
YESH, SHIR!
ムニーッ
TUUUG
SO, WHAT NOW?
IT'S SO LATE AND I HAVE TO COME BACK HERE TOMORROW.
GUESS MY RESOLVE'S WAVERING A BIT.
I'M GONNA CALL JIICHAN TO LET HIM KNOW.
YOU HEADING BACK HOME, MITSUOMI?
NO.
I'LL STAY WITH YOU UNTIL THE END.

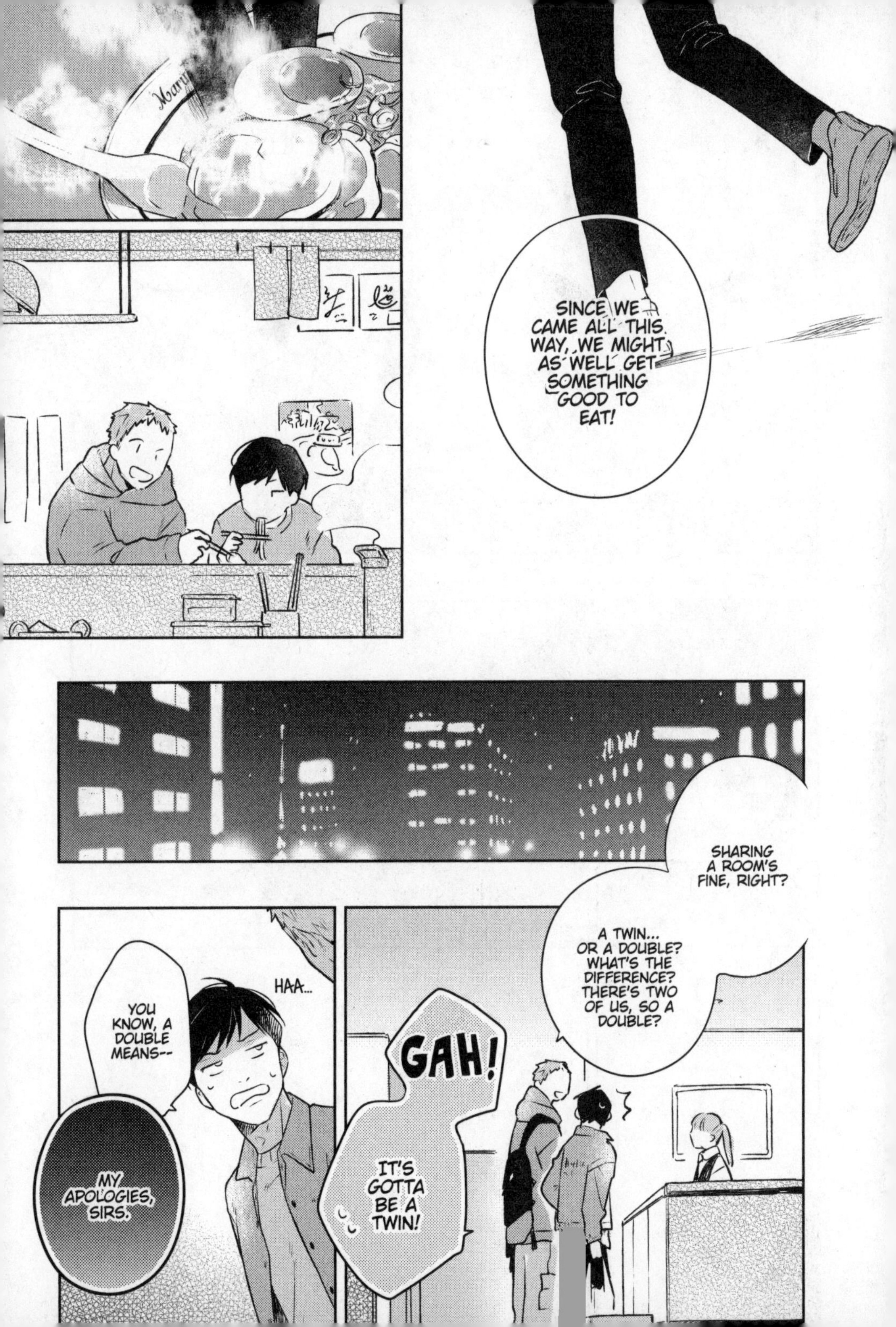
SINCE WE CAME ALL THIS WAY, WE MIGHT AS WELL GET SOMETHING GOOD TO EAT!
SHARING A ROOM'S FINE, RIGHT?
A TWIN... OR A DOUBLE? WHAT'S THE DIFFERENCE? THERE'S TWO OF US, SO A DOUBLE?
GAH!
IT'S GOTTA BE A TWIN!
HAA...
YOU KNOW, A DOUBLE MEANS--
MY APOLOGIES, SIRS.

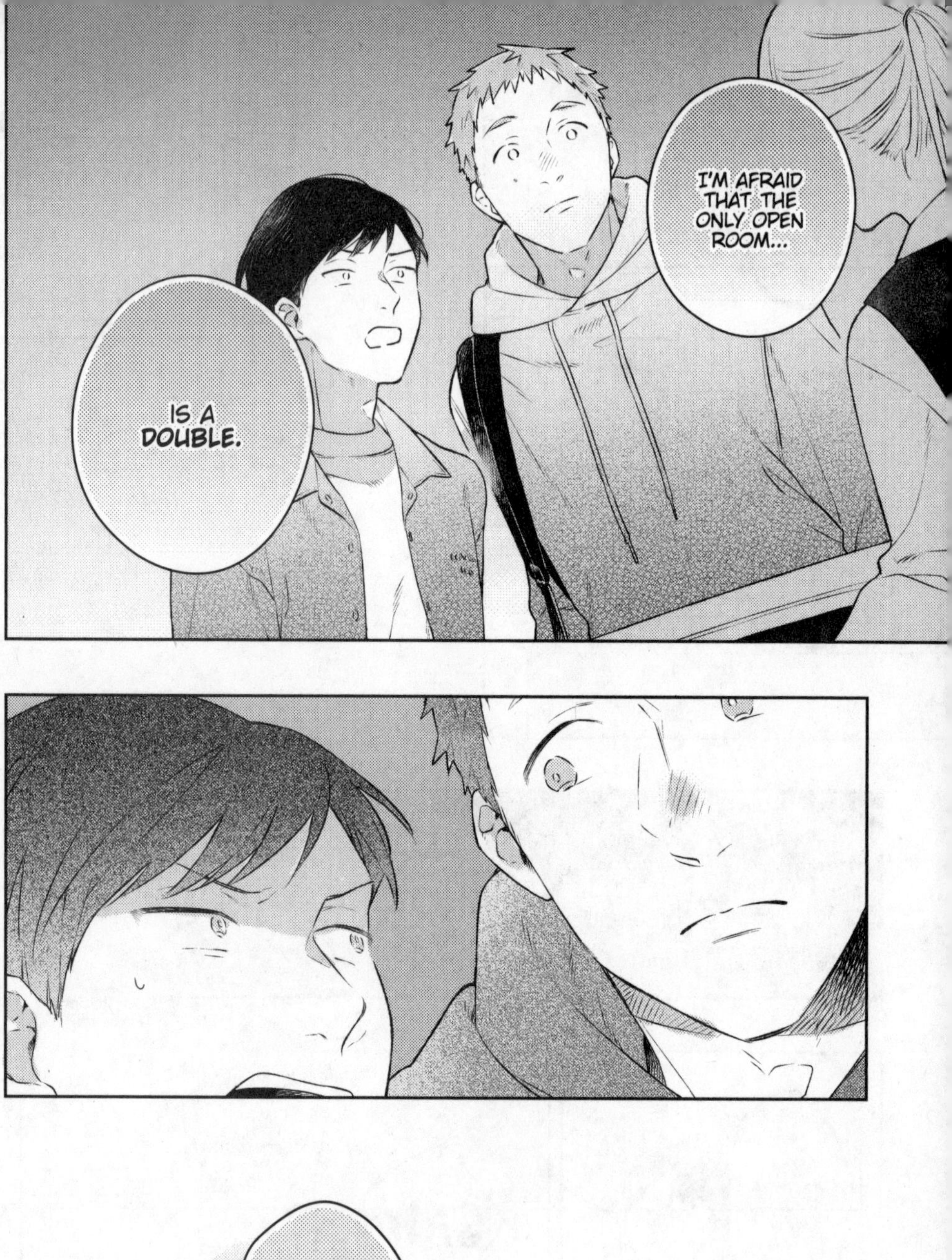
I'M AFRAID THAT THE ONLY OPEN ROOM...
IS A DOUBLE.
HUH?

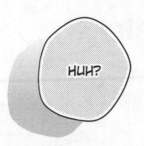

#006

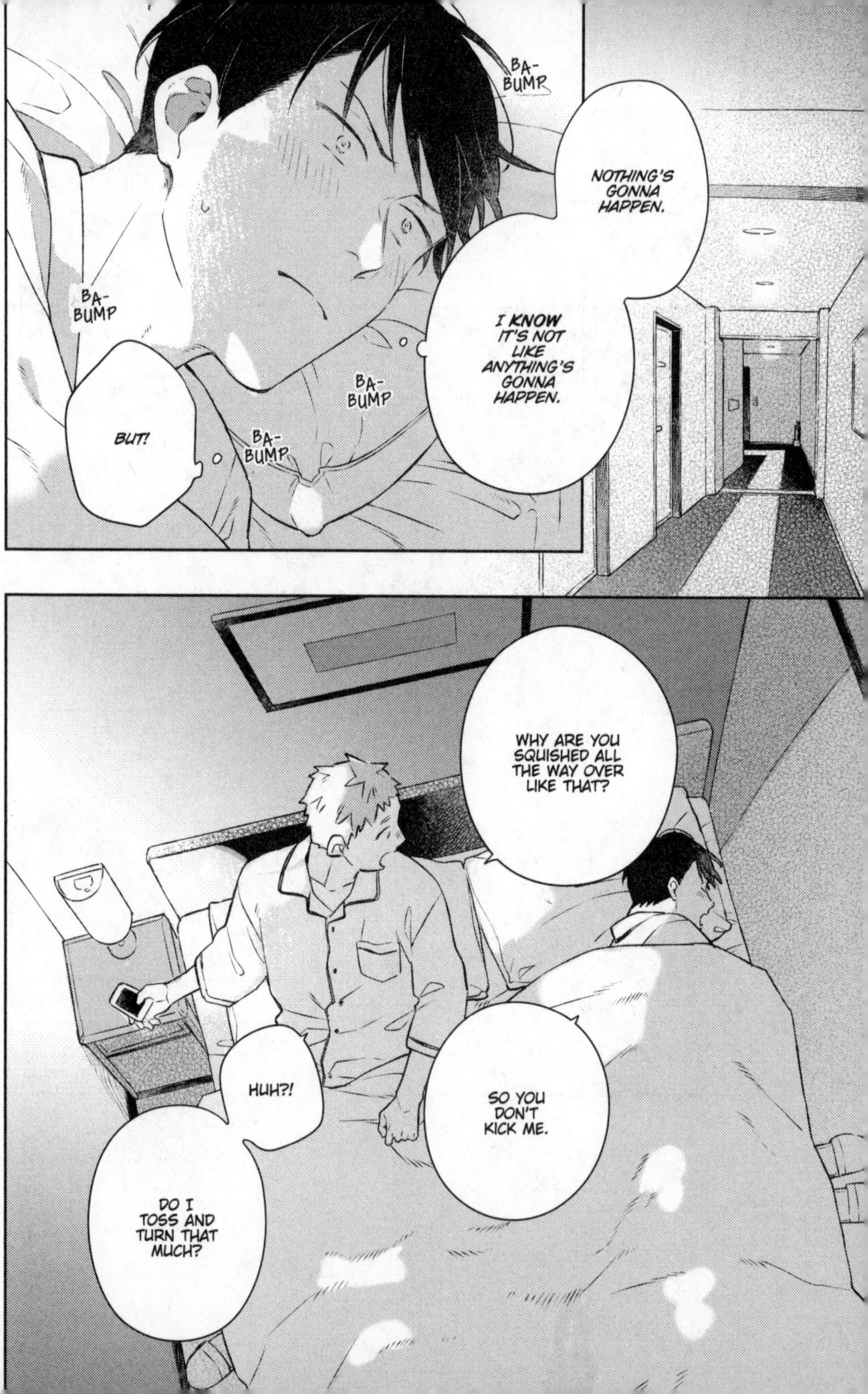
BA-BUMP
NOTHING'S GONNA HAPPEN.
I **KNOW** IT'S NOT LIKE ANYTHING'S GONNA HAPPEN.
BA-BUMP
BA-BUMP
BA-BUMP
BUT!
WHY ARE YOU SQUISHED ALL THE WAY OVER LIKE THAT?
SO YOU DON'T KICK ME.
HUH?!
DO I TOSS AND TURN THAT MUCH?

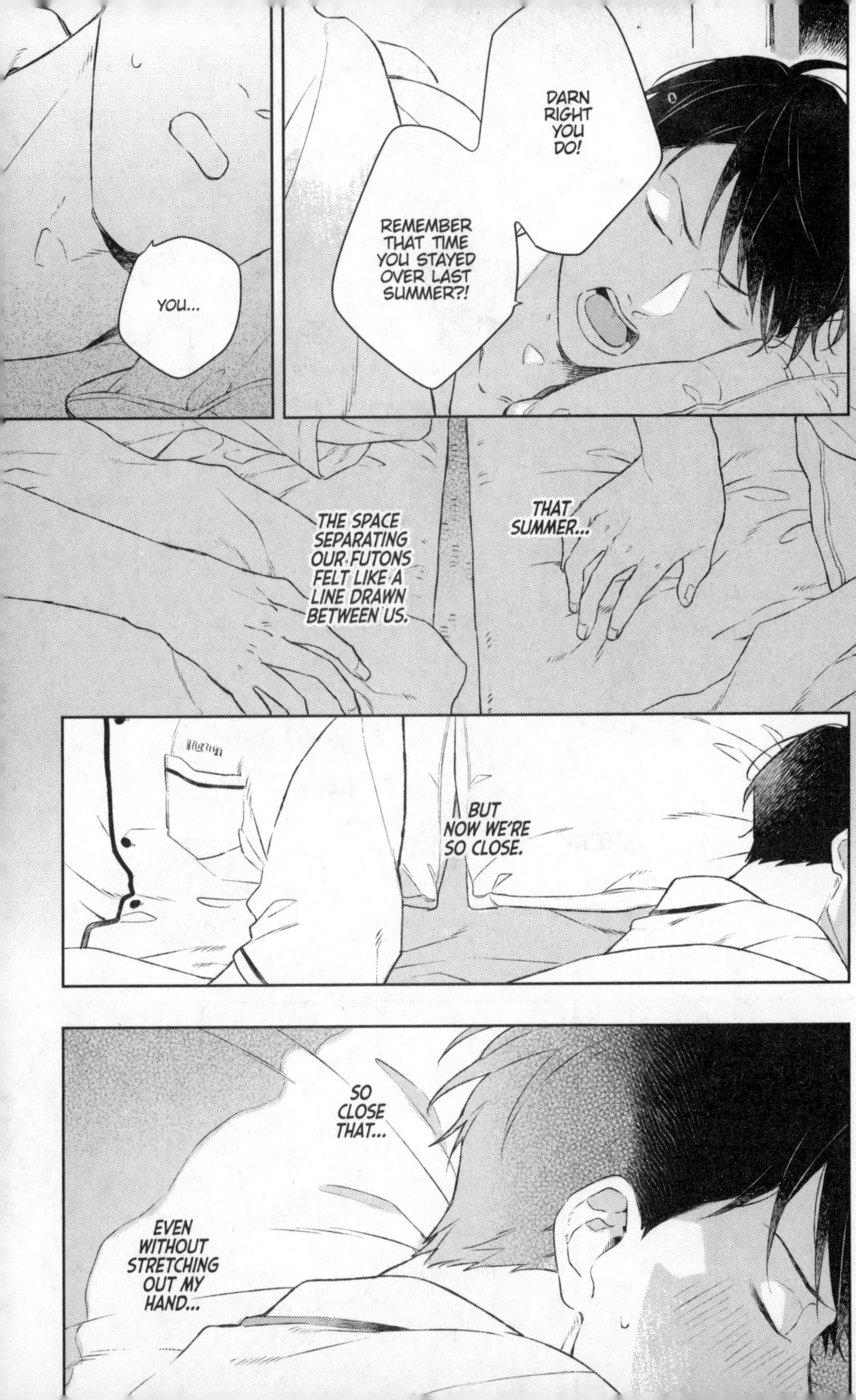
DARN RIGHT YOU DO!
REMEMBER THAT TIME YOU STAYED OVER LAST SUMMER?!
YOU...
THAT SUMMER...
THE SPACE SEPARATING OUR FUTONS FELT LIKE A LINE DRAWN BETWEEN US.
BUT NOW WE'RE SO CLOSE.
SO CLOSE THAT...
EVEN WITHOUT STRETCHING OUT MY HAND...

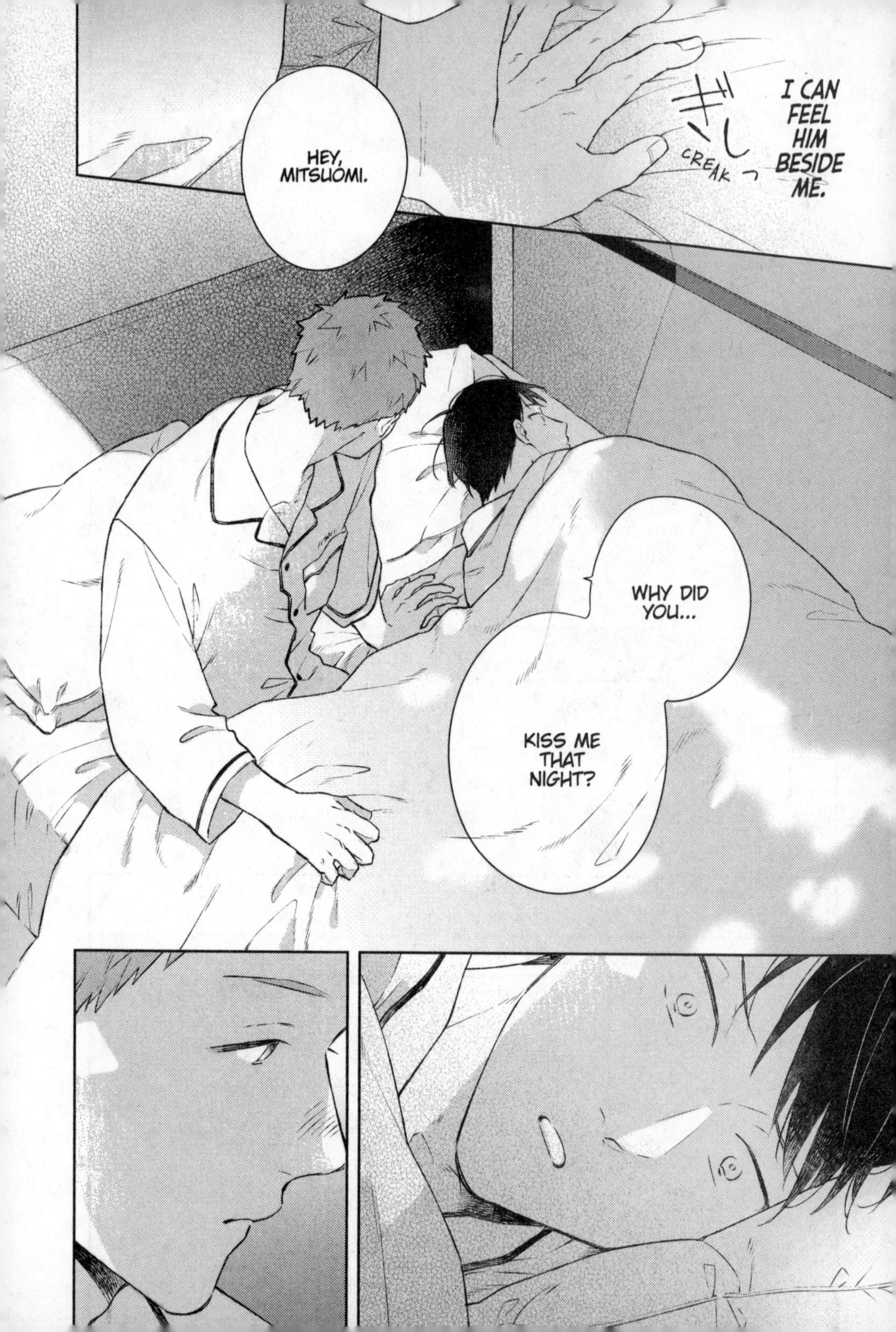

I CAN FEEL HIM BESIDE ME.
ぎしっ
CREAK
HEY, MITSUOMI.
WHY DID YOU...
KISS ME THAT NIGHT?

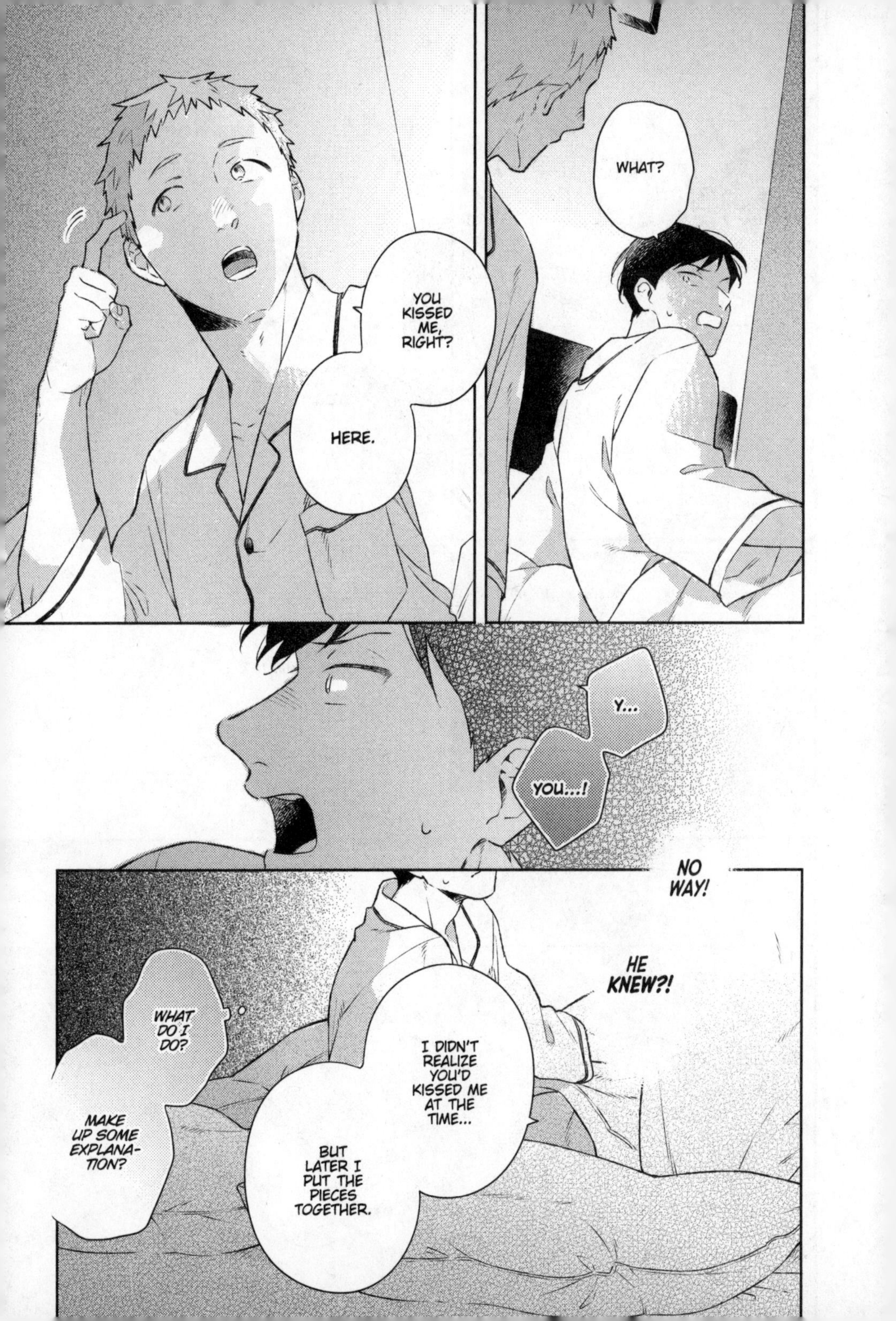
WHAT?
YOU KISSED ME, RIGHT?
HERE.
Y...
YOU...!
NO WAY!
HE KNEW?!
I DIDN'T REALIZE YOU'D KISSED ME AT THE TIME...
BUT LATER I PUT THE PIECES TOGETHER.
WHAT DO I DO?
MAKE UP SOME EXPLANATION?

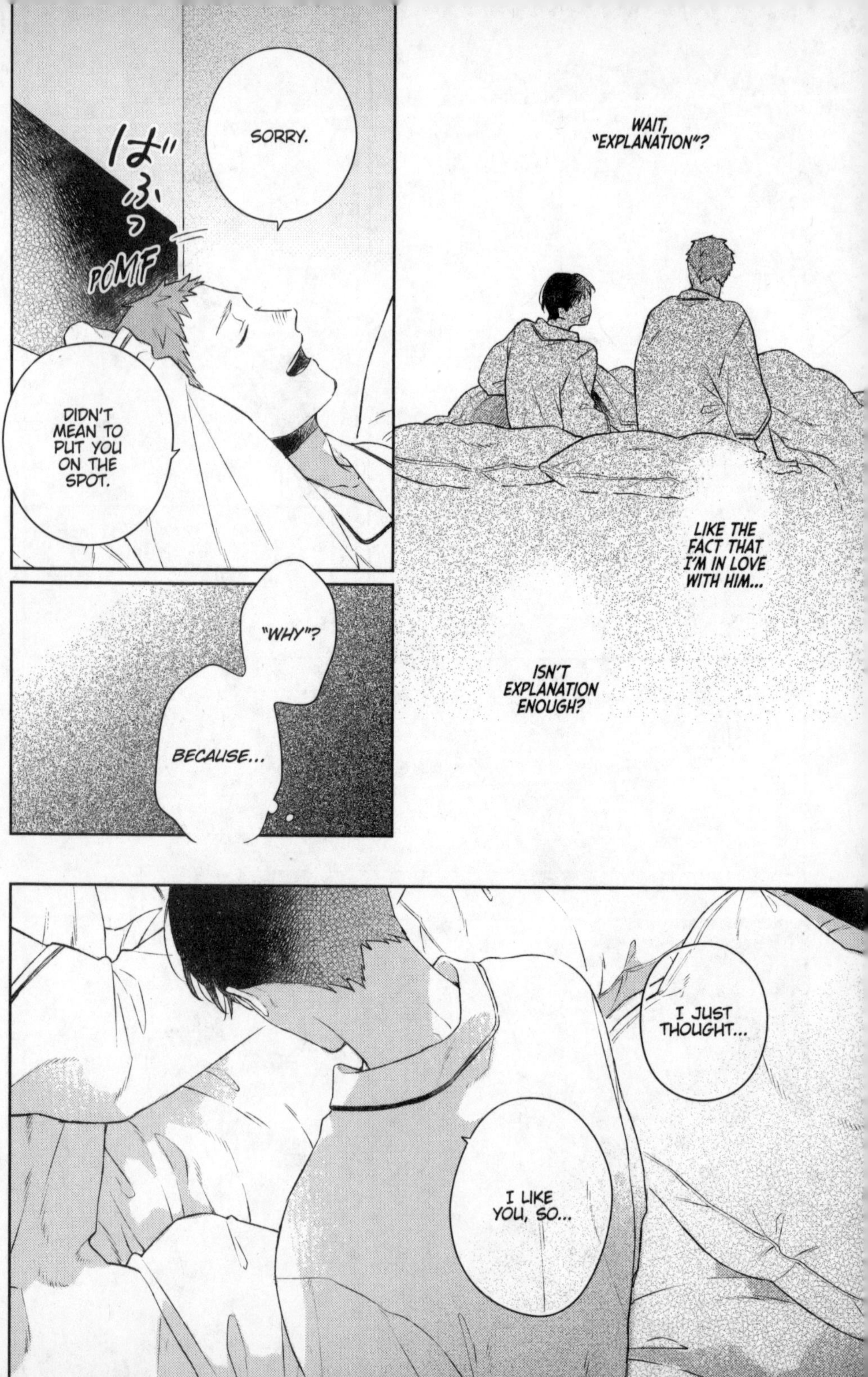
WAIT, "EXPLANATION"?
LIKE THE FACT THAT I'M IN LOVE WITH HIM...
ISN'T EXPLANATION ENOUGH?
SORRY.
ばふっ
POMF
DIDN'T MEAN TO PUT YOU ON THE SPOT.
"WHY"?
BECAUSE...
I JUST THOUGHT...
I LIKE YOU, SO...

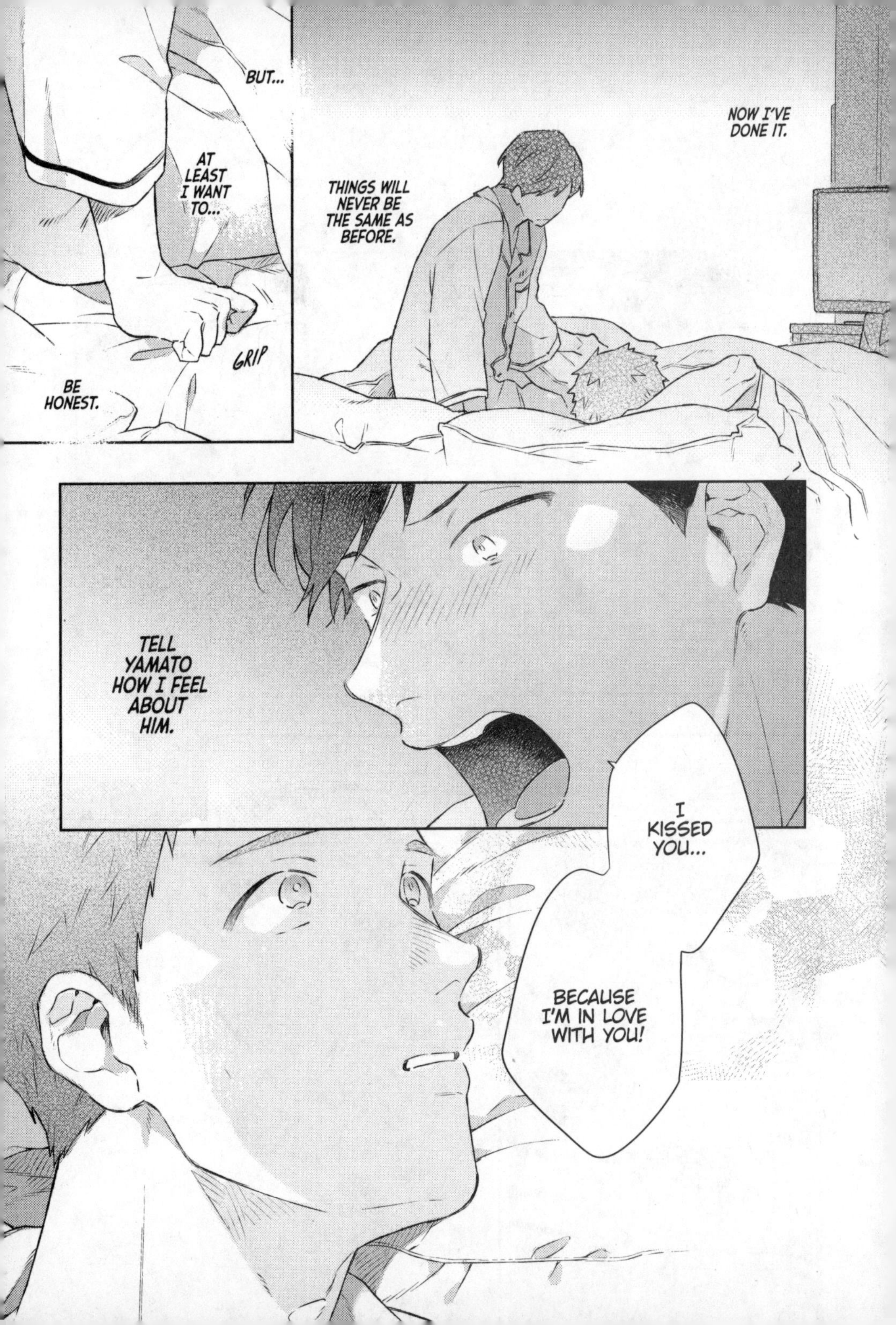
NOW I'VE DONE IT.
THINGS WILL NEVER BE THE SAME AS BEFORE.
BUT...
AT LEAST I WANT TO...
GRIP
BE HONEST.
TELL YAMATO HOW I FEEL ABOUT HIM.
I KISSED YOU...
BECAUSE I'M IN LOVE WITH YOU!

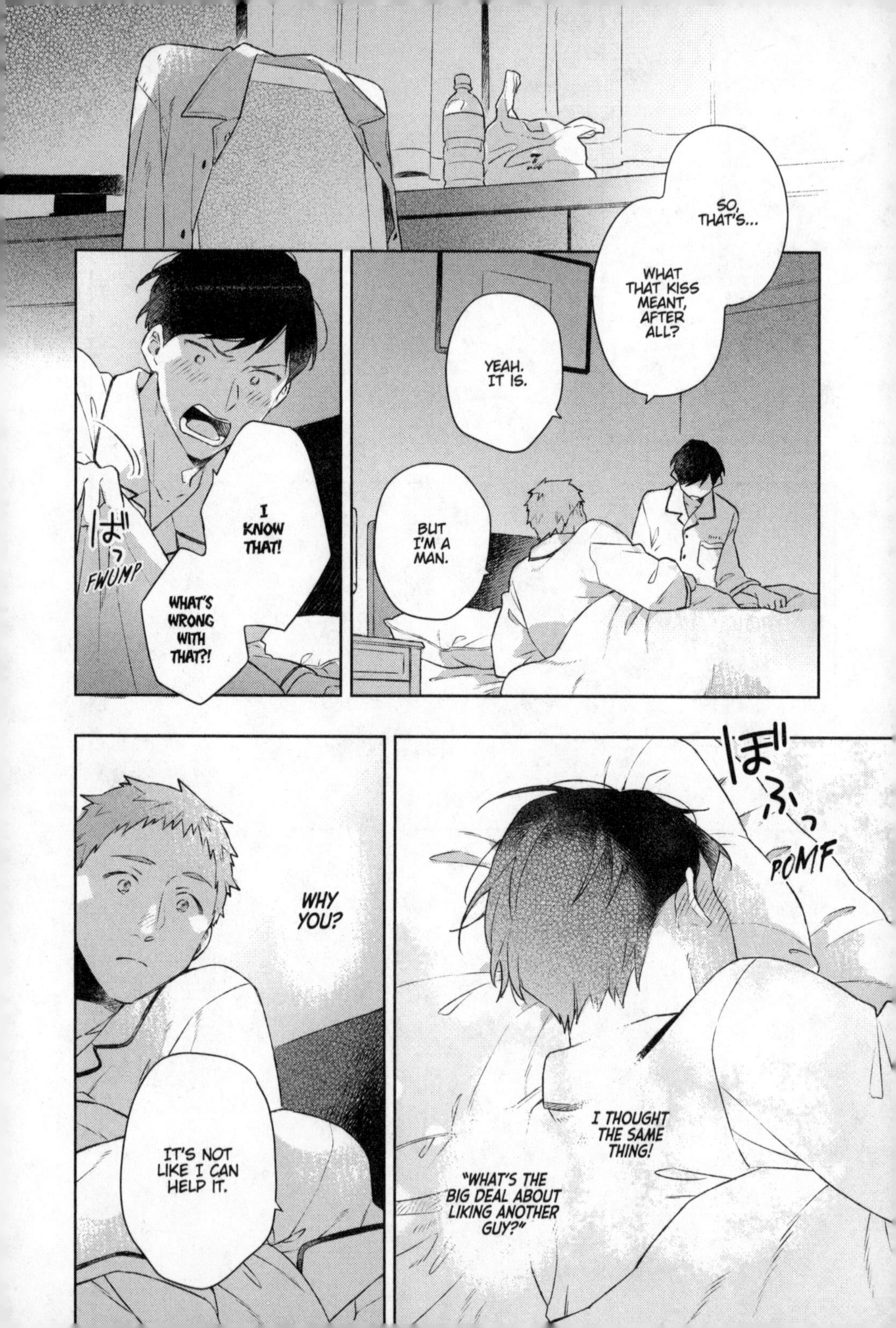

SO, THAT'S...
WHAT THAT KISS MEANT, AFTER ALL?
YEAH. IT IS.
BUT I'M A MAN.
I KNOW THAT!
ばっ
FWUMP
WHAT'S WRONG WITH THAT?!
ぼふっ
POMF
I THOUGHT THE SAME THING!
"WHAT'S THE BIG DEAL ABOUT LIKING ANOTHER GUY?"
WHY YOU?
IT'S NOT LIKE I CAN HELP IT.

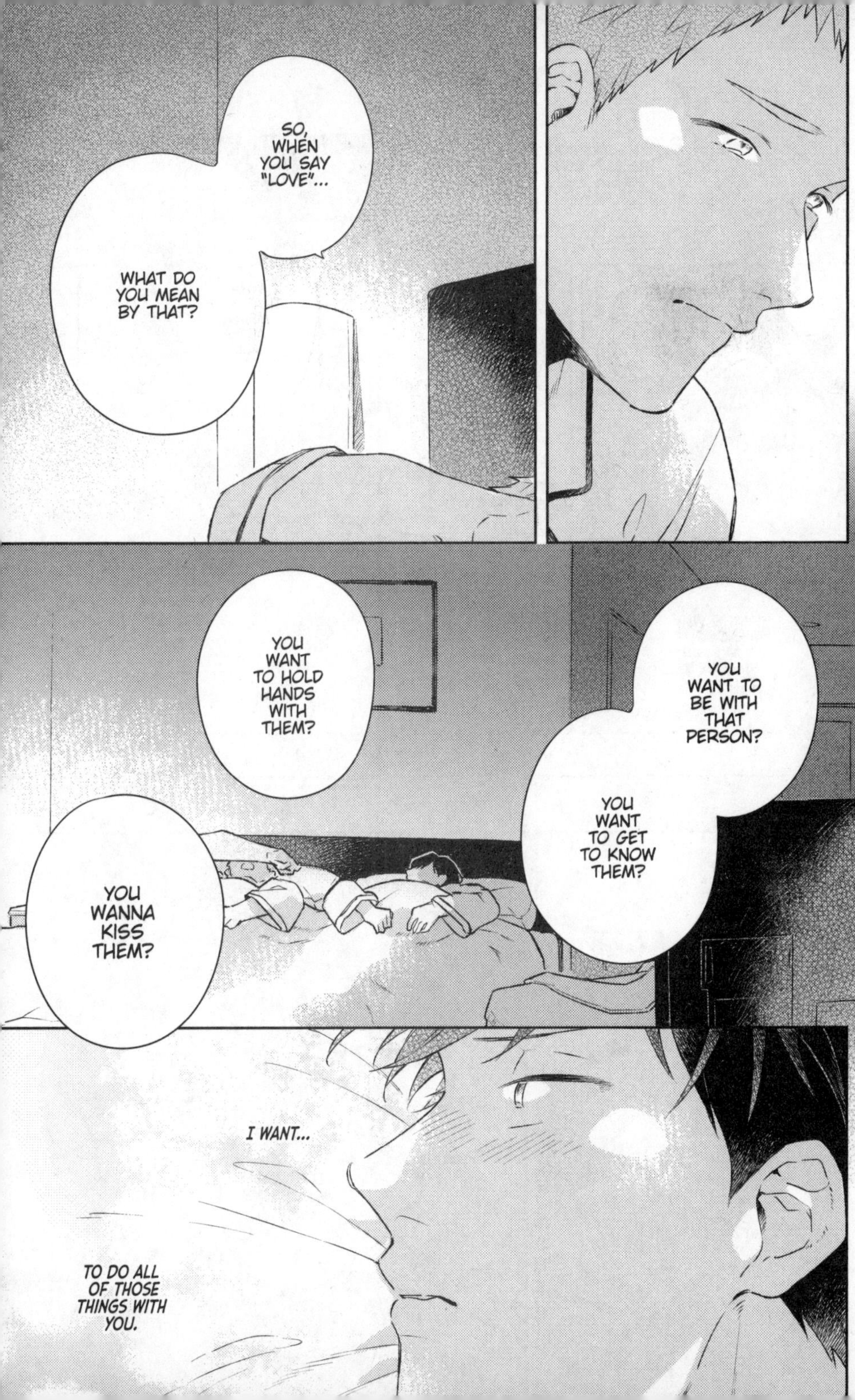
SO, WHEN YOU SAY "LOVE"...
WHAT DO YOU MEAN BY THAT?
YOU WANT TO BE WITH THAT PERSON?
YOU WANT TO GET TO KNOW THEM?
YOU WANT TO HOLD HANDS WITH THEM?
YOU WANNA KISS THEM?
I WANT...
TO DO ALL OF THOSE THINGS WITH YOU.

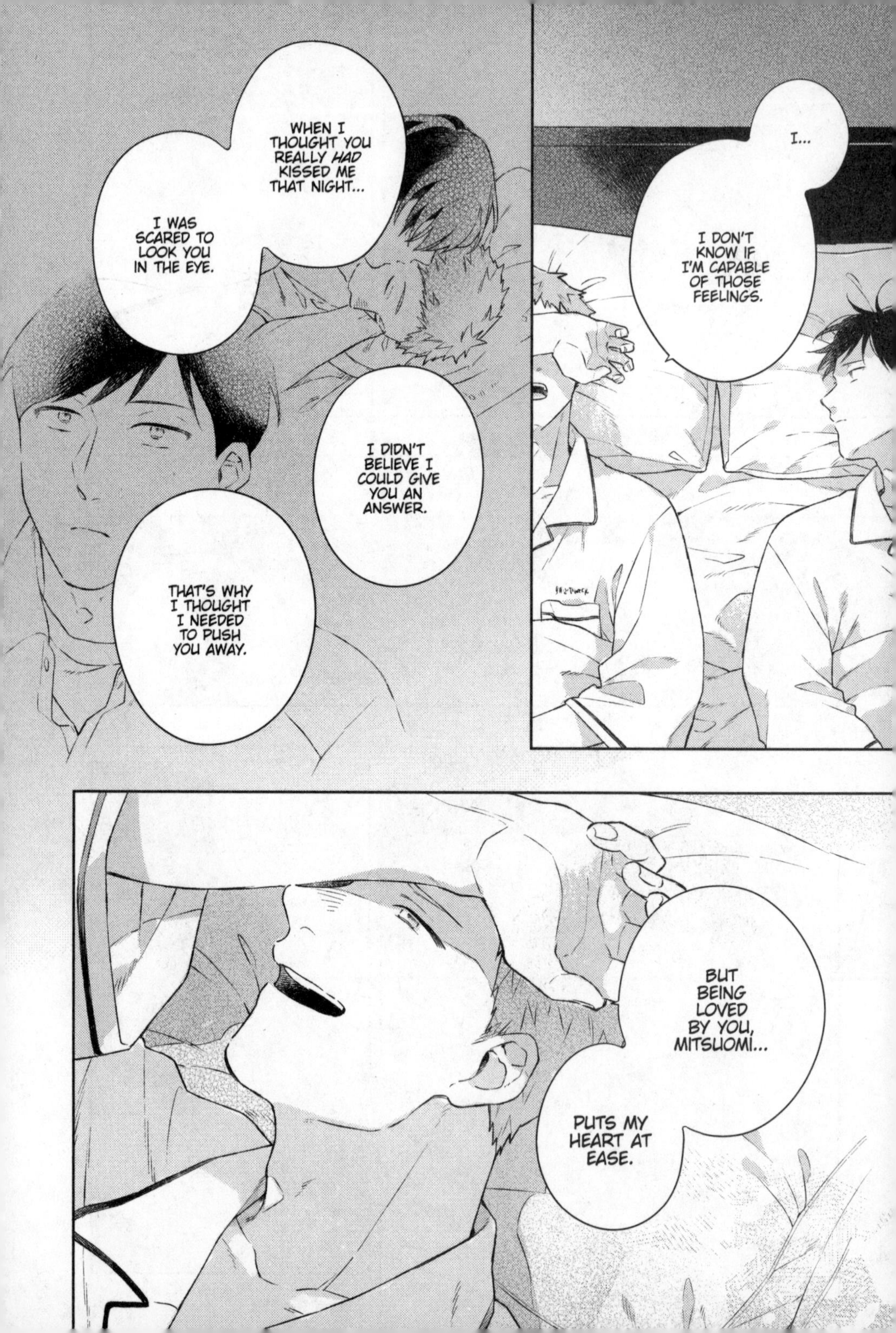
I...
I DON'T KNOW IF I'M CAPABLE OF THOSE FEELINGS.
WHEN I THOUGHT YOU REALLY *HAD* KISSED ME THAT NIGHT...
I WAS SCARED TO LOOK YOU IN THE EYE.
I DIDN'T BELIEVE I COULD GIVE YOU AN ANSWER.
THAT'S WHY I THOUGHT I NEEDED TO PUSH YOU AWAY.
BUT BEING LOVED BY YOU, MITSUOMI...
PUTS MY HEART AT EASE.

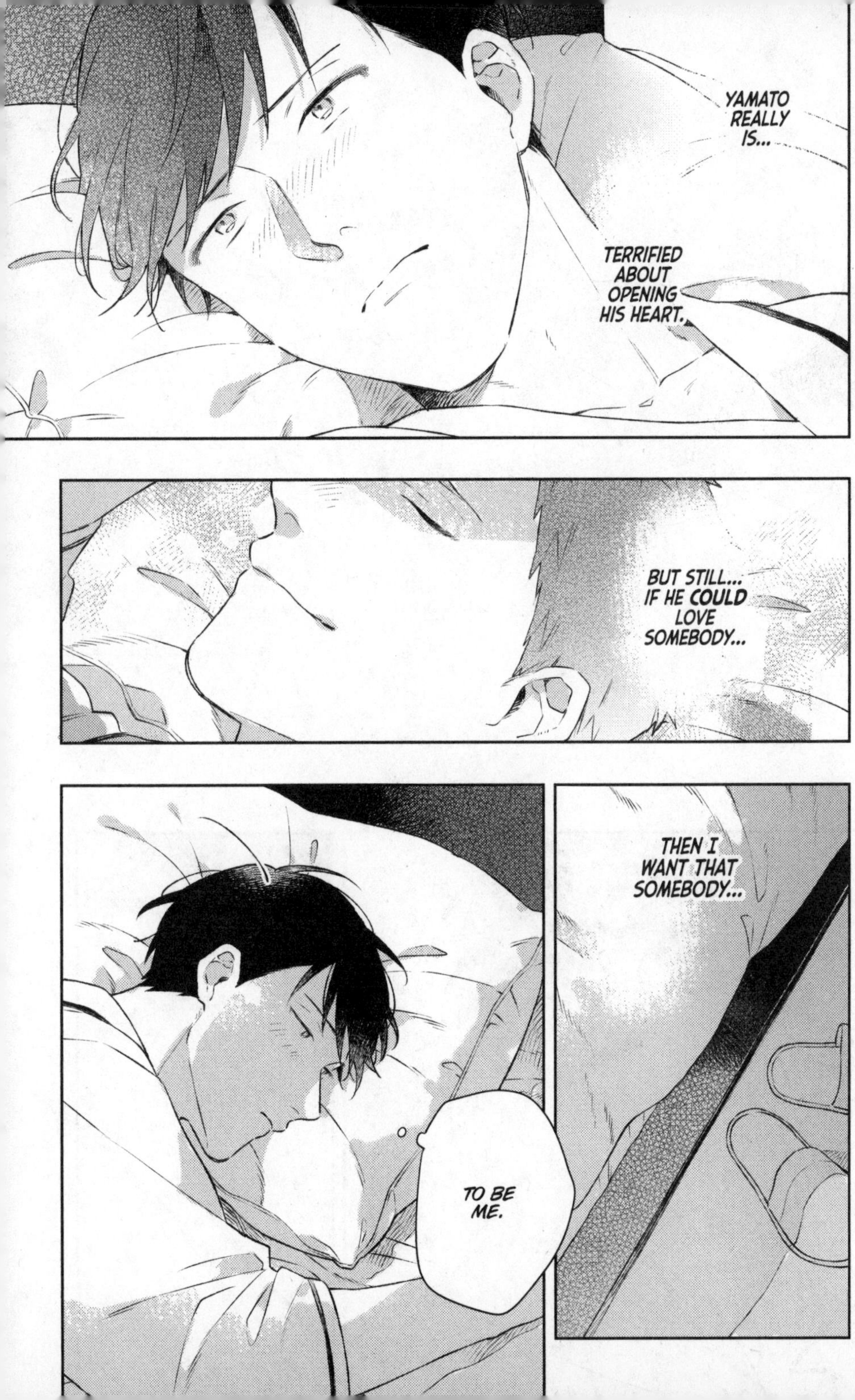
YAMATO REALLY IS...
TERRIFIED ABOUT OPENING HIS HEART.
BUT STILL... IF HE COULD LOVE SOMEBODY...
THEN I WANT THAT SOMEBODY...
TO BE ME.

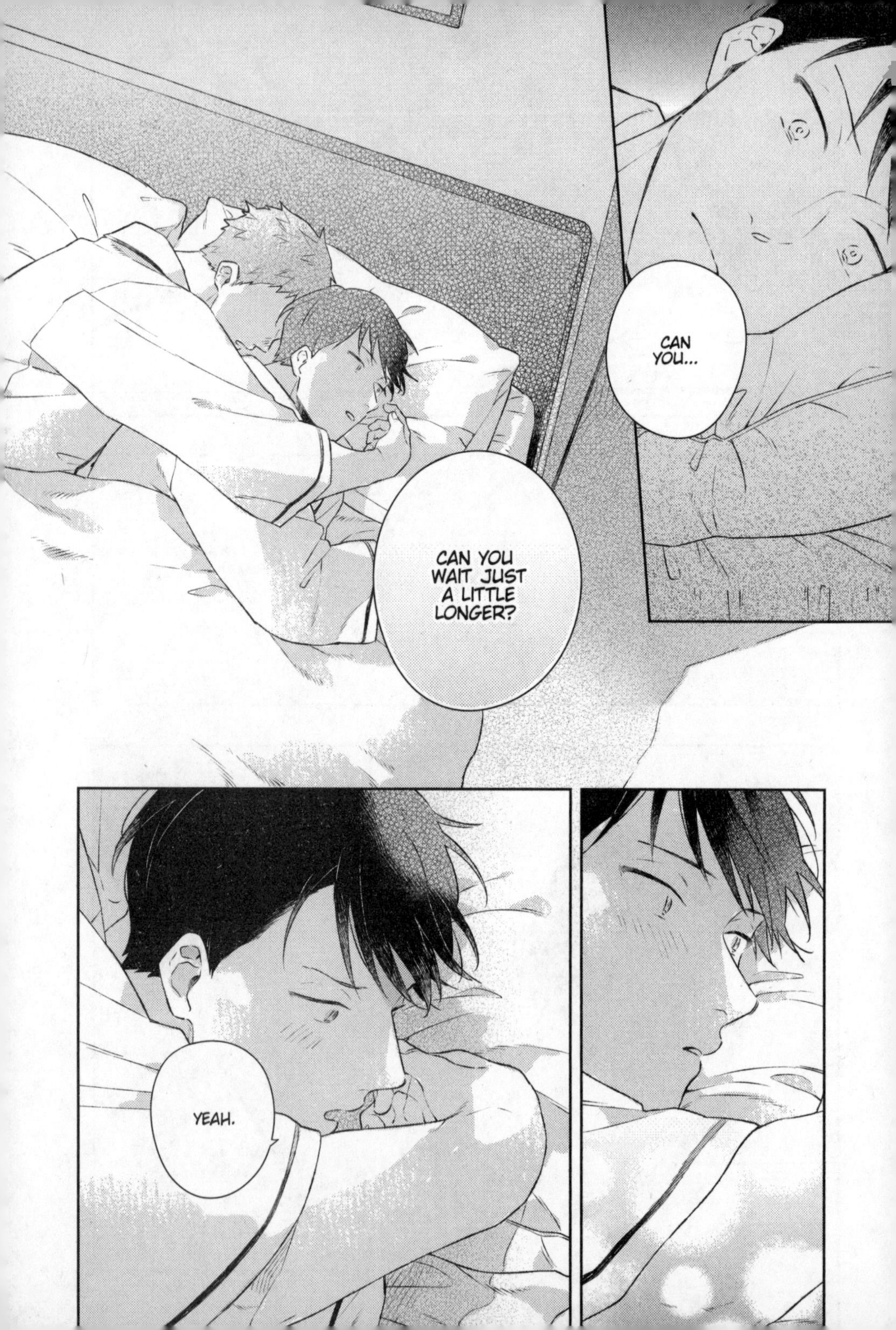
CAN YOU...
CAN YOU WAIT JUST A LITTLE LONGER?
YEAH.

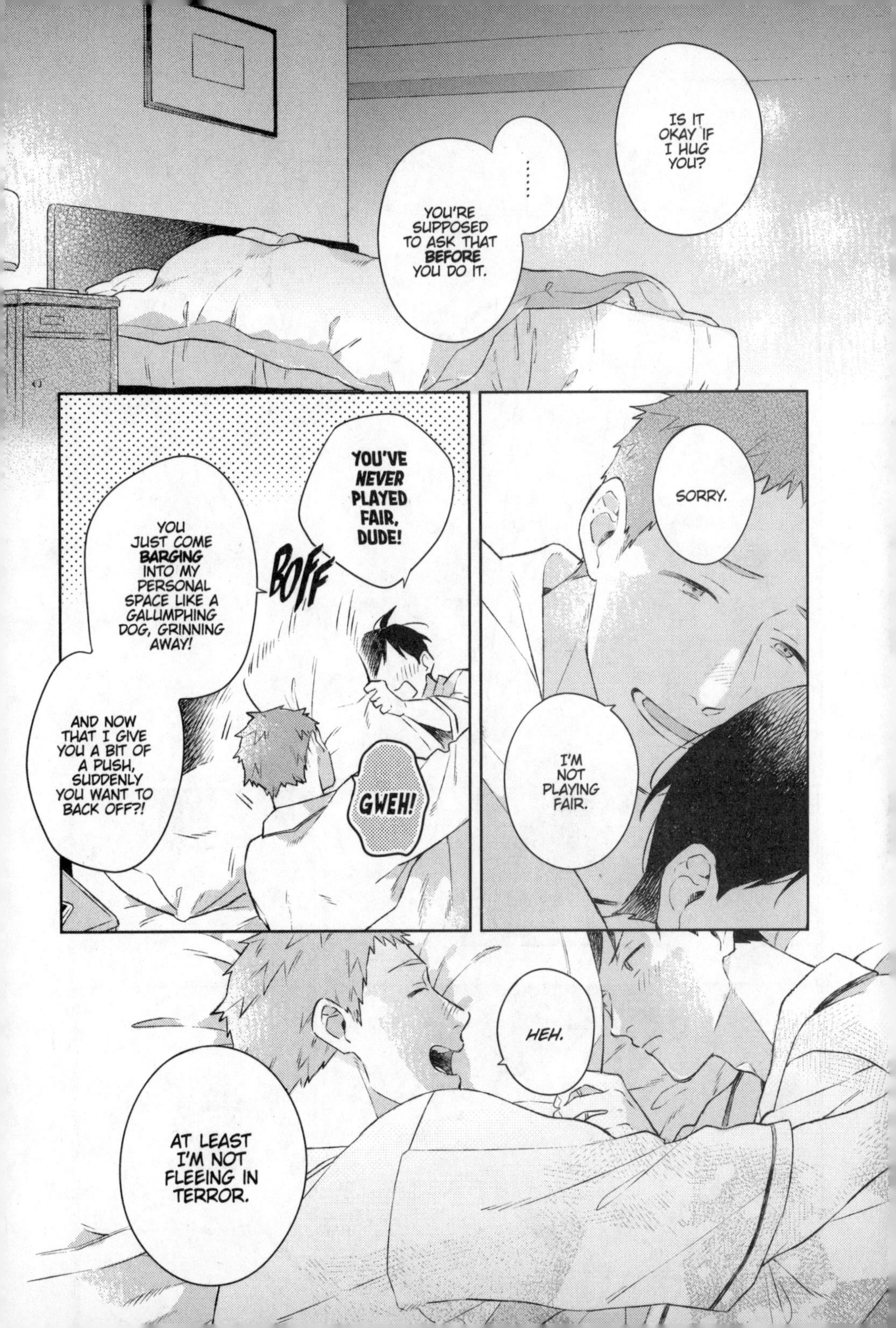
IS IT OKAY IF I HUG YOU?
......
YOU'RE SUPPOSED TO ASK THAT BEFORE YOU DO IT.
SORRY.
I'M NOT PLAYING FAIR.
YOU'VE NEVER PLAYED FAIR, DUDE!
BOFF
YOU JUST COME BARGING INTO MY PERSONAL SPACE LIKE A GALUMPHING DOG, GRINNING AWAY!
GWEH!
AND NOW THAT I GIVE YOU A BIT OF A PUSH, SUDDENLY YOU WANT TO BACK OFF?!
HEH.
AT LEAST I'M NOT FLEEING IN TERROR.

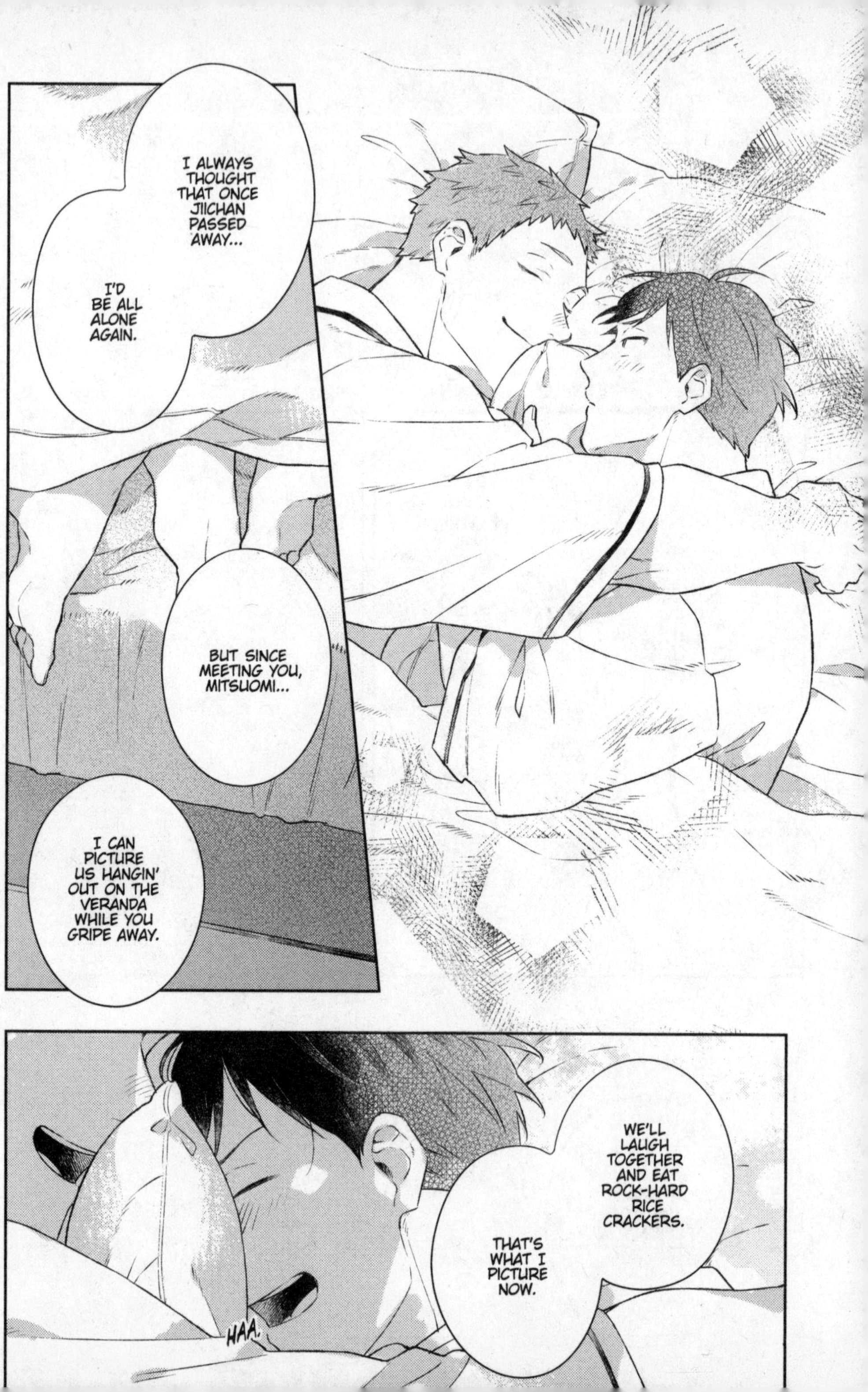
I ALWAYS THOUGHT THAT ONCE JIICHAN PASSED AWAY...
I'D BE ALL ALONE AGAIN.
BUT SINCE MEETING YOU, MITSUOMI...
I CAN PICTURE US HANGIN' OUT ON THE VERANDA WHILE YOU GRIPE AWAY.
WE'LL LAUGH TOGETHER AND EAT ROCK-HARD RICE CRACKERS.
THAT'S WHAT I PICTURE NOW.
HAA.

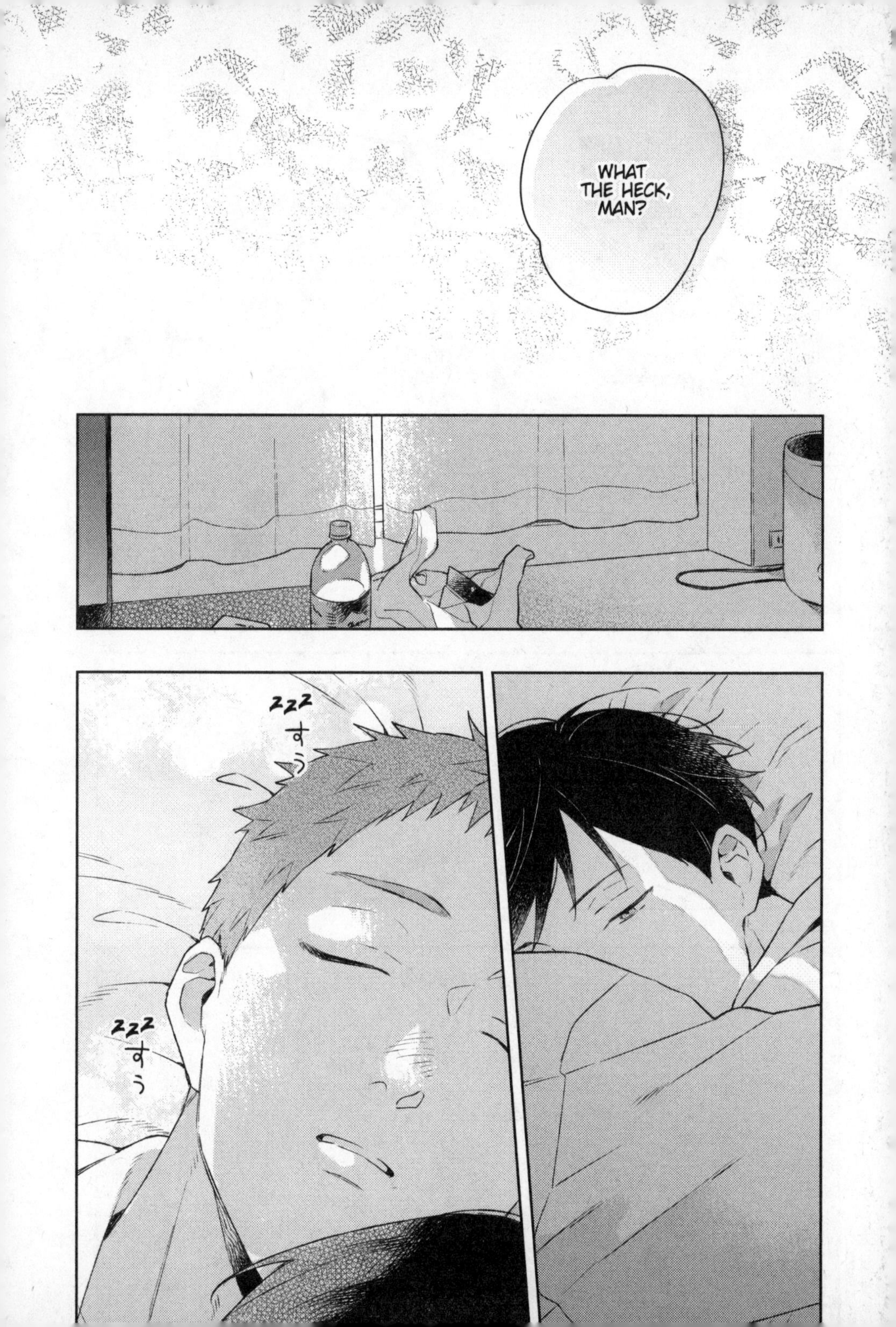
WHAT THE HECK, MAN?
ZZZ すう
ZZZ すう

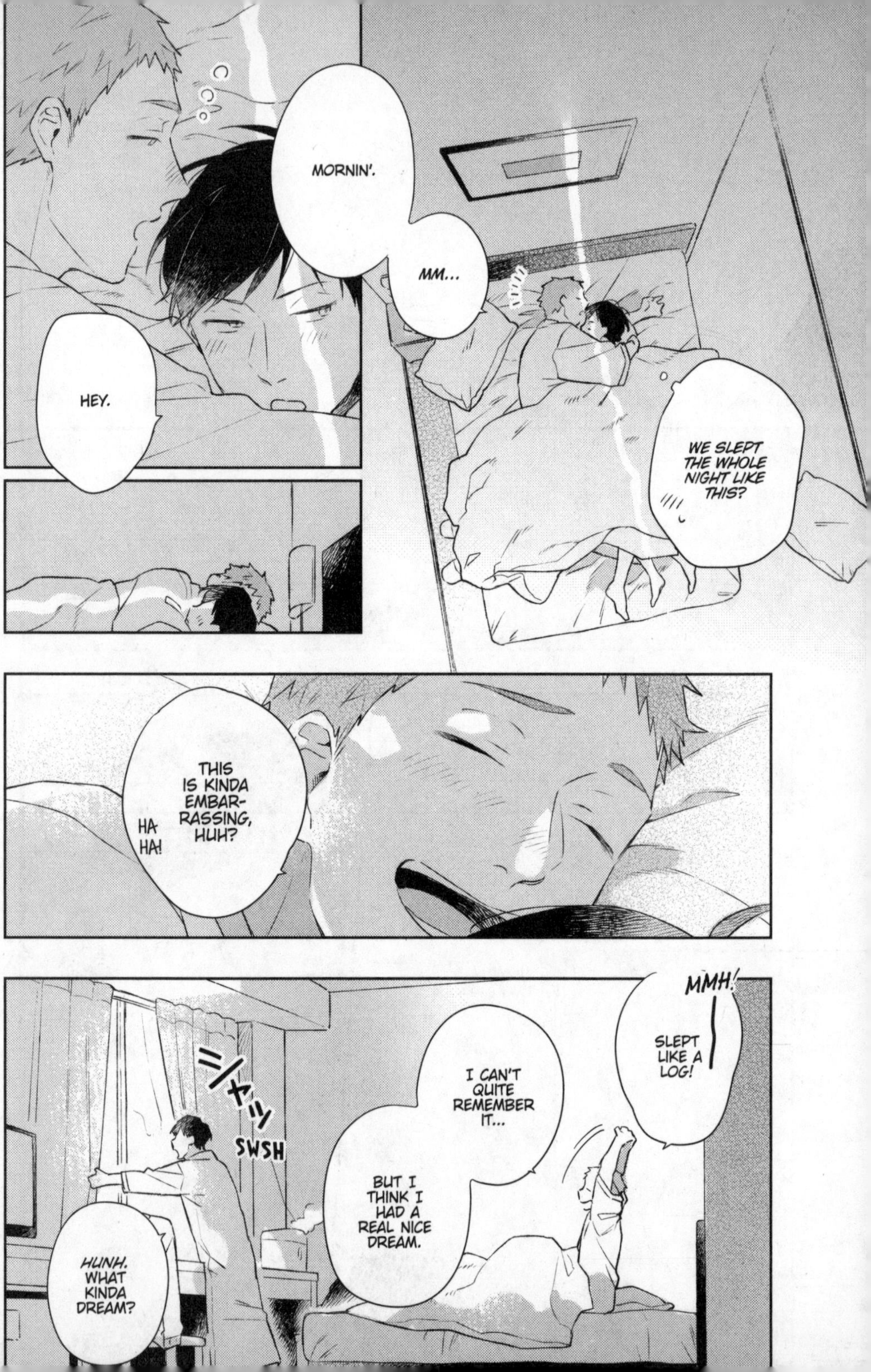
MORNIN'.
MM...
WE SLEPT THE WHOLE NIGHT LIKE THIS?
HEY.
THIS IS KINDA EMBARRASSING, HUH?
HA HA!
MMH! SLEPT LIKE A LOG!
I CAN'T QUITE REMEMBER IT...
BUT I THINK I HAD A REAL NICE DREAM.
シャッ
SWSH
HUNH. WHAT KINDA DREAM?

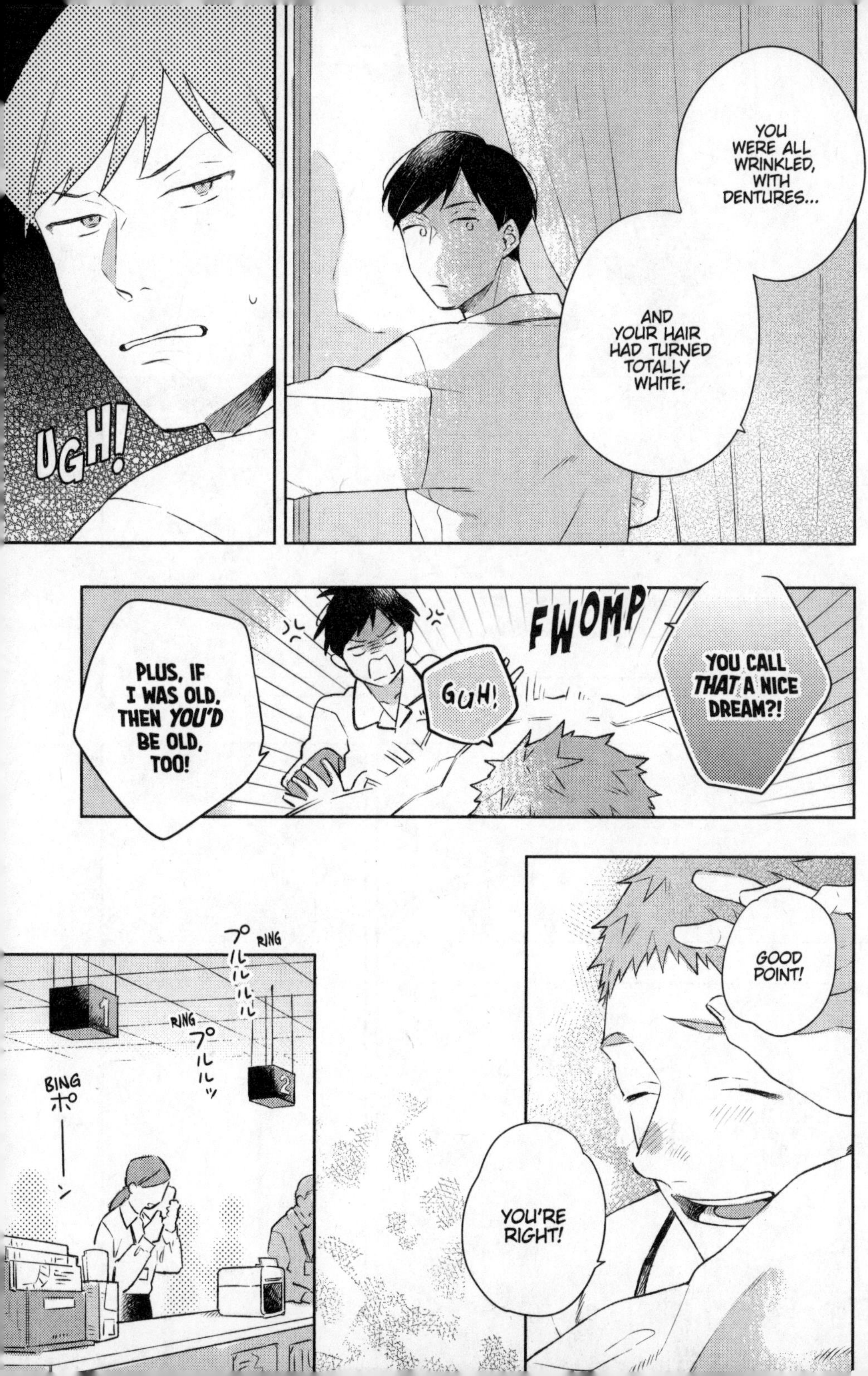
YOU WERE ALL WRINKLED, WITH DENTURES...
AND YOUR HAIR HAD TURNED TOTALLY WHITE.
UGH!
YOU CALL *THAT* A NICE DREAM?!
FWOMP
GUH!
PLUS, IF I WAS OLD, THEN *YOU'D* BE OLD, TOO!
GOOD POINT!
YOU'RE RIGHT!
RING プルルルル
RING プルルッ
BING ポーン

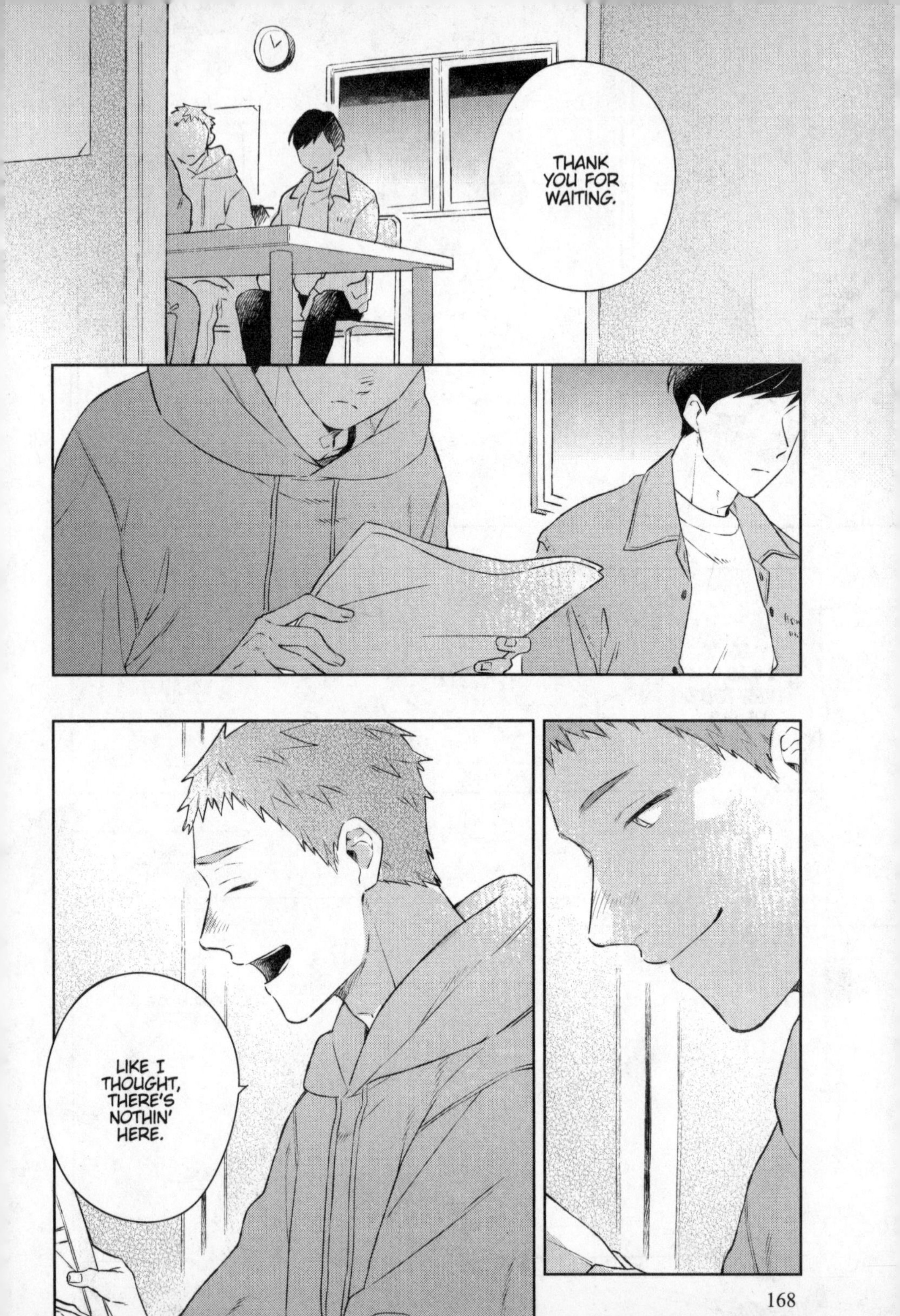
THANK YOU FOR WAITING.
LIKE I THOUGHT, THERE'S NOTHIN' HERE.

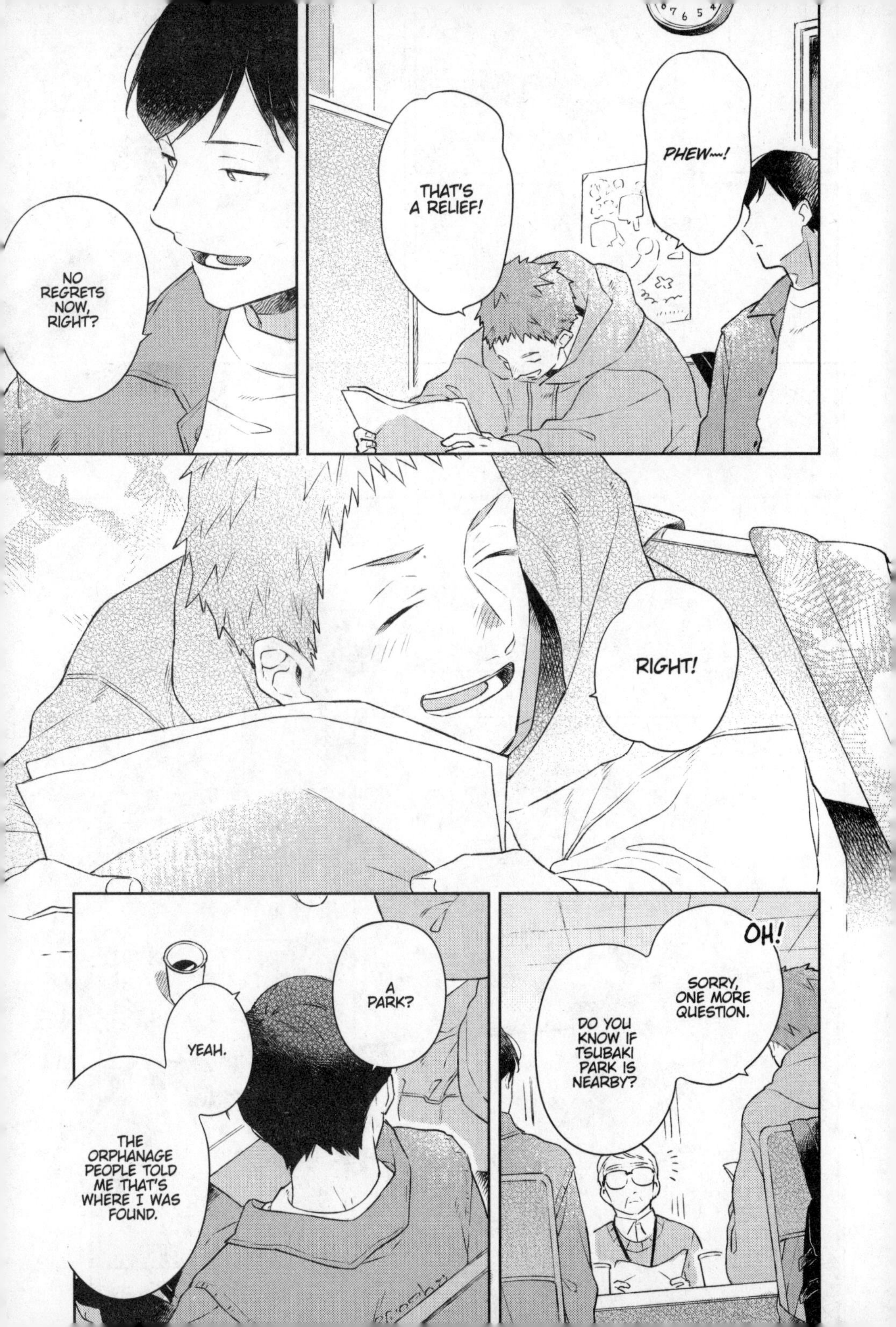
PHEW—!
THAT'S A RELIEF!
NO REGRETS NOW, RIGHT?
RIGHT!
OH!
SORRY, ONE MORE QUESTION.
DO YOU KNOW IF TSUBAKI PARK IS NEARBY?
A PARK?
YEAH.
THE ORPHANAGE PEOPLE TOLD ME THAT'S WHERE I WAS FOUND.

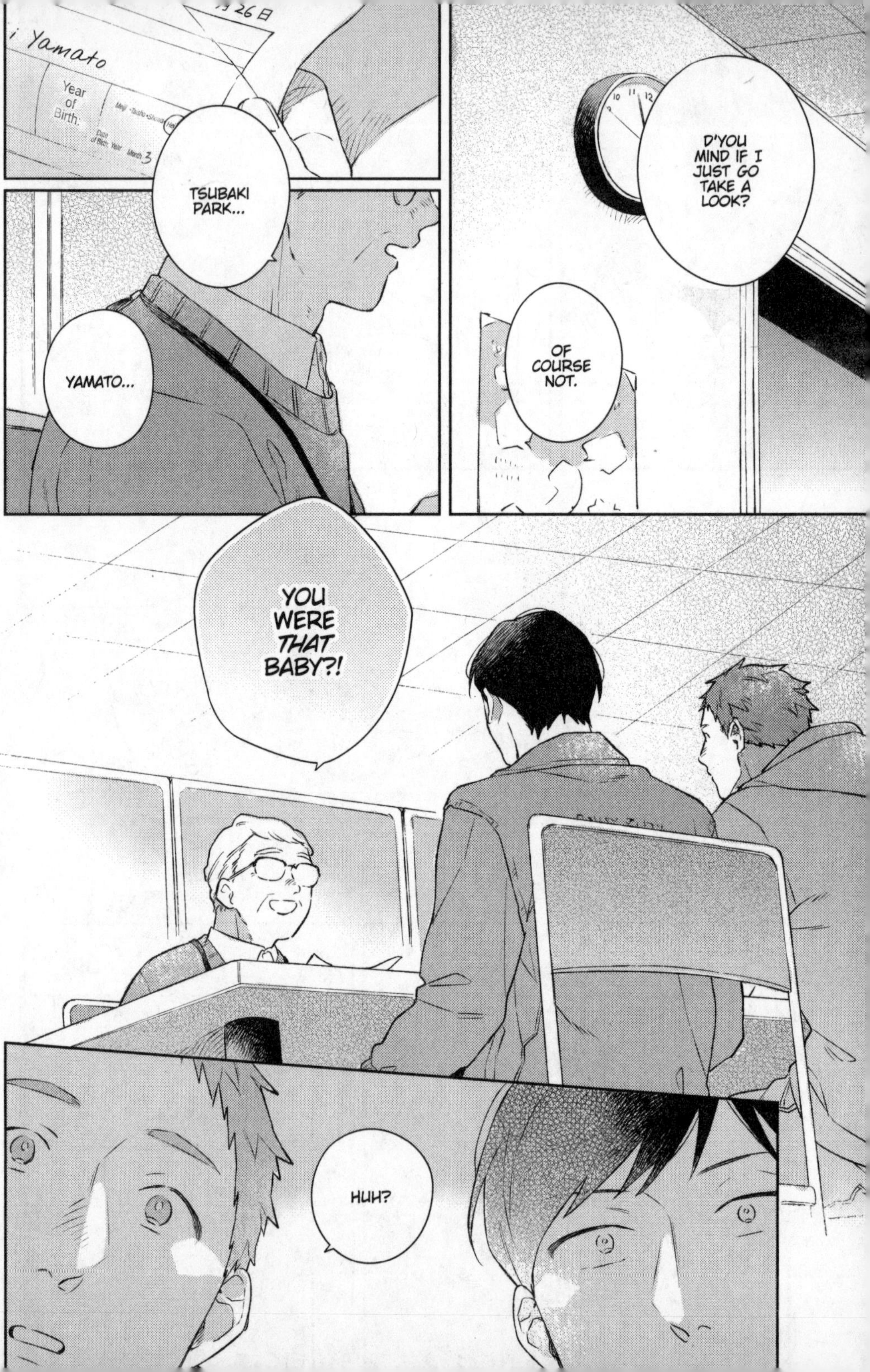

D'YOU MIND IF I JUST GO TAKE A LOOK?
OF COURSE NOT.
Yamato
Year of Birth:
TSUBAKI PARK...
YAMATO...
YOU WERE *THAT* BABY?!
HUH?

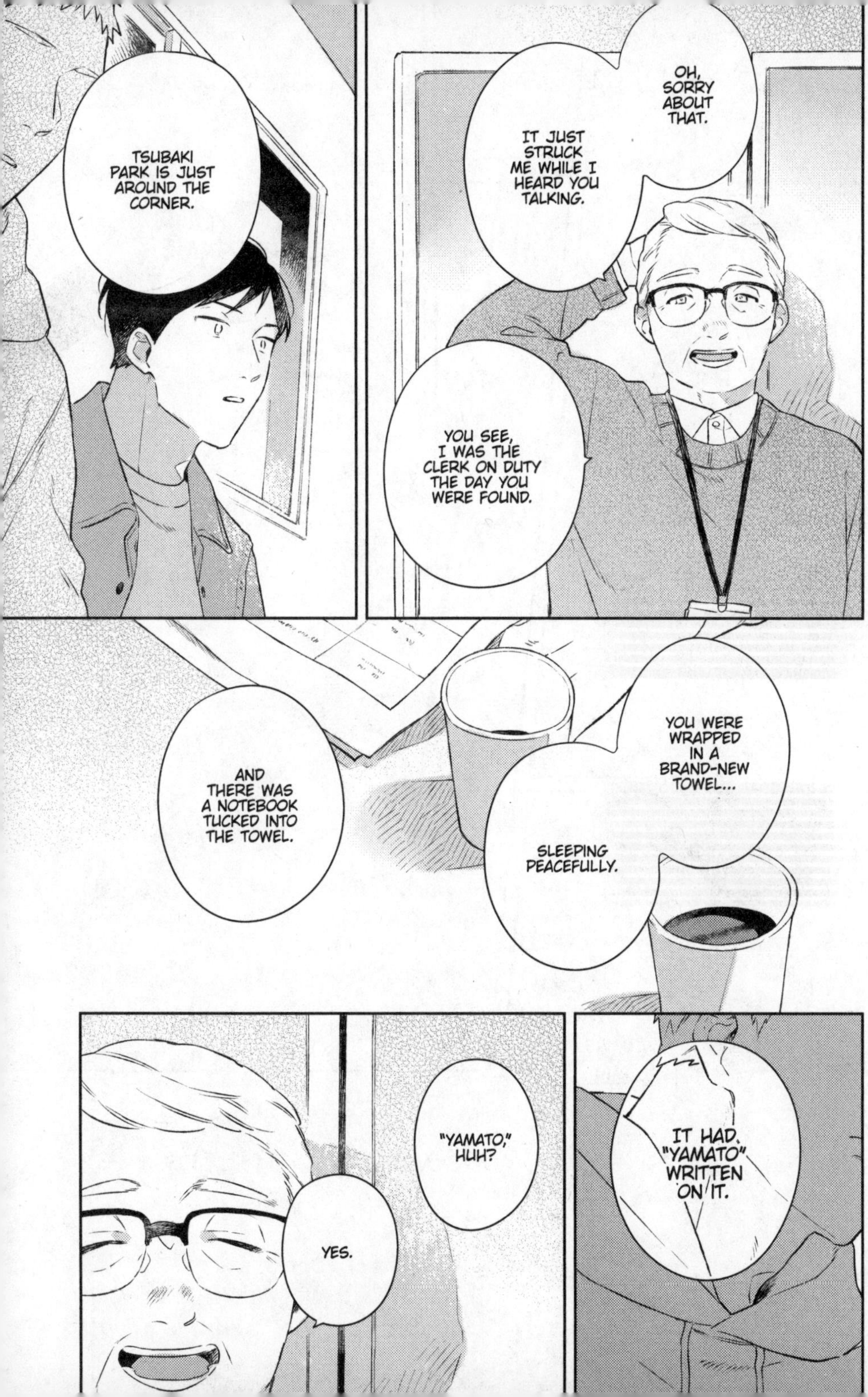
OH, SORRY ABOUT THAT.
IT JUST STRUCK ME WHILE I HEARD YOU TALKING.
YOU SEE, I WAS THE CLERK ON DUTY THE DAY YOU WERE FOUND.
TSUBAKI PARK IS JUST AROUND THE CORNER.
YOU WERE WRAPPED IN A BRAND-NEW TOWEL...
SLEEPING PEACEFULLY.
AND THERE WAS A NOTEBOOK TUCKED INTO THE TOWEL.
IT HAD "YAMATO" WRITTEN ON IT.
"YAMATO," HUH?
YES.

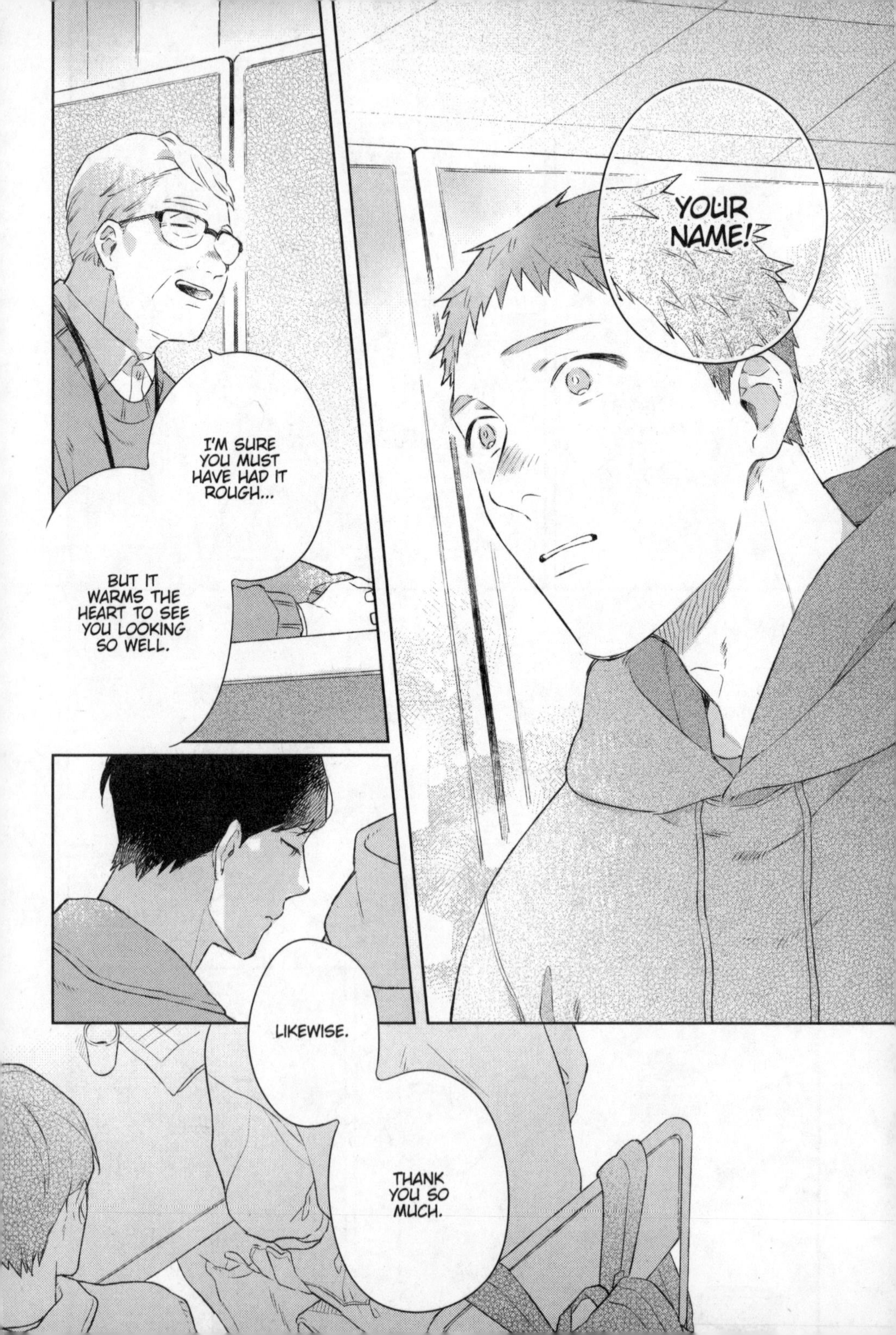
YOUR NAME!
I'M SURE YOU MUST HAVE HAD IT ROUGH...
BUT IT WARMS THE HEART TO SEE YOU LOOKING SO WELL.
LIKEWISE.
THANK YOU SO MUCH.

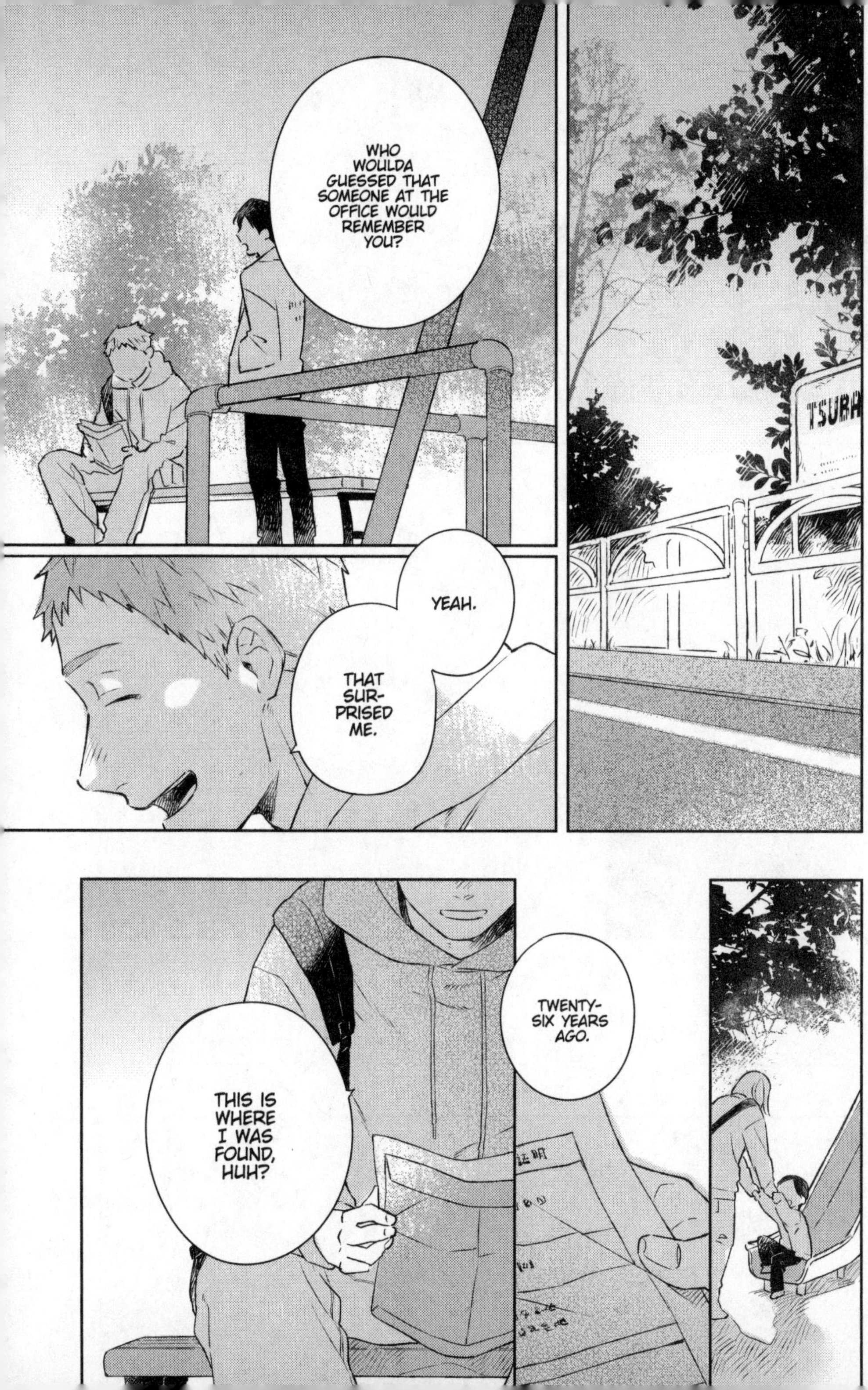
WHO WOULDA GUESSED THAT SOMEONE AT THE OFFICE WOULD REMEMBER YOU?
YEAH.
THAT SUR-PRISED ME.
TWENTY-SIX YEARS AGO.
THIS IS WHERE I WAS FOUND, HUH?

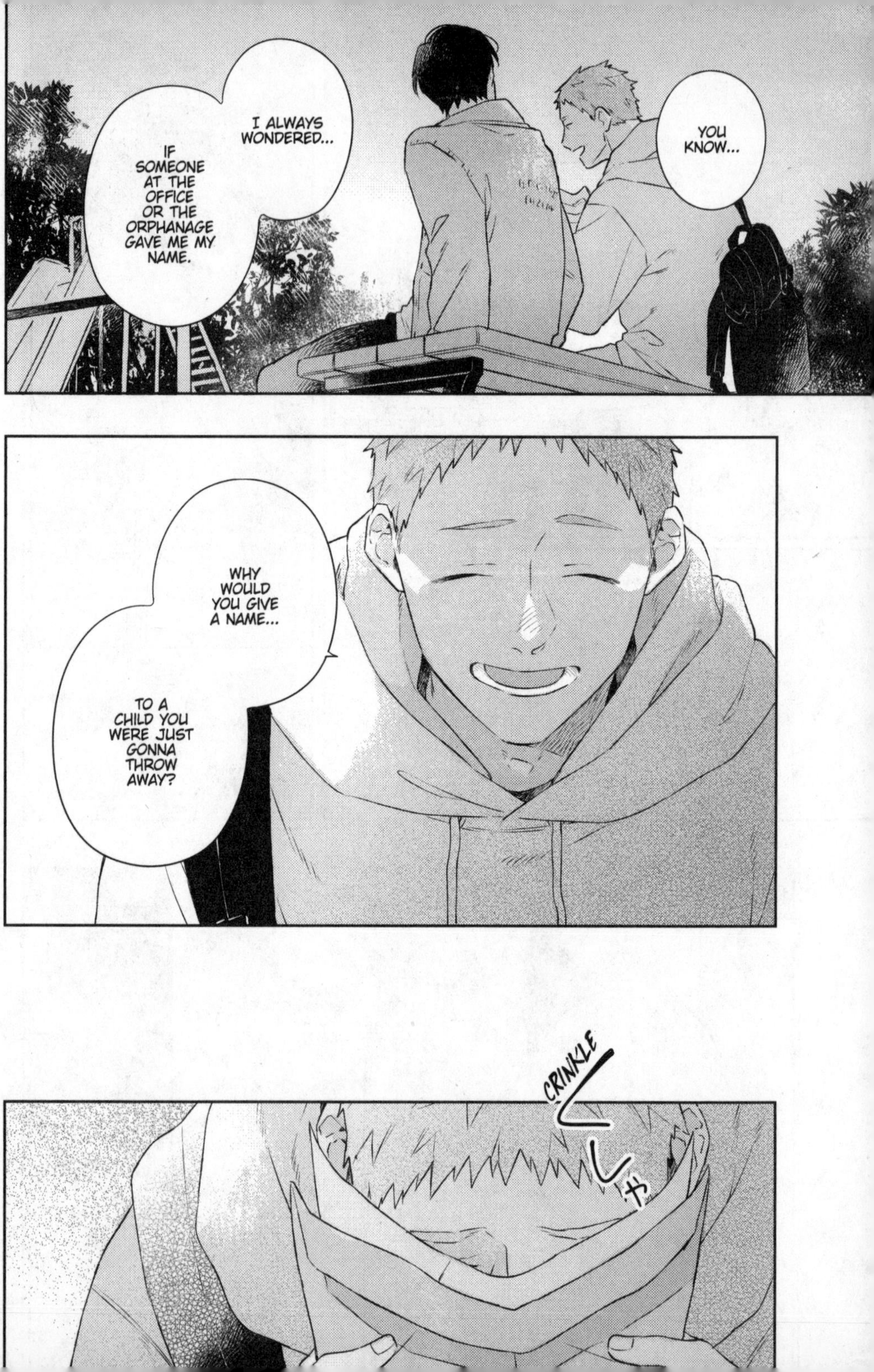
YOU KNOW...
I ALWAYS WONDERED...
IF SOMEONE AT THE OFFICE OR THE ORPHANAGE GAVE ME MY NAME.
WHY WOULD YOU GIVE A NAME...
TO A CHILD YOU WERE JUST GONNA THROW AWAY?
CRINKLE
くしゃ

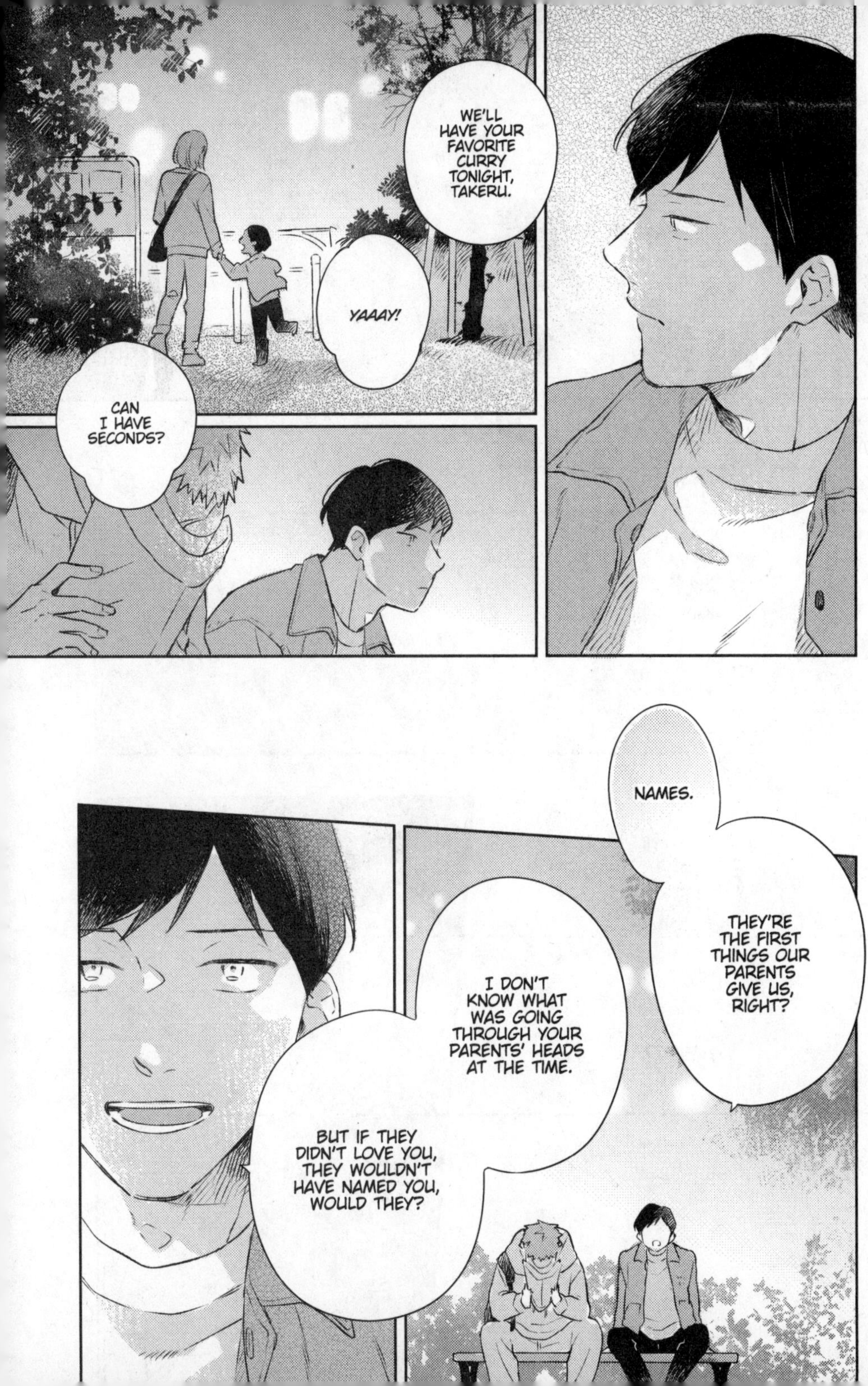
WE'LL HAVE YOUR FAVORITE CURRY TONIGHT, TAKERU.
YAAAY!
CAN I HAVE SECONDS?
NAMES.
THEY'RE THE FIRST THINGS OUR PARENTS GIVE US, RIGHT?
I DON'T KNOW WHAT WAS GOING THROUGH YOUR PARENTS' HEADS AT THE TIME.
BUT IF THEY DIDN'T LOVE YOU, THEY WOULDN'T HAVE NAMED YOU, WOULD THEY?

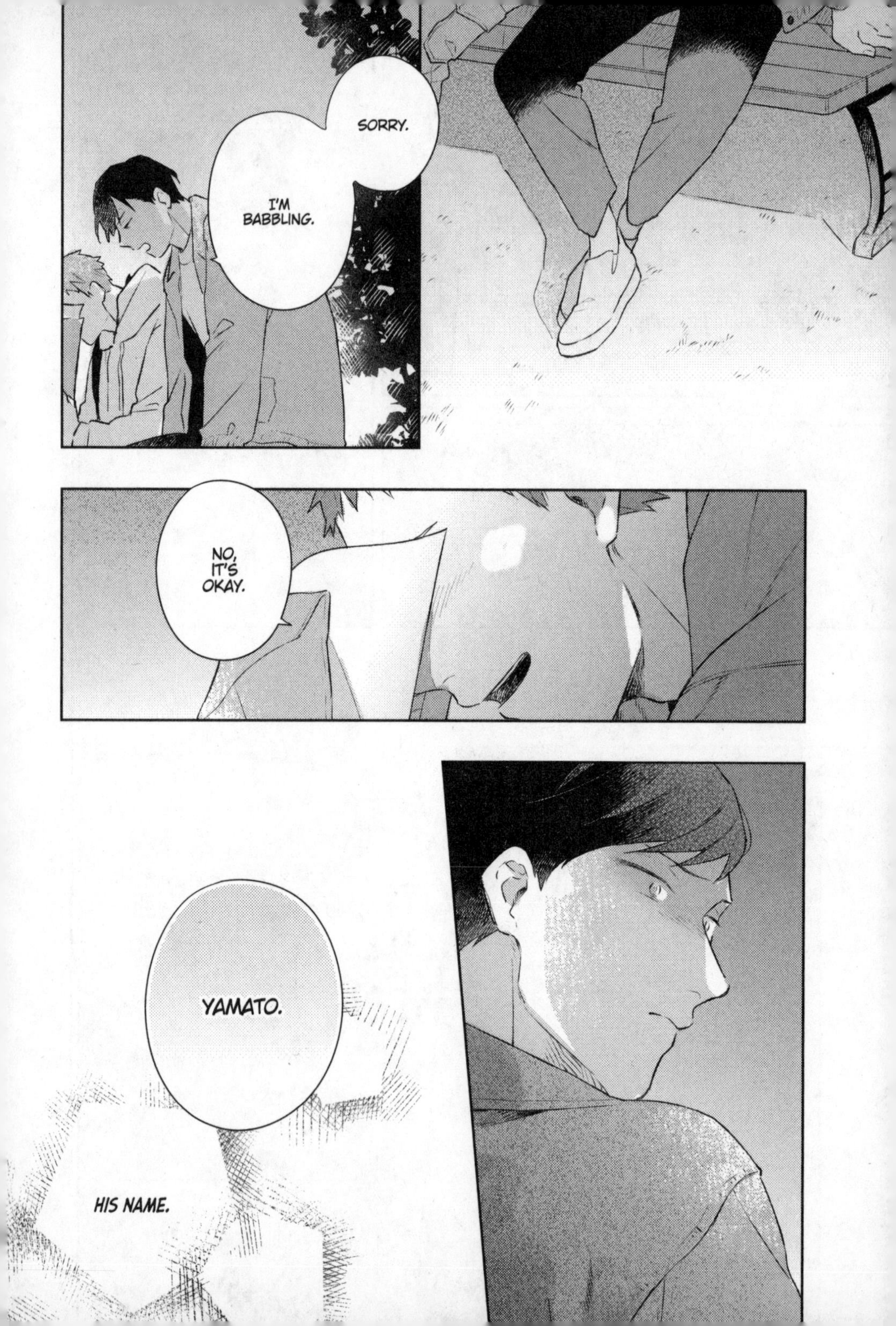
SORRY.
I'M BABBLING.
NO, IT'S OKAY.
YAMATO.
HIS NAME.

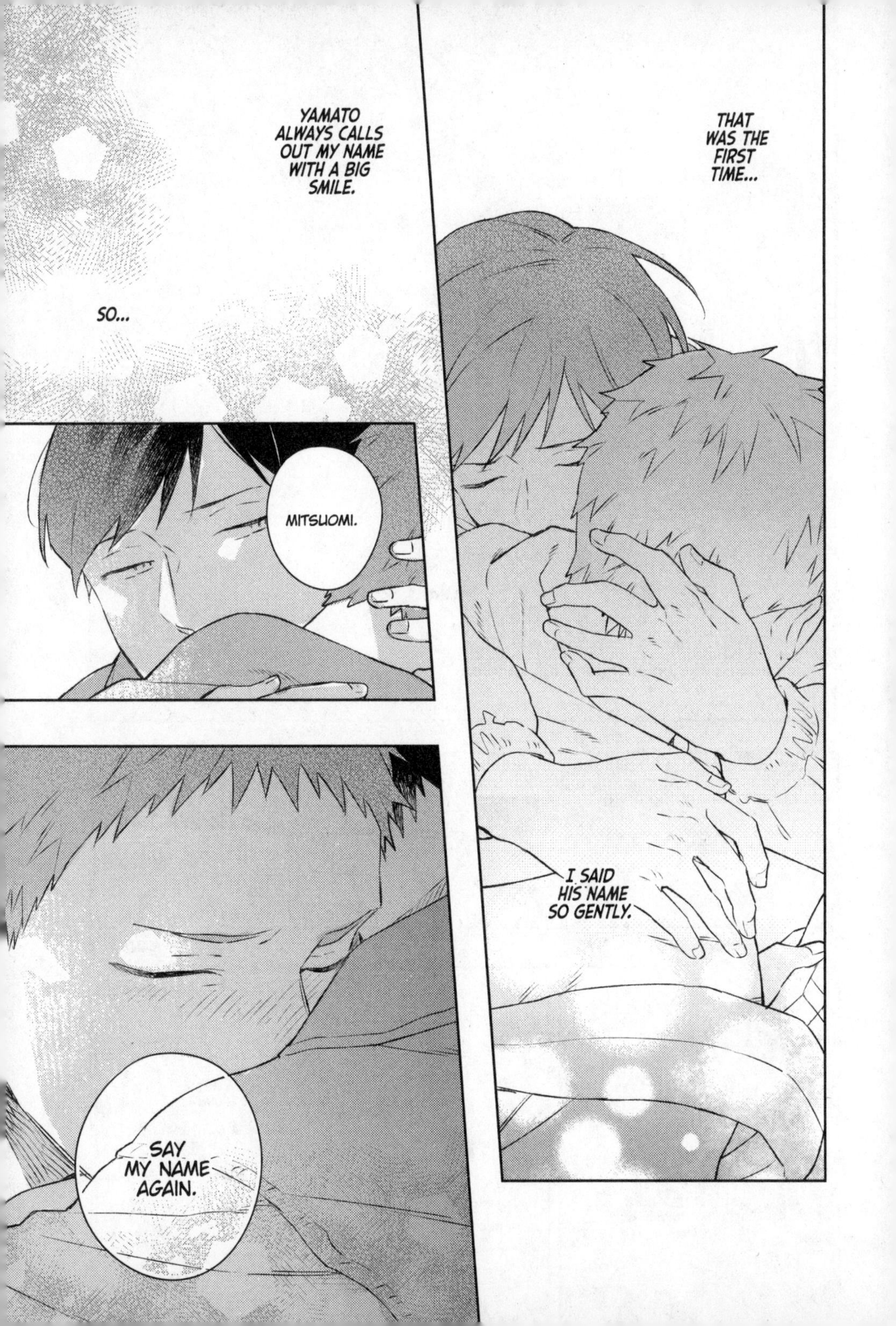
THAT WAS THE FIRST TIME...
I SAID HIS NAME SO GENTLY.
YAMATO ALWAYS CALLS OUT MY NAME WITH A BIG SMILE.
SO...
MITSUOMI.
SAY MY NAME AGAIN.

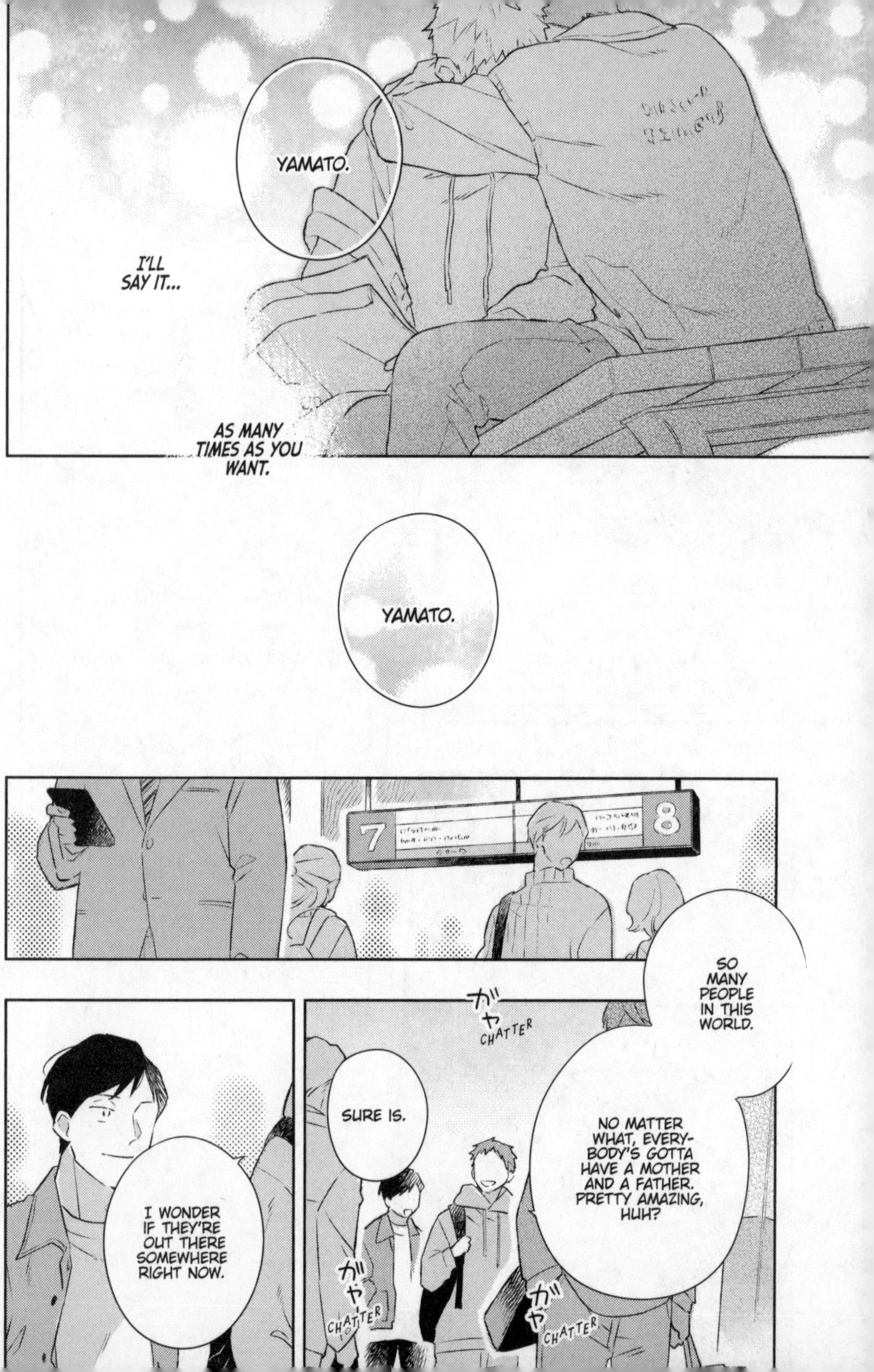
YAMATO.
I'LL SAY IT...
AS MANY TIMES AS YOU WANT.
YAMATO.
7
8
SO MANY PEOPLE IN THIS WORLD.
ガヤ
CHATTER
NO MATTER WHAT, EVERY-BODY'S GOTTA HAVE A MOTHER AND A FATHER. PRETTY AMAZING, HUH?
SURE IS.
ガヤ
CHATTER
ガヤ
CHATTER
I WONDER IF THEY'RE OUT THERE SOMEWHERE RIGHT NOW.

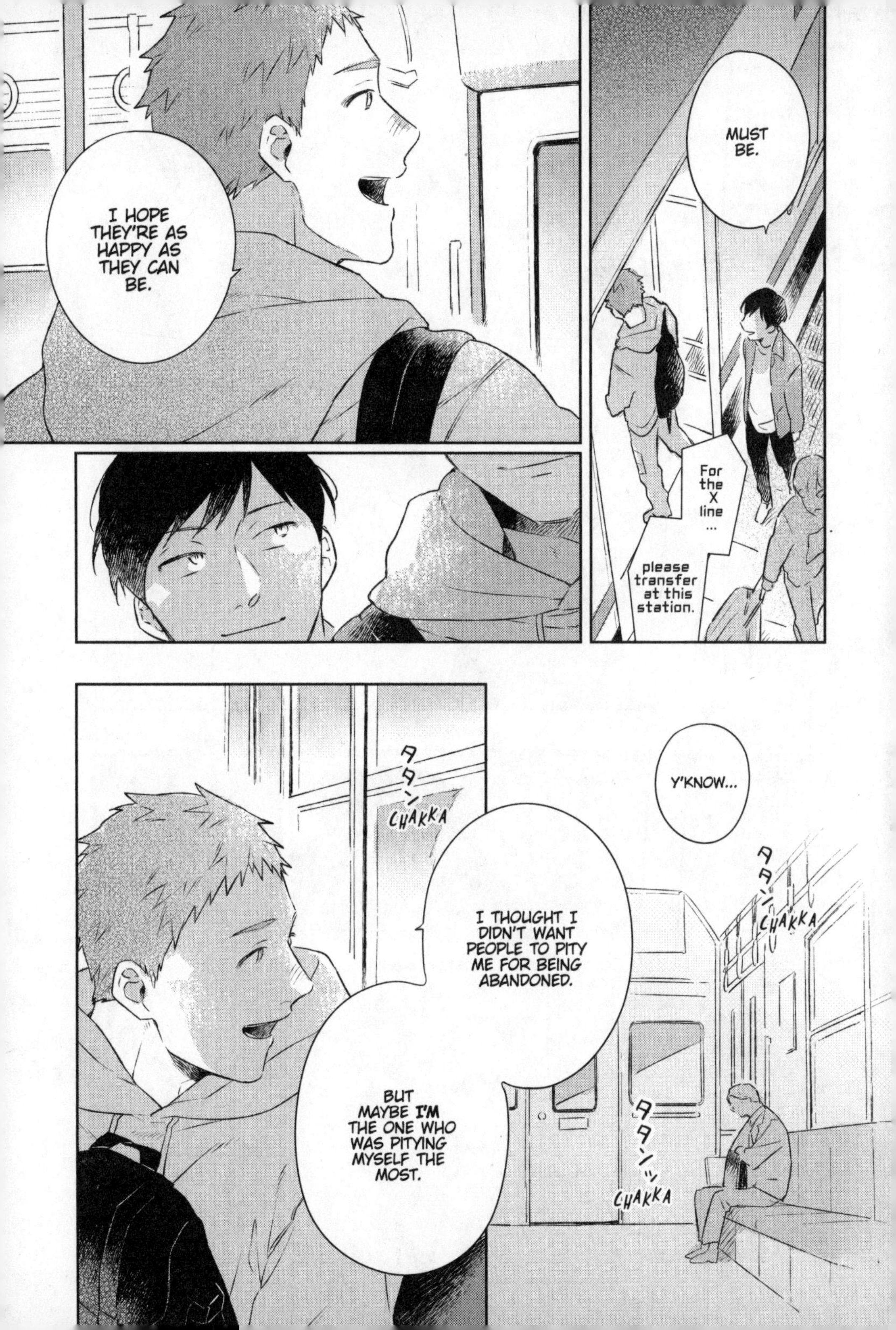
MUST BE.
For the X line... please transfer at this station.
I HOPE THEY'RE AS HAPPY AS THEY CAN BE.
Y'KNOW...
タタン CHAKKA
I THOUGHT I DIDN'T WANT PEOPLE TO PITY ME FOR BEING ABANDONED.
タタン CHAKKA
BUT MAYBE I'M THE ONE WHO WAS PITYING MYSELF THE MOST.
タタンッ CHAKKA

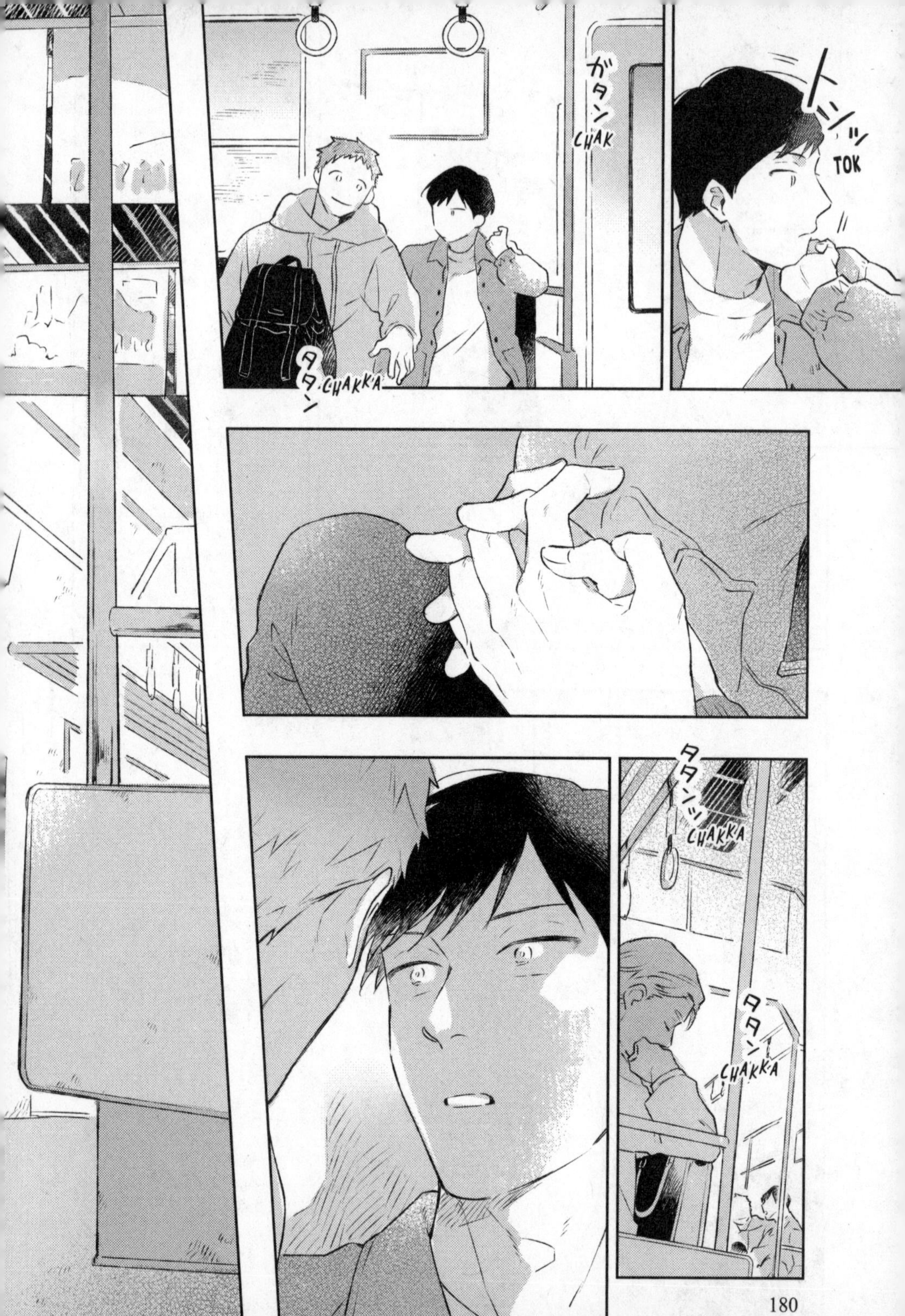
トンッ
TOK
ガタン
CHAK
タタン
CHAKKA
タタンッ
CHAKKA
タタン
CHAKKA

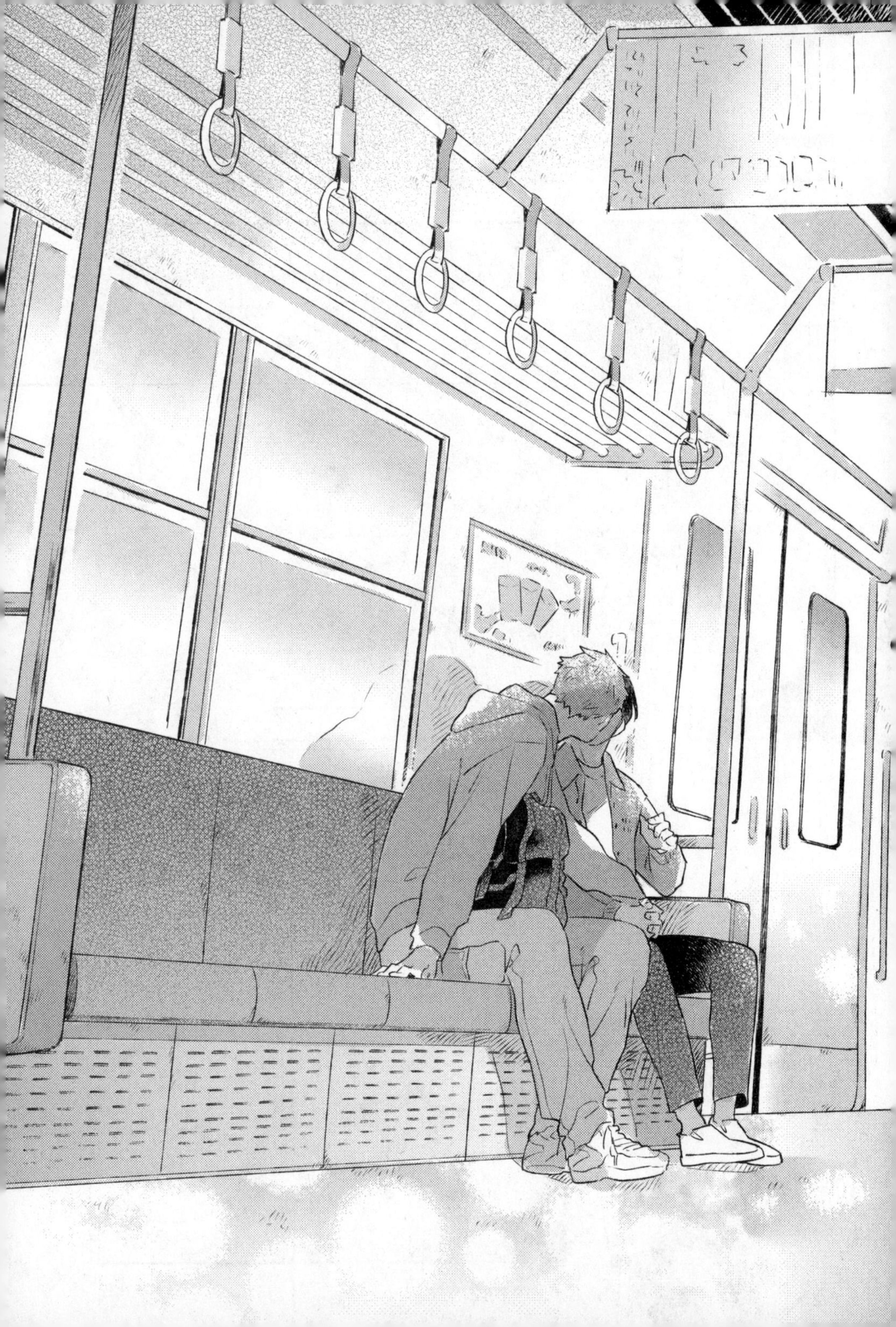

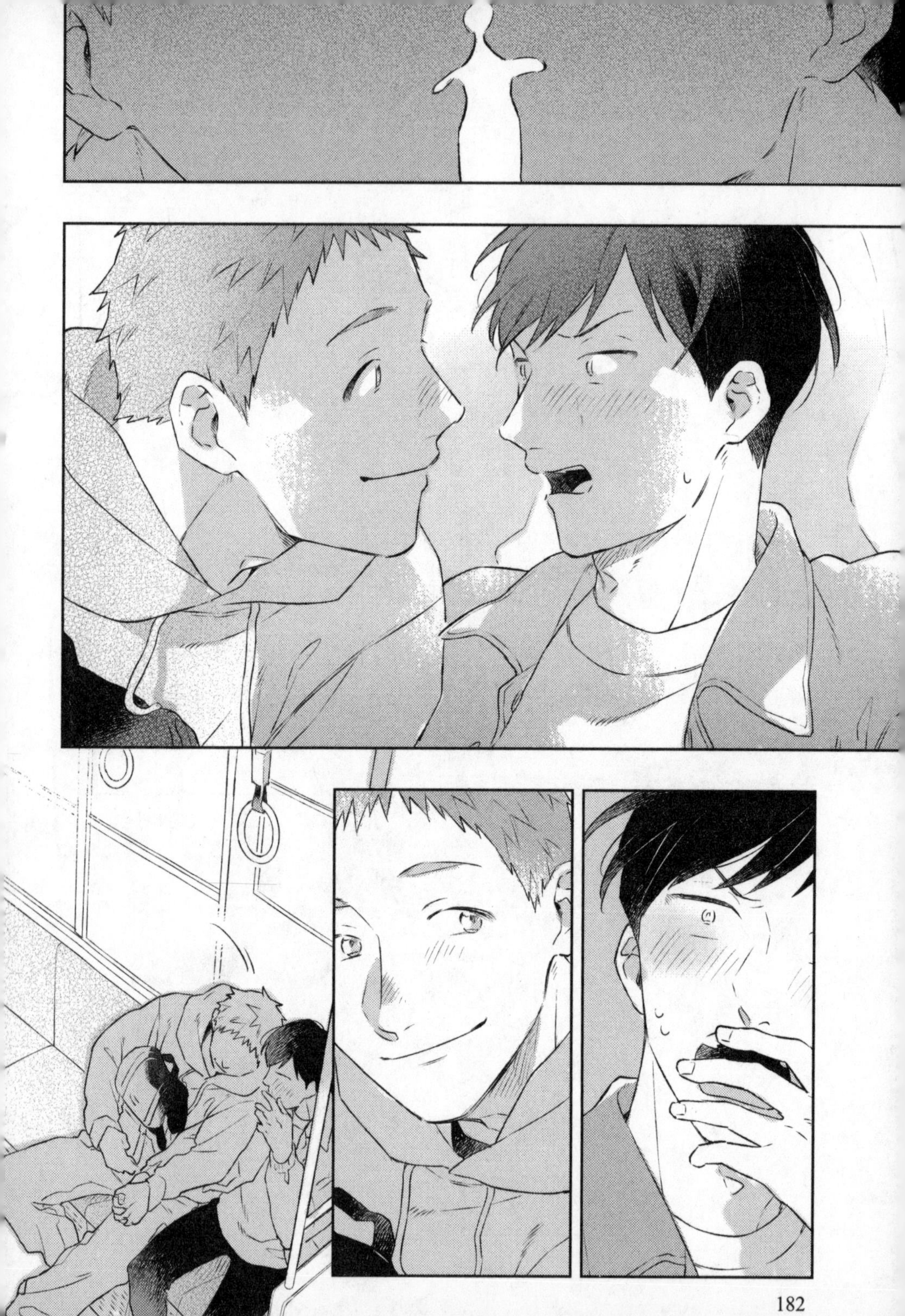

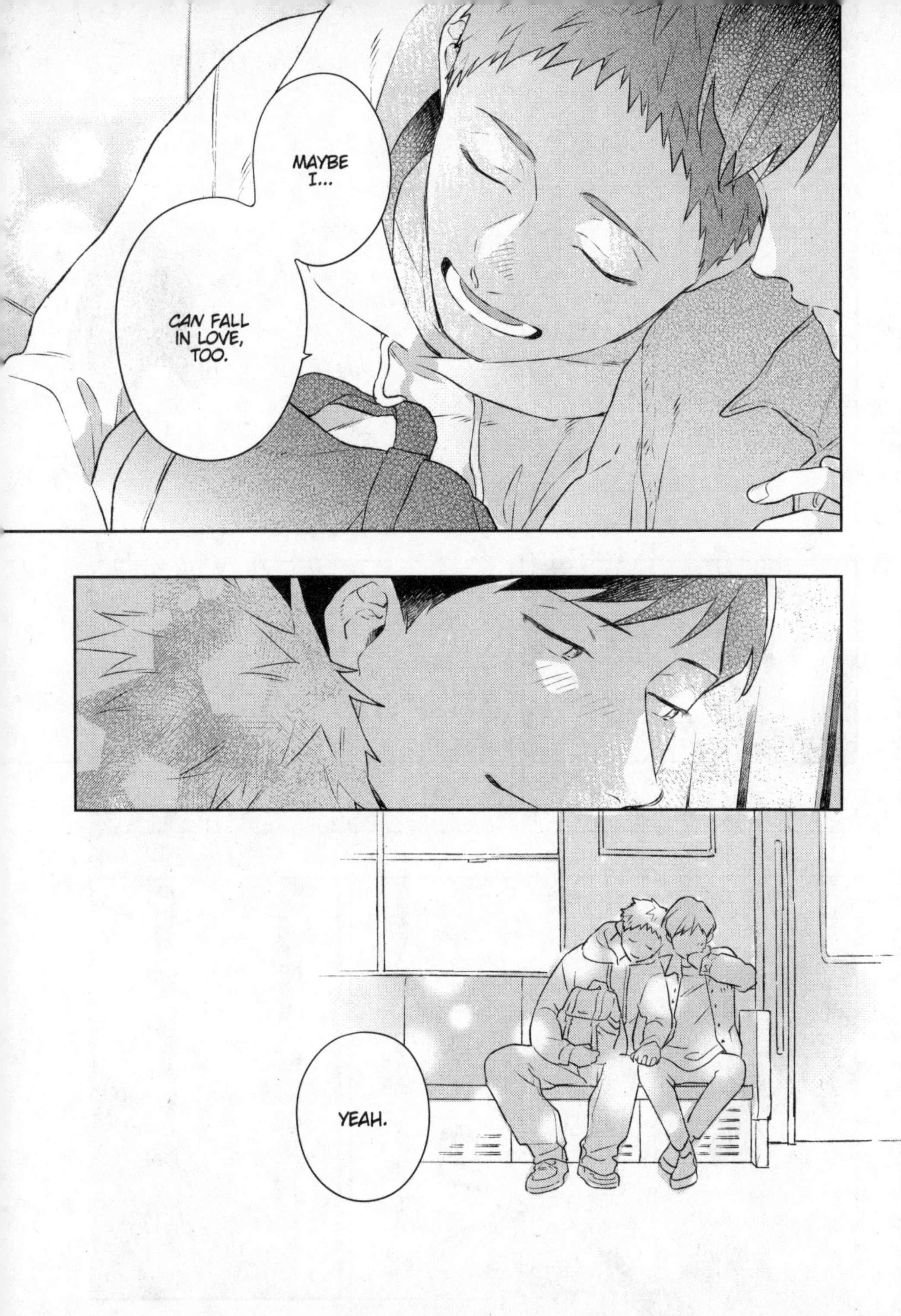
MAYBE I...
CAN FALL IN LOVE, TOO.
YEAH.

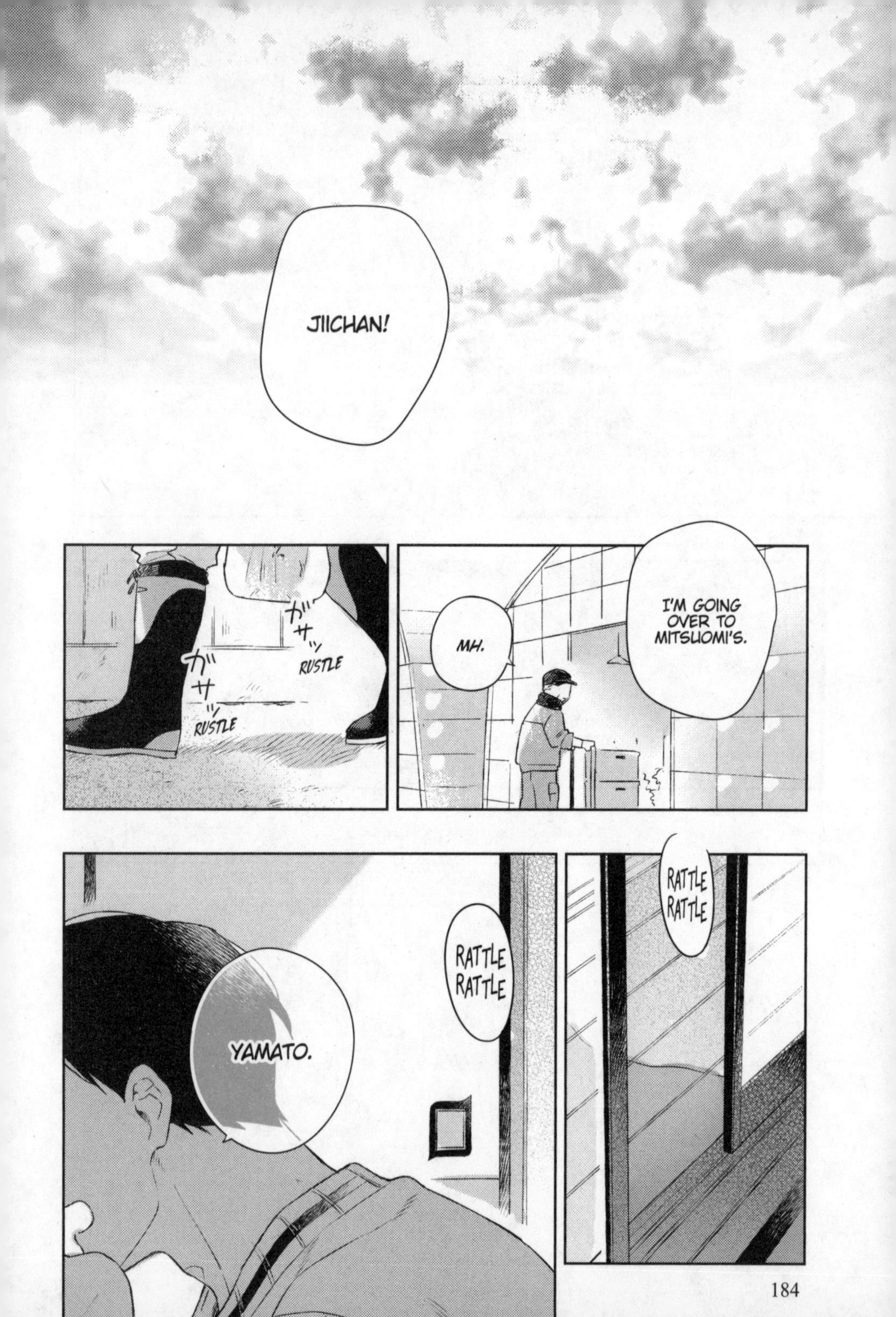

JIICHAN!
I'M GOING OVER TO MITSUOMI'S.
MH.
ガサッ
RUSTLE
ガサッ
RUSTLE
RATTLE RATTLE
RATTLE RATTLE
YAMATO.

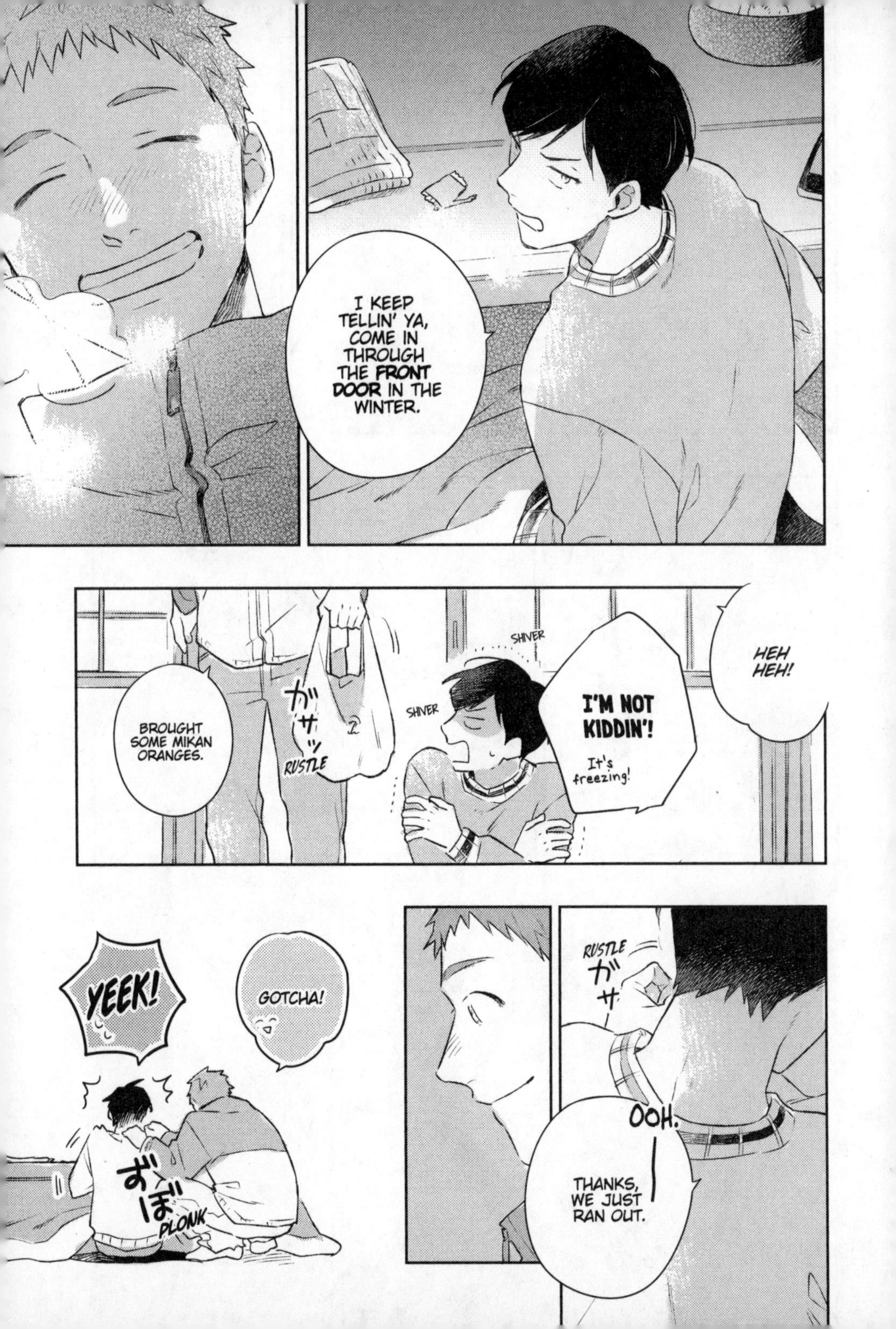
I KEEP TELLIN' YA, COME IN THROUGH THE FRONT DOOR IN THE WINTER.
HEH HEH!
SHIVER
I'M NOT KIDDIN'!
It's freezing!
SHIVER
ガサッ
RUSTLE
BROUGHT SOME MIKAN ORANGES.
RUSTLE
ガサ
OOH.
THANKS, WE JUST RAN OUT.
GOTCHA!
YEEK!
ずぼ
PLONK

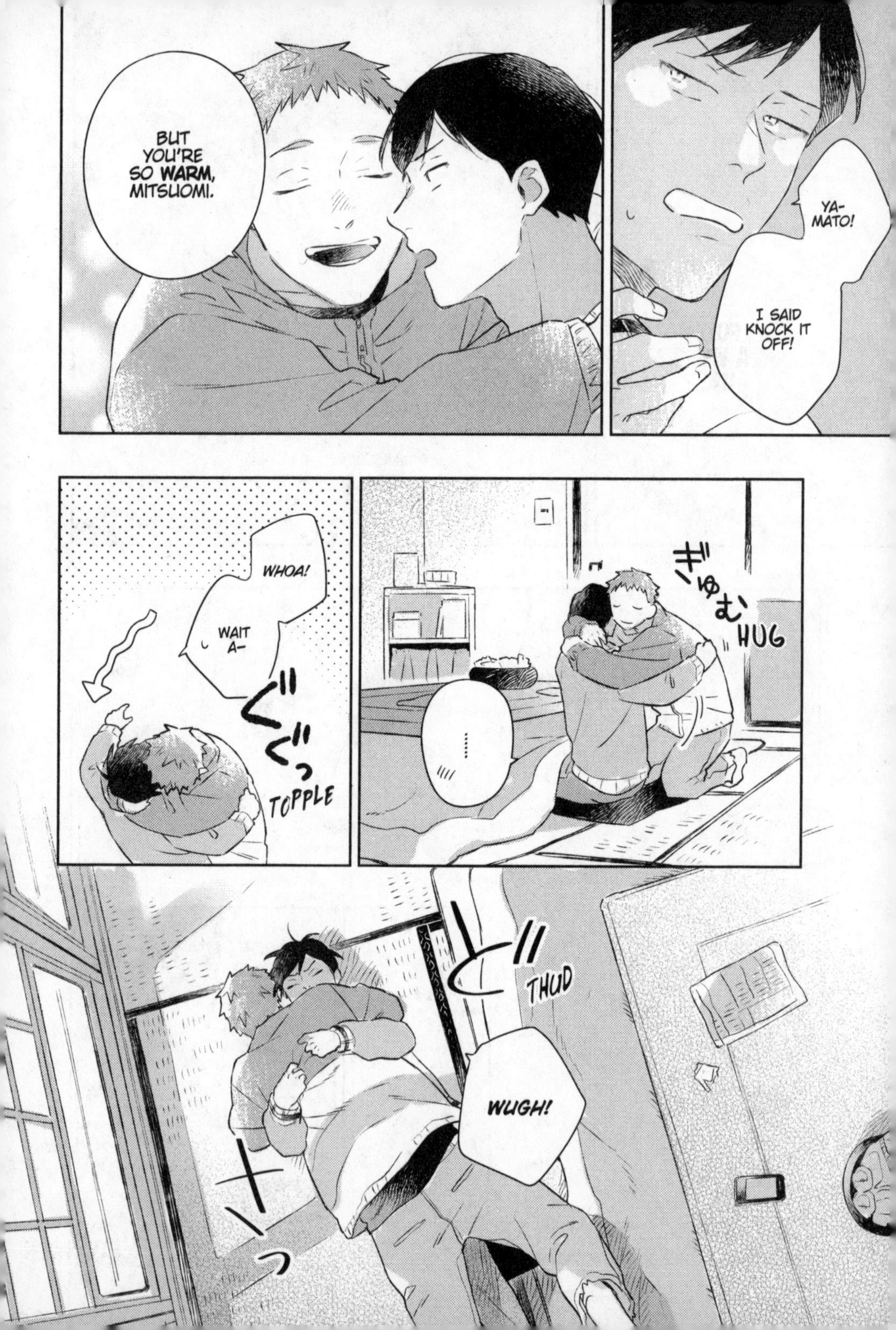
YA-MATO!
I SAID KNOCK IT OFF!
BUT YOU'RE SO WARM, MITSUOMI.
ぎゅむ HUG
......
WHOA!
WAIT A-
ぐぐっ TOPPLE
どっ THUD
WUGH!

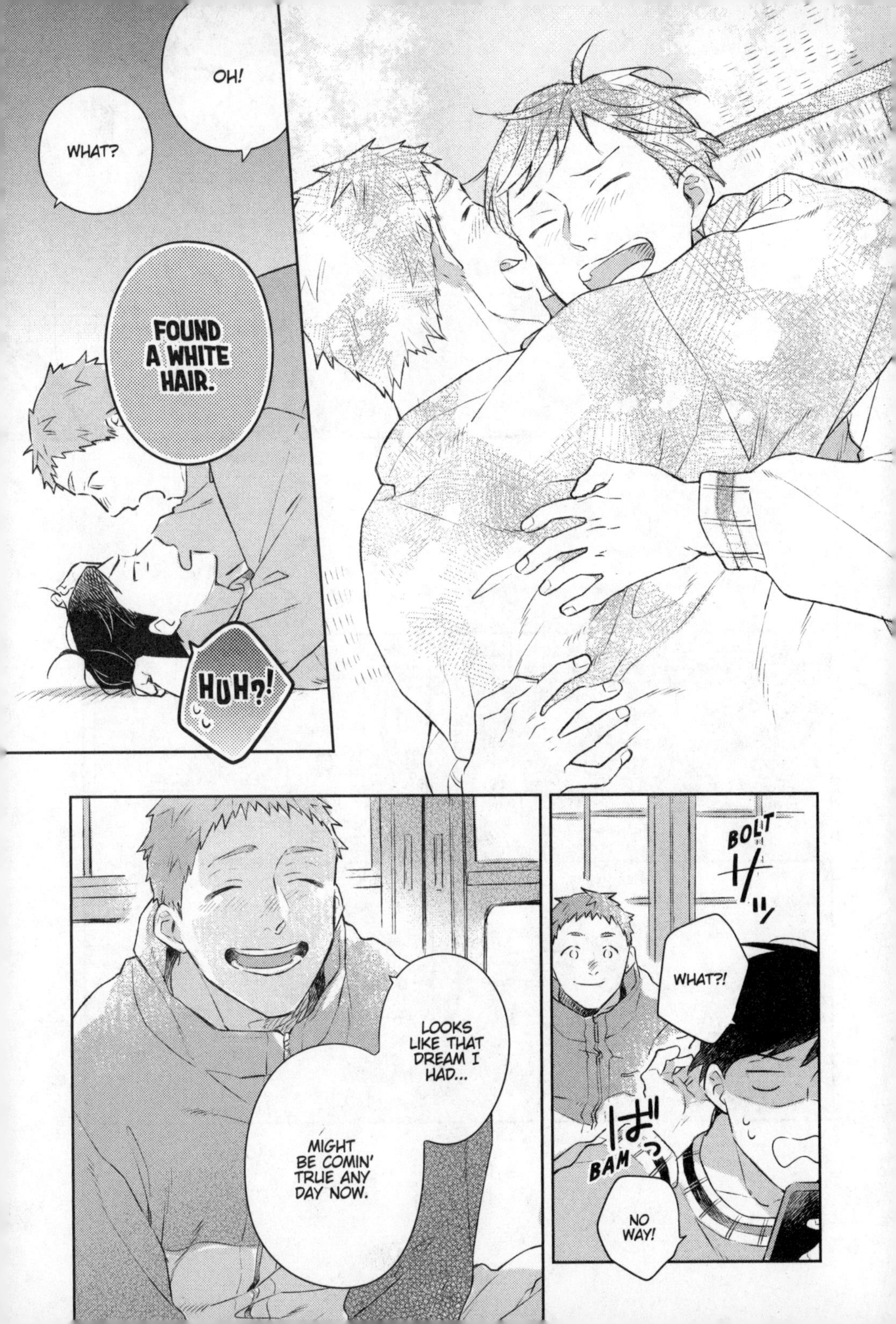
OH!
WHAT?
FOUND A WHITE HAIR.
HUH?!
BOLT
WHAT?!
ばっ
BAM
NO WAY!
LOOKS LIKE THAT DREAM I HAD...
MIGHT BE COMIN' TRUE ANY DAY NOW.

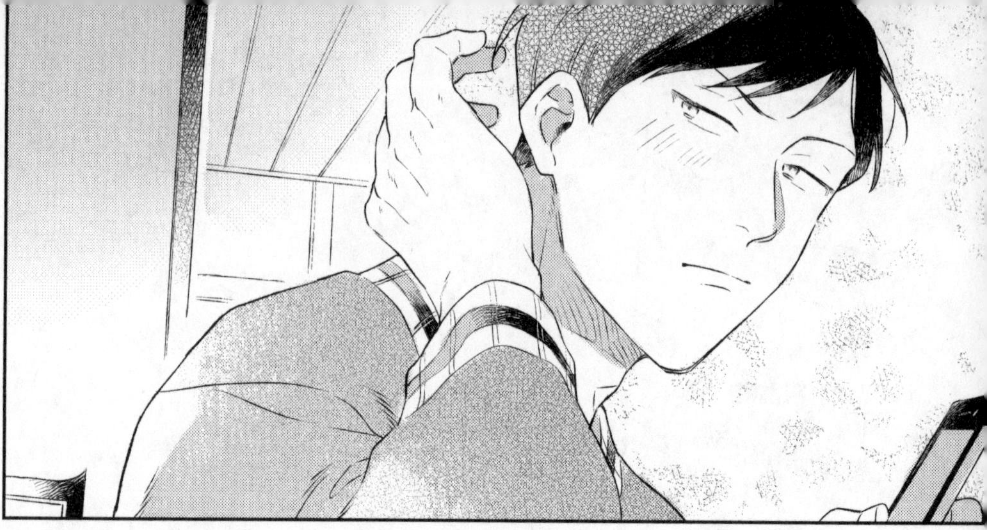

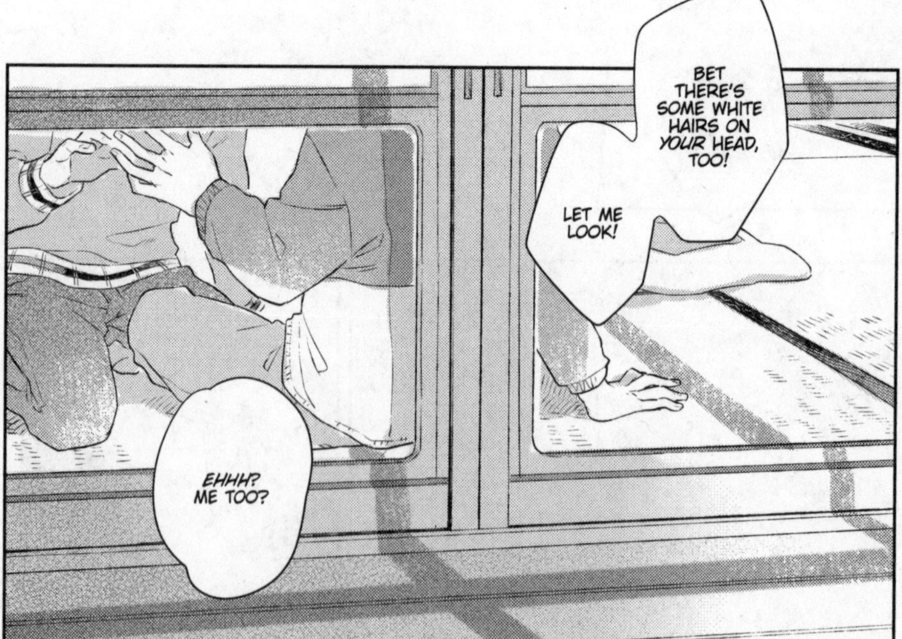
BET THERE'S SOME WHITE HAIRS ON *YOUR* HEAD, TOO!
LET ME LOOK!
EHHH? ME TOO?

Fin

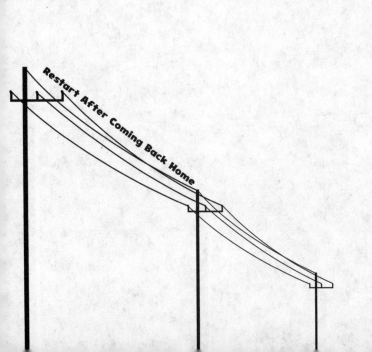

Restart After Coming Back Home

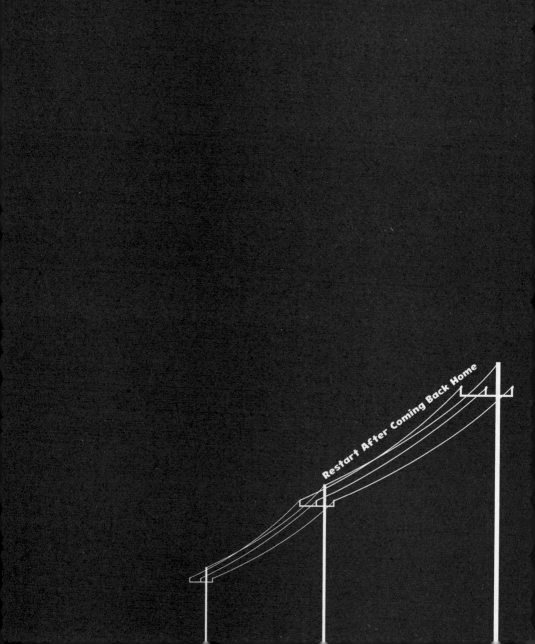
Restart After Coming Back Home

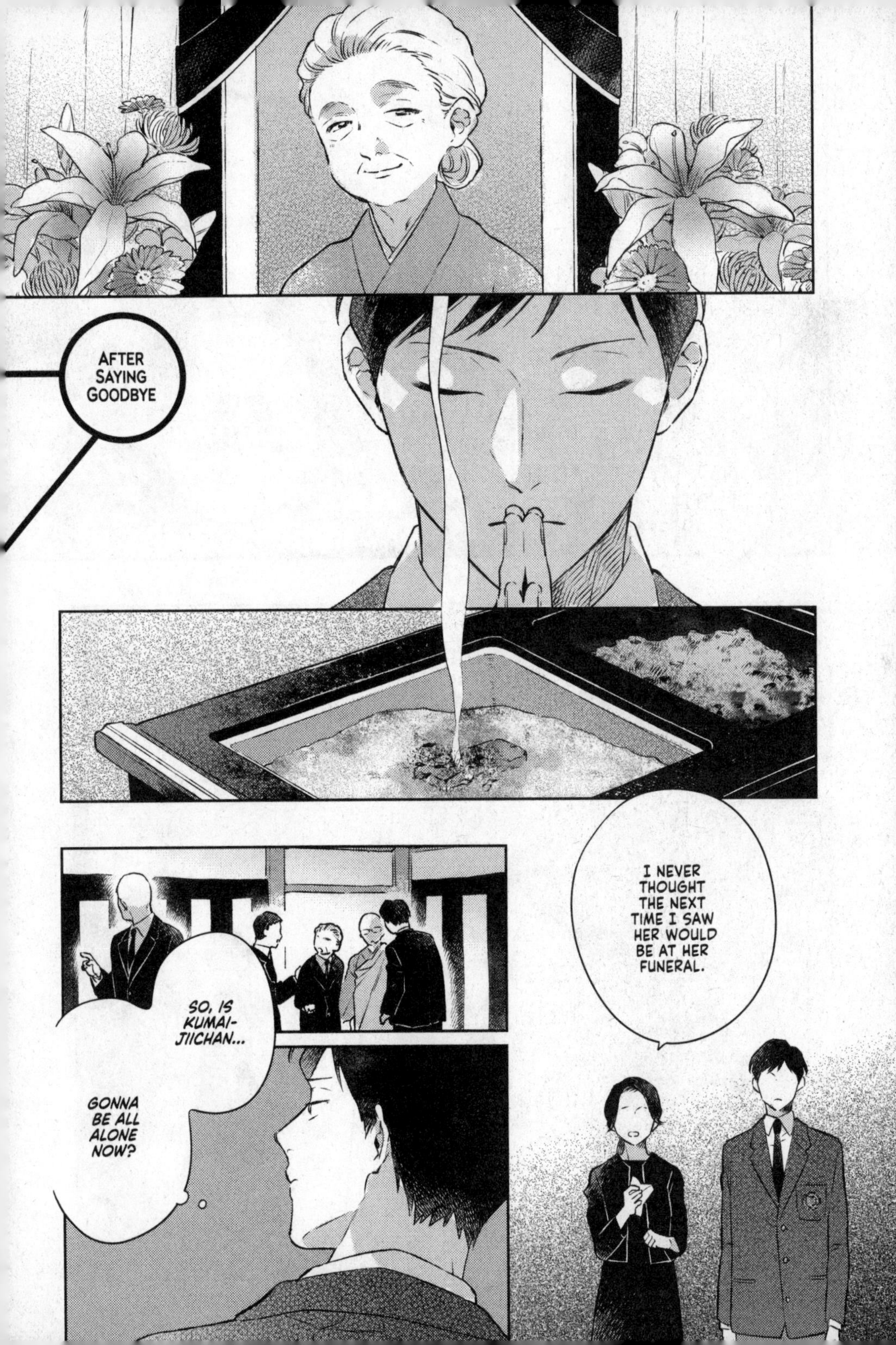
AFTER SAYING GOODBYE
I NEVER THOUGHT THE NEXT TIME I SAW HER WOULD BE AT HER FUNERAL.
SO, IS KUMAI-JIICHAN...
GONNA BE ALL ALONE NOW?

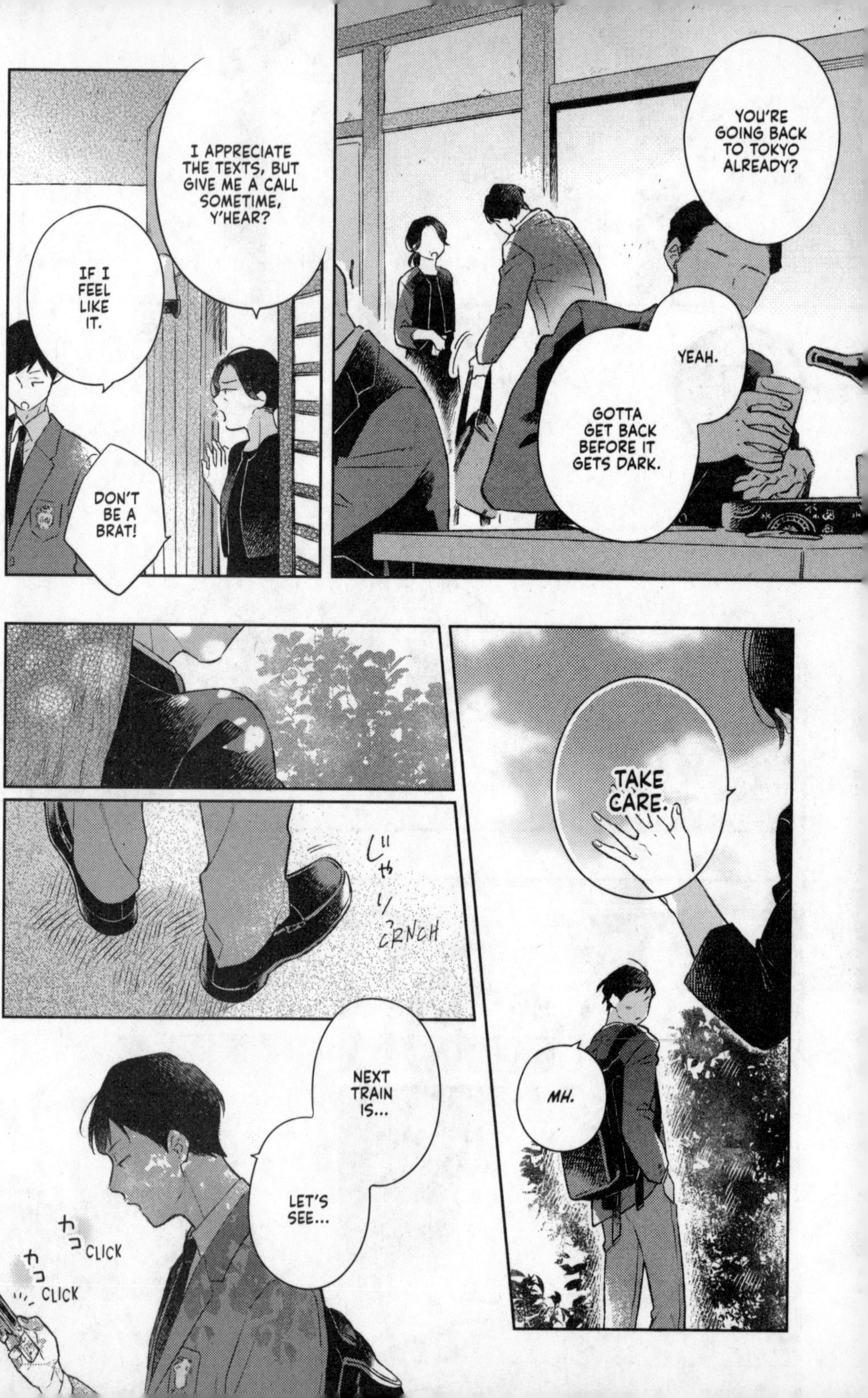
YOU'RE GOING BACK TO TOKYO ALREADY?
YEAH.
GOTTA GET BACK BEFORE IT GETS DARK.
I APPRECIATE THE TEXTS, BUT GIVE ME A CALL SOMETIME, Y'HEAR?
IF I FEEL LIKE IT.
DON'T BE A BRAT!
TAKE CARE.
MH.
じゃり CRNCH
NEXT TRAIN IS...
LET'S SEE...
カコ CLICK
カコ CLICK

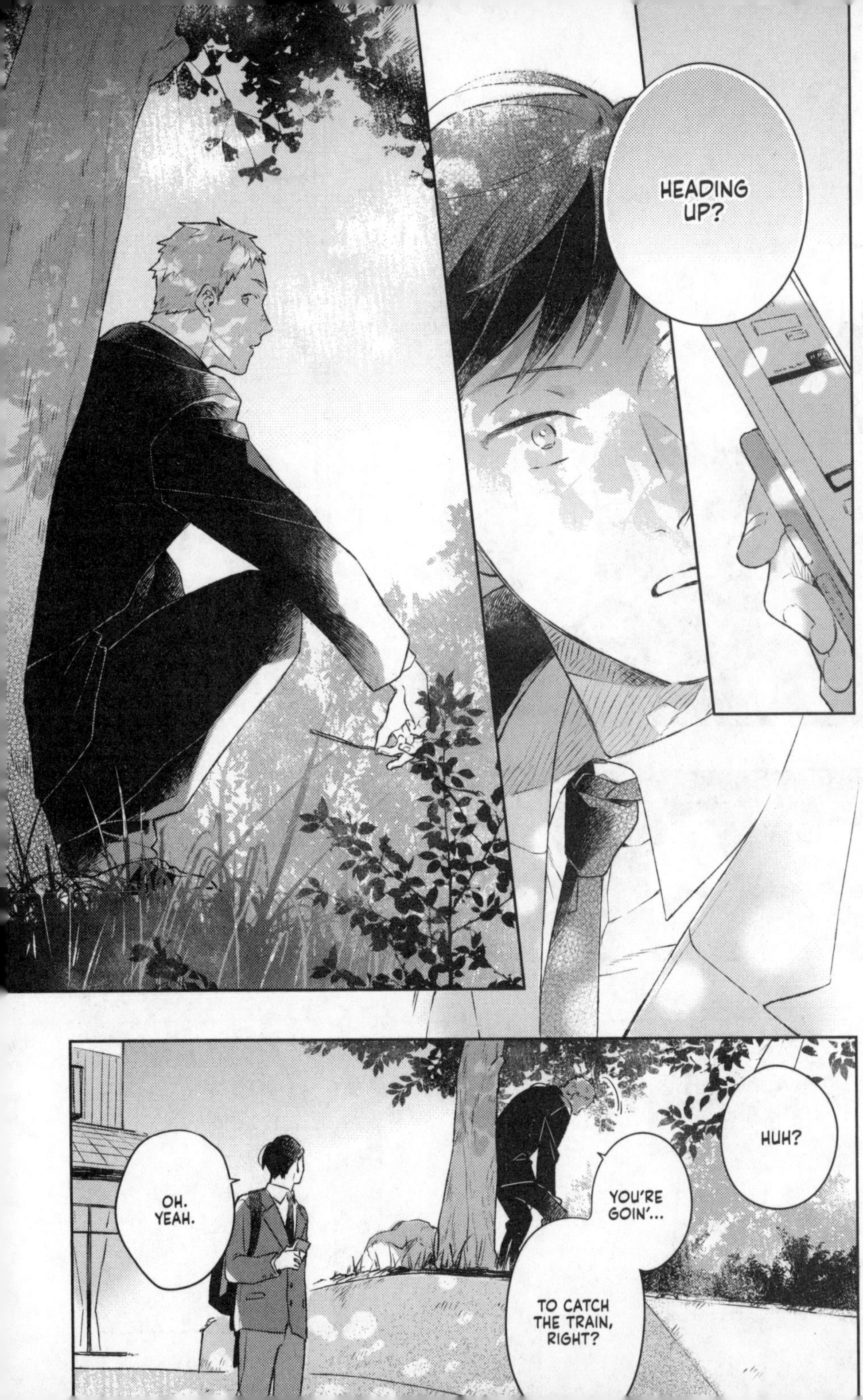
HEADING UP?
HUH?
YOU'RE GOIN'...
TO CATCH THE TRAIN, RIGHT?
OH. YEAH.

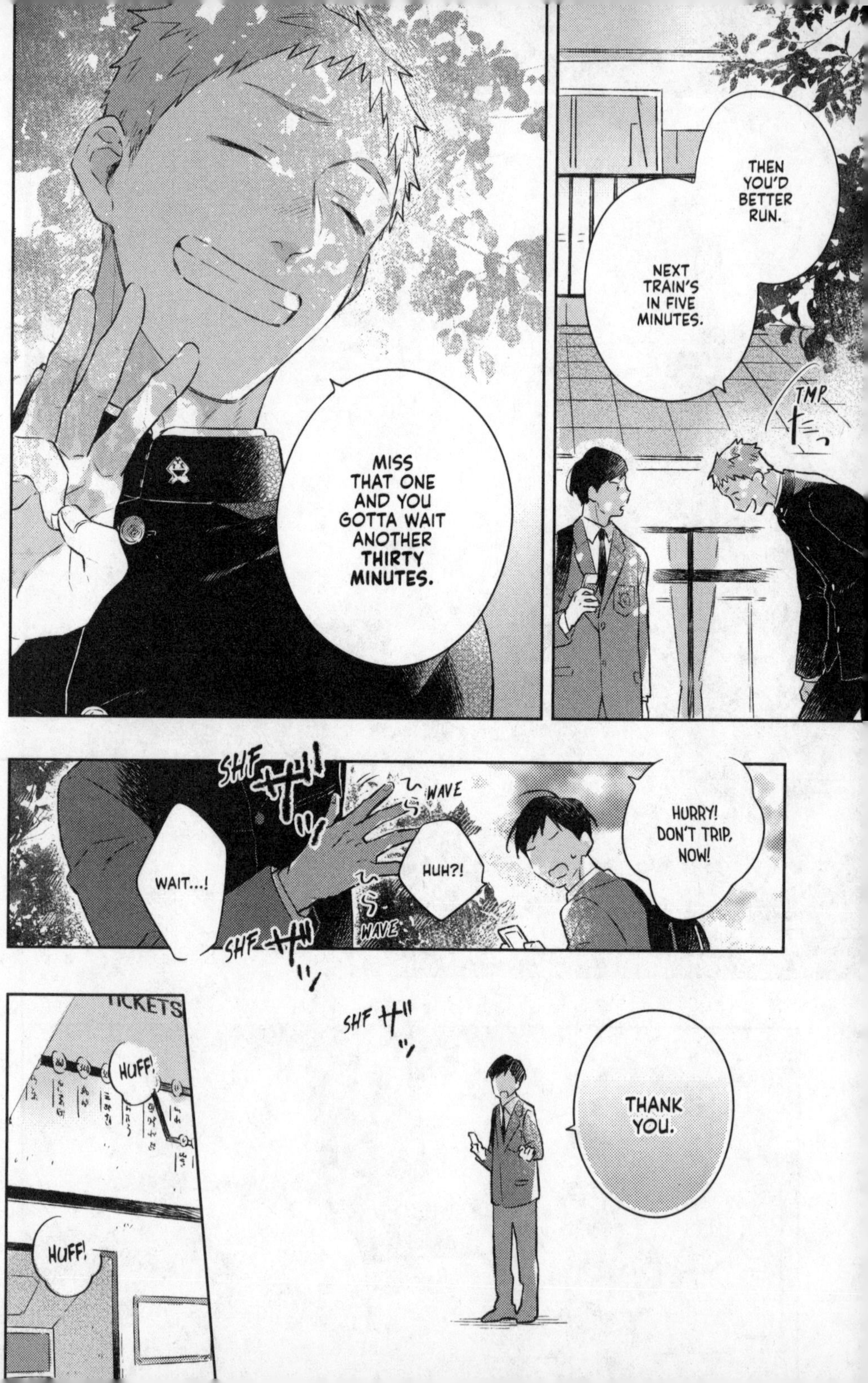
THEN YOU'D BETTER RUN.
NEXT TRAIN'S IN FIVE MINUTES.
TMP
MISS THAT ONE AND YOU GOTTA WAIT ANOTHER THIRTY MINUTES.
HURRY! DON'T TRIP, NOW!
HUH?!
WAVE
WAVE
SHF
WAIT...!
SHF
SHF
THANK YOU.
TICKETS
HUFF!
HUFF!

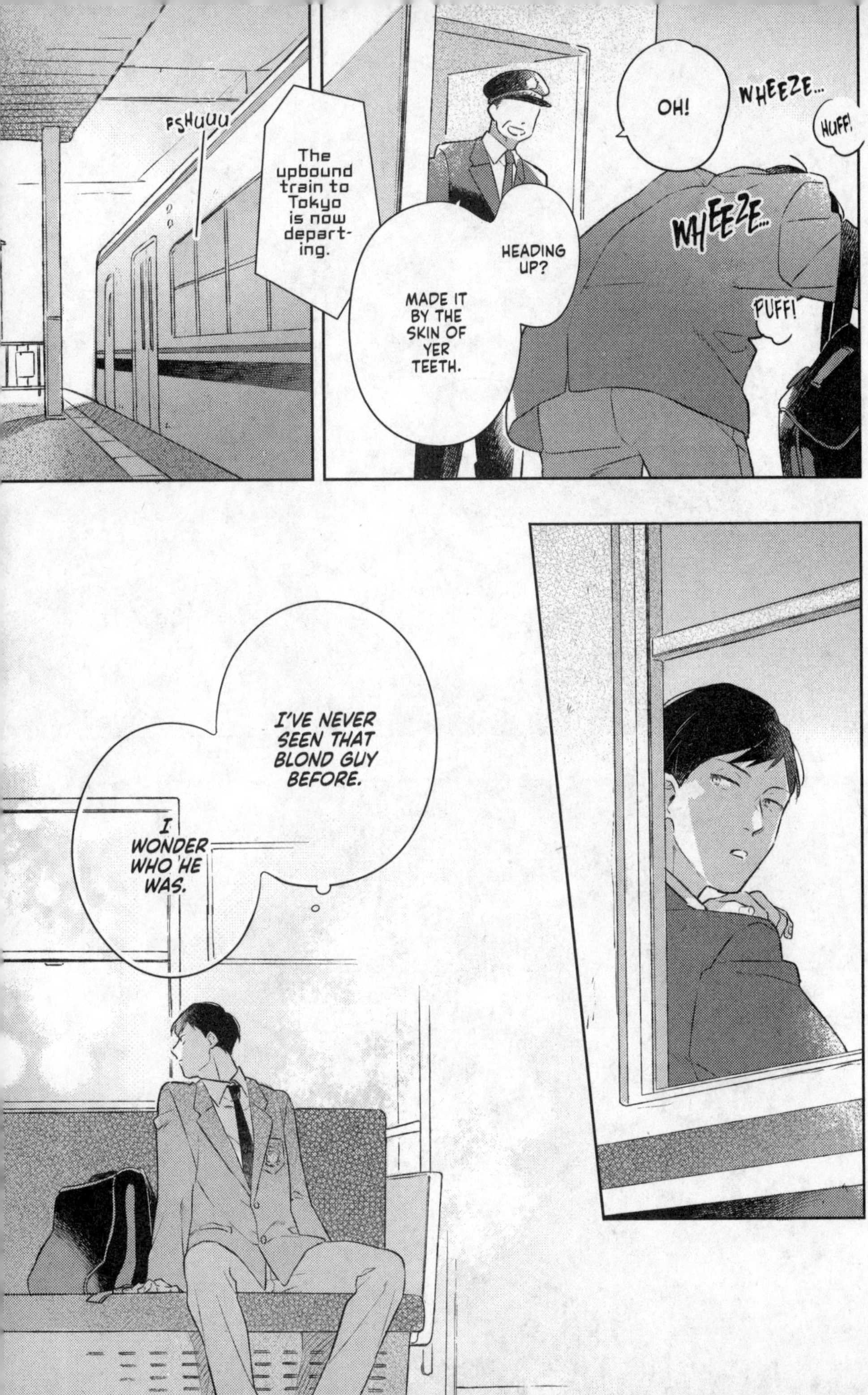
WHEEZE...
HUFF!
OH!
WHEEZE...
PUFF!
HEADING UP?
MADE IT BY THE SKIN OF YER TEETH.
The upbound train to Tokyo is now depart-ing.
FSHUUU
I'VE NEVER SEEN THAT BLOND GUY BEFORE.
I WONDER WHO HE WAS.

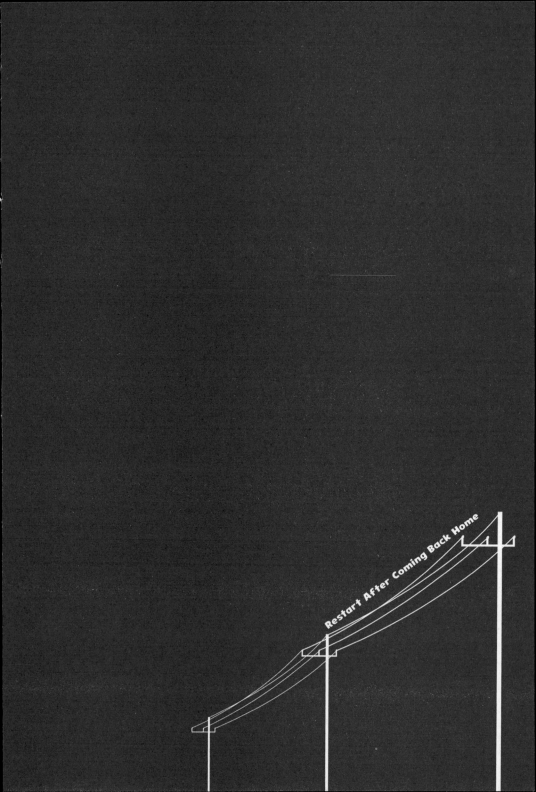

Restart After Coming Back Home

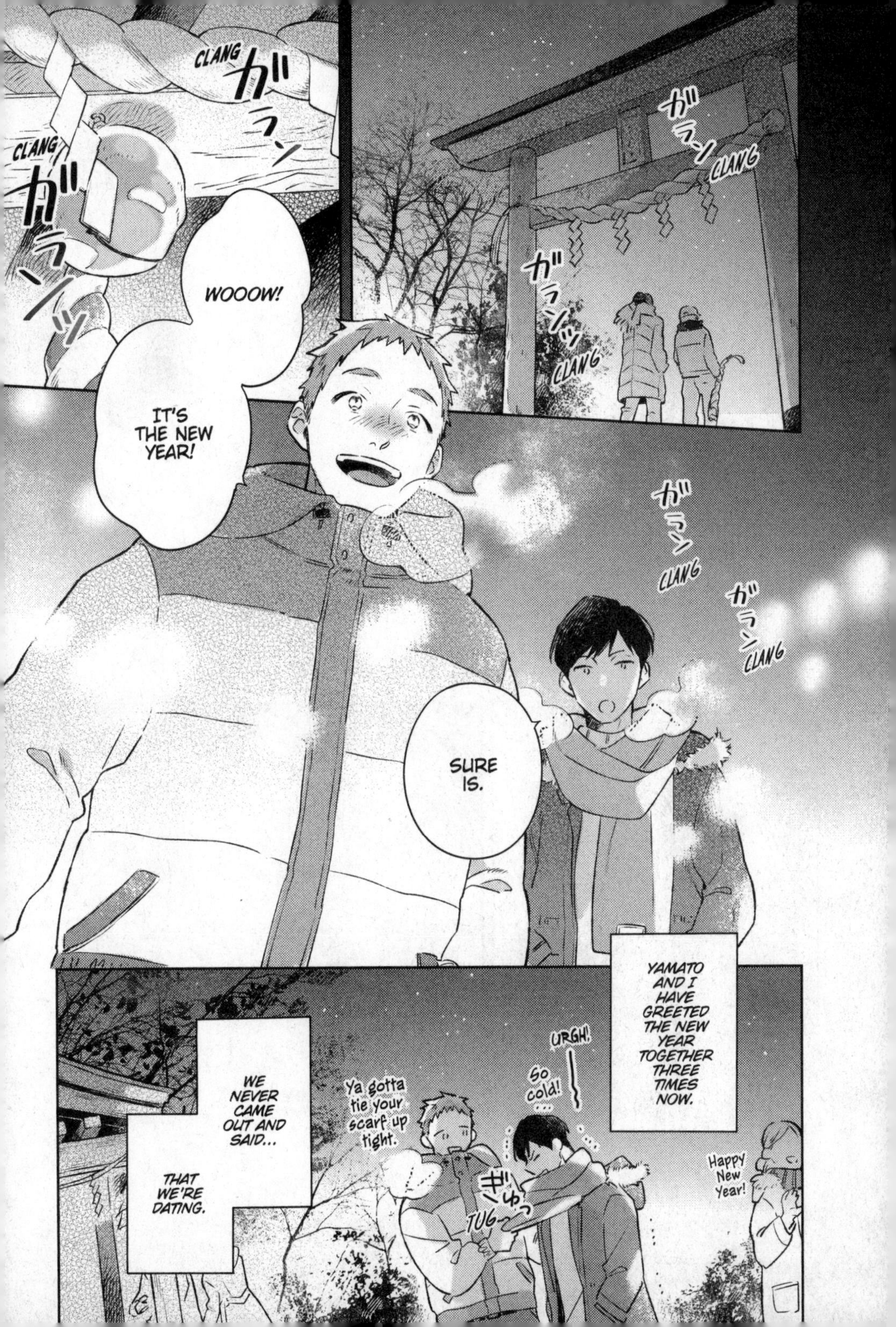
ガラン
CLANG
ガランッ
CLANG
CLANG
ガラン
CLANG
ガランッ
WOOOW!
IT'S THE NEW YEAR!
ガラン
CLANG
ガラン
CLANG
SURE IS.
YAMATO AND I HAVE GREETED THE NEW YEAR TOGETHER THREE TIMES NOW.
Happy New Year!
URGH!
So cold!...
Ya gotta tie your scarf up tight.
ぎゅっ
TUG
WE NEVER CAME OUT AND SAID...
THAT WE'RE DATING.

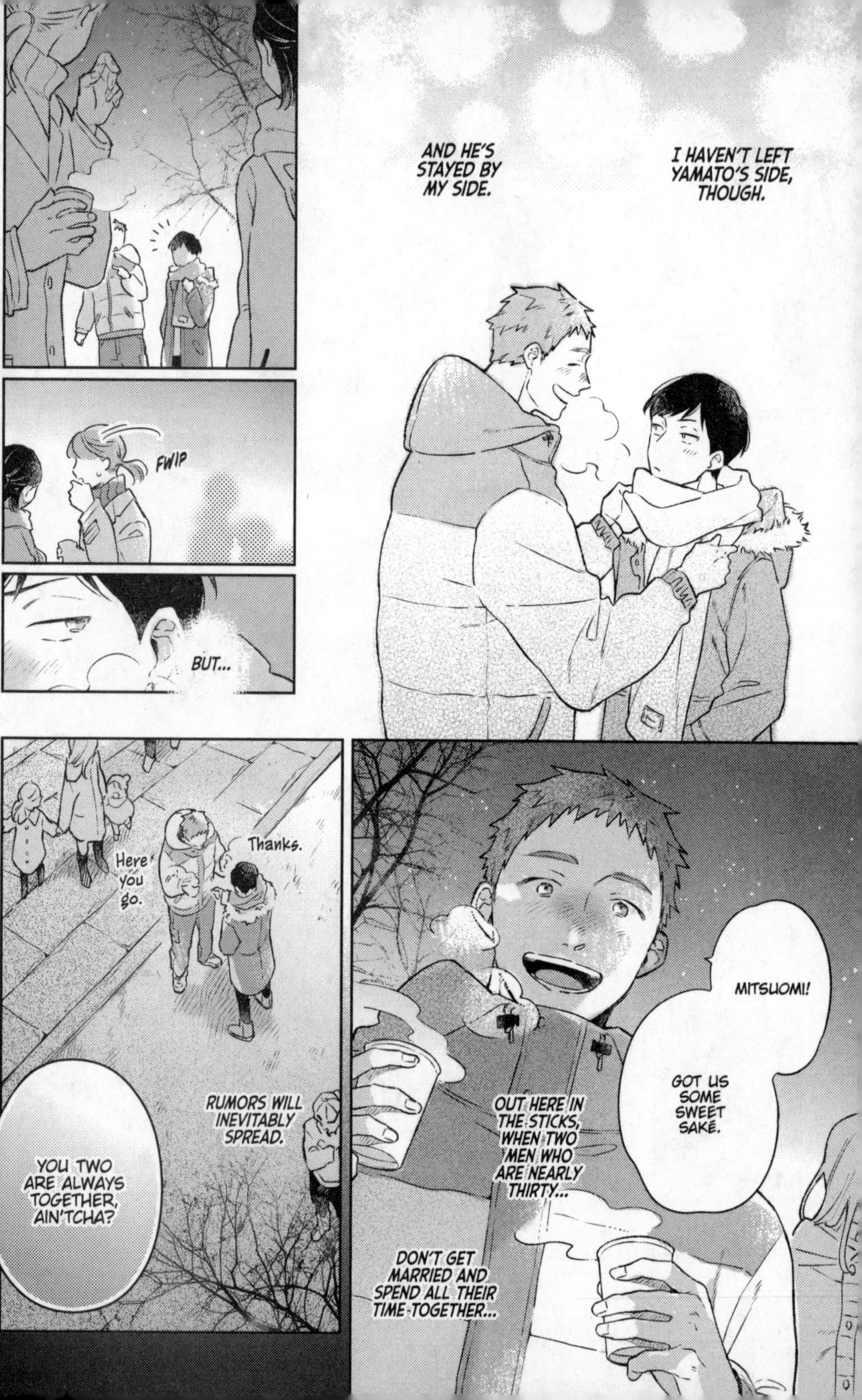
I HAVEN'T LEFT YAMATO'S SIDE, THOUGH.
AND HE'S STAYED BY MY SIDE.
FWIP
BUT...
MITSUOMI!
GOT US SOME SWEET SAKÉ.
OUT HERE IN THE STICKS, WHEN TWO MEN WHO ARE NEARLY THIRTY...
DON'T GET MARRIED AND SPEND ALL THEIR TIME TOGETHER...
Thanks.
Here you go.
RUMORS WILL INEVITABLY SPREAD.
YOU TWO ARE ALWAYS TOGETHER, AIN'TCHA?

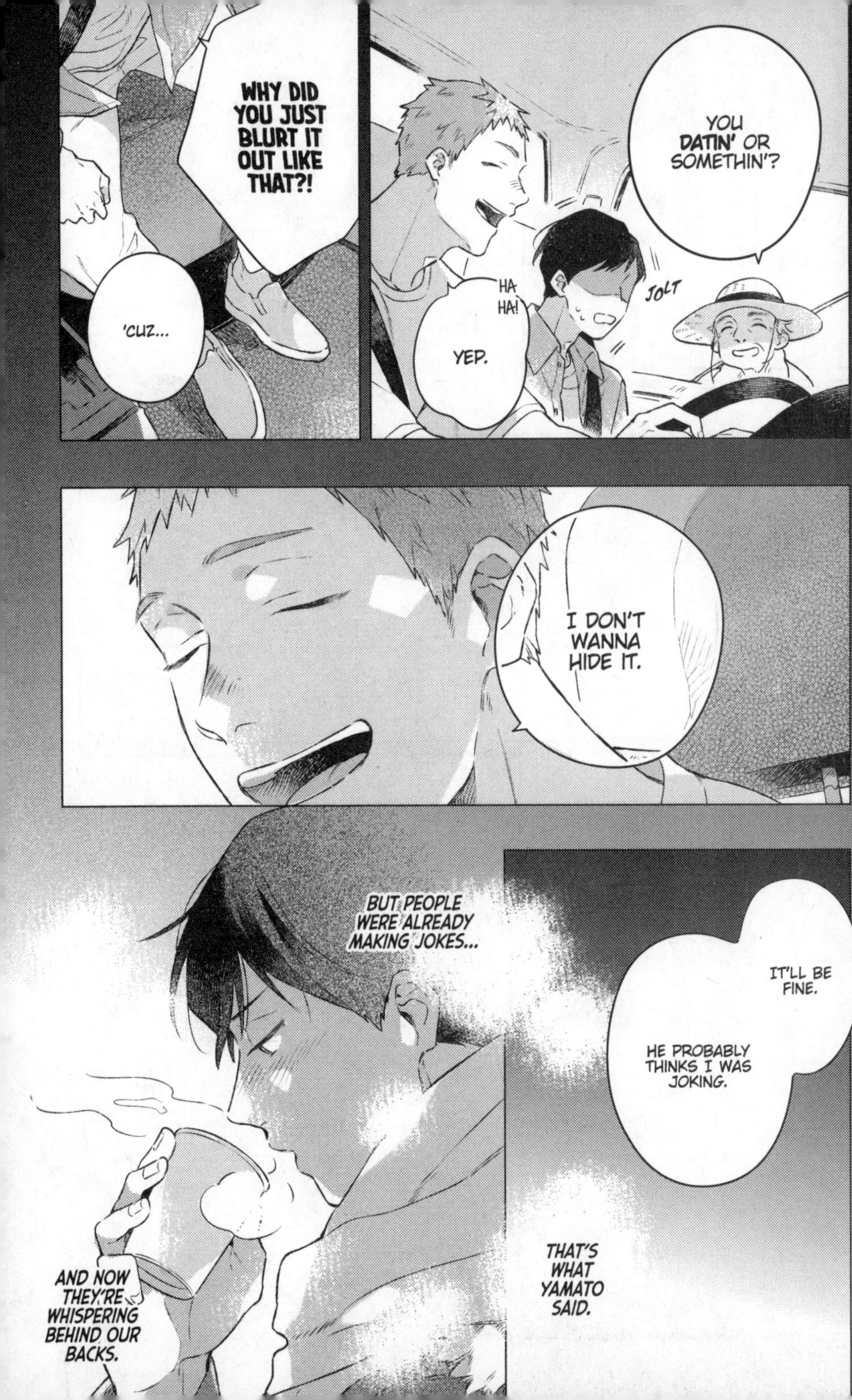
YOU DATIN' OR SOMETHIN'?
JOLT
HA HA!
YEP.
WHY DID YOU JUST BLURT IT OUT LIKE THAT?!
'CUZ...
I DON'T WANNA HIDE IT.
IT'LL BE FINE.
HE PROBABLY THINKS I WAS JOKING.
THAT'S WHAT YAMATO SAID.
BUT PEOPLE WERE ALREADY MAKING JOKES...
AND NOW THEY'RE WHISPERING BEHIND OUR BACKS.

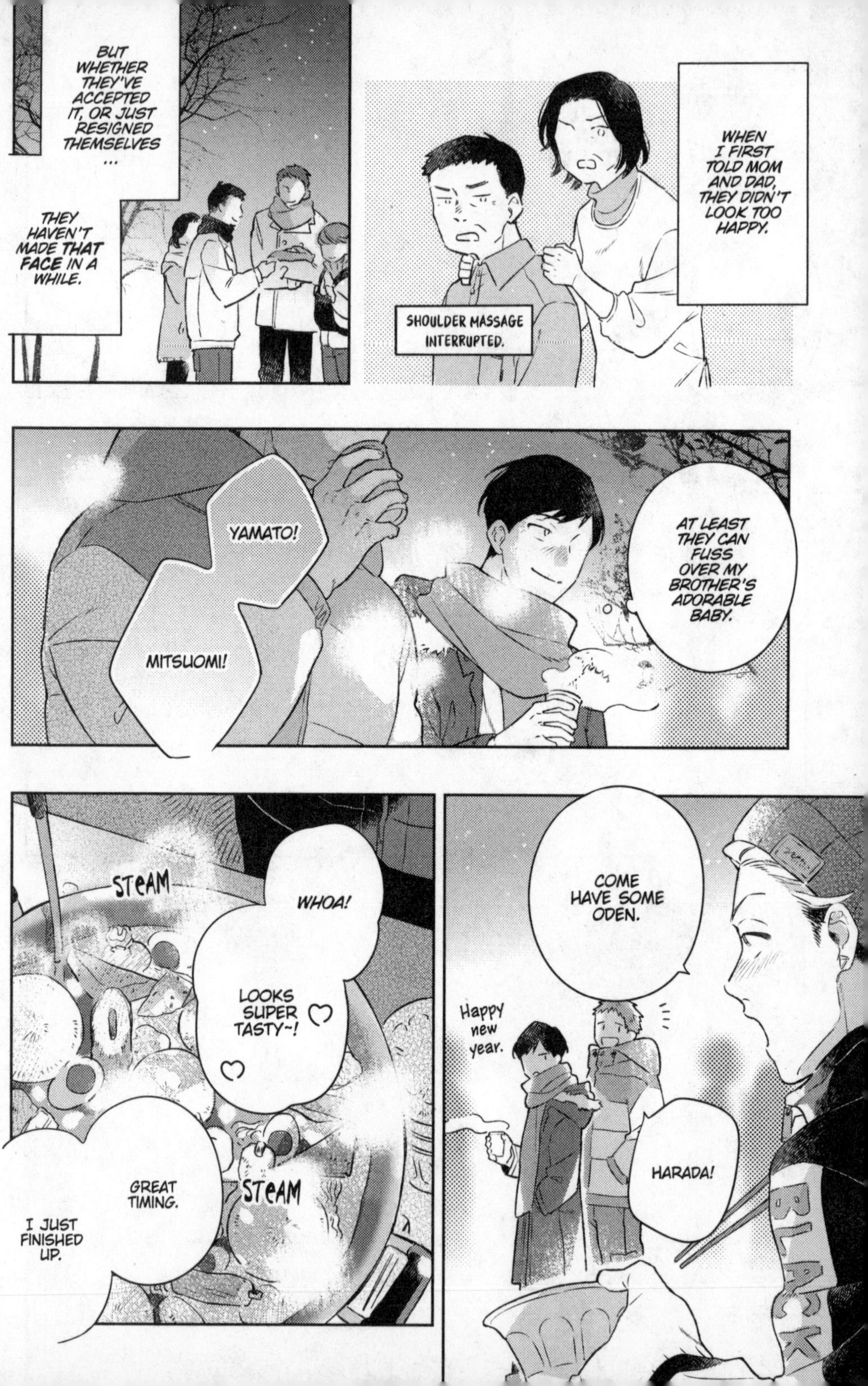
WHEN I FIRST TOLD MOM AND DAD, THEY DIDN'T LOOK TOO HAPPY.
SHOULDER MASSAGE INTERRUPTED.
BUT WHETHER THEY'VE ACCEPTED IT, OR JUST RESIGNED THEMSELVES...
THEY HAVEN'T MADE THAT FACE IN A WHILE.
AT LEAST THEY CAN FUSS OVER MY BROTHER'S ADORABLE BABY.
YAMATO!
MITSUOMI!
COME HAVE SOME ODEN.
Happy new year.
HARADA!
WHOA!
LOOKS SUPER TASTY~!
STEAM
STEAM
GREAT TIMING.
I JUST FINISHED UP.

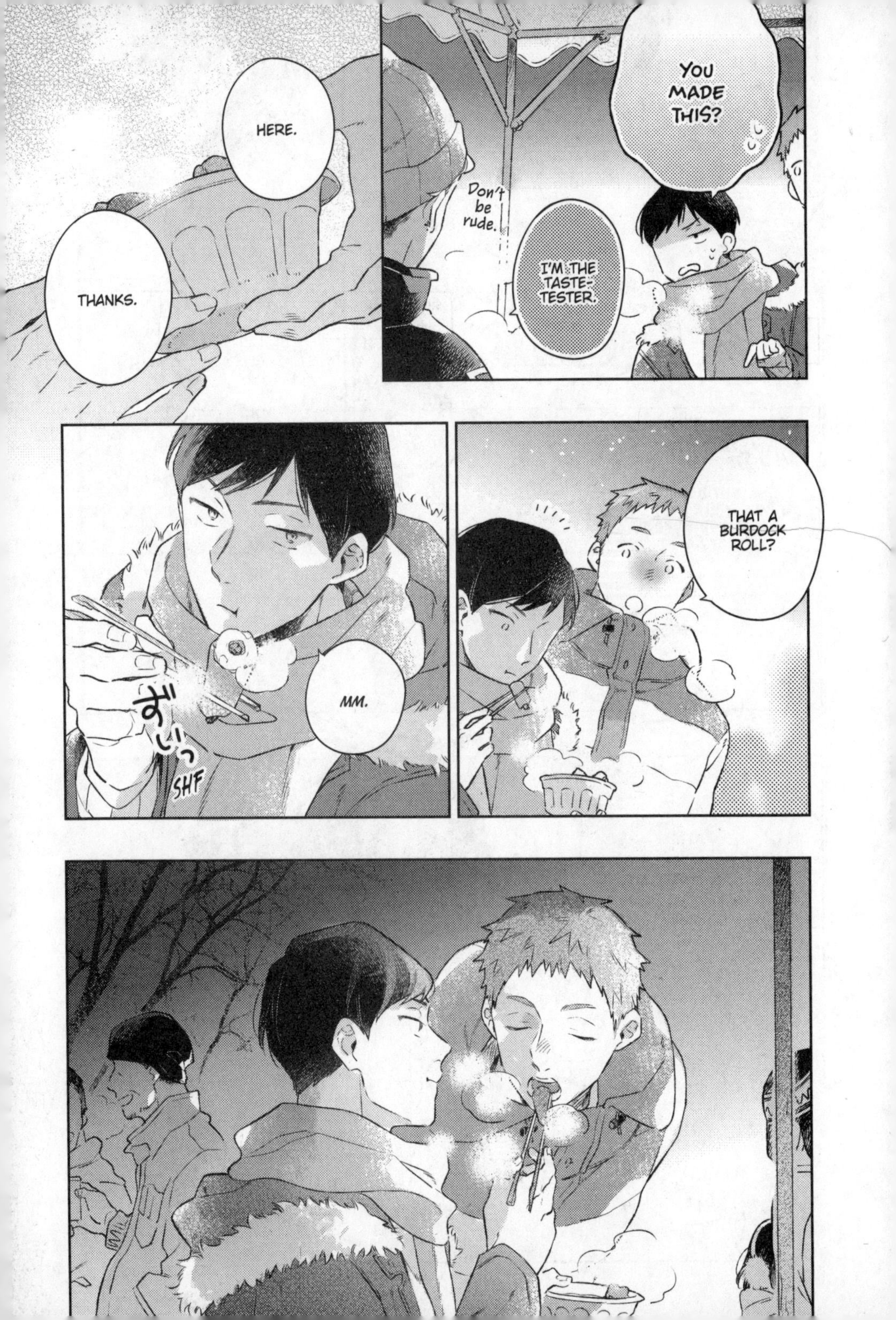
YOU MADE THIS?
Don't be rude.
I'M THE TASTE-TESTER.
HERE.
THANKS.
THAT A BURDOCK ROLL?
MM.
ずいっ
SHF

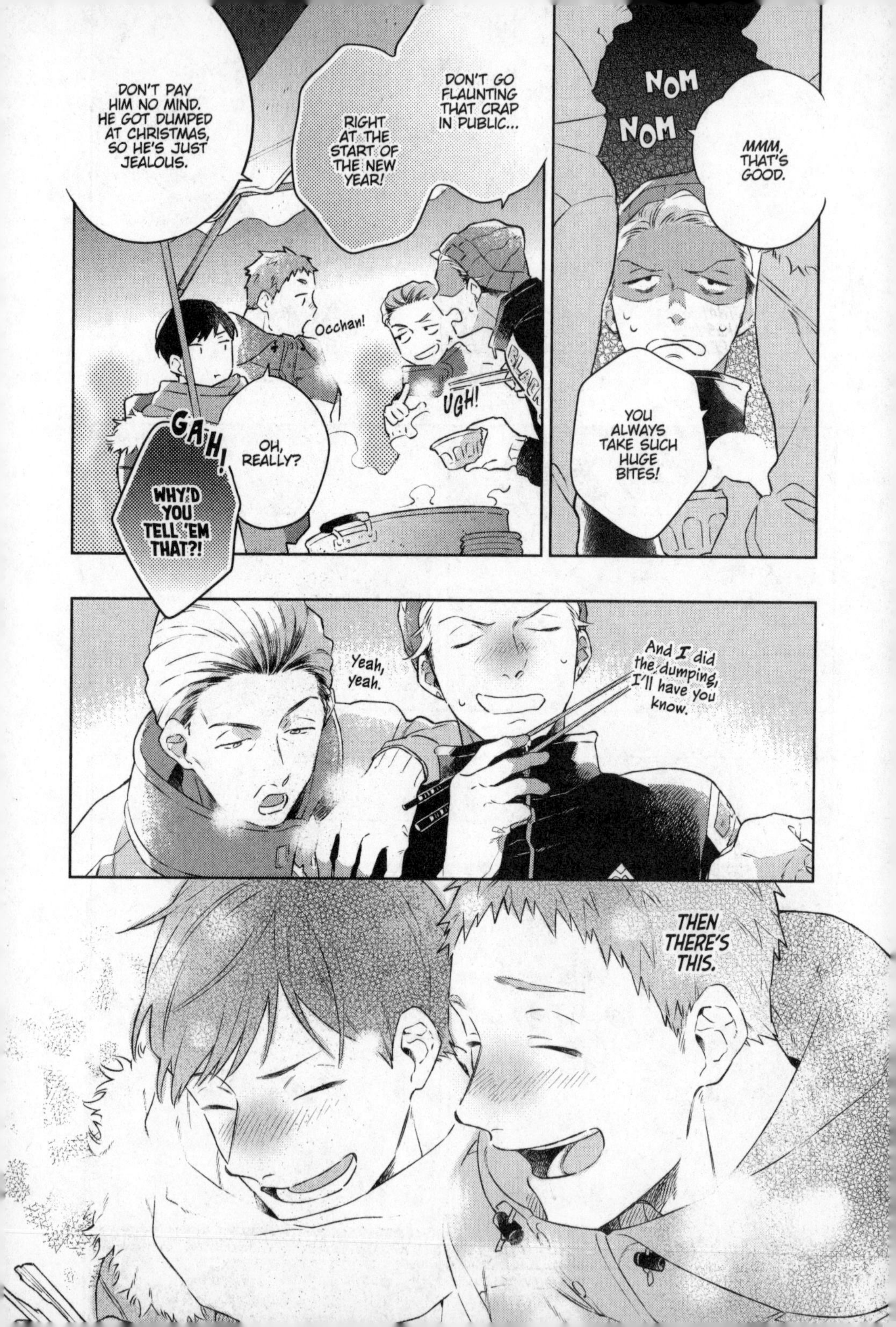
NOM NOM
MMM, THAT'S GOOD.
YOU ALWAYS TAKE SUCH HUGE BITES!
DON'T GO FLAUNTING THAT CRAP IN PUBLIC...
RIGHT AT THE START OF THE NEW YEAR!
DON'T PAY HIM NO MIND. HE GOT DUMPED AT CHRISTMAS, SO HE'S JUST JEALOUS.
Occhan!
UGH!
OH, REALLY?
GAH!
WHY'D YOU TELL 'EM THAT?!
And I did the dumping, I'll have you know.
Yeah, yeah.
THEN THERE'S THIS.

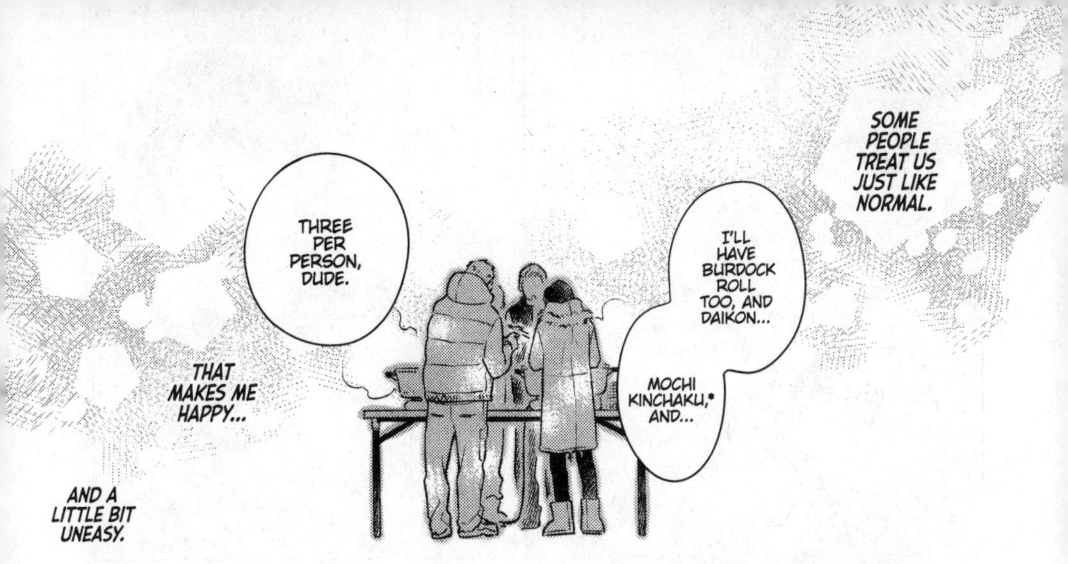
SOME PEOPLE TREAT US JUST LIKE NORMAL.
I'LL HAVE BURDOCK ROLL TOO, AND DAIKON...
MOCHI KINCHAKU,* AND...
THREE PER PERSON, DUDE.
THAT MAKES ME HAPPY...
AND A LITTLE BIT UNEASY.

* Mochi kinchaku is a pouch of fried tofu containing glutinous rice.

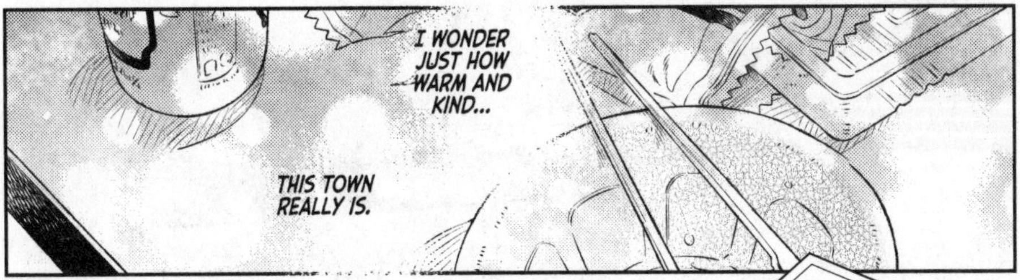
I WONDER JUST HOW WARM AND KIND...
THIS TOWN REALLY IS.

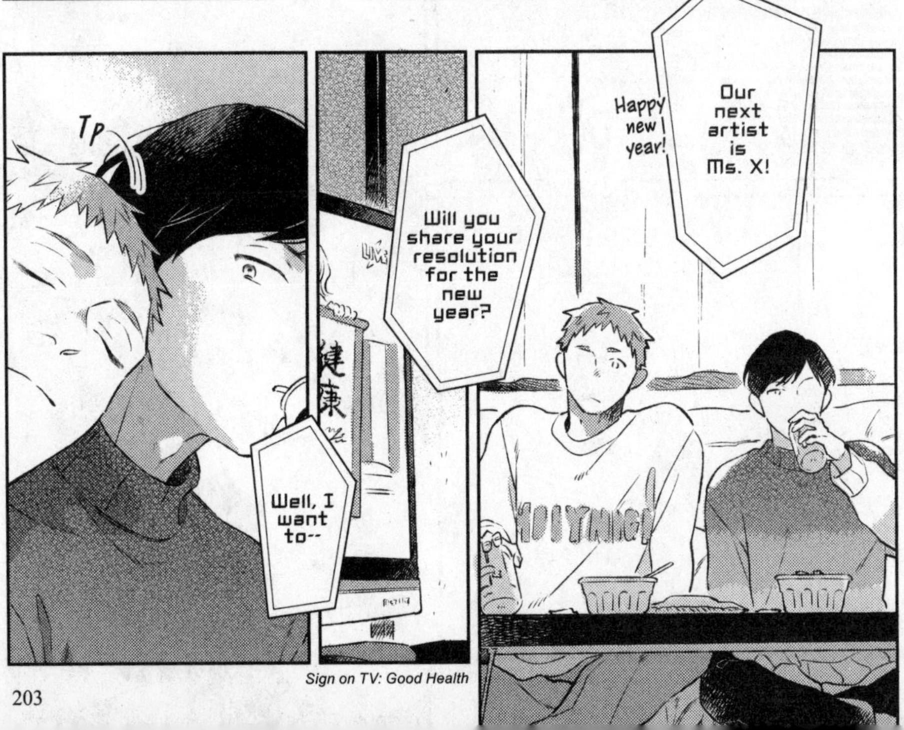
Our next artist is Ms. X!
Happy new year!
Will you share your resolution for the new year?
TP
Well, I want to--

Sign on TV: Good Health

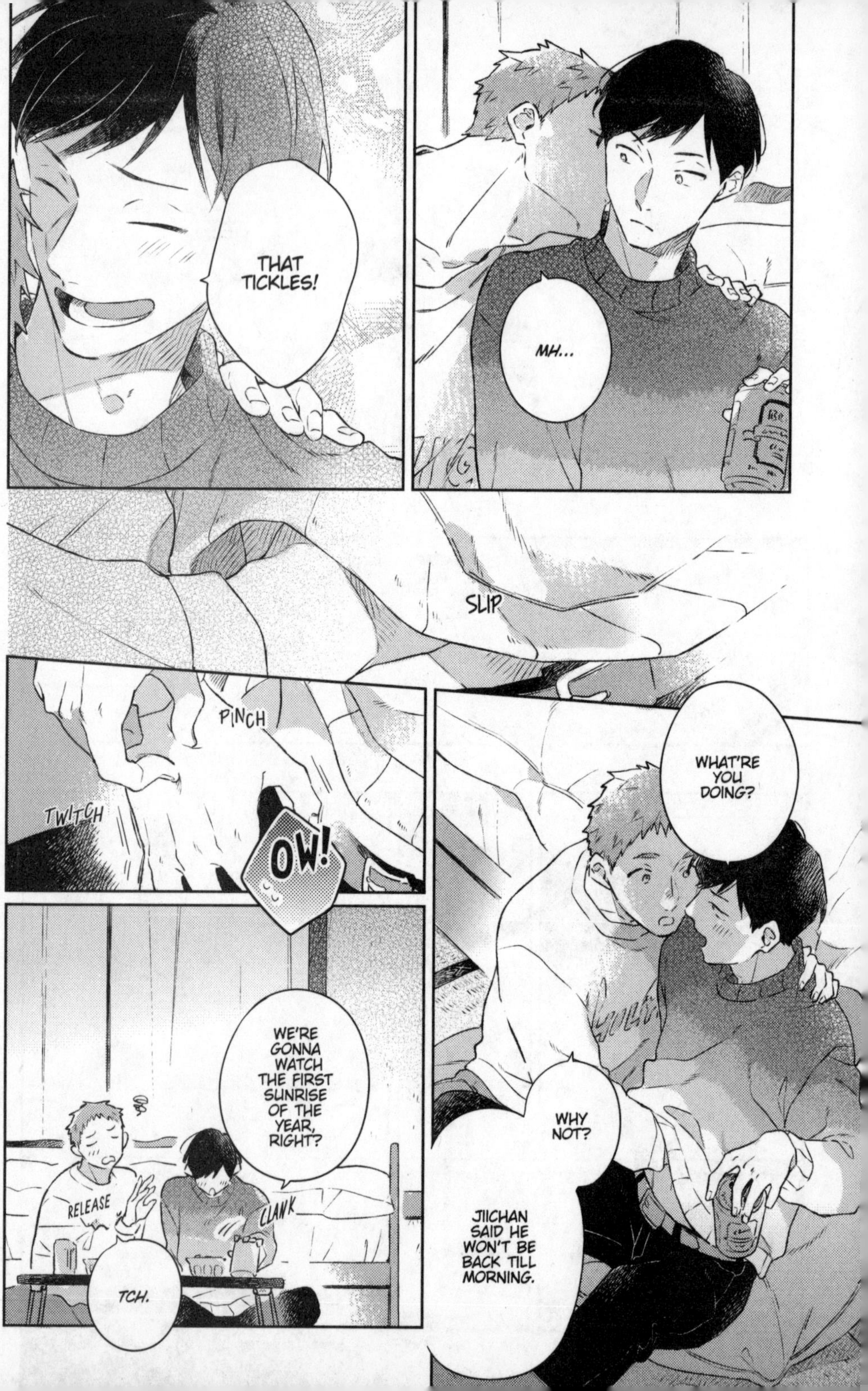
MH...
THAT TICKLES!
SLIP
WHAT'RE YOU DOING?
WHY NOT?
JIICHAN SAID HE WON'T BE BACK TILL MORNING.
PINCH
TWITCH
OW!
WE'RE GONNA WATCH THE FIRST SUNRISE OF THE YEAR, RIGHT?
RELEASE
CLANK
TCH.

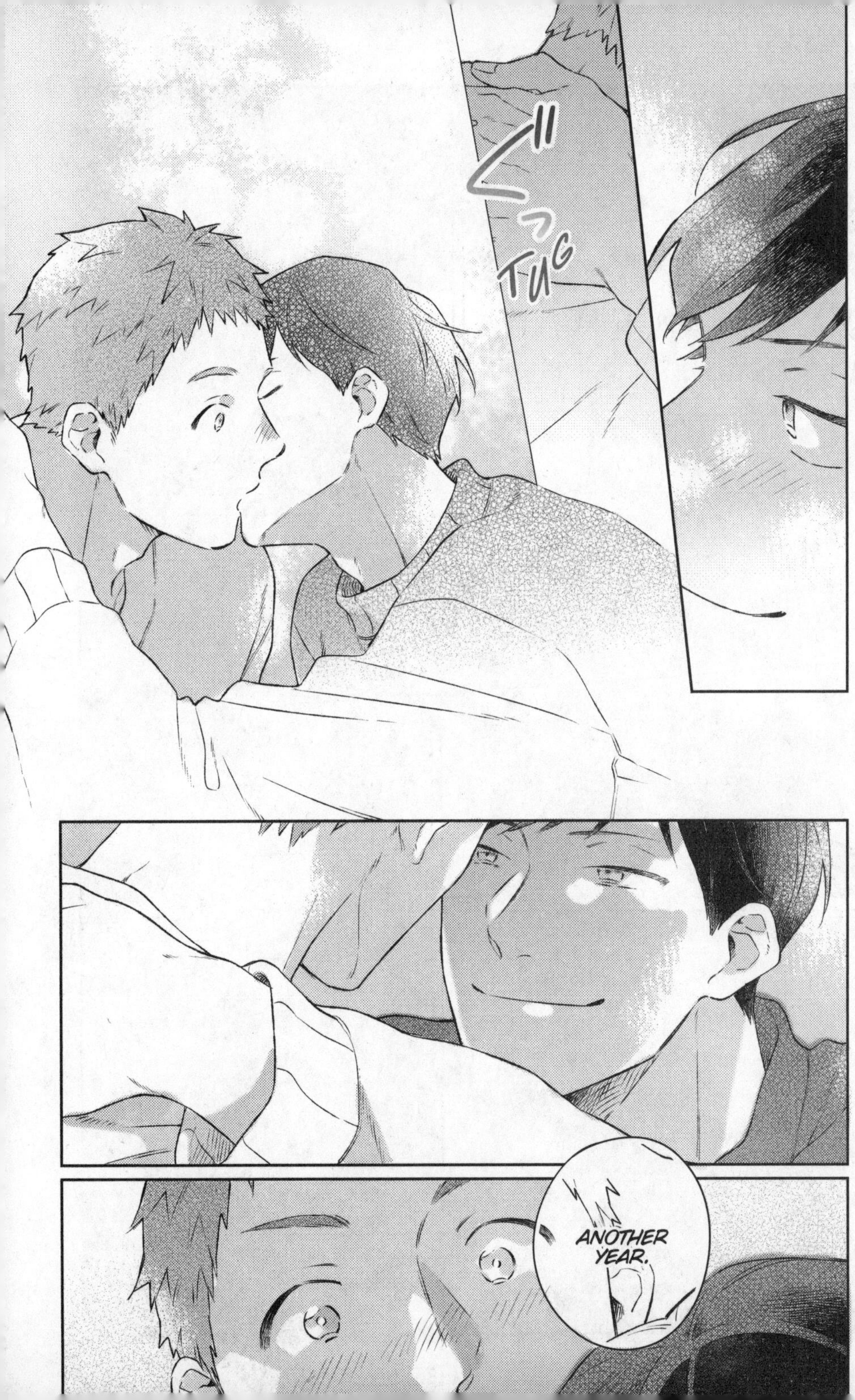
くっ
TUG
ANOTHER YEAR.

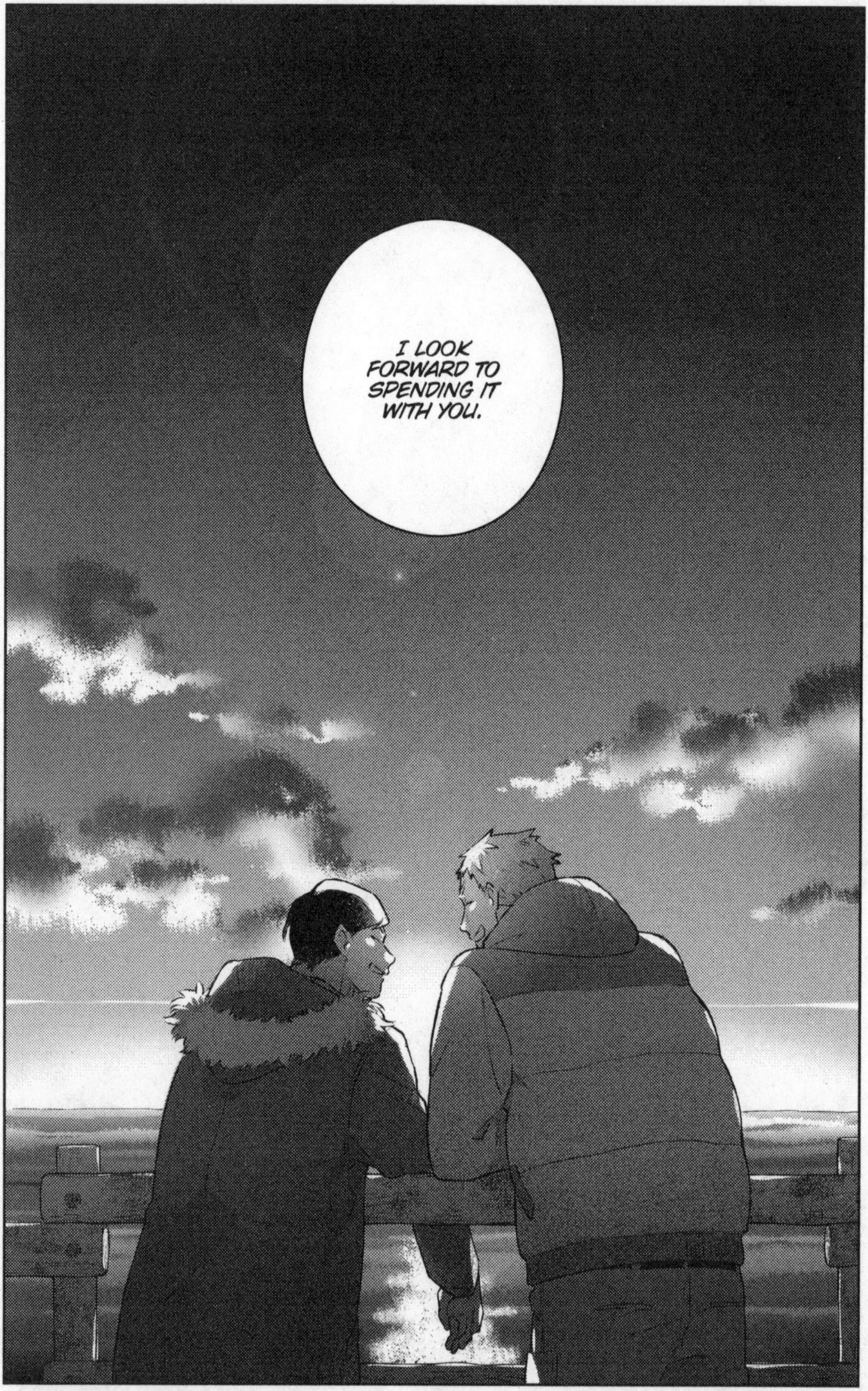
I LOOK FORWARD TO SPENDING IT WITH YOU.

Fin

thank you for reading.

THANK YOU SO MUCH...
FOR PICKING UP THIS BOOK.

I WAS SORTING OUT MY TANKOBON WORK FOLDER, WHEN...
OH! MY ROUGH DRAFTS.
THIS TAKES ME BACK...
Normal uke who returns home from Tokyo to the countryside. The seme is this feral child who tries to eat weeds and stuff. They grow closer...
Returns home after getting fired from his job. (Age twenty-five)
Mean
No confidence
Third son
Sharp tongue
EATING WEEDS?!
THAT'S NOT A FERAL CHILD THING, THAT'S JUST CRAZY!
Glad that didn't make it into the final draft.

I started drawing this story because I wanted to show two people who form an emotional bond based on each one making up for what the other lacks, while respecting each other, and which also explores this emotion we call love.

This book has a happy ending, but...maybe being lovers doesn't go so smoothly for them. Maybe they break up, maybe they get back together again, maybe they go through those stages more than once. I don't know what the future holds for them, but I hope that they can keep laughing together, side by side, the whole time. Not sure whether I pulled it off, but I'll be delighted if this book moves you in any way.

A big thank you to everyone I owe so much to—my editor "Y-sama," the editorial department, the designers, the printer, my friends, my family, and everyone else involved!

Cocomi Winter 2019

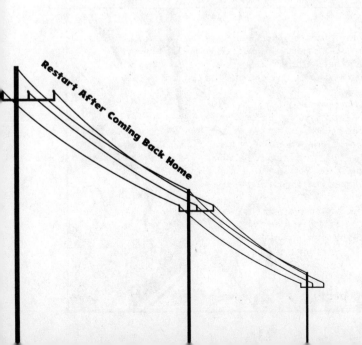

Restart After Coming Back Home

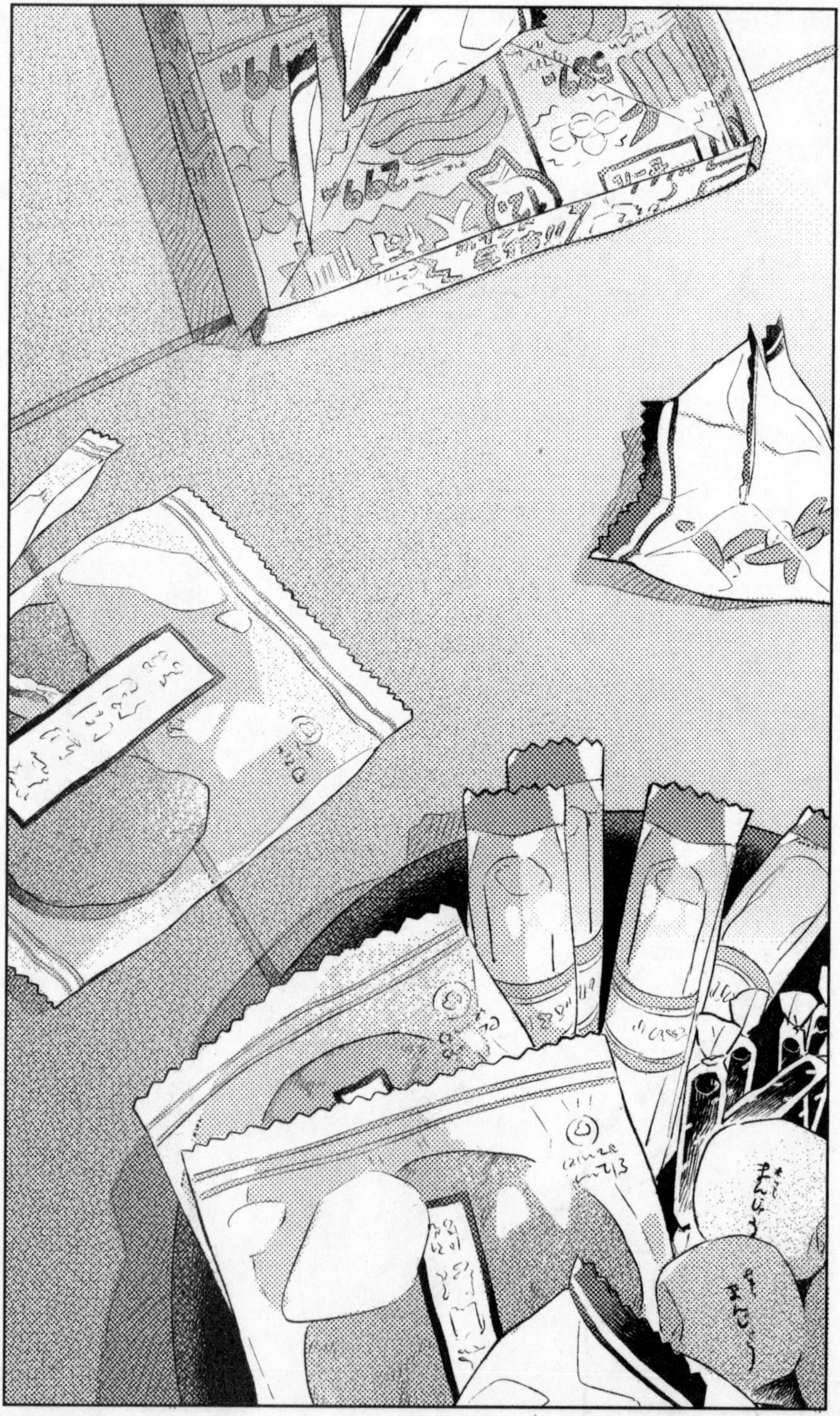
おまんじゅう

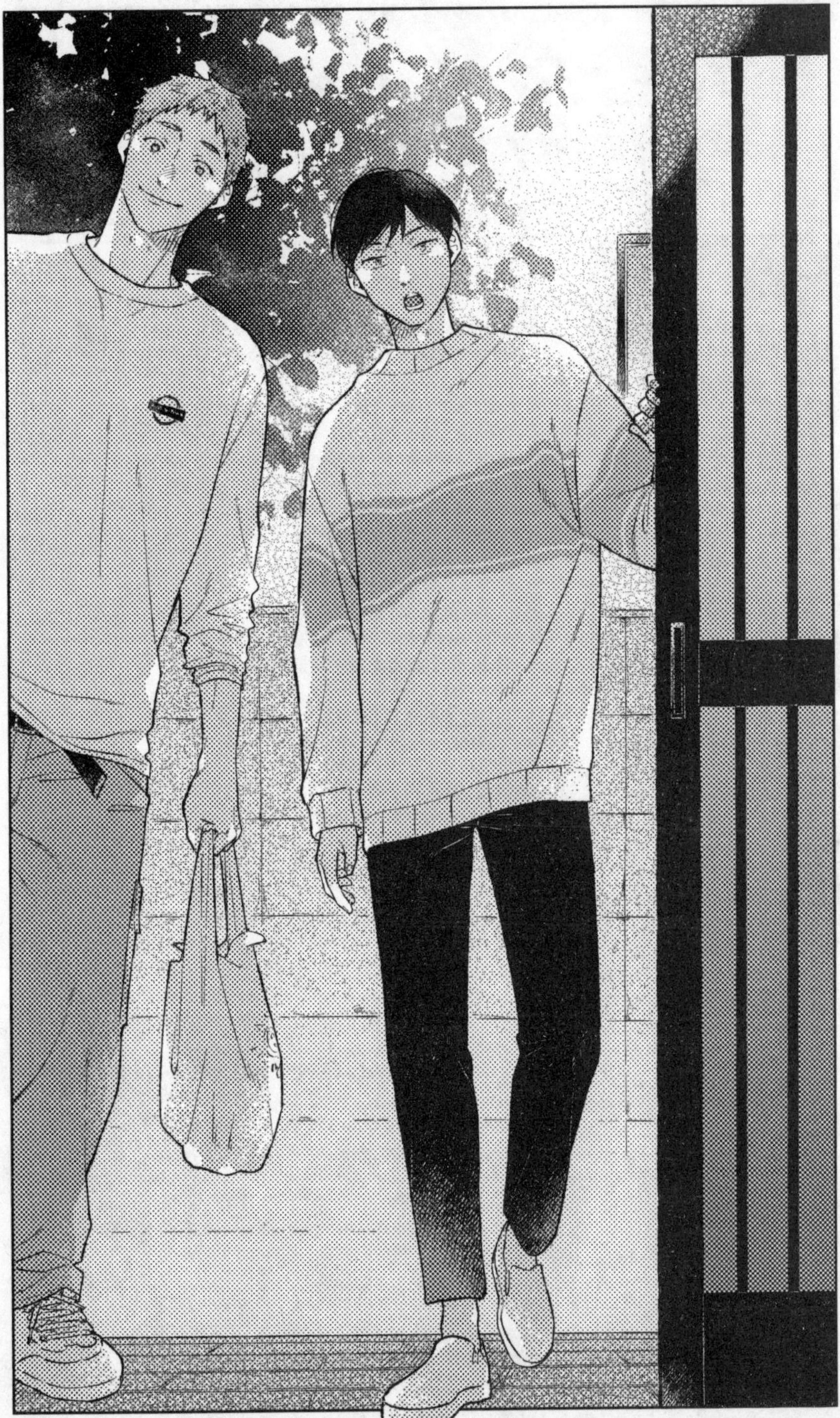

SEVEN SEAS ENTERTAINMENT PRESENTS

Restart After Coming Back Home

story and art by **COCOMI**

TRANSLATION
Anna Schnell

LETTERING
Nicole Roderick

COVER DESIGN
Hanase Qi

PROOFREADER
Alyssa Honsowetz

COPY EDITOR
Dawn Davis

EDITOR
Shanti Whitesides

PRINT MANAGER
Rhiannon Rasmussen-Silverstein

PRODUCTION ASSOCIATE
Christa Miesner

PRODUCTION MANAGER
Lissa Pattillo

MANAGING EDITOR
Julie Davis

ASSOCIATE PUBLISHER
Adam Arnold

PUBLISHER
Jason DeAngelis

Restart ha tadaima no atode

Originally published in Japan in 2019 by FRANCE SHOIN Inc., TOKYO.
English translation rights arranged through TOHAN CORPORATION, Tokyo.

Seven Seas press and purchase enquiries can be sent to Marketing Manager Lianne Sentar at press@gomanga.com. Information regarding the distribution and purchase of digital editions is available from Digital Manager CK Russell at digital@gomanga.com.

ISBN: 978-1-64827-676-7
Printed in Canada
First Printing: November 2021
10 9 8 7 6 5 4 3 2 1

READING DIRECTIONS

This book reads from ***right to left***, Japanese style. If this is your first time reading manga, you start reading from the top right panel on each page and take it from there. If you get lost, just follow the numbered diagram here. It may seem backwards at first, but you'll get the hang of it! Have fun!!

1
2
3
4
5
6
7
8
9

Follow us online: www.SevenSeasEntertainment.com

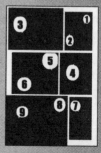